and Magic

Joscelyn Godwin was born in England and educated as a musicologist at Cambridge and Cornell universities. Since 1971 he has taught at Colgate University in New York State, where he is now Professor of Music. His books on the Western esoteric tradition have been translated into French, Spanish, Greek and Japanese.

JOSCELYN GODWIN

MUSIC, MYSTICISM
AND MAGIC

A SOURCEBOOK

SELECTED AND ANNOTATED BY
JOSCELYN GODWIN

ARKANA

ARKANA

Published by the Penguin Group
Penguin Books Ltd, 80 Strand, London WC2R 0RL, England
Penguin Group (USA) Inc., 375 Hudson Street, New York, New York 10014, USA
Penguin Books Australia Ltd, 250 Camberwell Road, Camberwell, Victoria 3124, Australia
Penguin Books Canada Ltd, 10 Alcorn Avenue, Toronto, Ontario, Canada M4V 3B2
Penguin Books India (P) Ltd, 11 Community Centre, Panchsheel Park, New Delhi – 110 017, India
Penguin Books (NZ) Ltd, Cnr Rosedale and Airborne Roads, Albany, Auckland, New Zealand
Penguin Books (South Africa) (Pty) Ltd, 24 Sturdee Avenue, Rosebank 2196, South Africa

Penguin Books Ltd, Registered Offices: 80 Strand, London WC2R 0RL, England

www.penguin.com

First published in 1986
Published by Arkana 1987
3

Printed in England by Clays Ltd, St Ives plc

CONTENTS

PREFACE AND
ACKNOWLEDGMENTS

This book documents the perennial wisdom associated with music, especially regarding the human being who is the potential worker of magic and the subject of mysticism. Taken in the natural, chronological order, the book shows that at the higher levels of music little changes: it is always the same vehicle for voyages to another world, the same revelation of divine and cosmic laws, the same powerful tool for self-transformation, as it was in ancient and even in prehistoric times. Only the soul of humanity does develop through time, as the individual's does, enabling ever new aspects of this wisdom to make themselves known.

The authors of the extracts collected here are anything but uniform, which makes it all the more remarkable when they meet so often on common ground. Among the composers, we hear from none less than Beethoven, Schumann, Wagner and Stockhausen. Of the poets, on the other hand, I have chosen some lesser-known, even decidedly inferior ones, in order to show some of the further ramifications of these ideas. Other authors here are novelists, philosophers and academics; monks, Kabbalists and Sufis; physicians, astronomers and wanderers. Part VI, "The Twentieth Century," represents the movements of Theosophy and Anthroposophy, the discovery of Eastern wisdom and the Gurdjieff Work, while looking, as one must, to the future.

Two other books should be mentioned as companions to this one. *Harmonies of Heaven and Earth: A New Philosophy of Music* (London, Thames & Hudson, 1986) contains my own reflections on this material and on much more, specifically the technicalities of the Harmony of the Spheres which are excluded here, but which could fill another sourcebook in themselves. Secondly, *Cosmic Music: Three Musical Keys to the Interpretation of Reality* (West Stockbridge, Mass., Lindisfarne Press, 1986) is a book of essays by the modern writers Marius Schneider, Rudolf Haase and Hans Erhard Lauer, edited by myself, which contains ideas on the metaphysics of sound, the harmony of the planetary motions, the occult aspects of music's evolution, etc., that supplement the last part of this sourcebook. These three books, moreover, treat almost exclusively the domain of the three Abrahamic religions (Judaism, Christianity, Islam), whereas there is just as much material – corroborating this in every respect – in the countries of the East and the South. I would mention Dane Rudhyar and Frank Denyer as pioneers in this broader field: Rudhyar for his books *The Rebirth of Hindu Music* and *The Magic of Tone and the Art of Music*, Denyer for his *The Rainbow Bridge: Myths and Images of Musical Creation* (as yet unpublished).

Unless otherwise attributed, all translations here are my own. I would like to thank my colleagues at Colgate University José Benavides, for his help with Spanish and his insight into Luis de León (no. 31), and Shimon Malin, for his translation from the Hebrew of Isaac ben Solomon (no. 13); and also Dr Masha Itzhaki, Professor of Hebrew Literature at Tel-Aviv University, for translating the Aramaic passage in the latter. I am grateful to my typists Betty Anne Morgan and Marilyn Jones. Todd Barton and Charles Mauzy kindly introduced me to Lemech (see no. 14); John Allitt to the Simon Mayr Circle, generously allowing me to use the translation of Marcazi (no. 38) from his forthcoming work on Mayr.

I
CLASSICAL

1

PLATO

c. 429-347 BC

In the Myth of Er we have the prototype of all the soul-journeys of
Western literature, with their oft-repeated theme of hearing celestial
music made by the souls of the spheres. If we allow that these
"spheres" may represent not only the physical orbits of the planets,
but also the powers of those planetary archetypes – the Mercurial,
the Solar, etc. – within the human soul itself, then the journey takes
on new meaning as an inner pilgrimage through the layers of the
psyche to the divine center within, which is also the all-encompassing
circumference of the Spirit.

The Myth of Er is a tale told by Socrates at the end of the *Republic*,
forming the conclusion and climax to a dialogue whose object has
been to examine the nature of Justice. In elevating the tone from
dialectic to myth, Socrates now rises from his consideration of justice
in the individual and in the State to a vision of cosmic justice. In the
world which Er visits, perfect balance and equity prevail: the good
and the wicked each receive their deserts; the souls of the stars sing
in harmony; the three Fates apportion the destiny of man and
cosmos in ideal symmetry; and above all presides Necessity, the
unmoving law which even the gods must obey. Freewill exists there
only for the human soul, which can choose, wisely or foolishly, the
pattern of its incarnation.

In including in the Notes a sketch of Ernest McClain's
interpretation of this entire myth as a musical allegory, I
acknowledge his discovery that music meant far more to Plato than
has hitherto been thought. This does not nullify other interpretations
of the myth, astronomical, psychological and theological, but adds a
fresh layer of meaning to these well-worked approaches: a plausible
one, in the light of Socrates' commendation of the science of
Harmonics in Book VII.

Source   Republic, X, 614b-619b, translated by Thomas Taylor[1] in *The Works of Plato*, London, 1804, vol. I, pp. 466-75.

The Myth of Er

614b I will not, said I, tell you the apologue of Alcinus;[2] but that, indeed, of a brave man, Er the son of Armenius, by descent a Pamphylian; who happening on a time to die in battle, when the dead were on the tenth[3] day carried off, already corrupted, he was taken up sound; and being carried home, as he was about to be buried on the twelfth day, when laid on the funeral pile, he revived; and being revived, he told what he saw in the other state;[4] and said that after his soul left

c the body, it went with many others, and that they came to a certain daemoniacal place, where there were two chasms in the earth, near to each other, and two other openings in the heavens opposite to them,[5] and the judges sat between these. When they gave judgment, they commanded the just to go to the right hand, and upwards through the heaven, fixing before them the accounts of the judgment pronounced; but the unjust they commanded to the left, and downwards, and these likewise had behind them the account of all

d they had done. But on his coming before the judges, they said, it behoved him to be a messenger to men concerning things there, and they commanded him to hear, and to contemplate every thing in the place. And he saw here, through two openings, one of the heaven, and one of the earth, the souls departing, after they were there judged; and through the other two openings he saw, rising through the one out of the earth, souls full of squalidness and dust; and through the other, he saw other souls descending pure from heaven;

e and always on their arrival they seemed as if they came from a long journey, and they gladly went to rest themselves in the meadow, as in a public assembly, and saluted one another, such as were acquainted, and those who rose out of the earth asked the others concerning the things above, and those from heaven asked them

615 concerning the things below, and they told one another: those wailing and weeping whilst they called to mind, what and how many things they suffered and saw in their journey under the earth; (for it was a journey of a thousand years) and these again from heaven explained their enjoyments, and spectacles of immense beauty. To narrate many of them, Glauco, would take much time; but this, he said, was the sum, that whatever unjust actions they had committed, and how many soever any one had injured, they were punished for

b all these separately tenfold, and it was in each, according to the rate of an hundred years, the life of man being considered as so long, that they might suffer tenfold punishment for the injustice they had done. So that if any had been the cause of many deaths, either by betraying cities or armies, or bringing men into slavery, or being

4

confederates in any other wickedness, for each of all these they reaped tenfold sufferings; and if, again, they had benefited any by good deeds, and had been just and holy, they were rewarded
c according to their deserts. Of those who died very young, and lived but a little time, he told what was not worth relating in respect of other things. But of impiety and piety towards the Gods and parents, and of suicide, he told the more remarkable retributions. For he said he was present when one was asked by another, where the great Aridaeus was? This Aridaeus had been tyrant in a certain city of Pamphylia a thousand years before that time, and had killed his
d aged father, and his elder brother, and had done many other unhallowed deeds, as it was reported: and the one who was asked, replied: "He neither comes,[6] nor ever will come hither. For we then surely saw this likewise among other dreadful spectacles: When we were near the mouth of the opening, and were about to ascend after having suffered every thing else, we beheld both him on a sudden, and others likewise, most of whom were tyrants, and some private persons who had committed great iniquity, whom, when they
e imagined they were to ascend, the mouth of the opening did not admit, but bellowed when any of those who were so polluted with wickedness, or who had not been sufficiently punished, attempted to ascend. And then," said he, "fierce men, and fiery to the view, standing by, and understanding the bellowing, took them and led
16 them apart, Aridaeus and the rest, binding their hands and their feet, and, thrusting down their head, and pulling off their skin, dragged them to an outer road, tearing them on thorns; declaring always to those who passed by, on what accounts they suffered these things, and that they were carrying them to be thrown into Tartarus." And hence, he said, amidst all their various terrors, this terror surpassed, lest the mouth should bellow, and when it was
b silent every one most gladly ascended. And the punishments and torments were such as these, and their rewards were the reverse of these. He also added, that every one, after they had been seven[7] days in the meadow, arising thence, it was requisite for them to depart on the eighth day, and arrive at another place on the fourth day after, whence they perceived from above through the whole heaven and earth, a light extended as a pillar,[8] mostly resembling the rainbow,
c but more splendid and pure; at which they arrived in one day's journey; and thence they perceived, through the middle of the light from heaven, the extremities of its ligatures extended; as this light was the belt of heaven, like the transverse beams of ships keeping the whole circumference united. From the extremities the distaff of necessity is extended, by which all the revolutions were turned round, whose spindle and point were both of adamant, but its whirl
d mixed of this and of other things; and the nature of the whirl was of such a mind, as to its figure, as is any one we see here. But you must

conceive it, from what he said, to be of such a kind as this: as if in some great hollow whirl, carved throughout, there was such another, but lesser, within it, adapted to it, like casks fitted one within another; and in the same manner a third, and a fourth, and four others, for the whirls were eight in all,[9] as circles one within

e another, having their lips appearing upwards, and forming round the spindle one united convexity of one whirl; the spindle was driven through the middle of the eight; and the first and outmost whirl had the widest circumference in the lip, the sixth had the second wide, and that of the fourth is the third wide, and the fourth wide that of the eighth, and the fifth wide that of the seventh, the sixth wide that of the fifth, and the seventh wide that of the third, and the eighth wide that of the second. Likewise, the circle of the largest is

617 variegated, that of the seventh is the brightest, and that of the eighth hath its colour from the shining of the seventh; that of the second and fifth resemble each other, but are more yellow than the rest. But the third hath the whitest colour, the fourth is reddish; the second in whiteness is the sixth [circle]; and the distaff must turn round in a circle with the whole it carries; and whilst the whole is turning round, the seven inner circles are gently turned round in a contrary motion to the whole. Again, of these, the eighth moves the swiftest;

b and next to it, and equal to one another, the seventh, the sixth, and the fifth; and the third went in a motion which as appeared to them completed its circle in the same way as the fourth.[10] The fourth in swiftness was the third, and the fifth was the second, and it was turned round on the knees of Necessity. And on each of its circles there was seated a Siren[11] on the upper side, carried round, and uttering a single sound on one pitch. But the whole of them, being eight, composed a single harmony.[12] There were other three sitting

c round at equal distance one from another, each on a throne, the daughters of Necessity, the Fates, in white vestments, and having crowns on their heads; Lachesis, and Clotho, and Atropos, singing to the harmony of the Sirens; Lachesis singing the past, Clotho the present, and Atropos the future. And Clotho, at certain intervals, with her right hand laid hold of the spindle, and along with her mother turned about the outer circle. And Atropos, in like manner, turned the inner ones with her left hand. And Lachesis touched both

d of these, severally, with either hand. After they arrive here, it is necessary for them to go directly to Lachesis. Then a certain prophet first of all ranges them in order, and afterwards taking the lots, and the models of lives, from the knees of Lachesis, and ascending a lofty tribunal, he says: – "The speech of the virgin Lachesis, the daughter of Necessity: Souls of a day! The beginning of another period of men of mortal race. The daemon shall not receive you as his lot, but you

e shall choose the daemon: He who draws the first, let him first make choice of a life, to which he must of necessity adhere: Virtue is

6

independent, which every one shall partake of, more or less, according as he honours or dishonours her: the cause is in him who makes the choice, and God is blameless." When he had said these things, he threw on all of them the lots, and each took up the one which fell beside him, and he was allowed to take no other. And when he had taken it, he knew what number he had drawn. After this he placed on the ground before them the models of lives, many more than those we see at present. And they were all various. For there were lives of all sorts of animals, and human lives of every kind. And among these there were tyrannies also, some of them perpetual, and others destroyed in the midst of their greatness, and ending in poverty, banishment, and want. There were also lives of renowned men, some for their appearance as to beauty, strength, and agility; and others for their descent, and the virtues of their ancestors. There were the lives of renowned women in the same manner. But there was no disposition of soul among these models, because of necessity, on choosing a different life, it becomes different itself. As to other things, riches and poverty, sickness and health, they were mixed with one another, and some were in a middle station between these.

There then, as appears, friend Glauco, is the whole danger of man. And hence this of all things is most to be studied, in what manner every one of us, omitting other disciplines, shall become an inquirer and learner in this study, if, by any means, he be able to learn and find out who will make him expert and intelligent to discern a good life, and a bad; and to choose every where, and at all times, the best of what is possible, considering all the things now mentioned, both compounded and separated from one another, what they are with respect to the virtue of life. And to understand what good or evil beauty operates when mixed with poverty, or riches, and with this or the other habit of soul; and what is effected by noble and ignoble descent, by privacy, and by public station, by strength and weakness, docility and indocility, and every thing else of the kind which naturally pertains to the soul, and likewise of what is acquired, when blended one with another; so as to be able from all these things to compute, and, having an eye to the nature of the soul, to comprehend both the worse and the better life, pronouncing that to be the worse which shall lead the soul to become more unjust, and that to be the better life which shall lead it to become more just, and to dismiss every other consideration. For we have seen, that in life, and in death, this is the best choice. But it is necessary that a man should have this opinion firm as an adamant in him, when he departs to Hades, that there also he may be unmoved by riches, or any such evils, and may not, falling into tyrannies, and other such practices, do many and incurable mischiefs, and himself suffer still greater: but may know how to choose always the middle life, as to

7

these things, and to shun the extremes on either hand, both in this
b life as far as is possible, and in the whole of hereafter. For thus man
becomes most happy.

2

MARCUS TULLIUS CICERO
106-43 BC

Cicero finished his *De Republica*, a treatise on the ideal republic, in 51 BC, under the stress of political troubles that were soon to exile him from Rome to a provincial proconsulate. Written partly in emulation of Plato's *Republic*, the work also follows the lead of the *Critias* in describing the author's own city in an idealized historical fantasy. Cicero looks back nostalgically to the recent heroic period of the Third Punic War, and takes as his central character Publius Cornelius Scipio Aemilianus Africanus (185/4-129 BC), a phil-hellenic politician who, like Cicero, came under the influence of Stoic philosophy – though Cicero professed himself primarily a follower of Plato. Both philosophies are in evidence here, the Stoic emphasis on virtue and patriotic duty gyving oddly with Platonic metaphysics and pneumatology.

In this dream-vision Scipio meets his grandfather by adoption, P.C. Scipio Africanus Major (236-184/3 BC), while visiting the latter's old friend King Masinissa of Numidia. Cicero uses the pretext of an ascent to the planetary spheres in order to put Earth and its affairs in perspective, and to show where man's true home lies. His brief but very compressed account also contains lessons in dream-lore, prophecy, time-cycles, cosmology, geography, and the doctrine of the soul. Surviving the loss of the remainder of *De Republica* through its inclusion in Macrobius' Commentary, it was valued as an authority on all these matters throughout the Middle Ages, and Scipio's remarks on astral music have been echoed and re-echoed by countless later writers. As our extract begins, Scipio is being introduced to the place where departed souls dwell: the Milky Way, "a circle of surpassing brilliance gleaming out amidst the blazing stars."

Source De Republica, VI. From Columbia University Records of Civilization: *Macrobius' Commentary on the Dream of Scipio*. Translated by William Harris Stahl. New York, Columbia University Press, 1952, pp. 72-4. By permission.

The Dream of Scipio

III   [7] As I looked out from this spot, everything appeared splendid and wonderful. Some stars were visible which we never see from this region, and all were of a magnitude far greater than we had imagined. Of these the smallest was the one farthest from the sky and nearest the earth, which shone forth with borrowed light.[1] And, indeed, the starry spheres easily surpassed the earth in size. From here the earth appeared so small that I was ashamed of our empire which is, so to speak, but a point on its surface.

IV   [1] As I gazed rather intently at the earth my grandfather said: "How long will your thoughts continue to dwell upon the earth? Do you not behold the regions to which you have come? The whole universe is comprised of nine circles, or rather spheres.[2] The outermost of these is the celestial sphere, embracing all the rest, itself the supreme god, confining and containing all the other spheres. In it are fixed the eternally revolving movements of the stars. [2] Beneath it are the seven underlying spheres, which revolve in an opposite direction to that of the celestial sphere. One of these spheres belongs to that planet which on earth is called Saturn. Below it is that brilliant orb, propitious and helpful to the human race, called Jupiter. Next comes the ruddy one, which you call Mars, dreaded on earth. Next, and occupying almost the middle region, comes the sun, leader, chief, and regulator of the other lights, mind and moderator of the universe, of such magnitude that it fills all with its radiance. The sun's companions, so to speak, each in its own sphere, follow – the one Venus, the other Mercury – and in the lowest sphere the moon, kindled by the rays of the sun, revolves. [3] Below the moon all is mortal and transitory, with the exception of the souls bestowed upon the human race by the benevolence of the gods. Above the moon all things are eternal.[3] Now in the center, the ninth of the spheres, is the earth, never moving and at the bottom. Towards it all bodies gravitate by their own inclination."

V   [1] I stood dumbfounded at these sights, and when I recovered my senses I inquired: "What is this great and pleasing sound that fills my ears?"

"That," replied my grandfather, "is a concord of tones separated by unequal but nevertheless carefully proportioned intervals, caused by the rapid motion of the spheres themselves. The high and low tones blended together produce different harmonies. Of course such swift motions could not be accomplished in silence and, as nature requires, the spheres at one extreme produce the low tones and at the other extreme the high tones. [2] Consequently the outermost sphere, the star-bearer, with its swifter motion gives forth a higher-pitched tone, whereas the lunar sphere, the lowest, has the deepest tone. Of course the earth, the ninth and stationary sphere, always clings to the same position in the middle of the universe. The other eight spheres, two of which move at the same speed, produce seven different tones, this number being, one might almost say, the key to the universe.[4] Gifted men, imitating this harmony on stringed instruments and in singing, have gained for themselves a return to this region, as have those of exceptional abilities who have studied divine matters even in earthly life.[5]

[3] The ears of mortals are filled with this sound, but they are unable to hear it. Indeed, hearing is the dullest of the senses: consider the people who dwell in the region about the Great Cataract[6] where the Nile comes rushing down from lofty mountains; they have lost their sense of hearing because of the loud roar. But the sound coming from the heavenly spheres revolving at very swift speeds is of course so great that human ears cannot catch it; you might as well try to stare directly at the sun, whose rays are much too strong for your eyes."[7]

I was amazed at these wonders, but nevertheless I kept turning my eyes back to earth.

3

PLUTARCH OF CHAERONEIA
before AD 50–after 120

Plutarch was a writer, lecturer, and for his last thirty years a priest at Delphi. Though best known as a biographer (Plutarch's *Lives*) his *Moralia* – essays on moral philosophy – include several works of considerable philosophical and even esoteric interest. *On the Daimon of Socrates* is a dramatic dialogue set in the Athens of 379 BC, in which philosophical conversation alternates with the vivid narration of a conspiracy which had just freed Thebes from Spartan domination. The narrator is Simmias, host to the conspirators, but Timarchus, also a Chaeroneian, is probably a fictitious character who takes the place of Plutarch himself: perhaps Plutarch, who was an initiate, was recounting experiences of his own.

Timarchus' vision bears many similarities to the Myth of Er (no. 1) and the Dream of Scipio (no. 2), such as his hearing the cosmic music and receiving instruction on the structure of the cosmos and the posthumous fate of man. Only a small part of it is given here. The beautiful description of the visible heavens partakes both of strict astronomical allegory (see our notes) and of an inspired, visionary quality found in accounts of the "astral world" (e.g. Steiner, no. 55).

Source *On the Daimon of Socrates*, 590a-f. Reprinted by permission of the publishers and The Loeb Classical Library from Plutarch's *Moralia*, translated by Phillip H. de Lacy and Benedict Einarson, Loeb Edition, Cambridge, Mass., and London, 1959, pp. 461-7.

The Vision of Timarchus

590 Timarchus, then, in his desire to learn the nature of Socrates' daimon[1] acted like the high-spirited young initiate in philosophy he was: consulting no one but Cebes and me, he descended into the crypt of Trophonius,[2] first performing the rites that are customary at the oracle. He remained underground two nights and a day, and

b most people had already given up hope, and his family were lamenting him for dead, when he came up in the morning with a radiant countenance. He did obeisance to the god, and as soon as he had escaped the crowd, began to tell us of many wonders seen and heard.

He said that on descending into the oracular crypt his first experience was of profound darkness; next, after a prayer, he lay a long time not clearly aware whether he was awake or dreaming. It did seem to him, however, that at the same moment he heard a crash and was struck on the head, and that the sutures parted and released his soul.[3] As it withdrew and mingled joyfully with air that c was translucent and pure, it felt in the first place that now, after long being cramped, it had again found relief, and was growing larger than before, spreading out like a sail; and next that it faintly caught the whir of something revolving overhead with a pleasant sound. When he lifted his eyes the earth was nowhere to be seen; but he saw islands[4] illuminated by one another with soft fire, taking on now one colour, now another, like a dye, as the light kept varying with their mutations. They appeared countless in number and huge in size, and though not all equal, yet all alike round; and he fancied that their circular movement made a musical whirring in the aether, for d the gentleness of the sound resulting from the harmony of all the separate sounds corresponded to the evenness of their motion.[5] In their midst lay spread a sea or lake,[6] through whose blue transparency the colours passed in their migrations; and of the islands a few sailed out in a channel and crossed the current, while many others were carried along with it, the sea itself drifting around, as it were, smoothly and evenly in a circle. In places it was very deep, mainly toward the south, but elsewhere there were faint shoals and shallows; and in many parts it overflowed and again receded, e never extending very far.[7] Some of it was of the pure hue of the high seas, while elsewhere the colour was not unmixed, but turbid and like that of a pool.[8] As they crested the surge the islands came back, without, however, returning to their point of departure or completing a circle; but with each new circuit they advanced slightly beyond f the old, describing a single spiral in their revolution.[9] The sea containing these was inclined at an angle of somewhat less than eight parts of the whole[10] toward the midmost and largest portion of the surrounding envelope, as he made out; and it had two openings receiving rivers of fire emptying into it across from one another so that it was forced far back, boiling, and its blue colour was turned to white.[11] All this he viewed with enjoyment of the spectacle.

4

CORPUS HERMETICUM
early centuries AD

The nineteen treatises attributed to Hermes Trismegistus (Thrice-greatest Hermes) and presented as Egyptian mystery-teaching come from the world of Alexandrian philosophy and religious syncretism. While they certainly embody Egyptian doctrines, inasmuch as Egypt was the source for much of Greek theology and initiatic wisdom, a more recent stamp is that of popular Neoplatonism with its leanings toward theurgy (see Iamblichus, no. 7). Their rediscovery at the Renaissance was one of the primary influences on the religious currents of the period *c.* 1470-1650. *Poimandres*, the first and most comprehensive treatise, relates a vision of Hermes (representing the initiate) in which he is shown the creation of the Cosmos and of Man, and the destiny of the Soul.

The image of the Soul ascending through the planetary spheres and hearing the planetary music on the way is one of the most powerful and recurrent in this collection. The ascent may take place during life, in a trance or dream, or else after death, as here. The Hermetic voyager transcends the planetary harmony – the realm where the Soul is made – to rise in his purified being to the harmony of the invisible world, whereupon another ladder of ascent leads eventually to his deification. Elsewhere in the treatise Poimandres also describes the descent of the Soul, which takes on the psychological qualities of each planet, to varying degrees, as it passes down through the spheres. It is these qualities or energies that are summarized in the natal horoscope, which charts the moment at which the Soul brings these tendencies into the earthly realm. Each incarnate being therefore sounds, as it were, a different chord of the planetary or psychological harmonies, and it is this that causes *musica humana* (the music of the human being) to resemble *musica mundana* (the music of the worlds or spheres).

The extract from the *Asclepius* draws a firm line between pure philosophy, which leads to God, and the inferior sciences which, diverting as they may be, only tell about the material cosmos below the Eighth Sphere. These sciences (which in modern terms include the arts) find their destined purpose in arousing wonder and reverence for the divine Creation. Whether the term "music" is used of this cosmic order simply as a pleasant metaphor, as here, or whether music as we know it on earth is truly and specifically a gateway to knowledge of higher realities, is one of the dilemmas that occupies many of our writers.

Source *Poimandres* and *Asclepius*, this version based on French translation by A.-J. Festugière in *Corpus Hermeticum*, ed. A.D. Nock, Paris, Les Belles Lettres, 1978, vol. I, pp. 15-16, and vol. II, pp. 311-12, and English translation by G.R.S. Mead in *Thrice Greatest Hermes*, London, Watkins, 1949, vol. II, pp. 15-17, 330-32.

The Ascent of the Soul

Poimandres sect. 24   Well hast thou taught me all as I desired, O *Nous* [Mind].[1] But speak to me further on the ascent [of the Soul], and how it occurs.

To this Poimandres replied: At first, when your physical body is dissolved, you surrender the body to change, and the form it used to have vanishes. Your *Ethos* [character], now devoid of power, is abandoned to the personal Daimon. The body's senses return to their respective sources, becoming absorbed in the [astral] Energies; passion and desire withdraw to the irrational Nature.

25.   And thus it is that man rises thereafter through the Harmony [i.e. the harmonious spheres of the planets]. To the first zone [Moon] he abandons the power of growth and decay; to the second [Mercury] return evil schemings, now de-energized; to the third [Venus] the illusions of desire, de-energized; to the fourth [Sun] the arrogance of power, de-energized; to the fifth [Mars] impious daring and presumption; to the sixth [Jupiter] the striving for wealth by evil means; and to the seventh zone [Saturn] ensnaring falsehood.

26.   And then, stripped of that which was given its energy by the Harmony and clothed in his proper power, he enters into the Eighth Sphere. Here he sings with the beings that are there, hymning the Father, and all rejoice at his coming. And now that he is made like his companions, he can also hear the Powers[2] above the Eighth Sphere beautifully singing their own hymns to God. And then, in order, they[3] ascend to the Father, surrendering themselves to the Powers; and, becoming Powers in their turn they are reborn in God. This is the happy end of those who have gained Gnosis: to become one with God. So now, why do you delay? Now that you have received the doctrine from me, should you not point the way to those who are worthy, that through thee the human race may be saved by God?

The True Knowledge of Music

Asclepius, 12b. Trismegistus: I will tell you, as if prophesying, that none after us will have that pure love of philosophy which consists only in knowing the divinity through repeated contemplation and sincere religion. For many confuse it with multifarious reasoning.

Asclepius: How then do many people make philosophy incomprehensible, and how do they confuse it with multifarious reasoning?
13. Trismegistus: In this way, Asclepius: by mixing it in subtle argument with other incomprehensible disciplines: arithmetic, music, and geometry. Pure philosophy, however, which derives solely from piety towards God, should only involve itself with other sciences in order to appreciate the workings of the stars, their pre-ordained stations, and their revolutions obedient to number; also to find out the dimensions, the qualities, and the quantities of the earth, the sea's depths, the strength of fire, and the effects and nature of all of these: that thus it should adore and praise the divine art and intelligence. For the true knowledge of music is nothing other than this: to know the ordering of all things and how the Divine Reason has distributed them; for this ordering of all separate things into one, achieved by skilful reason, makes the sweetest and truest harmony with the Divine Song.

5

CENSORINUS

flourished early third century AD

Censorinus was a Roman grammarian who wrote his one surviving
work, *On the Day of Birth*, as a birthday present to Quintus Caerullius
in AD 238. The book is mostly a careful compilation from the
encyclopedist Varro and others of anecdotes and doctrines concerning
human life and the phenomena of time. In this extract Censorinus
ranges in an extraordinary way over embryology, astrology, music
and number, but however bizarre the associations which he makes
between these realms, they are natural consequences of a syncre-
tistic, Neoythagorean world-view. He assumes that first in the
hierarchy of being come the numbers and pure geometrical figures.
Out of these arise, respectively, the musical consonances and the
patterns of astrology. Given the known effect of music on the soul,
and of the stars on human life, how could he not regard the two as
linked through their common ancestry?

The links are of several kinds. The aspects made by the transiting
Sun to its position at conception make angular harmonies which can
bring about birth. The numbers of days of gestation are musically
harmonious, too. The actual distances between the planets which
make up the nativity or horoscope are in musical proportion. Music
affects the Soul, the divine part of us, which is what enters at birth.
There is a deep underlying wholeness about this view of the world
which goes beyond mere compilation: a capacity to recognize
connections and to integrate disparate ideas which suggests that
Censorinus had a distinct contribution of his own to make.

Source *De die natali*, XI-XII, ed. Otto Jahn, Berlin, 1845.

Harmony and Embryology

XI,1 Now, returning to our theme,[1] I will show what Pythagoras thought
 2 pertinent to the number of days elapsing before birth. First, as noted
above, he said that there are generally two kinds of births: the

lesser one of seven months, issuing from the womb on the 210th day
after conception, and the greater one of ten months, issuing on the
3 274th day. The first, lesser one is notably divisible by six. Now that
which is conceived out of the seed is of a milky humor for the first six
days,[2] then for the following eight it is sanguine. This eight, joined
to the first six, makes the first consonance of a fourth. In the third
stage of nine days it is made into flesh, and these, combined with the
first six, make the sescuple [3:2] ratio and the consonance of a fifth.
Then in the following twelve days the body is formed. The twelve
4 compared to the six gives the third consonance of an octave, caused
by duple ratio. These four numbers (6, 8, 9, 12) added together
make 35 days. Not without reason is six the foundation of birth, for
it is a *teleios*, as the Greeks say, or as we call it a perfect number,
5 whose three factors – the sixth, the third, and the half, i.e. 1, 2, and 3
– add up to the number itself. For as the beginnings of the seed and
the milky basis of conception are first completed through this
number, so this beginning of man's formation lasting 35 days, is
multiplied by six for his complete growth; and so he is born mature
on reaching the 210th day.[3]
6 The other, greater period of gestation comprises the larger factor,
the septenary,[4] which as Solon wrote contains the whole life of
man. The Jews also divide by sevens in the numbering of all their
days, and the ritual books of the Etruscans will be found to say the
same. Hippocrates and other physicians declare no differently
concerning the health of the body, observing every seventh day as
7 critical. So whereas in the other period the time taken for the seed to
turn into blood is six days, here it is seven. Whereas there the infant
receives all its members in 35 days, here the portion of days is close
to 40. Hence in Greece they have 40 special days: a woman does not
enter the temple before the 40th day after giving birth: 40 days
during which most women are in pain, losing blood, while their
infants are usually feeble and sickly, do not smile, and are
endangered. Therefore they hold a celebration when that day is past,
calling the time *tesserakostaion*.
8 These 40 days multiplied by the seven initial ones make 280, or 40
weeks, but since the birth takes place on the first day of the last
week, six days are subtracted and the 274th day is counted. This
number of days corresponds exactly to the [astrological] square
9 aspects of the Chaldeans. The Sun circles the Zodiac in 365 days
and a few hours: if a quarter is subtracted (91 days and a few hours),
. it will take just short of 274 days to traverse the other three
quadrants until it reaches the point which makes a square aspect
with the place of conception.
0 That the human mind may perceive those days of change and
probe the secrets of nature should surprise no one. For there is a
phenomenon familiar to physicians, who have observed that many

women, having once received the seed, do not retain it. And when it is ejected within six or seven days, it has a milky quality (which they call *ekrysis*), whereas after that time it is sanguine (called *ektrosmos*).

11 Although both periods of birth seem to contain even numbers of days, and Pythagoras praises odd numbers,[5] yet his followers do not dispute it. The two odd numbers 209 and 273 are increased, they

12 say, by adding something of the days following; but they do not count a whole extra day. By observing nature we can see parallel examples in the durations of the year and of the month: for the odd number of 365 days in the year must be somewhat increased, and also something added to the lunar month of 29 days.

XII,1 It is by no means incredible to associate music with our birth. For whether music is only in the voice, as Socrates says, or, as Aristoxenus says, in the voice and the bodily motion, or whether, as Theophrastus[6] believes, in both these and more especially in the movement of the Soul [*animus*], it certainly partakes strongly of the

2 divine, and has the greatest power to excite souls. For if it were not agreeable to the immortal Gods, who are composed of divine Soul [*anima*], stage plays would certainly not have been instituted for the purpose of pleasing them, nor a piper employed for all the services in sacred temples. The triumph of Mars would not be celebrated with a piper or a trumpeter,[7] nor that of Apollo with the lyre, nor the Muses given pipes and other attributes of this kind. Neither would pipers, by whom the deities are appeased, be permitted to play publicly and feast on the Capitol, or to roam freely through the city at the Lesser Quinquatria (on the Ides of June), clad in masks and

3 intoxicated. And also the minds of men, which are divine (whatever Epicurus may say to the contrary), acknowledge their own nature in song. Finally, music serves to make toil as bearable as may be, as when it is used by the steersman in a moving galley; and the legions, fighting with the sword, even lose the fear of death when the trumpet is sounded.

4 On this account Pythagoras kept a lyre with him to make music before going to sleep and upon waking, in order always to imbue his soul with its divine quality. And with music Asclepiades the physician[8] often restored to sanity the minds of those made delirious

5 by disease. Herophilus,[9] a practitioner of this art, says that the pulse of the veins moves in musical rhythms. So if there is harmony in the motion both of the body and the soul, music is definitely not foreign to our nativities.

6

PLOTINUS
AD 205-269/270

In his *Enneads* – six groups of nine treatises each, collected and edited by his pupil Porphyry – Plotinus makes several uses of music as a metaphor – but only as that. He is far from being interested in such things as musical astrology or numerology; in fact, he is the least Pythagorean of all the Neoplatonists. But some of these metaphors have had a long life: the whole world as a stage upon which souls come or go as the actors; the universe as a musical instrument in which every string has its part to play; the explanation of sympathetic magic by the phenomenon of sympathetic vibration; the image of souls as a heavenly chorus surrounding God, their conductor.

His attitude to the magical use of music is in strong contrast to that of Iamblichus (no. 7). Plotinus is as firm in relegating it exclusively to the emotional realm as Iamblichus is in elevating it above this lowly use (whose efficacy he does not deny) to become a vehicle for divine possession. Plotinus' view is always from the loftiest standpoint, and he is careful not to confuse what his readers understand by music – the sung and sounded notes which can be numbered and analyzed – with the state of affairs in the wider cosmos and beyond it. His attitude is close to that expressed in our excerpt from the Hermetic *Asclepius* (no. 4), and was to become the norm for the early Christian writers, for whom the exercise of the Liberal Arts appeared to be a distraction from the more pressing duty of saving one's soul.

Source Reprinted by permission of Faber & Faber Ltd from *The Enneads*, translated by Stephen MacKenna, 4th revised ed., London, Faber & Faber, 1969, pp. 176-7, 271, 323-4, 621-2.

Universal Harmony

III.2.17   Just so[1] the Soul, entering this drama of the Universe, making itself a part of the Play, bringing to its acting its personal excellence or defect, set in a definite place at the entry and accepting from the author its entire role – superimposed upon its own character and conduct – just so, it receives in the end its punishment and reward.

But these actors, souls, hold a peculiar dignity: they act in a vaster place than any stage: the Author has made them masters of all this world; they have a wide choice of place; they themselves determine the honour or discredit in which they are agents since their place and part are in keeping with their quality: they therefore fit into the Reason-Principle[2] of the Universe, each adjusted, most legitimately, to the appropriate environment, as every string of the lyre is set in the precisely right position, determined by the Principle directing musical utterance, for the due production of the tones within its capacity. All is just and good in the Universe in which every actor is set in his own quite appropriate place, though it be to utter in the Darkness and in Tartarus the dreadful sounds whose utterance there is well.

This Universe is good not when the individual is a stone, but when everyone throws in his own voice towards a total harmony, singing out a life – thin, harsh, imperfect, though it be. The Syrinx does not utter merely one pure note; there is a thin obscure sound which blends in to make the harmony of Syrinx music: the harmony is made up from tones of various grades, all the tones differing, but the resultant of all forming one sound.[3]

Similarly the Reason-Principle entire is one, but it is broken into unequal parts: hence the difference of place found in the Universe, better spots and worse; and hence the inequality of souls, finding their appropriate surroundings amid this local inequality. The diverse places of this sphere, the souls of unequal grade and unlike conduct, are well exemplified by the distinction of parts in the Syrinx or any other instrument: there is local difference, but from every position every string gives forth its own tone, the sound appropriate, at once, to its particular place and to the entire plan.

What is evil in the single soul will stand a good thing in the universal system;[4] what in the unit offends nature will serve nature in the total event – and still remains the weak and wrong tone it is, though its sounding takes nothing from the worth of the whole, just as, in another order of image, the executioner's ugly office does not mar the well-governed state: such an officer is a civic necessity; and the corresponding moral type is often serviceable; thus, even as things are, all is well.

IV.3.12   We may know this also by the concordance of the souls with the ordered scheme of the Cosmos; they are not dependent, but, by their descent, they have put themselves in contact, and they stand henceforth in harmonious association with the cosmic circuit[5] – to the extent that their fortunes, their life-experiences, their choosing and refusing, are announced by the patterns of the stars – and out of this concordance rises as it were one musical utterance: the music, the harmony, by which all is described (the harmony of the spheres), is the best witness to this truth.

An Explanation of Magic

IV.4.40   But magic spells; how can their efficacy be explained?

By the reigning sympathy and by the fact in Nature that there is an agreement of like forces and an opposition of unlike, and by the diversity of those multitudinous powers which converge in the one living universe.

There is much drawing and spell-binding dependent on no interfering machination; the true magic is the "Friendship" and the "Strife" which exist within the All.[6] Here is the primal mage and sorcerer – discovered by men who thenceforth turn those same ensorcellations and magic arts upon one another.

Love is given in Nature; the qualities inducing love induce mutual approach: hence there has arisen an art of magic love-drawing whose practitioners apply by contact certain substances adapted to diverse temperaments and so informed with love as to effect a bond of union; they knit soul to soul as they might train two separate trees towards each other. The magician, too, draws on these patterns of power, and by ranging himself also into the pattern is able tranquilly to possess himself of these forces with whose nature and purpose he has become identified.[7] Supposing the mage to stand outside the All, his evocations and invocations would no longer avail to draw up or to call down; but as things are he operates from no outside standground, he pulls knowing the pull of everything towards any other thing in the living system.

The tune of an incantation, a significant cry, the mien of the operator, these too have a natural leading power over the Soul upon which they are directed, drawing it with the force of mournful patterns or tragic sounds; for it is the reasonless soul, not the will or wisdom, that is beguiled by music,[8] a form of sorcery which raises no question, whose enchantment, indeed, is welcomed, though not demanded, from the performers. Similarly with regard to prayers;

there is no question of a will that grants; the powers that answer to incantations do not act by will; a human being fascinated by a snake has neither perception nor sensation of what is happening; he knows only after he has been caught, and his highest mind is never caught. In other words, some influence falls from the being addressed upon the petitioner – or upon someone else – but that being itself, sun or star, perceives nothing of it all.

41 The prayer is answered by the mere fact that part and other part are wrought to one tone like a musical string which, plucked at one end, vibrates at the other also. Often, too, the sounding of one string awakens what might pass for a perception in another, the result of their being in harmony and tuned to one musical scale; now, if the vibration in a lyre affects another by virtue of the sympathy existing between them, then certainly in the All – even though it is constituted in contraries – there must be one melodic system; for it contains its unisons as well, and its entire content, even to those contraries, is a kinship.

Thus, too, whatever is hurtful to man – the passionate spirit, for example, drawn by the medium of the gall into the principle seated in the liver – comes with no intention of hurt; it is simply as one transferring fire to another might innocently burn him: no doubt, since he actually set the other on fire he is a cause, but only as the attacking fire itself is a cause, that is by the merely accidental fact that the person to whom the fire was being brought blundered in taking it.

The Individual and the Supreme

VI.9.8 Every soul that knows its history is aware, also, that its movement, unthwarted, is not that of an outgoing line; its natural course may be likened to that in which a circle turns not upon some external but on its own centre, the point to which it owes its rise. The soul's movement will be about its source; to this it will hold, poised intent towards that unity to which all souls should move and the divine souls always move, divine in virtue of that movement; for to be a god is to be integral with the Supreme; what stands away is man still multiple, or beast.

Is then this "centre" of our souls the Principle for which we are seeking?

We must look yet further: we must admit a Principle in which all these centres coincide: it will be a centre by analogy with the centre of the circle we know. The soul is not a circle in the sense of the geometric figure but in that its primal nature (wholeness) is within it and about it, that it owes its origin to what is whole, and that it will be still more entire when severed from body.

In our present state – part of our being weighed down by the body, as one might have the feet under water with all the rest untouched – we bear ourselves aloft by that intact part and, in that, hold through our own centre to the centre of all the centres, just as the centres of the great circles of a sphere coincide with that of the sphere to which all belong. Thus we are secure.

If these circles were material and not spiritual, the link with the centres would be local; they would lie round it where it lay at some distant point: since the souls are of the Intellectual, and the Supreme still loftier, we understand that contact is otherwise procured, that is by those powers which connect Intellectual agent with Intellectual object; indeed soul is closer to the Supreme than Intellect to its object – such is its similarity, identity, and the sure link of kindred. Material mass cannot blend into other material mass: unbodied beings are not under this bodily limitation; their separation is solely that of otherness, of differentiation; in the absence of otherness, it is similars mutually present.

Thus the Supreme as containing no otherness is ever present with us; we with it when we put otherness away. It is not that the Supreme reaches out to us seeking our communion: we reach towards the Supreme; it is we that become present. We are always before it: but we do not always look: thus a choir, singing set in due order about the conductor, may turn away from that centre to which all should attend; let it but face aright and it sings with beauty, present effectively. We are ever before the Supreme – cut off is utter dissolution; we can no longer be – but we do not always attend: when we look, our Term is attained; this is rest, this is the end of singing ill; effectively before Him, we lift a choral song full of God.

7

IAMBLICHUS OF CHALCIS

AD *c.* 250–*c.* 325

Iamblichus stands at only one remove from Plotinus, linked through his master and Plotinus' pupil, Porphyry (232/3-305). But with him the focus of Neoplatonism has altered greatly from Plotinus' *theoria*, the ascent to the One through knowledge, to *theurgia*, the ritualistic and magical approach to Divinity. For this reason Iamblichus has received harsh treatment at the hands of scholars who can admire the pure and beautiful ideas of Plotinus, and indeed almost assimilate him to Christian mysticism, but cannot take seriously Iamblichus' respect for pagan ceremonial magic and his too blatant polytheism. Iamblichus, however, is far more a figure of his age than the timeless Plotinus, and deserves credit for rising to the challenge of an epoch of unprecedented religious variety, with its almost chaotic proliferation of sects and cults. Knowing, from experiences which his critics lack, that there was efficacy in the ceremonies of the Mysteries, he set out to bring these practices under the wing of Platonism, to give them an intellectual justification, and to assimilate their gods with his own. Thus began a movement of comparative religious study and theological synthesis that was to underlie the philosophical revival of Iamblichus' admirer the Emperor Julian (ruled 361-3), and reach its zenith in Proclus (410/12-485).

Iamblichus also bridges the dichotomy between Pythagoras and Plato: he is both Neopythagorean and Neoplatonist, and it never occurs to him that the two masters could have had any fundamental differences. (Recent research tends to confirm Plato's own Pythagoreanism; see notes to *Republic*.) But Plato and Socrates were historical figures, whereas the life of Pythagoras, like those of Jesus and Apollonius of Tyana, had long since assumed a symbolic and mythical overlay in which historical truth was subservient to a message. Iamblichus' hagiographical *Life*, based on a shorter version by Porphyry, is a collection of the numerous tales, legends and myths which had accrued through seven centuries (Pythagoras was born in 569 BC and may have lived 100 years).[1]

The chronological order of our authors has made Pythagoras appear later than he should. Two features of his activity concern us in particular here: his use of music to affect the psyche, and his hearing the harmony of the spheres. Both are described in these chapters by Iamblichus.

If, as seems certain from Ernest McClain's discoveries,[2] the Babylonians and Egyptians were familiar with the connection of tone with number and had developed an elaborate symbolism of tuning-systems two millennia or more before Pythagoras, then in view of his extensive travels and initiations in both these countries Pythagoras must be regarded not as the inventor but as the importer of such knowledge to Greece. This in no way lessens his achievement as one of the fathers of the Greek intellectual miracle, but it does remind us that, here as in other subjects, the Greeks were indeed as children to those venerable but by then quite decadent civilizations.

Sources   Iamblichus' Life of Pythagoras, or Pythagoric Life, translated by Thomas Taylor, London, 1818, pp. 43-8, 80-3; Iamblichus on the Mysteries of the Egyptians, Chaldeans, and Assyrians, translated by Thomas Taylor, London, 1821, pp. 129-34.

Pythagoras' Use of Music

Ch. 15.   Conceiving that the first attention which should be paid to men, is that which takes place through the senses; as when some one perceives beautiful figures and forms, or hears beautiful rhythms and melodies, he (Pythagoras) established that to be the first erudition which subsists through music, and also through certain melodies and rhythms, from which the remedies of human manners and passions are obtained, together with those harmonies of the powers of the soul which it possessed from the first. He likewise devised medicines calculated to repress and expel the diseases both of bodies and souls. And, by Jupiter![3] that which deserves to be mentioned above all these particulars is this, that he arranged and adapted for his disciples what are called apparatus and contrectations,[4] divinely contriving mixtures of certain diatonic, chromatic, and enharmonic melodies, through which he easily transferred and circularly led the passions of the soul into a contrary direction,[5] when they had recently and in an irrational and clandestine manner been formed; such as sorrow, rage, and pity, absurd emulation and fear, all various desires, angers, and appetites, pride, supineness, and vehemence. For he corrected each of these by the rule of virtue, attempering them through appropriate melodies, as through certain salutary medicines. In the evening, likewise, when his disciples were retiring to sleep, he liberated them by these means from diurnal perturbations and tumults, and purified their intellective power from the influxive and effluxive waves of a corporeal nature; rendered their sleep quiet, and their dreams pleasing and prophetic. But when they again rose from their bed, he freed them from nocturnal heaviness, relaxation and torpor, through certain peculiar songs and modulations, produced either by simply striking the lyre, or employing the voice. Pythagoras, however, did not procure for himself a thing of this kind through instruments or the voice, but employing a certain ineffable divinity, and which it is difficult to apprehend, he extended his ears, and fixed his intellect in the sublime symphonies of the world, he alone hearing and understanding, as it appears, the universal harmony and consonance of the spheres, and the stars that are moved through them, and which produce a fuller and more intense melody than any thing effected by mortal sounds.[6] This melody also was the result of dissimilar and variously differing sounds, celerities, magnitudes, and intervals, arranged with reference to each other in a certain most musical ratio, and thus producing a most gentle, and at the same time variously beautiful motion and convolution. Being therefore irrigated as it were with this melody, having the reason of his intellect well arranged through it, and as I may say, exercised, he determined to exhibit certain images of these things to his disciples as much as possible, especially producing an imitation of them through instruments, and through the mere voice alone. For he conceived that by him alone, of all the inhabitants of the earth, the mundane sounds were understood and heard, and this from a natural fountain itself and root. He therefore thought himself worthy to be taught, and to learn something about the celestial orbs, and to be assimilated to them by desire and imitation, as being the only one on the earth adapted to this by the conformation of his body, through the daemoniacal power that inspired him. But he apprehended that other men ought to be satisfied in looking to him, and the gifts he possessed, and in being benefited and corrected through images and examples, in consequence of their inability to comprehend truly the first and genuine archetypes of things. Just, indeed, as to those who are incapable of looking intently at the sun, through the transcendent splendour of his rays, we contrive to exhibit the eclipses of that luminary, either in the profundity of still water, or through melted pitch, or through some darkly-splendid mirror; sparing the imbecility of their eyes, and devising a method of representing a certain repercussive light, though less intense than its archetype, to those who are delighted with a thing of this kind. Empedocles also appears to have obscurely signified this about Pythagoras, and the illustrious and divinely-gifted conformation of his body above that of other men, when he says:

27

"There was a man among them (i.e. among the Pythagoreans) who was transcendent in knowledge, who possessed the most ample stores of intellectual wealth, and who was in the most eminent degree the adjutor of the works of the wise. For when he extended all the powers of his intellect, he easily beheld every thing, as far as to ten or twenty ages of the human race."[7]

For the words transcendent, and he beheld every thing, and the wealth of intellect, and the like, especially exhibit the illustrious nature of the conformation of his mind and body, and its superior accuracy in seeing, and hearing, and in intellectual perception.

Ch. 25.   Pythagoras was likewise of opinion that music contributed greatly to health, if it was used in an appropriate manner. For he was accustomed to employ a purification of this kind, but not in a careless way. And he called the medicine which is obtained through music by the name of purification. But he employed such a melody as this about the vernal season. For he placed in the middle a certain person who played on the lyre, and seated in a circle round him those who were able to sing. And thus, when the person in the centre struck the lyre, those that surrounded him sung certain paeans,[8] through which they were seen to be delighted, and to become elegant and orderly in their manners. But at another time they used music in the place of medicine. And there are certain melodies devised as remedies against the passions of the soul, and also against despondency and lamentation, which Pythagoras invented as things that afford the greatest assistance in these maladies. And again, he employed other melodies against rage and anger, and against every aberration of the soul. There is also another kind of modulation invented as a remedy against desires. He likewise used dancing; but employed the lyre as an instrument for this purpose. For he conceived that the pipe was calculated to excite insolence, was a theatrical instrument, and had by no means a liberal sound.[9] Select verses also of Homer and Hesiod were used by him, for the purpose of correcting the soul.

Among the deeds of Pythagoras likewise, it is said, that once through the spondaic song of a piper he extinguished the rage of a Tauromenian lad, who had been feasting by night, and intended to burn the vestibule of his mistress, in consequence of seeing her coming from the house of his rival. For the lad was inflamed and excited [to this rash attempt] by a Phrygian song; which however Pythagoras most rapidly suppressed. But Pythagoras, as he was astronomizing, happened to meet with the Phrygian piper at an unseasonable time of night, and persuaded him to change his Phrygian for a spondaic song;[10] through which the fury of the lad being immediately repressed, he returned home in an orderly manner, though a little before this he could not be in the least restrained, nor would, in short, bear any admonition; and even stupidly insulted Pythagoras when he met him. When a certain youth also rushed with a drawn sword on Anchitus, the host of Empedocles, because, being a judge, he had publicly condemned his father to death, and would have slain him as a homicide, Empedocles changed the intention of the youth, by singing to his lyre that verse of Homer,

> Nepenthe, without gall, o'er every ill
> Oblivion spreads;

(*Odyssey*, IV, 220-1)

and thus snatched his host Anchitus from death, and the youth from the crime of homicide. It is also related that the youth from that time became the most celebrated of the disciples of Pythagoras. Farther still, the whole Pythagoric school produced by certain appropriate songs, what they called *exartysis*, or adaptation; *synarmoge*, or elegance of manners; and *epaphe*, or contact, usefully conducting the dispositions of the soul to passions contrary to those which it before possessed. For when they went to bed, they purified the reasoning power from the perturbations and noises to which it had been exposed during the day, by certain odes and peculiar songs, and by this means procured for themselves tranquil sleep, and few and good dreams. But when they rose from bed, they again liberated themselves from the torpor and heaviness of sleep, by songs of another kind.[11] Sometimes, also, by musical sounds alone, unaccompanied with words, they healed the passions of the soul and certain diseases, enchanting, as they say, in reality. And it is probable that from hence this name *epode*, i.e. enchantment, came to be generally used. After this manner, therefore, Pythagoras through music produced the most beneficial correction of human manners and lives.

Music in the Mysteries

Ch. 9.   What you afterwards say[12] is as follows: "That some of those who suffer a mental alienation, energize enthusiastically on hearing cymbals or drums, or a certain modulated sound, such as those who are Corybantically inspired, those who are possessed by Sabazius, and those who are inspired by the mother of the Gods."[13] It is necessary, therefore, to discuss the causes of these things, and to show how they are definitely produced.

That music, therefore, is of a motive nature, and is adapted to excite the affections, and that the melody of pipes produces or heals the disordered passions of the soul, changes the temperaments or dispositions of the body, and by some melodies causes a Bacchic fury, but by others occasions this fury to cease; and, likewise, how the differences of these accord with the several dispositions of the soul, and, that an unstable and variable melody is adapted to ecstasies, such as are the melodies of Olympus, and others of the like kind; all these appear to me to be adduced in a way foreign to enthusiasm. For they are physical and human, and the work of our art; but nothing whatever of a divine nature in them presents itself to the view.

We must rather, therefore, say, that sounds and melodies are appropriately consecrated to the Gods. There is, also, an alliance in these sounds and melodies to the motions in the universe itself, and to the harmonious sounds which proceed from the motions. Conformably, therefore, to such like adaptations of melodies to the Gods, the Gods themselves become present. For there is not any thing which intercepts; *so that whatever has but a casual similitude to, directly participates of, them.*[14] A perfect possession, likewise, immediately takes place, and a plenitude of a more excellent essence and power. Not that the body and the soul are in each other, and sympathize, and are copassive with the melodies; but because the inspiration of the Gods is not separated from divine harmony, but is originally adapted and allied to it, on this account it is participated by it in appropriate measures. Hence also, it is excited and restrained according to the several orders of the Gods. But this inspiration must by no means be called an ablation, purgation, or medicine. For it is not primarily implanted in us from a certain disease, or excess, or redundance; but the whole principle and participation of it are supernally derived from the Gods.

Neither is it proper to say that the soul primarily consists of harmony and rhythm. For thus enthusiasm would be adapted to the soul alone. It is better, therefore, to deny this, and to assert that the soul, before she gave herself to body, was an auditor of divine harmony; and that hence, when she proceeded into body, and heard melodies of such a kind as especially preserve the divine vestige of harmony, she embraced these, from them recollected divine harmony, and tends and is allied to it, and as much as possible participates of it. Hence the cause of divine divination may, after this manner, be assigned in common.

8

SYNESIUS OF CYRENE
AD *c*. 370-413

Synesius was born into an upper-class Libyan family, and his life followed in many respects the predictable lines of marriage, estate-management, keen horsemanship and hunting, and energetic public service. But he was also a meeting-point for the two most powerful spiritual influences of his time. As a youth he went to Alexandria and studied in the Neoplatonic school of philosophy which was enjoying a last flowering under the philosopher-martyr Hypatia (d. 415), an expounder of the purest Plotinian doctrines as well as an adept in various arts and sciences. And in 410, although he was not even baptised as a Christian, a public election created him Bishop of Ptolemais. Synesius accepted the honor with misgivings, but acquitted himself nobly in the political wrangles which such a position brought upon him, devoting himself wholeheartedly to his people for his few remaining years.

In his Hymns he shows himself a Christian of a strongly Neoplatonic cast, filled with loving aspiration for the God above the gods and with longing for release from the mire of material existence. The Hymn on the Ascension, probably his latest and finest, fuses the imagery of Christ's Resurrection, his Ascension, and the Platonic ascent of the Soul. Here the ascent is not, as in *Poimandres* and Plotinus, through one music to a higher one, but to the Silence which transcends all sound. Yet perhaps these are not so different, for as Synesius himself says in Hymn no. 2: "I sing to thee, Blessed one, with my voice, and I also sing to thee, Blessed one, through my silence; for all that my intellect sings with its voice thou hearest also in its silence."

Source *Synésios de Cyrène Tome I: Hymnes*, ed. and translated (French) by Christian Lacombrade, Paris, Les Belles Lettres, 1978, pp. 92-7.

Christ's Ascension through the Spheres

Best-loved, renowned, and blessed Son
Of Solyme's[1] Virgin, thee I sing.
Who banished from the Garden
That false, infernal Serpent
5   Which gave forbidden fruit,
A bitter food, to Eve.

Crowned and renowed Father,[2] born
Of Solyme's Virgin, thee I sing.

Thou cam'st to Earth to live
10   With mortals as a mortal;
And harrowed Tartarus
Where souls enslaved by Death
Languished in their thousands.
Aeonian Hades shrank
15   Before thee, with its guardian,
A mighty demon hound.[3]
And after thou hadst loosed
The blameless choirs of souls
From torment, thou didst raise
20   Thy hymns unto the Father.

Crowned and renowned Father, born
Of Solyme's Virgin, thee I sing.

During thy Ascension,[4] Lord,
Th'aerial demons[5] trembled;
25   The choir of deathless stars
Was struck dumb with amaze.
The laughing Aether, wise
Engenderer of harmony,
Struck its seven-stringed lyre
30   And played a tune of triumph.[6]
Lucifer, day's herald,
Smiled at golden Hesperus,
Evenstar of Venus.
Her crescent filled with fire,
35   There went ahead the Moon,
The pasture of nocturnal gods.
The Sun spread out his hair
Flaming beneath thy feet.
He knew the Son of God,

40   The all-creating Spirit,
      His fire's archetype.

      But thou, with spreading wings,
      Broke through the azure dome[7]
      And rested in the spheres
45   Of pure Intelligence:
      The source of all things good,
      The silence-filled Heaven.[8]
      There is no longer found
      Deep-flowing Time, who leads
50   With heavy tread the things of Earth.
      Nor is there Matter, whose
      Deep waters bring such ill.

      Only eternity
      Of immemorial birth,
55   Ever both young and old,
      Guards the immortal home
      Of all the Gods.

9

MARTIANUS CAPELLA
flourished fifth century AD

Martianus Minneus Felix Capella, whose own character and biography are unknown, wrote in Carthage between 410 and 439[1] one of the most bizarre, yet one of the most influential works of Latin literature: *De Nuptiis Philologiae et Mercurii* (The Marriage of Philology and Mercury). It is an allegorical tale of the search for a suitable bride for Mercury, the young god of eloquence; of the choosing of Philology (i.e. learning) and her ascent from earth to heaven; the assembly of wedding guests and the entertainment at the marriage, consisting of seven speeches in which the personified Liberal Arts (Grammar, Dialectic, Rhetoric, Geometry, Arithmetic, Astronomy and Harmony) expound their subjects. The preparations take two books. The seven books of speeches were to enjoy the undeserved status of primary textbooks on their subjects during the Middle Ages.

Martianus' work, like Boethius' *Consolations of Philosophy*, is written in the alternating verse and prose form known as Menippean Satire. He has two styles: one for the allegorical setting, excessively elaborate, wordy, and obscure to a degree (so his translator says) unmatched by any other Latin writer: the other straightforward (and often directly plagiarized) for the technical accounts which his seven learned maidens give of their arts. As is generally the case with the Latin transmitters of Greek learning, Martianus' treatises are in no way original, and he has been censured for his uncritical and often uncomprehending treatment of the seven subjects. William Stahl, whose translation and edition of Martianus crowned his life's work as a scholar, came to despise his subject as a third-rate textbook writer. But without Martianus, and without the equally inadequate or incomplete accounts which Calcidius, Macrobius, Boethius, Cassiodorus, and Isidore of Seville prepared in their efforts to preserve learning during a time of cultural collapse, there would have been nothing for the scholars of the ninth-century intellectual revival to draw on as they attempted to retrieve what they could of ancient wisdom. It is probably thanks to Martianus, incidentally, that the Middle Ages knew of seven liberal arts and not the nine which formed Varro's own canon, adding the more earthly pair, Architecture and Medicine. St Augustine had also planned to write on seven, replacing Astronomy with Philosophy, but since he abandoned his project after writing a Grammar and part of a book on Music, he was a lesser influence.

While Martianus was a dilettante in book-learning, his account of the betrothal and marriage is a marvelous Neoplatonic fairy-tale, resembling nothing so much as the great entertainments of the Renaissance which preceded the birth of opera. It is picturesque, imaginative, and often humorous in a self-mocking way, as when, near the end of some of the long expository speeches, wedding-guests break in to say that they have had more than enough: a sentiment shared, no doubt, by generations of readers of these dry tractates. Another wry comment on all this book-learning occurs when Philology is about to step into the carriage prepared for her voyage to the heavens: she is made to vomit up a stream of writings – papyri, parchments, hieroglyphs, diagrams in countless volumes – which are all eagerly collected by the Muses and personifications of the Arts and Disciplines. Then she drinks the egg-like Cup of Immortality and begins her ascent (sections 135-138). All this is eloquent of philosophical reflections on the nature and function of learning. Martianus sounds like a retired schoolmaster, weary of teaching the same material year after year, who finally has the opportunity to use his wit and imagination. This vivid and mildly erotic setting certainly gave great pleasure to medieval readers, while occupying an important place in the literature of the heavenly ascent.

The important role which Martianus accords to music is everywhere echoed in this literature, as our anthology shows. Instrumental and vocal music is ever-present in the *Marriage* as an adornment of the ceremony, while allusions to theoretical music occur in the book on Arithmetic, in the description of the trees of Apollo's grove, and in the ascent through the planetary spheres (see notes). Harmony's eulogy of the marvelous powers of music was plundered for the opening chapters of music treatises throughout the Middle Ages and Renaissance, and many of his examples were still taken seriously by Baroque writers such as Kircher (no. 35) and Nassarre (see no. 31).

Source The Marriage of Philology and Mercury, Book IX, from Columbia University
Records of Civilization: *Martianus Capella and the Seven Liberal Arts*, Vol. II, translated
by W.H. Stahl and R. Johnson with E.L. Burge, New York, Columbia University
Press, 1977, pp. 350-9. By permission.

The Marvelous Powers of Music

[904] While Hymen, in a sportive mood appropriate to the
occasion, was singing this hymn repeatedly and for some length of
time, thinking that he had brought pleasure to the gods, a large
company of bystanders followed the Tritonian and Dione[2] out of the
hall. In the excitement over the return of Harmony, a throng quickly
gathered. A crowd of maidens who had followed after the goddesses
and were standing close by them, and of heroes, under orders to be
present, bustled in expectation; the former to learn the theme of the
songs, the latter to confirm their recollection of Harmony's features.
[905] Immediately a sweet new sound burst forth, like the strains
of auloi; and echoing melodies, surpassing the delight of all sounds,
filled the ears of the enchanted gods. For the sound was not a simple
one, monotonously produced from one instrument, but a blending of
all instrumental sounds creating a full symphony of delectable
music. As this melody soothed the breasts of the mortal bystanders
and the gods for some time, the throngs of those who had gone out a
little while earlier, anticipating the arrival of the maiden, were seen
again in the van, walking ahead of the vast retinue. But their return
was not unaccompanied by sweet and melodious sounds. For
Eratine, daughter of the Cyprian, and Himeros, attendant of Cupid,
and Terpsis, one of the household servants of Dione, were the first to
enter, singing in pleasing harmony; but the lad was [906] playing on
a single aulos. Next came Persuasion, Pleasure, and the Graces,
singing to the accompaniment of a lyre and dancing hither and
thither with the rhythmic beat. At the same time companies of
heroes and of philosophers with flowing locks were moving along in
the van, to the left and the right, all chanting in soft and sweet tones,
many of them singing hymns and praises of the gods, others singing
melodies they had just learned. In the middle were some rustic and
tuneful demigods, playing on appropriate instruments, the Goat-
Footed one [Pan] on a pandura, Silvanus on a reed pipe smoothed of
knots, and Faunus on a rustic flute. A company of heroes that
followed after, attracted great wonder and surprise; for Orpheus,
Amphion, and Arion, most skillful musicians,[3] were harmoniously
playing a moving melody on their golden lyres.

[907] The same song with which the forgetful Thracian bard invaded
the realms of grim Erebus and gained his dear Eurydice; with which the
wrath of the dumb-struck tiger subsided; with which Orpheus is said to

have subdued fierce beasts; with which Mount Ismaros saw the foliage on her trees grow stiff and her forests course up and down her sides; with which the Strymon checked the flow of her waters and the Tanais was often reversed; with which the lamb lay down securely beside the ravenous wolf and the hare drew near to the cruel hunting dog – with this song Orpheus now delighted his audience, adding hymns of praise to Jove.

[908]   And so with song Amphion brought life again to bodies stiff with cold, made mountains animate, and gave to hard rocks sensibilities, teaching them to follow his refrains. The walls of Thebes, obedient to his song, were raised to the strains of his sweet lyre, and he provided a protection. And the billows were not deaf to Arion's lyre, when he in desperate straits cried out for help. Though the frothing waters of Scylla's strait churned about him, blasted by a dreadful storm sent by the unbridled south wind, Arion attracted dolphins from all the seas, and one accommodating creature heeded his tuneful song. O Harmony, verily surpassing the great divinities whose praises you have sounded; you have been able with your song to subdue Erebus, the seas, the stones, the wild beasts, and to bring sensation to rocks.

After them the even more honored chorus of fount-sprung maidens [the Muses] poured forth the nectar of Pierian song; accompanied by the twin pipes of the Phrygian,[4] they surpassed all the sweetness of the delights that had gone before.

[909]   Harmony walked along between Phoebus and Pallas, a lofty figure, whose melodious head was adorned with ornaments of glittering gold. Her garment was stiff with incised and laminated gold and it tinkled softly and soothingly with every measured step and movement of her body. Her radiant mother the Paphian[5] – who followed her closely – though she too moved with graceful measure and balanced steps, could scarcely match the gait of her daughter. In her right hand Harmony bore what appeared to be a shield, circular over-all, with many inner circles, the whole interwoven with remarkable configurations. The encompassing circles of this shield were attuned to each other, and from the circular chords there poured forth a concord of all the modes.[6] From her left hand the maiden held, suspended at equal length, several small models of theatrical instruments, wrought of gold. [910] No lyre or lute or tetrachord appeared on that circular shield, yet the strains coming from that strange rounded form surpassed those of all musical instruments. As soon as she entered the hall, a symphony swelled from the shield. All other music – which, by contrast with its sweetness, sounded dissonant – now became silent. Then Jupiter and the other heavenly beings, recognizing the grandeur of the more exalted melodies, which were pouring forth in honor of a certain secret fire and inextinguishable flame, reverenced the profound

ancestral song, and one by one arose in homage to extramundane intelligence.[7]

[911]   Concluding this stirring symphony, impossible to describe, Harmony turned to Jove and, lending her voice to a new melody and meter, began the following hymn:

"I worship you, O Jupiter, resounding with heavenly song; through you the sacred swirling of the heavens has set the glittering stars in predetermined motion. You, all-powerful Father of the multifarious gods, move and bind kingdoms beneath your scepter-bearing diadem, while Mind, which you instill with heavenly force, revolves the universe in ceaseless whirl.

[912]   The gleaming stars recall your scattering and kindling of the seeds of fire. Phoebus' light beneficently restores the luster of lovely daylight to the earth, bearing witness to your majesty. And Cynthia [Diana], jewel of the night, moves on ahead in her monthly course, a beautiful ornament with gilded horns. Under your dominion the Dragon tears asunder the Parrhasian beasts,[8] rivaling the Bears in brilliance. The earth, yielding its solid body to soft envelopment, is pierced by an axis, and controls and is in turn controlled by the poles. Thus Nereus can know the limits of the seas, and the fiery bodies of the sky can draw nourishment, so that dissonant elements may not teem with strife, that parts remote may cherish lasting bonds and always dread the ruptive forces of Chaos. Ruler of the heavens, best Father, gathering the stars in fond embrace, you quicken your offspring with eternal bodies. Hail! For you our lyre is attuned, for you the gamut of our song resounds in double diapason.[9]

[913]   I pray you, venerable offspring of the heavens, who know how to play upon the barbiton [cithara] of many sounds, make your hearts propitious to our song, as the mixed harmonies of the heavenly senate are being presented to gladden your company. And I in turn will celebrate you next in order of gods after Jupiter with my divided fiction,[10] and my song will attract and delight all of you with its tones, and will goad and stimulate emotions in places, and again will gently soothe them.

[914]   And now, you benevolent luminaries that crown the senate of the gods with venerable crest, although Etruscan rituals celebrate you as the twelve divinities[11] and honor you with sacrificial offerings, nevertheless the two lights that gleam in twin courses, bearing Phoebean names, have been elevated to high rank by their nature: flashing Phoebus and Latona's comely daughter [Diana].[12] Indeed the lunar partner is coming in this direction; the blazing Delian will mount the chariot of Phaethon. I shall beseech you now, chaste pair, our celestial crown, let not what the songs may tell to the divine couple bring a frown to your revered faces, and let not Hymen offend us with his lewdness. The wedding will be celebrated in lyric song; the wanton banter will come forth to the accompaniment of the lyre.

[915]   And now, alluring Dione, enjoy my melody.
        Stern primness yields to love.

The tossing sea that bore Cytherean Venus knows how to commend my
tender song; while Galatea stirs the Muse with Nereus' lyre, flaming
passion draws the swimming Tritons, blowing on their conch shells, and
the chorus of Phorcus; and love ungovernable prevails in the frothy
billows.

[916]   And now, alluring Dione, enjoy my melody.
        Stern primness yields to love.

Maenalian pines[13] have borne my song, and the Arcadian grove, old
haunt of shepherds' pipes, resounds with Lycaean modes. The swift
mistress [Syrinx] of half-beast Pan, is turned into speaking reeds and gives
out sound, and as the god presses her with his lips she sighs forth song as
if from kisses.

[917]   And now, alluring Dione, enjoy my melody.
        Stern primness yields to love.

Cupid, changeable boy, is eager for the strings. Binding his sweetly
strung bow with shoots of roses, he lays his weapons to rest as the Muse
prepares the reeds. Entranced by song, he disregards his arrows and
leaves his tender quiver at our melody. Ardor and song combine to
delight our breasts. Pleasure and beauty in turn: let us sing and let us
love.

[918]   And now, alluring Dione, enjoy my melody.
        Stern primness yields to love.

The mother of the Spartan beauty was a discreet girl;[14] but, lured by
song, she knew not how to protect herself from guile. For a swan,
assuming snow-white plumage (aware that silvery wings were less
attractive and could not greatly please her beautiful eyes), prepared his
plot, and feigning imminent death, suddenly began a tender song,
invoking Apollo's Muses. Then, drawing close to the face of the
perplexed girl, he stole a kiss from her rosy lips and, holding her in firm
embrace, took away her chastity.

[919]   And now, alluring Dione, enjoy my melody.
        Stern primness yields to love.

The goddess of the second light[15] preferred Endymion's song to life
among the stars. Leaving the summit of the sky, she sought out her
lover's cave and, burning with passion, gave her prize to his shepherd's
pipe. Casting off her golden splendor, she entered the sheepfold, and
covering herself with a sordid garment, she delights in the rustic life. By
night, Cynthia feeds the mountain goats and, looking up at the stars,
lashes at them vigorously with her crook. The seductive charm of his

ampler song compelled the lovesick goddess to give no heed to tasks assigned by the gods and to endure their whispering. She spurns the honor that she holds by night, preferring the grotto of a swineherd, and rests her head upon a hard rock. After leaving the Thunderer's kingdom, she finds the grass a sweeter bed."

[920]   Harmony's songs delighted and soothed the spirits of all the gods, and the strains that poured forth from her stringed instruments were no less sweet than the melody of her voice. Hereupon a discussion ensued, to which Jupiter listened with admiration, regarding the pains and labor involved in the production of that music and the effort and unabated concentration that must have gone into the mastery and attainment of harmonies so soft and caressing as to enthrall the innermost emotions of their hearts. Then, when Harmony perceived that those present were seeking the precepts of her art by way of putting her learning to test, refraining somewhat from songs and with encouragement from the Delian and Pallas, she thus began her discourse.

[921]   "A loathsome and detestable creature to earthborn mortals, I have been striking against the star-studded heavenly spheres, where I am forbidden to discourse on the precepts of my art – this despite the fact that the swirling celestial mechanism, in the swiftness of its motion, produces a harmony which it recognizes as concordant with the gamut of all proportions. But inasmuch as a maiden has risen up from the earth who is about to be wed, it behoves me now with my celestial powers to dispel the darkness, which is beginning to lift after a long intermission. I shall run through my precepts in accordance with your request, if you will first permit me to call to your attention the boons accruing to ungrateful mankind from the knowledge that is being restored.

[922]   From the time that the limitless universe of the ineffable Creator begot me as the twin sister of heaven, I have not forsaken numbers; I followed the courses of the sidereal spheres and the whirling motion of the entire mass, assigning tones to the swiftly moving celestial bodies. But when the Monad[16] and first hypostasis of intellectual light was conveying to earthly habitations souls that emanated from their original source, I was ordered to descend with them to be their governess. It was I who designated the numerical ratios of perceptible motions · and the impulses of perfect will, introducing restraint and harmony into all things, [923] a subject which Theophrastus elaborated upon as a universal law for all mankind. The Pythagoreans too assuaged the ferocity of men's spirits with pipes and strings and taught that there is a firmly binding relationship between souls and bodies. [924] I deigned to have numbers underlie the limbs of human bodies, a fact to which Aristoxenus and Pythagoras attest. At last, with a generous

outpouring of my favor, I revealed the concepts of my art to men, in a manner which they could understand. For I demonstrated the use of stringed instruments at Delphi, through the Delian's cithara; flutes were blown by my companion the Tritonian and by the Lydian Marsyas; the Mariandynians and Aonians blew upon reed pipes their hymns to the heavenly deities; I permitted the Egyptians to try their skill with the pandura; and I did not deny myself to shepherds imitating on their pipes the calls of birds or the rustling of trees or the gurgling of rivers. I invented the art of cithara players, of players on stringed instruments, on sambukes, and on water organs throughout the world, for the benefit of lowly mankind. [925] Through me, in fact, men have inveigled the support of you deities and have quelled the anger of the underworld deities through mournful songs.

[17]And were not military campaigns and victories in all parts of the world accomplished through my songs? The Cretans used to engage the enemy to the strains of the cithara; the Lacedaemonians, to the sound of the aulos – the latter would not advance to the test of battle until they had made propitious sacrifice to the Muses. And did not the Amazons make a practice of brandishing their weapons to the tune of reedpipes? One of these women, who had come to Alexander in the hope of conceiving by him, when she greeted him, was given a flute and went away as elated as if she had received a great gift. Is anyone unaware that the Spartans in Greece and the Sybarites in Italy are led into battle by aulos players? It has recently been learned that trumpets rouse the spirits of prancing steeds and battle [sic] and also sharpen the keen edge of wrestlers and other competitors in public games.

[926] And were not peacetime functions performed to the accompaniment of my songs? In many Greek cities, laws and public decrees were recited to the strains of a lyre. I have frequently recited chants that have had a therapeutic effect upon deranged minds and ailing bodies; I have restored the mad to health through consonance, a treatment which the physician Asclepiades learned from me. When an unruly mob of the common people were raging at the city fathers as they were deliberating, the sound of music that rose above their obstreperous clamor held them in check. Some young men in a drunken condition who were behaving in a rowdy manner were brought to their senses by the musicianship of Damon, one of my disciples. He ordered them to sing some spondaic measures to the accompaniment of a flute, and brought their noisy brawling to an abrupt halt. Have not I myself brought healing to diseased bodies by prolonged therapy? The ancients were able to cure fever and wounds by incantation. Asclepiades healed with the trumpet patients who were stone deaf, and Theophrastus used the flute with mentally disturbed patients. Is anyone unaware that gout in the hip is

removed by the sweet tones of the aulos? Xenocrates cured insane patients by playing on musical instruments. Thales of Crete is known to have dispelled diseases and pestilence by the sweetness of his cithara playing. Herophilus checked the pulse of his patients by comparing rhythms.

[927] The Thracian lyre player was one who demonstrated that animals are sensitive to my songs and are drawn to follow directly. In this case it was not a myth but actual fact that established his reputation. How is it that stags are caught through the use of shepherds' pipes, that clattering sounds cause fish to stop swimming in the stagnant pools of Alexandria, and that the melodious strains of a cithara attract Hyperborean swans? It is a fact that Indian elephants are restrained by the soothing effects of musical instruments; it is also common knowledge that birds are attracted by reed pipes and that rattles pacify crying infants; and stringed instruments have won dolphins over to the friendship of man. [928] It is even reported that cobras are charmed by music and their bodies burst asunder from the effect, and that trees and crops move from place to place. And is it not a fact that spirits are exorcised and that the moon suffers eclipses from the use of that age-old expedient? In Lydia there are said to be isles of nymphs which Varro, the most recent reporter, claims to have observed floating off from the mainland at the first strains of flutes, out to the middle of a lake and then round about and back again to the main land. [929] Along the shore at Actium the sea has a sound like that of a cithara. In Megaris there is a rock that produces musical sounds when anyone strikes it. I could mention countless benefactions that I have given to mankind to show you that I did not leave the earth merely because of a desire to get away, but because I was justified in censuring ungrateful mankind for their apathetic attitude. But now I shall plunge into the precepts of my discipline, to bestow upon the bride-to-be the gift I have promised her.

10

BOETHIUS
c. 480-524/5

Anicius Manlius Torquatus Severinus Boethius, born in Rome, became Consul in 510 and subsequently counselor to Theodoric, King of the Ostrogoths, who had him executed on charges of treason. Early in life Boethius conceived the ambition of preserving Greek learning by translating Plato and Aristotle, reconciling them in commentaries, and writing treatises on the Seven Liberal Arts (see introduction to Martianus, no. 9). How much of this he finished, we do not know. We have extensive translations and writings on logic, a *Principles of Arithmetic* that is a translation from Nicomachus of Gerasa (between AD 50 and 150), the incomplete *Principles of Music*, as well as Christian theological treatises and the celebrated *Consolations of Philosophy.*

Boethius' music treatise is a purely theoretical work, following the Platonic use of music as a speculative and mathematic science divorced from practice. As it stands, it is mainly concerned with the calculation of scales and intervals, and is probably in the main a translation of Nicomachus' lost work on music. But the incomplete fifth book is a translation from Ptolemy's *Harmonics*, Book I, suggesting that it was Boethius' intention to continue through Ptolemy's subsequent discussions of *musica humana* and *musica mundana.* These higher realms of speculative music, to which Boethius alludes in Book I, chapter 2, are never discussed in the work as it stands. Boethius may have left it unfinished, preferring to proceed with his translations of Plato and Aristotle.[1]

Since *The Principles of Music* was to become the primary textbook on the subject for the Latin Middle Ages (still being used at Oxford in the seventeenth century), the result was, in Bower's words, that "the Middle Ages inherited a translation of Nichomachus' *Introduction to Music* and an incomplete translation of Ptolemy's *Harmonics.* Rather than the complete translation of Ptolemy's *Harmonics* they received translations of Aristotle's logical works."[2] From the point of view of our subject this was most unfortunate, since it focussed the

43

attention of Medieval scholars on the dry bones of musical calculation: certainly a necessary school for the Soul, in the Platonic view, but one that never led, as it should, to a proper consideration of the subsequent realm, symbolized by the planetary spheres, where the qualities of the soul are imaged in figure and tone. This, together with the victory of Scholastic Aristotelianism over the Platonism of the School of Chartres, accounts for the poverty of the Medieval period in sources for our subject.

On the other hand, Boethius' work, even as far as it goes, did have an incalculable effect on the general estimation of music as an influence on the Soul and as a reflection of the cosmic harmony, his dicta being repeated again and again by Medieval and Renaissance writers. To this extent it assured the perpetuation of an elementary musical Pythagoreanism and Platonism right through the Middle Ages.

Source *De Institutione Musica*, translated by Calvin M. Bower in "Boethius' *The Principles of Music*, an Introduction, Translation, and Commentary," PhD diss., George Peabody College for Teachers, 1967, pp. 31-6, 44-7, 101-4. Reprinted by kind permission of Professor Bower.

Music and Character

I.1 Introduction: That music is related to us by nature, and that it can ennoble or debase our character

An ability to perceive through the senses is so spontaneously and naturally present in certain living creatures that an animal without these senses cannot be imagined. But a knowledge and clear perception of these senses themselves is not so easily acquired, even with an investigation of the mind. It is obvious that we use our senses in perceiving sensible objects. But what is the exact nature of these senses in connection with which we carry out our actions? And what is the actual property of these objects sensed? The answers to these questions are not so obvious; and they cannot become clear to anyone unless the contemplation of these things is guided by a comprehensive investigation of reality.

Now sight is present in all mortals. But whether we see by images coming to the eye or by rays sent out from the eye to the object seen, this problem is in doubt to the learned, although the common man is not conscious of doubt. Again if someone sees a triangle or square, he can easily identify it by sight. But what is the essence of a triangle or a square? This he must learn from a mathematician.

The same thing can be said of the other senses, especially concerning aural perception. For the sense of hearing can apprehend sounds in such a way that it not only judges them and recognizes their differences, but it very often takes pleasure in them if they are in the form of sweet and well-ordered modes, whereas it finds displeasure if the sounds heard are unordered and incoherent. Thus it follows that, since there are four mathematical disciplines,[3] the others are concerned with the investigation of truth, whereas music is related not only to speculation but to morality as well. For nothing is more consistent with human nature than to be soothed by sweet modes and disturbed by their opposites. And this affective quality of music is not peculiar to certain professions or ages, but it is common to all professions; and infants, youths and old people as well are so naturally attuned to the musical modes by a certain spontaneous affection that there is no age at all that is not delighted by sweet song. Thus we can begin to understand that apt doctrine of Plato which holds that the soul of the universe is united by a musical concord.[4] For when we compare that which is coherently and harmoniously joined together within our own being with that which is coherently and harmoniously joined together in sound – that is, that which gives us pleasure – so we come to recognize that we ourselves are united according to this same principle of similarity. For similarity is pleasing, whereas dissimilarity is unpleasant and contrary.

From this same principle radical changes in one's character also occur. A lascivious mind takes pleasure in the more lascivious modes or is often softened and moved upon hearing them. On the other hand, a more violent mind finds pleasure in the more exciting modes or will become excited when it hears them. This is the reason that the musical modes were named after certain peoples, such as the "Lydian" mode, and the "Phrygian" mode; for the modes are named after the people that find pleasure in them. A people will find pleasure in a mode resembling its own character, and thus a sensitive people cannot be united by or find pleasure in a severe mode, nor a severe people in a sensitive mode. But, as has been said, similarity causes love and pleasure. Thus Plato held that we should be extremely cautious in this matter, lest some change in music of good moral character should occur.[5] He also said that there is no greater ruin for the morals of a community than the gradual perversion of a prudent and modest music.[6] For the minds of those hearing the perverted music immediately submit to it, little by little depart from their character, and retain no vestige of justice or honesty. This will occur if either the lascivious modes bring something immodest into the minds of the people or if the more violent modes implant something warlike and savage.

For there is no greater path whereby instruction comes to the mind than through the ear. Therefore when rhythms and modes enter the mind by this path, there can be no doubt that they affect and remold the mind into their own character. This fact can be recognized in various peoples. For those peoples which have a more violent nature delight in the more severe modes of the Thracians. Gentler peoples, on the other hand, delight in more moderate modes, although in these times this almost never occurs. Indeed today the human race is lascivious and effeminate (*molle*), and thus it is entertained totally by the representational and theatrical modes. Music was prudent and modest when it was performed on simple instruments; but since it has come to be performed in various ways with many changes, it has lost its mode of gravity and virtue, and having almost fallen into a state of disgrace, it preserves almost nothing of its ancient splendor.[7] For this reason Plato prescribed that boys must not be trained in all modes but only in those which are vigorous and simple.[8] Moreover, it should be especially remembered that if some melody or mode is altered in some way, even if this alteration is only the slightest change, the fresh change will not be immediately noticed; but after some time it will cause a great difference and will sink down through the ears into the soul itself. Thus Plato held that the state ought to see that only music of the highest moral character and prudency be composed, and that it should be modest, simple and masculine, rather than effeminate, violent or fickle.[9]

The Three Types of Music

2 That there are three types of music, and concerning the power of music

It seems that one discussing the musical discipline should discuss, to begin with, the kinds of music which we know to be contained in this study. Indeed there are three types of music. The first type is the music of the universe (*musica mundana*), the second type, that of the human being (*musica humana*), and the third type is that which is created by certain instruments (*musica instrumentis constituta*), such as the kithara, or tibia or other instruments which produce melodies.

Now the first type, that is the music of the universe, is best observed in those things which one perceives in heaven itself, or in the structure of the elements, or in the diversity of the seasons.[10] How could it possibly be that such a swift heavenly machine should move silently in its course? And although we ourselves hear no sound – and indeed there are many causes for this phenomenon[11] – it is nevertheless impossible that such a fast motion should produce absolutely no sound, especially since the orbits of the stars are joined by such a harmony that nothing so perfectly structured, so perfectly united, can be imagined. For some stars drift higher, others lower, and they are all moved with such an equal amount of energy that a fixed order of their courses is reckoned through their diverse inequalities. Thus there must be some fixed order of musical modulation in this celestial motion.

Moreover if a certain harmony does not join together the diversities and contrary qualities of the four elements, how is it possible for them to unite in one body machine? But all this diversity produces a variety of both seasons and fruits, so that the year in the final analysis achieves a coherent unity. Now if you would imagine one of these things that gives such a diversity to everything taken away, then they would all seem to fall apart and preserve none of their "consonance." Moreover, just as the lower strings are not tuned too low, lest they descend to a pitch that would be inaudible, and the higher strings are not tuned too high, lest they break under the excessive tension, but rather all the strings are coherently and harmoniously tuned, so we discern in the universal music that nothing can be excessive; for if it were, it would destroy something else. Everything either bears its own fruit or aids other things in bearing theirs. For what winter confines, spring releases, summer heats, and autumn ripens, and so the seasons in turn either bring forth their own fruit, or give aid to the others in bringing forth their own. But these things ought to be discussed later more studiously.

Now one comes to understand the music of the human being[12] by examining his own being. For what unites the incorporeal existence of the reason with the body except a certain harmony (coaptatio) and, as it were, a careful tuning of low and high pitches in such a way that they produce one consonance? What unites the parts of man's soul, which, according to Aristotle, is composed of a rational and irrational part?[13] In what way are the elements of man's body related to each other or what holds together the various parts of his body in an established order? But these things also will be discussed later.

Now the third type of music is that which is said to be found in various instruments. The governing element in this music is either tension, as in strings, or breath, as in the tibia or those instruments which are activated by water, or a certain percussion, as in those instruments consisting of concave brass which one beats and thus produces various pitches.

The Three Types of Musician

34 What a musician is

Every art and discipline ought naturally to be considered of a more honorable character than a skill which is exercised with the hand and labor of a craftsman.[14] For it is much better and nobler to know about what someone else is doing than to be doing that for which someone else is the authority. For the mere physical skill serves as a slave, while the reason governs all as a sovereign. And unless the hand acts according to the will of reason, the thing done is in vain. Thus how much nobler is the study of music as a rational science than as a laborious skill of manufacturing! It is nobler to the degree that the mind is nobler than the body. For he who is without reason spends his life in servitude. Indeed the reason reigns and leads to right action, for unless reason's commands are obeyed, the action, void of reason, will be senseless.

Thus we can see that rational speculation is not dependent upon an act of labor, whereas manual works are nothing unless they are determined by reason. The great splendor and merit of reason can be perceived in the fact that the so-called men of physical skill are named according to their instrument rather than according to the discipline. For the kitharist is named after the kithara, the aulos player from the tibia, and the others according to the names of their instruments. But that person is a musician, who, through careful rational contemplation, has gained the knowledge of making music, not through the slavery of labor, but through the sovereignty of reason.

Indeed this fact can be seen in the building of monuments and waging of wars, since they are given other names; for monuments are inscribed with the names of those with whose authority and reason they were ordained, and military triumphs are also similarly commemorated. But monuments and triumphs are not named or commemorated for the servitude of labor of those who carried these things to completion.

Thus there are three kinds of people who are considered in relation to the musical art. The first type performs on instruments, the second composes songs, and the third type judges the instrumental performances and composed songs.

But the type which buries itself in instruments is separated from the understanding of musical knowledge. Representatives of this type, for example kithara players and organists and other instrumentalists, devote their total effort to exhibiting their skill on instruments. Thus they act as slaves, as has been said; for they use no reason, but are totally lacking in thought.

The second type is that of the poets. But this type composes songs not so much by thought and reason as by a certain natural instinct. Thus this type is also separated from music.

The third type is that which has gained an ability of judging,[15] whereby it can weigh rhythms and melodies and songs as a whole. Of course since this type is devoted totally to reason and thought, it can rightly be considered musical. And that man is a musician who has the faculty of judging the modes and rhythms, as well as the genera of songs and their mixtures, and the songs of the poets, and indeed all things which are to be explained subsequently; and this judgment is based on a thought and reason particularly suited to the art of music.

11

SIMPLICIUS
flourished first half of sixth century

When the School of Athens, founded by Plato, was closed in 529 by order of the Emperor Justinian, it was still the scene of philosophical and mystical teaching of a high order under the leadership of Damascius. Of Simplicius we know only that he was one of six pupils of Damascius who upon the Academy's dissolution accepted the hospitality of King Khosroes of Persia. They spent three years in the more tolerant atmosphere of Khosroes' Mazdaean court, then, following a peace treaty between the Eastern Empire and Persia, they were specifically mentioned as being permitted to return and continue to live in Athens unmolested. Simplicius worked there until about 560. During their exile these Platonists may have planted the seed on Persian soil that would later flower in the synthesis of Zoroastrianism, Platonism, and Sufi Islam made by Suhrawardī (see no. 18); and within the Eastern Empire some continuity, at least in book-learning, may connect them with the Byzantine revival of Platonism by Michael Psellus in the eleventh century.

Simplicius belongs to the last phase of Neoplatonism, begun by Proclus, which attempted the marriage of Stoic ethics and Aristotelian logic with Platonic, Orphic and Chaldean theology. He himself left several commentaries on Aristotle and one on Epictetus' *Morals*. In this extract we have one of the most intelligent insights yet on the nature of the Harmony of the Spheres, avoiding the sterile arguments about whether or not it is audible by introducing an order of existence and of experience quite unknown to profane commentators.

Source Commentary on Aristotle's *On the Heavens'* translated by Thomas Taylor in *The Theoretic Arithmetic of the Pythagoreans*, London, 1816, reprinted New York, Weiser, 1972, "Additional Notes", pp. 239-40 of reprint. Virtually the same extract is found in Iamblichus' *Life of Pythagoras*, trans. Thomas Taylor, London, 1818, pp. 44-6 nn.; and in *The Mystical Hymns of Orpheus*, trans. Thomas Taylor, 2nd ed. London, 1824, pp. 80-3 nn.

How Pythagoras heard the Harmony of the Spheres

II, 9. The Pythagoreans said, that an harmonic sound was produced from the motion of the celestial bodies, and they scientifically collected this from the analogy of their intervals; since not only the ratios of the intervals of the sun and moon, of Venus and Mercury, but also of the other stars, were discovered by them.[1] Perhaps the objection of Aristotle[2] to this assertion of the Pythagoreans may be solved as follows, according to the philosophy of those men: All things are not commensurate with each other, nor is every thing sensible commensurate to every thing, even in the sublunary region. This is evident from dogs, who scent animals at a great distance, and which are not smelt by men. How much more, therefore, in things which are separated by so great an interval as those which are incorruptible from the corruptible, and celestial from terrestrial natures, is it true to say that the sound of divine bodies is not audible by terrestrial ears? But if any one, like Pythagoras, who is reported to have heard this harmony, should have his terrestrial body exempt from him, and his luminous and celestial vehicle,[3] and the senses which it contains, purified, either through a good allotment, or through probity of life, or through a perfection arising from sacred operations, such a one will perceive things invisible to others, and will hear things inaudible by others.[4] With respect to divine and immaterial bodies, however, if any sound is produced by them, it is neither percussive nor destructive, but it excites the powers and energies of sublunary sounds, and perfects the sense which is coordinate with them.[5] It has also a certain analogy to the sound which concurs with the motion of terrestrial bodies. But the sound which is with us, in consequence of the sonorific nature of the air, is a certain energy of the motion of their impassive sound. If then, air is not passive there, it is evident that neither will the sound which is there be passive. Pythagoras, however, seems to have said that he heard the celestial harmony, as understanding the harmonic proportions in numbers, of the heavenly bodies, and that which is audible in them.[6] Some one, however, may very properly doubt why the stars are seen by our visive sense, but the sound of them is not heard by our ears? To this we reply, that neither do we see the stars themselves; for we do not see their magnitudes, or their figures, or their surpassing beauty. Neither do we see the motion through which the sound is produced; but we see,

51

as it were, such an illumination of them as that of the light of the sun about the earth, the sun himself not being seen by us. Perhaps too, neither will it be wonderful, that the visive sense, as being more immaterial, subsisting rather according to energy than according to passion, and very much transcending the other senses, should be thought worthy to receive the splendour and illumination of the celestial bodies, but that the other senses should not be adapted for this purpose. Of these, however, and such like particulars, if anyone can assign more probable causes, let him be considered as a friend, and not as an enemy.

II

JUDAIC AND ISLAMIC

12

PHILO JUDAEUS
c. 30 BC – AD 45

Philo was the head of the Jewish community in Alexandria, and spent his life attempting a reconciliation of his ancestral faith with Hellenistic philosophy – Platonic, Aristotelian, and Stoic. His exegetical methods had considerable influence on later philosophers, Jewish, Pagan, Christian and Islamic. Our first extract comes from a long series of expositions of problematic passages in Genesis. He is commenting on Genesis 15.9: "Take for me a heifer three years old and a she-goat three years old and a ram three years old and a turtle-dove and a dove." (The instructions are to Abraham as part of his covenant with God.) Philo points out earlier in his Answer that three is the full and perfect number, and that the ox, goat, and ram stand for the elements of earth, water, and air. His interpretation is that the Law is "gnostic and describes the various forms of knowledge, since the sacrificial act is to be interpreted as conjecture and opportune reasoning" (R. Marcus in ed. cit., p. 179). Therefore the five creatures represent the whole known cosmos, which is being revealed to Abraham in this mystical experience.

Philo's words on the danger of hearing celestial music are supplemented in an aside to his treatise *On Dreams*, where he is discussing the four wells dug by Abraham and Isaac (Genesis 21.25, 26.19-23) as symbolic of the four constituents of the universe: earth, water, air, heaven. To these he compares (V, 25) the four constituents of man: body, the senses, reason or speech (*logos*), and mind or intellect (*nous*), calling the latter, like the heavens, incomprehensible. Such allegorizations were to become a model for medieval philosophers as they approached the seemingly trivial details of Torah, New Testament and Quran.

The beautiful description of the death of Moses is on another plane altogether, and is intended as a direct account of the attunement of Perfect Man with the entire created order. In this Philo is writing as the father of the Kabbalistic doctrine of mutual influence between the levels of being.

Source   *Questions and Answers on Genesis*, reprinted by permission of the publishers and
The Loeb Classical Library from *Philo*, translated by Ralph Marcus, Cambridge,
Mass., and London, Loeb Edition, 1953, suppl. vol. II, pp. 180-1; *On Dreams*,
translated by F.H. Colson and G.H. Whitaker, ed. cit., 1934, vol. V, pp. 313-15; *On
the Virtues*, translated by F.H. Colson, ed. cit., 1939, vol. VIII, pp. 207-9, with
alterations based on partial translation by Erwin R. Goodenough in his *By Light,
Light: the Mystic Gospel of Hellenistic Judaism*, New Haven, Yale University Press,
1935, pp. 196-7.

The Heavenly Singing

from Questions and Answers on Genesis

III, 3   But to the birds, such as the dove and the turtle-dove, the
whole heaven is equally appropriated, being divided into the circuits
of the planets and the fixed stars. And so (Scripture) assigns the
dove to the planets, for this is a tame and domesticated creature, and
the planets also are rather familiar to us, as though contiguous to
terrestrial places, and sympathetic. But the turtle-dove (is related) to
the fixed stars, for this animal is something of a lover of solitude, and
avoids meeting and mixing with the multitude. (So too) is the
inerrant sphere distant (from us) and at the ends of the world, at the
very extremes of nature. And both orders of the two birds are likened
to the heavenly forces, wherefore, as the Socratic Plato says, it is
likely that "Heaven is a flying chariot"[1] because of its very swift
revolution which surpasses in speed even the birds in their course.
Moreover, the aforesaid birds are singers, and the prophet is
alluding to the music which is perfected in heaven and is produced
by the harmony of the movement of the stars.[2] For it is an indication
of human skill that all harmonic melody is formed by the voices of
animals and living[3] organs through the mechanism of the intelligence. But the heavenly singing does not extend or reach as far as
the Creator's earth, as do the rays of the sun, because of His
providential care for the human race. For it rouses to madness those
who hear it, and produces in the soul an indescribable and
unrestrained pleasure. It causes them to despise food and drink and
to die an untimely death through hunger in their desire for the song.
For did not the singing of the Sirens,[4] as Homer says, so violently
summon listeners that they forgot their country, their home, their
friends and necessary foods? And would not that most perfect and
most harmonious and truly heavenly music, when it strikes the
organ of hearing, compel them to go mad and to be frenzied?

from On Dreams

I, VI, 35   For it is in the heaven and in the mind that capacity
resides to set forth in solemn strains hymns of praise and blessing in

honour of the Father who is the author of our being. For man is the recipient of a privilege which gives him distinction beyond other living creatures, that, namely, of worshipping Him that IS; while the heaven is ever melodious, producing, as the heavenly bodies go through their movements, the full and perfect harmony. 36. If the sound of it ever reached our ears, there would be produced irrepressible yearnings, frantic longings, wild ceaseless passionate desires, compelling to abstain even from necessary food, for no longer should we take our nourishment from meat and drink through the throat after the fashion of mortals, but, as beings awaiting immortality, from inspired strains of perfect melody coming to us through our ears.[5] To such strains it is said that Moses was listening, when, having laid aside his body,[6] for forty days and as many nights he touched neither bread nor water at all (Exodus 24.18). VII, 37. It seems, then, that the heaven, the original archetype of all musical instruments, was tuned with consummate skill for no other purpose than that the hymns sung in honour of the Universal Father may have a musical accompaniment.

The Death of Moses[7]

from On the Virtues

XI, 72.   Having discoursed thus suitably to his subjects and the heir of his headship [Joshua], he proceeded to hymn God in a song in which he rendered the final thanksgiving of his bodily life for the rare and extraordinary gifts which which he had been blest from his birth to his old age. 73. He gathered together a divine company, that is the elements of the universe and the chiefest parts of the cosmos, namely earth and heaven, earth the hearth of mortals and heaven the house of immortals. In the midst of these he composed hymns in every mode and interval,[8] in order that men and ministering angels might hear, 74. men as learners that he might teach them a similarly grateful attitude, and the angels as critics to watch how, judged by their own technique, he made not a single false note. The angels would also be strengthened in their faith if a man clothed in his mortal body could have a power of song like the sun, the moon, and the sacred choir of the other stars, and could attune his soul to the divine instrument, namely the heaven and the whole cosmos. 75. Thus in his post amid the ethereal choristers the Hierophant blended with the choral hymns of thankfulness to God his own true emotions of good will to the Nation. He reproved them for their past sins, gave them warnings and corrections for the present, and advice for the future based upon good hopes which were bound to be fulfilled. XII, 76. When he had ended his songs, a blend we may call them of religion and humanity, he began to pass over from mortal existence to life immortal, and gradually became conscious of the dissolution of the elements of which he was composed. The body, which had grown about him like an oyster-shell, was being stripped away, while his soul was laid bare and yearned for its natural removal hence.[9]

13

ISAAC BEN SOLOMON IBN SAHULA

1244-after 1284

Although music as such has never played as large a part in Jewish speculative thought as it has, for example, in Greek,[1] the period of Babylonian exile left an indelible stamp on the Hebrew scriptures as they were revised and compiled into the form they have today. The Babylonians were obsessed with number and its relationship on the one hand to astrology, on the other to music. Consequently when the learned Jews responsible for the "Priestly" source of scriptural material returned from exile, they took pains to adjust all the numbers in the sacred books so as to accord with the symbolism they had learnt in Babylon.[2] Probably the same knowledge lies behind the Kabbalistic books as well: the *Sepher Yezirah* (Book of Formation) and the *Zohar*.[3] But since the basis of Kabbalistic numerology is not tone but the numerical values of the letters of the Hebrew alphabet, the medieval Kabbalists use music more in a metaphorical way, as a general acknowledgment of the principle of universal harmony within and between the levels of being.

This is a part of the philosophical heritage common to Muslims, Jews and Christians alike, for which, if an outward line of transmission is sought, the obvious meeting-place is medieval Spain, under the rule of the Muslims and of certain Christian kings such as Alfonso the Wise. In this tolerant atmosphere the three "Peoples of the Book" exchanged their knowledge, exoteric and esoteric. Ibn Sahula lived in Guadalajara at this high point of Sephardic culture, active as a poet, commentator and Kabbalist.

Much of this strange text is enigmatic, and it therefore seems best to give a literal translation rather than an interpretative one. It is partially a commentary on a passage from the *Zohar* III, 18b-19a, which it paraphrases in sections 8-12. But whereas in the *Zohar* the emphasis is on the community of angels and men, here it is on the personal experience of song as something which can be realized by the soul at various levels, the highest of them being that attained by Solomon and reflected in his Song of Songs. "Song" is here a metaphor for transcendent knowledge, though this does not discount the possibility that the experience of such knowledge may actually take musical form.

Source *Commentary on the Song of Songs*, translated by Shimon Malin from Israel Adler, *Hebrew Writings concerning Music*, Munich, Henle, 1975, pp. 172-4. This publication (part of the *RISM* series of bibliographies) contains a number of other relevant writings in their complete Hebrew texts, with English summaries.

Song as Transcendent Knowledge

1.   It was right for the Sage to have called it the "Song of Songs," and not another name, because of the knowledge of song which was known to the nation at that time, and the Levites used to sing it in the Temple during service. As it is said, "And thou shalt sing in the name of the Lord your God"; and in the Kabbalah, "What service is there which is in the name of God? You have to say singing."

2.   And this Song was a most awesome, great and marvelous thing, because through the melody of the song which is in the mouth and in the instrument, the soul awakens and the Holy Spirit shines in it. And it goes higher and attains supreme understanding, which it could not reach before.

3.   And this excellent Song is a voice coming out of the mouth of singers in fear, awe and holiness. It goes up and down, lengthens and shortens, as if it is inspired by a song of the higher ministers [angels]. And while it moves by degrees which are known and understood by the drawing of the points [of notation] in those phrases which the pleasant voices [sing], these phrases are ordered in correspondence with the spiritual virtues, as is explained in the teaching of music.[4]

4.[5]   And thus said our Rabbis of blessed memory, "Rabbi Yochanan said, three things calm the heart, an instrument, a voice, and a throat, as it is written [II Kings, 3.15] 'But now bring me a minstrel. And it came to pass, when the minstrel played,' which means three things; an instrument, a voice, and a throat – this is a melody."

5.   Certain of the holy singers knew this wisdom better than others. As they said, "Agras, son of Levi, had a chapter[6] in singing," which means to say more than the chapters of the singers who were his friends. And this shows that they had books which were written about the Receiving [*Kabbalah*] of the song, arranged like the chapters of the Mishna.[7]

6.   And all of this is designed to awaken the soul to its [higher] level and arrive at its power of understanding. And then the Holy Spirit awakens and shines, and desires it with great desire, fondness,

and much love. And then it reaches a still higher level, power, and *gevurah*.[8]

7. And to King Solomon – may he rest in peace – it was given to know this song, more than any in his generation. As they of blessed memory said:[9] "Nine angels who sing by night sing down on all those who can sing; and when [men] begin singing, the high ones add to it, that they may know and understand and reach what Heaven and Earth do not reach. By singing, they add power." (*Mishna* Yoma, chs 3, 4)

8. [Rabbi Nehemiah said:] "Happy is he to whom it is given to know this song, because whoever knows this song knows things of the Torah and wisdom, and will listen and investigate, and will gain power and *gevurah* about what has been and what will be."

9. And what Solomon knew, as Rabbi Shimon said, David used to know too; [and he made] many songs and extollings of God, and hinted in them about future happenings; and he added power and *gevurah* in the Holy Spirit. To Solomon was given more about this song, as it is said, "I made myself men and women singers" (Koheleth 2.9/Ecclesiastes 2.8); which means "I acquired knowledge of one of those supreme songs and [those which are beneath them]." He means the Song of Songs, which means a song of those ministers of above; a song which includes [all] things of the Torah, and wisdom and power and *gevurah* about what was and what will be. [lacuna].

10. And Eleazar said: "This is how these singers were until Levi was born." [But] when Levi was born he [they] burst into song; when Moses was born and Aaron was anointed and Levites sanctified, the song was completed, and the singers used to stand in ranks [and because they came from the tribe of Levi, the singers of below were all sanctified and stood in their places]. They were all one, facing one another [connected as one]; and the worlds are one, and one King rules over them. Solomon came and made a book from the song of those singers, and fulfilled the wisdom thereof.

11. And Rabbi Jehuda said: "Why were the singers below called Levites ['accompaniers']? Because they accompany [and join] as one with the higher ones, and whoever hears, he accompanies too, and his soul becomes attached to [what is] on high."

12. And we have adduced the commentary of our Rabbis of blessed memory on the fact that the Sage gave this book of songs the name of "Song of Songs," and it will be solved as follows: a song which is given as an adumbration of the higher songs, chosen [by God] to be sung in the holy Temple of King Solomon; the Lord of Hosts [*Elchai Sabaoth*] is his name, and including in his mercy all kinds of completing parts, he makes peace in his heavens.

13. And our Rabbis of blessed memory said: "Solomon's Song of Songs, a song which the Blessed One recites every day". And one

should study these sayings, because a great principle is included in them, and we have received something about which we will not lie. "Because every Solomon which is in the Song of Songs is holy, save one." [*sic*]

14

ISAAC LOEB PERETZ
1851-1915

I.L. Peretz, called by his translator Rappoport "one of the most modern, most powerful and most European of Yiddish authors," draws here on the age-old traditions of the Jewish Kabbalists. The setting of this short story is the timeless one of the Jewish Diaspora, which could as well be the ancient Alexandria of Philo Judaeus (no. 12) or the medieval Spain of our previous extract, as Peretz's own nineteenth-century Poland. The hungry Kabbalists, as Philo says, "no longer take [their] nourishment from meat and drink through the throat after the fashion of mortals, but, as beings awaiting immortality, from inspired strains of perfect melody." And Reb Yekel's description of the higher degrees of mystical knowledge as "knowing an entire melody" is entirely analogous to "Agras, son of Levi, [who] had a chapter in singing" (see no. 13, paragraph 5).

In other respects, the musical details of this story are intimately linked with others widely different in time and place. The wordless melody that is "sung without any voice . . . in the interior of man" is the state of *canor* described by the Christian mystic Richard Rolle (see no. 25), for whom "these songs shall swell to his mouth, and his prayers he shall sing with a ghostly symphony, and of his tongue he shall be slow." The "melody with which the Lord once created the Universe," celebrated by the heavenly hosts, is the discourse of God, "the sweetest melody the inhabitants of paradise possess," as the encyclopedia of the Ikhwān al-Ṣafā' puts it (no. 15). The student's feeling that his body had lost its heaviness and could fly, his merry, happy and lively state, recall that of Henry Suso (no. 26) joyously dancing with the angels. But such music is very close to death, for when "they require a new choir-boy in the celestial choir" his must be a soul purified from all the dross of the spheres; then, in the words of Poimandres, "he sings with the beings that are there, hymning the Father, and all rejoice at his coming." (See no. 4, paragraph 26.)

Source *The Cabbalists*, translated by A.S. Rappoport in I.L. Peretz, *Bontshe the Silent*, Freeport, New York, Books for Libraries Press, 1971 (reprint of 1927 edn.), pp. 115-20.

The Kabbalists

In bad times the finest merchandise loses its value, even the *Torah* – which is the best *Sckhorah* [reward]. And thus of the big *Jeshibah* [Rabbinical college] of Lashtshivo, there remained only the principal, Reb Yekel, and one of his students.

The principal is an old, lean Jew, with a long unkempt beard and extinguished eyes. Lemech, his favourite pupil, is a tall, slight, pale-faced youth, with black curly locks, sparkling, dark-rimmed eyes, dry lips, and an emaciated throat, showing the pointed Adam's apple. Both the principal and his pupil are wearing tattered garments showing the naked breasts, as they are too poor to buy shirts. With great difficulty the principal is dragging on his feet a pair of peasant's boots, whilst the student, with stockingless feet, is shuffling along in a pair of sabots much too big for him. The two alone had remained of all the inmates of the once famous *Jeshibah*.

Since the impoverished townspeople had begun to send less and less food to the *Jeshibah* and to offer fewer *days* to the students, the latter had made tracks for other towns. Reb Yekel, however, was resolved to die and be buried at Lashtshivo, whilst his favourite pupil was anxious to close his beloved master's eyes.

Both now very frequently suffer the pangs of hunger. And when you take insufficient nourishment your nights are often sleepless, and after a good many hungry days and sleepless nights you begin to feel an inclination to study the *Kabbalah*. If you are already forced to lie awake at night and go hungry during the day, then why not at least derive some benefit from such a life? At least avail yourself of your long fasts and mortifications of the body to force open the gates of the invisible world and get a glimpse of all the mysteries it contains, of angels and spirits.

And thus the two had been studying the *Kabbalah* for some time. They are now seated at a long table in the empty lecture-room. Other Jews had already finished their mid-day meal, but for these two it was still before breakfast! They are, however, quite used to it. His eyes half-shut, the principal is talking, whilst the pupil, his head leaning on both his hands, is listening.

"There are," the principal is saying, "four degrees of perfection. One man knows only a small portion, another a half, whilst a third knows an entire melody. The *Rebbe* [Rabbi], of blessed memory, knew, for instance, an entire melody. And I," he added sadly, "I have only been vouchsafed the grace of knowing but a small piece, a very small piece, just as big as ——"

He measured a tiny portion of his lean and emaciated finger, and continued:

"There are melodies which require words. That is the lowest degree. There is also a higher degree; it is a melody that requires no words, it is sung without words – as a pure melody.[1] But even this melody requires a voice and lips to express itself. And the lips, you understand me, are appertaining to *matter*. The voice itself, though a nobler and higher form of matter, is still material in its essence. We may say that the voice is standing on the border-line between matter and spirit. Anyhow, the melody which is still dependent upon voice and lips is not yet pure, not yet entirely pure, not real spirit.

"The true, highest melody, however, is that which is sung without any voice. It resounds in the interior of man, is vibrating in his heart and in all his limbs.

"And that is how we are to understand the words of King David, when he says in his Psalms: 'All my bones are praising the Lord.' The melody should vibrate in the marrow of our bones, and such is the most beautiful song of praise addressed to the Lord, blessed be His name. For such a melody has not been invented by a being of flesh and blood; it is a portion of that melody with which the Lord once created the Universe; it is a part of the soul which He has breathed into His creation.[2] It is thus that the heavenly hosts are singing ——"

The sudden arrival of a ragged fellow, a carrier, his loins girt with a cord, interrupted the lecture. Entering the room, the messenger placed a dish of gruel soup and a piece of bread upon the table before the *Rosh-Jeshibah* [Principal of the Rabbinical College] and said in a rough voice:

"Reb Tevel sends this food for the *Rosh-Jeshibah*." Turning to the door, he added: "I will come later to fetch the dish."

Torn away from the celestial harmonies by the sound of the fellow's voice, the principal slowly and painfully rose from his seat and dragged his feet in their heavy boots to the water basin near the door, where he performed the ritual ablution of his hands. He continued to talk all the time, but with less enthusiasm, whilst the pupil was following him with shining, dreamy eyes, and straining his ears.

"I have not even been found worthy," said the principal sadly, "to know the degree at which this can be attained, nor do I know through which of the celestial gates it enters. You see," he added with a smile, "I know well enough the necessary mortifications and prayers, and I will communicate them to you even to-day."

The eyes of the student are almost starting out of their sockets, and his mouth is wide open; he is literally swallowing every word his master is uttering. But the master interrupts himself. He performs the ritual ablution of his hands, dries them, and recites the

65

prescribed benediction; he then returns to the table and breaking off a piece of bread, recites with trembling lips the prescribed blessing. His shaking hands now seize the dish, and the moist vapour covers his emaciated face. He puts down the dish upon the table, takes the spoon into his right hand, whilst warming his left at the edge of the dish; all the time he is munching in his toothless mouth the morsel of bread over which he had said a blessing.

When his face and hands were warm enough, he wrinkled his brow and extending his thin, blue lips, began to blow. The pupil was staring at him all the time. But when the trembling lips of the old man were stretching out to meet the first spoonful of soup, something squeezed the young man's heart. Covering his face with his hands, he seemed to have shrivelled up.

A few minutes had scarcely elapsed when another man came in, also carrying a basin full of gruel soup and a piece of bread.

"Reb Joisseff sends the student his breakfast," he said.

The student never removed his hands from his face. Putting down his own spoon, the principal rose and went up to him. For a moment he looked down at the boy with eyes full of pride and love; then touching his shoulder, he said in a friendly and affectionate voice:

"They have brought you food."

Slowly and unwillingly the student removed his hands from his face. He seemed to have grown paler still, and his dark-rimmed eyes were burning with an even more mysterious fire.

"I know, Rabbi," he said, "but I am not going to eat to-day."

"Are you going to fast the fourth day?" asked the *Rosh-Jeshibah*, greatly surprised. "And without me?" he added in a somewhat hurt tone.

"It is a particular fast-day," replied the student. "I am fasting to-day for penance."

"What are you talking about? Why must you do penance?"

"Yes, Rabbi, I must do penance, because a while ago, when you had just started to eat, I transgressed the commandment which says, 'Thou shalt not covet ——' "

Late in the night the student woke up his master. The two were sleeping side by side on benches in the old lecture-hall.

"Rebbe, Rebbe!" called the student in a feeble voice.

"What is the matter?" The *Rosh-Jeshibah* woke with a start.

"Just now, I have been upon the highest summit."

"How's that?" asked the principal, not yet quite awake.

"There was a melody, and it has been singing in me."

The principal sat up.

"How's that? How's that?"

"I don't know it myself, Rebbe," answered the student in an almost inaudible voice. "As I could not find sleep I plunged myself into your lecture. I was anxious at any cost to learn that melody.

Unable, however, to succeed, I was greatly grieved and began to weep. Everything in me was weeping, all my members were weeping before the Creator of the Universe. I recited the prayers and formulas you taught me; strange to say, not with my lips, but deep down in my heart. And suddenly I was dazzled by a great light. I closed my eyes, yet I could not shut out the light around me, a powerful dazzling light."[3]

"That's it," said the old man leaning over.

"And in the midst of the strange light I felt so strong, so light-hearted. It seemed to me as if I had no weight, as if my body had lost its heaviness and that I could fly."

"That right; that's right."

"And then I felt so merry, so happy and lively. My face remained motionless, my lips never stirred, and yet I laughed. I laughed so joyously, so heartily, so frankly and happily."

"That's it; that's it. That is right, in the intensest joy ———"

"Then something began to hum in me, as if it were the beginning of a melody."

The *Rosh-Jeshibah* jumped up from his bench and stood up by his pupil's side.

"And then? And then?"

"Then I heard how it was singing in me."

"And what did you feel? What? What? Tell me!"

"I felt as if all my senses were closed and stopped; and there was something singing in me, just as it should be, without either words or tunes, only so ———"

"How? How?"

"No, I can't say. At first I knew, then the song became ———"

"What did the song become? What? ———"

"A sort of music, as if there had been a violin in me, or as if Joyné, the musician, was sitting in my heart and playing one of the tunes he plays at the Rebbe's table. But it sounded much more beautiful, nobler and sadder,[4] more spiritual; and all this was voiceless and tuneless, mere spirit."

"You lucky man ———!"

"And now it is all gone," said the pupil, growing very sad. "My senses have again woke up, and I am so tired, so terribly tired that I.... Rebbe!" the student suddenly cried, beating his breast, "Rebbe, recite with me the confession of the dying. They have come to fetch me; they require a new choir-boy in the celestial choir. There is a white-winged angel – Rebbe – Rebbe – *Shmah Yissroel* [Hear, O Israel], *Shmah* ———"

Everybody in the town wished to die such a death, but the *Rosh-Jeshibah* found that it was not enough.

"Another few fast-days," he said, "and he would have died quite a different death. He would have died by a Divine Kiss."[5]

15

THE IKHWĀN AL-ṢAFĀ'
(Brethen of Purity)
tenth century

The Brethren of Purity of Basra (SE Iraq) remain a mystery in
several respects. Debates continue on their date, the identity of their
members, their connections (or non-connections) with Ismā'īlism,
Twelver Shī'ism, Sufism, and the pre-Islamic Sabaeans of Harran.[1]
Their surviving achievement consists of a 51- or 52-volume
encyclopedia of universal knowledge, the *Rasā'il*. This collection was
read, and still is read, in many languages throughout the Muslim
world (the only complete Western version so far is Dieterici's
German), and is one of the foundations of Islamic learning.

The ambition of the Ikhwān was to reconcile the teachings of the
ancient philosophers, especially the more mystical ones, with the
Quranic revelation. They acknowledged a perennial revelation of
truth and wisdom to all ages and races, recognizing it as the
inspiration of Hermes Trismegistus, Pythagoras, Plato, Abraham
and Jesus as well as Muhammad and his successors. They were
"Hermetic" in the sense that they embraced a cosmology of many
levels of being, linked by correspondences and permeated with one
divinity, in which the human being is a microcosm whose destiny is
to rejoin his own inner divinity which is also the One God. In
another sense, they shared the practical and scientific outlook of
Hermetism – Hermes was, after all, the god of technique and craft
– in their curiosity about the world and their program for
understanding it in all its aspects. In their treatment of music, for
example, we do not find the contempt for the practical side that we
do in most of the Greek theorists, from Plato to Boethius. Their
encyclopedia itself had a practical goal: it was not a mere
assemblage of learning, but a treatise composed to further man's
development on every level through appropriate use of the arts and
sciences.

The *Epistle on Music*, the fifth treatise, comes near the beginning of
the course (which proceeds from mathematics and logic through
natural science and psychology to theology and magic) and serves to

focus many aspects of knowledge, including psychology, cosmology and mysticism. Amnon Shiloah, in his Introduction, calls it "one of the most magnificent achievements in Arabic musical literature," and we would agree that the Middle Ages, East or West, offers no more complete or beautiful summation of the world-view with which this anthology is concerned.

Source *The Epistle on Music of the Ikhwān al-Safā'*, translated by Amnon Shiloah, Jerusalem, Tel-Aviv University, 1978, pp. 12-15, 71-3. Reprinted by kind permission of Professor Shiloah.

The Powers and Effects of Music

In the name of God, the compassionate, the merciful.

1 Preface

Having completed our study of the theoretical spiritual arts, which are the genres of the sciences, and the study of the practical corporeal arts, which are the genres of the arts, and after having also clearly explained the nature of each of them and the number of their respective species as well as the aims sought by means of them, in two of our Epistles, we propose in this Epistle, called "Music", to study the art which is constituted at one and the same time of the corporeal and the spiritual. This is the art of harmony (*ta'līf*) which can be defined in terms of proportions. Our intention in this Epistle is not therefore the teaching of the practice of music (*ghinā'*), nor of the instrumental art (*sinā'at al-malāhī*),[2] although the study of this aspect is indispensable, but our purpose is to make known the science of proportions and the modality of harmony, the knowledge of which presides at mastery in all the arts.

Know, my brother – may God assist you and assist us through a spirit emanating from Himself[3] – that the matter which is the subject of every art that is practised with the hands is composed of natural bodies, and its products are all physical forms, except for the matter which is the subject of the musical art, which is entirely composed of spiritual substances which are the souls of the hearers, their effects also being entirely spiritual manifestations. In effect, melodies which are composed of notes and rhythms (*aswāt wanaghamāt*) leave an impression on the soul similar to that made by the artisan's work on the material which is the substratum of his art.

Among melodies, some stimulate the soul in the accomplishment of difficult toil and laborious crafts, render men alert and resolute in hard and extenuating undertakings which demand the consecration of great effort and material sacrifice. Other melodies bestow courage. It is these that are used during periods of war at the moment of great

69

battles and combats, especially if these melodies are associated with metrical verses that describe wars or vaunt the merits of heroes, such as this line of the poet:[4]

If I were of the tribe of the Māzin the people of this clan would not have allowed the Banū l-lakīta to take my camels.

Or these lines by al-Basūs:

By my life! if I were in the dwelling-place of Munkidh, Sa'd would not have been oppressed while he enjoyed the protection of my people.
But alas! I live in a strange camp where the running wolf throws himself on my she-camel. O Sa'd, do not indulge in illusions and go! you are sheltering among people who are like dead men towards the client.

It is said that these verses and others like them were at the origin of the declaration of wars between populations and of combats between Arab tribes for many years. Metrical verses also exist that are capable of exciting hatreds, of agitating the tranquil soul and of kindling the fire of anger, such as these words of the poet:

Remember the heroic death of Husayn and of Zayd and of the martyr near Mihrās.

These lines and others like them cause hatred to arise between tribes, and agitate their souls, kindle the fire of anger, and incite them to kill cousins, relatives and members of their families so greatly that they exterminate them for the parents' faults or their grandparents' crime without taking pity on any of them. Among melodies and rhythms there are also some that possess the virtue of appeasing the fever of wrath, of dissipating hatred, of leading to reconciliation and of making friendship and love gain the upper hand. It is said on this matter that two men who had wrought violence on each other and cherished for each other an ancient hatred and a latent rancour, met at a banquet. When they had become intoxicated with drink their rancour awoke, the fire of anger flamed up and each prepared to kill his adversary. The musician, having sensed their intention and being a master of his art, modified the tuning of his strings and played the melody that softens [the heart] and brings appeasement; he let them hear it and pursued his performance until he had warded off their access of anger. Then they rose, embraced, and were reconciled.

Other melodies and rhythms have the power of transporting the soul from one state to another and of transforming its character by making it pass from one extreme to the other. It is recounted, to this effect, that a certain number of musicians were gathered at a feast

given by a great sovereign who took care to place them according to
their degree of mastery of their respective arts, when a man of
wretched appearance, clad in rags, entered. The master of
ceremonies raised him up above all the participants, whose faces
expressed their evident disapproval. Wishing to display the man's
merit and calm his guests' anger, the master asked him to let them
hear a sample of his art. He took out some pieces of wood that he
had with him, set them out before him and stretched strings over
them. Then he set these strings vibrating and performed an air that
made all those present burst into laughter because of the pleasure,
the joy and the well-being that took possession of their souls. Then
he changed his tuning and played another air which made everyone
weep for the tenderness of the melody and the sadness which settled
in their hearts. Then he changed the tuning, and played another air
which plunged everyone into slumber; so doing he rose, went out
and was never heard spoken of again.[5]

It appears from what we have just said that music leaves diverse
impressions in the souls of its hearers, similar to those produced by
the work of an artisan in the material that is the substratum of his
art.

For this reason, all the peoples of the world have recourse to music
and even many animals find pleasure in it. We can find the proof of
the effect of music on the soul in the use that people make of it,
sometimes in moments of joy and mirth, during marriages, banquets
and feasts, sometimes in moments of affliction, at the time of
misfortunes, or in sad assembles (ma'ātim), sometimes in holy places,
on the occasions of religious festivals, sometimes in the market-
places and in their houses, during journeys and in the populous
cities at the time of meals or of weariness, in royal gatherings and in
the dwellings of the common people. Music is used by men and
women, young and old, learned and ignorant, artisans and
merchants and all the strata of human society.

18 *The Various Effects of Music* (al-anghām)[6]

Know, my brother – may God assist you and assist us through a
spirit [emanating] from Himself – that the effects imprinted by the
rhythms and melodies (naghamāt) of the musician in the souls of
hearers are of different kinds. In the same way, the pleasure that the
soul draws from these rhythms and melodies and the manner in
which it enjoys them, are variable and divergent. All this depends on
the degree that each soul occupies in the domain of gnosticism (al-
ma'ārif) and of the nature of the good actions that form the
permanent object of its love. Each soul, then, listening to the
descriptions that correspond to the object of its desires and the
melodies that accord with the object of its delight, rejoices, exalts

and is delighted in terms of the image which it has made for itself of its beloved, and firmly believes in it. Doing this, it may happen to a certain person to be disowned by others when these latter are ignorant of his religious conception and the aim to which it tends. Here are some examples: It is told that an ecstatic sufi (*radjul min ahl al-wadjd*) having heard a reader reciting "O Soul at peace, return unto thy Lord, well-pleased, well-pleasing!" (Koran, 89, 27) begged the reader to repeat this verse several times, then began to say: How many times have I said to it: return, and it did not do so. And after this, he was rapt in ecstasy (*tawādjada*), gave a great cry, shrieked, and his soul left his body. Another ecstatic sufi, having heard a man reciting "What shall be its recompense [of this theft] if you are liars? They [Joseph's brothers] said, 'This shall be its recompense – in whoever's saddlebag the goblet is found, he shall be its recompense [i.e. will remain here a slave]' ". (Koran, 12, 74-75) He asked the reader to repeat this verse, gave a cry, shrieked, and his soul left (his body). The ecstatics say that the man in question applied the meaning of the words "in whoever's saddlebag the goblet is found, he shall be its recompense" to the beloved who is the recompense of the lover, for it is he who is found in his "baggage". They mean by this that the image of the beloved is imprinted in the soul of the lover and the features of his visage are engraved in his heart and this is his recompense. Do you not see, my brother, how the man in question applied the meaning of the words to his religious concept and to the purpose that he pursued, even though the apparent (*zāhir*) sense of this verse is well known.[7]

Another ecstatic heard the words of one who spoke, singing: "The messenger said: you will visit tomorrow. I say then: do you understand what you are saying?" These words and this melody excited him, then he was rapt in ecstasy and began to repeat the words, changing the *tā'* (of *tazūr* – you will visit) to *nūn*, saying that tomorrow we will visit (*nazūr*) until he fainted from the intensity of his joy, the pleasure and the well-being (that took hold of him). When he had come to himself he was questioned as to the cause of his ecstasy. "I remembered", he replied, "the word of the Apostle – may the blessing of God be on him. In effect, the inhabitants of paradise pay a visit to their Lord once every Friday."

Tradition teaches that the sweetest melody the inhabitants of paradise possess, and the most beautiful chant they hear is the discourse of God – may He be greatly praised. It is thus that the word of the most high God pronounces: "Their cry therein (that shall welcome them), 'Glory to Thee, O God,' their greeting, 'Peace' and their cry ends, 'Praise belongs to God, the Lord of Being.'" (Koran, 10, 10-11) It is said that Moses – may he be blessed – when he heard the discourse of his Lord, was possessed with joy, happiness and pleasure to such a point that he could no longer contain himself; he was exalted with emotion, and was in transports hearing this serene melody (*tarannama*) and thereafter considered all rhythms, all melodies and all songs as insignificant.[8]

May God aid you, O brother, to understand the meanings (*ishārāt*) of these discreet mystical signs and of these hidden secrets. May God so do that you may read them, you, we and all our brothers, everywhere wherever they may be and in all the countries where they may live. God is compassionate to his servants.

16

ABŪ ḤĀMID AL-GHAZĀLĪ
1058-1111

The prolific and celebrated al-Ghazālī (also spelt Ghazzālī) was a
Sunnite Sufi and jurist, born at Tūs near Mashhad (Iran). By his
early thirties he was already a recognized authority on Islamic law,
and held an important lecturing post in the *Nizāmīya* (law school) of
Baghdad. Quite suddenly he left, for reasons that have never been
fully explained, and spent the next eleven years in obscure
wanderings. Then he returned to the *Nizāmīya*, and finally ended his
days in Tūs.[1]

It was during his years of wandering that al-Ghazālī consolidated
his learning in the enormous *Ihyā' 'ulūm ad-dīn* (The Revival of the
Religious Sciences), a book whose forty chapters – of which this one
on music is over 100 pages long – form a complete guide to the devout
Muslim, ranging from prescriptions for the minutiae of daily life to
the practice of Sufi mysticism.

Al-Ghazālī drew on two sources for this work: Aristotelian logic,
and the Islamic tradition of Quran and Hadith (legends and sayings
of Muhammad). Although a Sufi, he had a distaste for the
Neoplatonic tendencies of his time (thus we find here no Harmony of
the Spheres), and for the independence from tradition shown by the
Ismailis. In his *Revival* he attempted to bridge the gap that was
forming – and which would continue to widen, despite his efforts –
between the narrow, legalistic world of exoteric Islam and the
transcendent world of the Sufis. Like certain of the Christian
Fathers, he bypasses entirely the cosmic dimension of music – *musica
mundana* – and proceeds straight from the emotional level to the
mystical perceptions which defy description. This directness is the
privilege, or some would say the illusion, of the monotheistic
religions, which ignore the gods in order to aspire to the one God.

Source Duncan B. Macdonald, "*Emotional Religion in Islam as affected by Music and Singing*. Being a Translation of a Book of the *Ihya 'Ulūm ad-Dīn* of al-Ghazzālī. . ," *Journal of the Royal Asiatic Society*, vol. 22 (1901), pp. 195-252, 705-48; vol. 23 (1902), pp. 1-28. This extract is from vol. 22, pp. 729-30. Reprinted by kind permission of the Royal Asiatic Society.

Music and the Soul's Longing

In the soul are strange states, and this is their description. The well-recognized ideas of fear and grief and joy occur only in the case of that Hearing which proceeds from singing that has a meaning. But as for vibrating strings and the other musical tones which have no meaning, they make on the soul a wonderful impression, and it is not possible to express the wonders of that impression. Sometimes it is expressed as a longing; but a longing which he who feels does not know for what he longs, is wonderful. And he whose heart is disturbed when he hears stringed instruments and the *shāhīn* and their like does not know for what he is longing. He finds in his heart a state as though it demanded a thing he does not know what; this befalls even the common herd and those over whose hearts the love neither of man nor of God Most High can get control. There is a mystery in this, and it is that to every longing belong two fundamental bases: the one of them is a quality in him that longs, a kind of relationship with that which is longed for; and the second is a knowledge of the thing longed for, and a knowledge of what attaining to it would be like. Then given the quality in which is the longing and given the knowledge of the appearance of the thing longed for, the matter is clear. But if the knowledge of the thing longed for is not given, and the quality of longing is given and the quality moves the heart and its flame flares up, that entails confusion of mind and bewilderment without fail. If a human being grew up alone so that he never saw the form of women and knew not what sexual intercourse was, and thereafter approached puberty and lust overcame him, verily he would feel in himself the fire of lust, but would not know that he was longing for sexual intercourse, because he did not know what sexual intercourse was and had not experience of the form of women. There is a relationship like this in the soul of the human being with the upper world and the pleasures which he is promised there at the Lote-tree of the Extremity[2] and in the upper Paradises. Only he cannot imagine these things to himself except as qualities and names, like him who has heard the expression "sexual intercourse" and the name "woman," but has not seen the form of a woman even, nor the form of a man, nor his own form in a mirror that he might know by analogy. So Hearing moves in him longing, but abounding ignorance and the being occupied with this world have made him forget himself, and have made him forget his Lord, and have made him forget his abiding-place to which is his desire and his longing by nature. Then his heart demands from him a thing he does not know what, and he is confused and bewildered and distu.bed like one who is choking, who does not know how to be saved. This, and things like it, belong to the states, a perception of the completeness of the verities of which is not to be attained, and he who is affected by them is not able to give them expression.

The division of ecstasy into that which can be made manifest and that which cannot be made manifest is now clear.

17

MAJD AL-DĪN
AL-GHAZĀLĪ
died 1126

Majd al-Dīn (also known as Aḥmad ibn Muḥammad) al-Ghazālī
was brother of the more famous Abū Ḥāmid, to whose chair at the
Baghdad law school he succeeded on Abū Ḥāmid's death. A
theologian and preacher, he wrote a (lost) abbreviation of the *Revival
of the Religious Sciences*, but in other respects seems to have been of
quite an independent bent. In addition to sermons, books on music
and on divine love, he wrote a defence of Satan. The *Bawāriq al-Ilmā*
is a treatise on a lively question of the time: whether music and
dancing are admissible in a religious context. Abū Ḥāmid had
already given his approval to such practices, backed by all the
weight of his jurisprudential learning; but Majd al-Dīn goes a stage
further in his description and analysis of the states which *samā'* can
induce. He obviously writes from personal experience.

His references to a world of lights and spirits which *samā'* enables
one to enter concern what the Iranian philosophers of a generation
later would call *Hūrqalyā*, the "imaginal world" of Archetypal or
Autonomous Images. We will find an exposition of the musical
significance of this world in Suhrawardī (no. 18), but in Majd al-
Dīn's view, music is merely the means for getting there.

Source *Bawāriq al-Ilmā* (Treatise on Sufi music and dance), translated by James
Robson in *Tracts on Listening to Music*, London, Royal Asiatic Society, 1938 (Oriental
Translation Fund, New Series, vol. 34), pp. 97-104. Reprinted by kind permission of
the Royal Asiatic Society.

Sufi Music and Dance: the Samā'

It is then established from the declarations, proofs, and traditions we
have mentioned[1] that audition is absolutely permissible, and that he
who disapproves of it is either an infidel, or a profligate. And this is
rather a matter of approval regarding the novices,[2] necessary
regarding the saints of Allāh (Exalted is He!) with reference to their

77

stations, because they are detached from what is other than Allāh towards Allāh (Exalted is He!). Allāh (Exalted is He!) said, "They seek His face."[3] As often as they come upon anything of the forms, they apply it to the hidden meanings,[4] as he (Allāh bless him, etc.) said concerning Usaid ibn Al-Hudair[5] when he said, "O apostle of Allāh, I was reciting Sūra Al-Kahf[6] last night, and lo, over my head was a cloud in which was the likeness of lamps"; he said, "That was the sakīna,"[7] and he did not treat the cloud as a mere cloud. Sakīna is [of the form] fa'līla from [the root] sukūn, and it is repose in the lights of the unseen world which come down upon one because of one's going backwards and forwards and passing their forms, which are the words of the Qur'ān.[8] And similarly the saints of Allāh (Exalted is He!) apply the forms to the realities (ma'ānī) on account of their abandoning the ranks of the forms and their moving in the ranks of the branches of gnosis. So among them the tambourine[9] is a reference to the cycle of existing things (dā'ira al-akwān); the skin which is fitted on to it is a reference to general existence (al-wujūd al-muṭlaq), the striking which takes place on the tambourine is a reference to the descent of the divine visitations (wāridāt) from the innermost arcana (bāṭin al-buṭūn) upon general existence to bring forth the things pertaining to the essence from the interior to the exterior, the five small bells (jalājil) are a reference to the prophetical ranks, the saintly ranks, the apostolic ranks, the khalifate ranks, and the imāmate ranks, and their combined sound is a reference to the appearance of the divine revelations and unrestricted knowledge by means of these realities in the hearts of the saints and the people of perfection. And the soul of the reality is the form of the rank of the Truth (Exalted and holy is He!), since it is He who sets the things in motion, brings them into existence, and enriches them. And the voice of the singer is a reference to the divine (rabbānīya) life which comes down from the innermost arcana to the levels (marātib) of the spirits, the hearts, and the consciences (asrār). The flute (qaṣab) is a reference to the human essence, and the nine holes are a reference to the openings in the outer frame (ẓāhir), which are nine, viz. the ears, the nostrils, the eyes, the mouth, and the private parts (al-qubl wa'l-dubr). Nine other holes are inverted from the exterior to the interior, viz. the armpits, the inner part of the elbows, under the knees, the inner part of the wrists and the navel. And there are nine ranks inside [the body] viz. the heart, the mind, the spirit, the soul, the conscience, the human essence, the memory, the interior of the heart (fu'ād), and the pericardium (shaghāf). And the breath which penetrates the flute is a reference to the light of Allāh (Exalted is He!) penetrating the reed of man's essence.[10] And their being moved in audition is a reference to the bird of human reality in the station of the eternal address, "Am I not your Lord?"[11] and to the excitement of the spirit on account of the cage of the body being broken and its return to the true home, since he said, "Love of home pertains to faith," i.e. the home of the spirits in which the spirit was brought into existence, since He said, "And I breathed into him of my spirit."[12] And the dancing[13] is a reference to the circling of the spirit round the cycle of existing things on account of receiving the effects of the unveilings and revelations; and this is the state of the gnostic. The whirling is a reference to the spirit's standing with Allāh in its inner nature (sirr) and being (wujūd), the circling of its look and thought, and its penetrating the ranks of existing things; and this is the state of the assured one. And his leaping up is a reference to his being drawn from the human station to the unitive station and to existing things acquiring from him spiritual effects and illuminative helps. Then when his spirit goes forth from the veil and reaches the ranks of what is right, his head is uncovered. Then when he is detached from what is other than Allāh and reaches Allāh (Exalted is He!), he takes off his clothing; and if the singer is the possessor of a state (ḥāl) and a station (maqām), he throws his clothing to him; but if he is not such, throwing it to him is a wrong, because the garment of the possessor of a state is the form of his state, and only he who is of his rank deserves to receive his state.[14] Then if he rises to a higher station and the singer is speaking in a lower station, he suggests to him a verse suitable for his state. But if something about which he sang becomes dubious to him and his state comes to a stop, he takes someone else and circles with him that their states may be united and his bond may be loosed. Then when he becomes thirsty and asks for a drink of water, it indicates that he is overpowered, because the station of the spirit is the station of serenity and dryness from the lights;[15] so when he becomes thirsty it indicates that he has returned to the station of the body, since the station of the spirit is [that of] getting nourishment from the unseen,[16] so that it does not require the seen; while the station of the body is [that of] getting nourishment from the form. So when he returns from the unseen to the seen, he asks for water, and that indicates defect.

As for the signification understood by the intellect which indicates the nobility of audition, its nature is contrast from various points of view.

I.   One is that the states which are connected with a thing are of two kinds, movement and quiescence. Movement is a characteristic of spirits and inner natures, and quiescence is a characteristic of bodies and crass forms. And heat and rendering delicate are among the requisites of movement, while solidification and deterioration are among the requisites of quiescence. On this account, should water remain in its jar, even though it were a large quantity, it would deteriorate with the passage of time; while if it is flowing a little, it does not deteriorate. So when a measured sound affects the inner being, it moves the spirit to seek ascent, and the body is moved by the movement of the spirit. Then heat arises within it and the superfluities of its nature are loosed, and marks which are seen appear in its heart; and that is by the agency of audition.

II. The second is that sensual nourishment strengthens the body, which results from coming in contact with food, while spiritual nourishment strengthens the heart and the inner nature. That arises from coming in contact with the instruments of bringing down spirit, light, and life from the unseen world. And it is the stirring of the spirit by listening to wonderful realities in delicate poems and the abandonment of the attachments of created things, and being drawn to the spiritual stages (manāzil). Now the instrument of obtaining these lights is the association of the brethren and the seeking of help from Allāh, the Merciful.

III. The third is that audition detaches one from external things and inclines one to accept the hidden lights and secrets. Then as often as one's ecstasy (wajd) increases in audition, one's travelling and flying in the world of spirits increases. And when one's increase is abundant, the heart is made fine, and one receives some of the marks of the outpouring and revelations of Allāh (Exalted is He!): then one attains the station of union (wuṣūl) without a new religious exercise (riyāḍa).

IV. The fourth is that the sound Huwā[17] is penetration from the exterior to the interior and is joined to the heart; then the heart and the spirit are joyful by means of the variation of measured notes and by the number of the realities which come down upon the spirit in the ranks of existing things. So when the spirit follows the body in movement and the body follows the spirit in presence, light, and joy it is detached from suppositions and imaginations, and the realities which are combined in the spirit penetrate the bodily powers. Then when the body is drawn to the station of the spirit the veil is removed, and it sees those realities and truths all at once. This is the station of the perfection of actual vision which does not arise by many religious exercises.

V. The fifth is that audition is quiescence in the internal and movement in the external; and other acts of worship, except fasting, are a movement in the external, and the movement in the external corresponds to abundance. So as often as the movement is abundant in audition and quiescence becomes strong in the heart, it is detached from everything but Allāh (Exalted is He!), ecstasy appears in it, and it is drawn to the Unique Presence. Then by the sight of the inner nature it sees the divine worlds and comprehends the divine (rabbānīya) secrets which intellects and understandings cannot grasp. And as for the three pillars,[18] like prayer, pilgrimage, and the two testimonies, even if they are a movement in the external and the internal, yet sometimes a spiritual and facial quiescence which leads its possessor to annihilation (fanā') and immortality (baqā')[19] appears between two movements. As for fasting, it is a quiescence in the external and the internal, and sometimes a movement from Allāh, in Allāh, to Allāh comes forth between two periods of quiescence, and that is the complete liberation and the universal law. So the inner nature (sirr) of audition in its various ranks (marātib) comprises the verities of the five pillars; for prayer, pilgrimage, and the two testimonies pertain to external ranks, and fasting and almsgiving to internal ranks; and sometimes a man gets from audition perfections such as are not obtained from persistence in many acts of devotion.[20]

VI.   The sixth is that audition comprises the perfect states which are the limits of the stations. Its sīn and mīm[21] indicate samm (poison), meaning that the inner nature of audition is like poison which causes one to die to the attachments of things which are other than Allāh and causes one to reach the unseen stations. Its 'ain and mīm indicate ma'a (with), meaning that audition causes one to reach the Essential, divine co-existence (ma'īya). He (Peace be upon him!)[22] said, "I have a time with Allāh in which no angel who is brought near [Allāh's presence] or prophet who is sent on a mission is enough for me." Its sīn, mīm, and alif indicate samā' (heaven) to make known that audition causes one to become supernal and heavenly, and one comes forth from the lower ranks. And its alif and mīm indicate umm (mother) to tell that he who engages in audition is the mother of everything else, gets support from the unseen by his spiritual nature, and pours forth on everything else life and knowledge which the word mā' (water) indicates. Its 'ain and mīm indicate 'amm (inclusive), i.e. he who engages in audition includes in his spiritual nature supernal things, in the life of his heart human things, and in the light of his pure soul bodily things and other states. So he who engages in audition rises to the high stations and the divine favours which one cannot attain to by a thousand efforts and the most perfect religious exercises. And the benefits of audition reach a hundred benefits and a hundred thousand states which he who has taste, ecstasy, and insight discovers. Only he disapproves of audition who is blind of heart, lacking in light, thickly veiled, neglectful of Allāh (Exalted is He!), and inclining to the appetite and passion. Allāh (Exalted is He!) said, "And when they hear what has been sent down to the apostle, you see their eyes pouring with tears from what they know of the truth. They say, 'Our Lord, we believe, so write us down among the testifiers. And why should we not believe in Allāh and the truth which has come to us, and desire that our Lord should cause us to enter along with the upright people?' "[23]

18

SUHRAWARDĪ
1153-91
with Quṭbuddīn Shīrāzī

Shihābuddīn Yahyā Suhrawardī, sometimes known as "the Martyr" and as *Shaikh al-ishrāq*, "Master of Illumination," was the founder of the "Oriental Theosophy" of Iran, a development of Shīʿite Sufism in conjunction with Zoroastrian, Platonic and Hermetic theology. For Suhrawardī, as for many Sufis, Islam crowned but by no means annulled the previous Revelations, which could serve it in turn by providing means for interpreting its scriptures in their inner sense. But his zeal in restoring the wisdom of ancient Persia and his enthusiastic exposition of esoteric doctrines brought him the enmity of the doctors of the law, who petitioned Saladin for his execution.[1]

Here the Harmony of the Spheres is placed within a context in which it makes perfect sense. With the preliminary explanations of Suhrawardī and of his commentator, Quṭbuddīn Shīrāzī, we are introduced to the world of *Hūrqalyā*, whose ontological position is between the pure world of Angelic Intelligences (where, as he says at the outset, the Ideas of Plato belong) and our material universe. Hūrqalyā is the place of visions and theophanies, of Heavens and Hells, perceived by the Active or Creative Imagination. But far from being "imaginary," it is even more real than what the bodily senses perceive. Its "earth" contains the vast cities Jābalqā and Jābarṣā; its "heaven" is Hūrqalyā proper. Dreams may touch the fringes of it, but most people enter it fully only after death, when it is the setting for their posthumous experiences. Prophets, sages and mystics may enter it during life and know it, as Suhrawardī evidently did, as the superior reality underlying the entire material world, whose every person, every entity and event has its root and its *raison d'être* in Hūrqalyā.

When at the end of this extract Suhrawardī turns to the Harmony of the Spheres, he disposes at a stroke of the tedious arguments about whether it is audible on earth. His commentator in turn amplifies this and gives the exact situation of this music and the condition of one such as Pythagoras who hears it.

It now becomes plain in what realm we should interpret the visions of Er, Scipio and Timarchus; where we should look for the *musica mundana* that is palely shadowed in our *musica instrumentalis*; and what must be done to ascertain the truth of the matter for ourselves.

Source *Hikmat al-ishrāq* (Book of Oriental Philosophy), translated by Henry Corbin (French) and Nancy Pearson (English) from Henry Corbin, *Spiritual Body and Celestial Earth*, trans. Nancy Pearson, Bollingen Series XCI, 2, pp. 129-34. Copyright © 1977 by Princeton University Press. Reprinted by permission of Princeton University Press.

Music and the Imaginal World

These autonomous Images and Forms are not the Platonic Ideas, for the Ideas of Plato are of pure, immutable light, whereas among the Forms in question there are some which are dark – those which torment the reprobate; these are hideous, repulsive, the sight of them causes the soul suffering, whereas others are luminous and their sweetness is tasted by the blessed and these are beautiful, resplendent Forms.[2]

Quṭbuddīn Shīrāzī: The Sages of old, such as Plato, Socrates, Empedocles and others, not only affirmed the existence of the Platonic Ideas, which are intelligible and made of pure light, but also the existence of autonomous imaginative Forms which are not immanent in a material substratum of our world. They affirmed that these are separate substances, independent of "material matters," that they have their seat in the meditative faculty and in the soul's active Imagination, in the sense that these two faculties are the epiphanic places where these Forms appear; undoubtedly and concretely they exist, although this does not mean that they are immanent in a substratum. The Sages affirmed the existence of a twofold universe: on the one hand, a purely suprasensory universe, including the world of the Deity and the world of angelic Intelligences; on the other hand, a world of material Forms, that is, the world of the celestial Spheres and Elements and the world of apparitional forms, namely, the world of the autonomous Image. . . . These Forms and Images have no substratum in our material world, for otherwise they would necessarily be perceptible to the outer senses and would not need places for their epiphany. They are, therefore, spiritual substances, subsisting in and by themselves in the world of imaginative perception, that is, in the spiritual universe.

Suhrawardī: I have witnessed in my soul some authentic and unquestionable experiences which prove that the universes are four in number:[3] there is the world of dominant or archangelic Lights (*Luces victoriales*, the *Jabarūt*); there is the world of the Lights governing bodies (the Souls, that is to say, the *Malakūt*); there is a double *barzakh* and there is the world of autonomous Images and Forms, some of them dark, some luminous, the first constituting the imaginative torment of the reprobate, the second the imaginative sweetness enjoyed by the blessed. . . . This last world is the one we call the world of the *Apparentiae reales* which are independent of matter ('*ālam al-ashbāḥ al-mujarrada*); this is the universe in which the resurrection of bodies and divine apparitions are realized and where all the prophetic promises are fulfilled.

Quṭbuddīn Shīrāzī: So we have to understand that the first of these universes is that of the separated intelligible Lights which have no attachment of any kind of bodies; they are the cohorts of the divine Majesty, Angels of the highest rank (*Angeli intellectuales*). The second universe is the world of the Lights governing bodies, whether they be the *Ispahbad* [commander] of a celestial Sphere (*Angeli coelestes*) or of a human body. The double *barzakh* constitutes the third universe; it is the world of bodies perceptible to the senses (because everything which has a body forms an interval, a distance, a *barzakh*). It is divided into the world of the celestial Spheres with the astral bodies they enclose, and the world of the Elements with their compounds. Finally, the fourth universe is the world of the active Imagination; this is an immense world, infinite, whose creatures are in a term-for-term correspondence with those enclosed by the sensory world in the double *barzakh* – the stars and the compounds of the Elements, minerals, vegetables, animals, and man. . . .

It is to this last world that the Sages of old referred when they say that there exists a world having dimensions and extent other than the material sensible world. Infinite are its marvels, countless its cities. Amongst these are Jābalqā and Jābarṣā, two immense cities, each with a thousand gates. They are peopled by countless creatures who are not even aware that God has created terrestrial Adam and his posterity.

This world corresponds to the sensory world: its imaginative celestial Spheres (that is to say, Hūrqalyā) are in perpetual movement; its Elements (that is, Jābalqā and Jābarṣā) and their compounds receive from Hūrqalyā the influx and at the same time the illuminations of the intelligible worlds. It is there that the various kinds of autonomous archetypal Images are infinitely realized, forming a hierarchy of degrees varying according to their relative subtlety or density. The individuals peopling each degree are infinite, although the degrees themselves are finite in number. (*Same work*, p. 240: "On each of these levels species exist analogous to those in our world, but they are infinite. Some are peopled by Angels and the human Elect. Others are peopled by Angels and genii, others by demons. God alone knows the number of these levels and what they contain. The pilgrim rising from one degree to another discovers on each higher level a subtler state, a more entrancing beauty, a more intense spirituality, a more overflowing delight. The highest of these degrees borders on that of the intelligible pure entities of light and very closely resembles it.") The prophets, the Initiates, the mystical theosophists have all acknowledged the existence of this universe. The pilgrims of the spirit find there everything they need, all the marvels and wondrous works they could wish. . . .

Through this universe are realized the divine apparitional forms – sometimes majestic and dazzlingly beautiful, sometimes awesome and horrifying – under which the First Cause manifests itself. The same is true of the *apparentiae reales* under which it pleases the First Intelligence and the other archangelic Intelligences to show themselves, because for each of them there is a multitude of apparitions corresponding to the diverse forms under which it may please them to manifest themselves. The divine apparitional forms may have epiphanic places in our world; when they are manifested here, it is possible to perceive them visually. This was so in the case of Moses when God manifested Himself to him on Mount Sinai, as described in the Torah. Thus it was for the Prophet, who perceived the reality of the Angel Gabriel when the latter manifested himself in the form of the youth, Daḥya al-Kalbī. It could be said that the whole Imaginative universe is the epiphanic place of the Light of Lights and of the immaterial beings of light, each manifested in a definite form, at a definite moment, always corresponding to the correlative fitness of the receptacle and of the agent.

Lastly, when it is said that the promises of prophecy are fulfilled in this universe, if this is understood as the torments suffered by the people in hell and the delights tasted by those in paradise, it is because the condition of the *subtle body* available to the soul *post mortem* corresponds to that of the material, sensory body. The subtle body also has outer senses and inner senses and the fact remains that in the one case as in the other the perceiving, feeling subject is never anything other than the soul itself.

Suhrawardī: The suprasensory realities encountered by the prophets, the Initiates, and others appear to them sometimes in the form of lines of writing, sometimes in the hearing of a voice which may be gentle and sweet and which can also be terrifying. Sometimes they see human forms of extreme beauty who speak to them in most beautiful words and converse with them intimately about the invisible world; at other times these forms appear to them like those delicate figures proceeding from the most refined art of the painters. On occasion they are shown as if in an enclosure; at other times the forms and figures appear suspended. Everything which is perceived in dream – mountains, oceans, and continents, extraordinary voices, human personages – all these are so many figures and forms which are self-subsistent and need no substratum. The same is true of perfumes, colors, and flavors. How can the brain, or one of its cavities, contain the mountains and oceans seen in a dream, whether the dream be true or false, no matter how one conceives of, or explains, this capacity? Just as the sleeper on awakening from his dreams, or the imaginative man and the contemplative man, between the waking state and sleep, returning from their vision, leave the world of autonomous Images without having to make any movement or without having the feeling of material distance in relation to it, in the same way he who dies to this world meets the vision of the world of Light without having to make any movement because he himself is in the world of Light. . . .

The celestial Spheres give out sounds which are not caused by anything existing in our sublunar world. Moreover, we have already proven that sound is something other than the undulation of air. The most that can be said on this point is that here below sound is conditioned by the undulation of air. But if a thing is the condition of another in a certain place, it does not follow that it remains a condition for its analogue. Just as anything in general can have multiple, interchangeable causes, so also its conditions can change. Just as the colors of the stars are not conditioned by that which conditions the colors in our terrestrial world, so it is as regards the sounds emitted by the celestial spheres. We cannot say that the tremendous terrifying sounds heard by the visionary mystics are caused by an undulation of air in the brain. For an air-wave of such force due to some disturbance in the brain is inconceivable. No, what we have here is the archetypal Image of the sound, and this autonomous Form is itself a sound [*Commentary*: Just as the archetypal Image of man is certainly a man, and that of each thing is certainly respectively that thing]. Thus, it is conceivable that there are sounds and melodies in the celestial Spheres which are not conditioned by the air nor by a vibratory disturbance. And one cannot imagine that there could be melodies more delightful than theirs, just as one cannot conceive that there could be a burning desire more ardent than the desire of the *Angeli coelestes*. Hail! then, to the company of all who have become mad and drunk with desire for the world of Light, with their passionate love for the majesty of the Light of Lights, and who, in their ecstasy, have become like the "Seven Very Firm Ones."[4] Because in their case there is a lesson for those who are capable of understanding.

Qutbuddīn Shīrāzī: As the author mentioned in the *Book of Conversations*, all the Spirituals of the different peoples have affirmed the existence of these sonorities, not on the plane of Jābalqā and Jābarṣā, which are cities of the world of the Elements in the universe of the archetypal Forms, but on the plane of Hūrqalyā, the third city, with its many marvels, the world of the celestial Spheres of the universe of archetypal Forms. To him who reaches this universe are revealed the spiritual entities of these Spheres with their beautiful forms and exquisite sonorities. Pythagoras related that his soul rose as far as the higher world. Due to the purity of his being and to the divinatory power of his heart, he heard the melodies of the Spheres and the sonorities produced by the movements of the heavenly bodies; at the same time he became aware of the discreet resonance of the voices of their angels. Afterwards he returned to his material body. As a result of what he had heard he determined the musical relationships and perfected the science of music.[5]

19

JALĀLU'DDĪN RŪMĪ

1207-73

The supreme Persian poet and one of Islam's greatest mystics, Rūmī turned to music and verse in middle life in reaction to the loss of his spiritual companion, Shāmsoddīn. His *Mathnawī* (spiritual couplets) is a work of some 26,000 verses which Persian Sufis regard as inferior only to the *Quran* in inspiration.

In the town of Konya, Turkey, to which the Mongol invasion had driven his family, Rūmī founded the Mevlevī Order – the "whirling Dervishes" – which still celebrates there a *samā'* of ecstatic dance accompanied by song and the music of the *nay* (reed flute). The well-known "Song of the Nay" which opens the *Mathnawī* is inscrutable enough in its poetic symbolism as it brings together the tumultuous and contradictory emotions felt by the ecstatic auditor. As the earlier Sufi writers explain (see no. 17), passive listening would often culminate in the activity of ecstatic dance – equally a part of the *samā'*. The dance of the Mevlevī Dervishes, in particular, is said to symbolize the movements of the planetary spheres as they circle in perfect order and love for their Lord. Its object is to raise the consciousness of the participant to the level referred to here in the tale of Ibrāhīm ibn Adham, at which the memory of one's pre-existent state is realized, even in this life, in all its beauty and perfection.

Source The Mathnawī of Jalālu'ddīn Rūmī, translated by Reynold A. Nicholson, London, Luzac, 1968 reprint of 1926-30 ed., vol. II, p. 5; vol. IV, pp. 312-13, and commentary in vol. VII (1937), pp. 8-11; vol. VIII (1940, repr. 1971), pp. 143-5. Reprinted by permission of the Gibb Memorial Trust.

The Song of the Reed-Flute

Book I, Verse 1

In the name of God, the merciful, the compassionate.

Listen to the nay[1] how it tells a tale, complaining of separations –

Saying, "Ever since I was parted from the reed-bed, my lament hath caused man and woman to moan.

I want a bosom torn by severance, that I may unfold (to such a one) the pain of love-desire.

Every one who is left far from his source wishes back the time when he was united with it.

In every company I uttered my wailful notes, I consorted with the unhappy and with them that rejoice.

Every one became my friend from his own opinion; none sought out my secrets from within me.

My secret is not far from my plaint, but ear and eye lack the light (whereby it should be apprehended).

Body is not veiled from soul, nor soul from body, yet none is permitted to see the soul.

This noise of the nay is fire, it is not wind: whoso hath not this fire, may he be naught!

10   'Tis the fire of Love that is in the nay, 'tis the fervour of Love that is in the wine.

The nay is the comrade of every one who has been parted from a friend: its strains pierced our hearts.[2]

Who ever saw a poison and antidote like the nay? Who ever saw a sympathiser and a longing lover like the nay?

The nay tells of the Way full of blood and recounts stories of the passion of Majnūn.[3]

Only to the senseless is this sense confided: the tongue hath no customer save the ear.

In our woe the days (of life) have become untimely: our days travel hand in hand with burning griefs.

If our days are gone, let them go! — 'tis no matter. Do Thou remain, for none is holy as Thou art!

Whoever is not a fish becomes sated with His water; whoever is without daily bread finds the day long.

None that is raw understands the state of the ripe: therefore my words must be brief. Farewell!

Remembering the Melodies of Paradise

The cause of the emigration of (Ibrāhīm son of) Adham,[4] may God sanctify his spirit, and his abandoning the kingdom of Khurāsān.

Book IV,
Verse 726   Quickly dash to pieces the kingdom (of this world), like (Ibrāhīm son of) Adham, that like him thou mayst gain the kingdom of everlasting life.

At night that king was asleep on his throne, (while) on the roof (of the palace) the guards were exercising authority.

The king's purpose in (having) the guards was not that he might thereby keep off robbers and ne'er-do-wells.

He knew that the man who is just is free from (fear of) attack and secure in his heart.

730 Justice is the guardian of pleasures; not men who beat their rattles on the roofs at night.

But his object in (listening to) the sound of the rebeck[5] was, like (that of) ardent lovers (of God), (to bring into his mind) the phantasy of that (Divine) allocution;

(For) the shrill noise of the clarion and the menace of the drum somewhat resemble that universal trumpet.[6]

Hence philosophers have said that we received these harmonies from the revolution of the (celestial) sphere,

(And that) this (melody) which people sing with pandore and throat is the sound of the revolutions of the sphere;

(But) the true believers say that the influences of Paradise made every unpleasant sound to be beautiful.

We all have been parts of Adam, we have heard those melodies in Paradise.[7]

Although the water and earth (of our bodies) have caused a doubt to fall upon us, something of those (melodies) comes (back) to our memory;

But since it is mingled with the earth of sorrow, how should this treble and bass give (us) the same delight?

When water is mingled with urine and stalings, its temperament is made bitter and acid by the commixture.

740 There is a small quantity of water in his (a man's) body: suppose it is urine, (yet) it will extinguish a fire.

If the water has been defiled, (still) this natural property of it remains, for by its nature it allays the fire of grief.

Therefore *samā* (music) is the food of lovers (of God), since therein is the phantasy of composure (tranquillity of mind).

From (hearing) sounds and pipings the mental phantasies gather a (great) strength; nay, they become forms (in the imagination).[8]

The fire of love is made keen (inflamed) by melodies, just as the fire (ardour) of the man who dropped walnuts (into the water).[9]

III

MEDIEVAL

20

DIONYSIUS THE AREOPAGITE
fifth or sixth century

This Christian writer was identified in the Middle Ages both with Dionysius, the Athenian convert of St Paul (Acts 17.34), and with Saint Denis, the martyr and Patron Saint of France. Peter Abelard was the first to question his identity, then in the fifteenth century the new historical and philological criticism attributed the Dionysian (or, now, "Pseudo-Dionysian") corpus to a Christian Neoplatonist, probably influenced by Proclus (410/12-85). Our translators suggest that he may have been a pupil of Damascius, on whom see our introduction to Simplicius (no. 11). The Dionysian writings include, in addition to *The Celestial Hierarchies*, *Mystical Theology* and *The Ecclesiastical Hierarchy*. The first two of these are the fountainhead of that stream of Christian mysticism that espouses the inward way to a God who transcends all categories of rational thought – to "the superessential Radiance of the Divine Darkness," as Dionysius puts it in Chapter 1 of *Mystical Theology*.

In Dionysian cosmogony, as in Neoplatonic, Kabbalistic and Sufi thought, the universe emanates from God in an orderly hierarchy, and flows back to its source. The first members of the hierarchy, starting immediately below God, are the Nine Angelic Orders, divided into three Hierarchies:

> Seraphim, Cherubim, Thrones
> Dominions, Virtues, Powers
> Principalities, Archangels, Angels.

Music enters in here in two ways: first, as one of their activities as they form into choirs and perform dances; second, as providing the image of the harmony that exists between their different levels of being.

Source Mystical Theology and the Celestial Hierarchies, translated by the Editors of the Shrine of Wisdom, Brook, Surrey, Shrine of Wisdom, 2nd ed., 1965, pp. 50-1. Reprinted by kind permission of the Editors of the Shrine of Wisdom.

The Angelic Hierarchies

Ch. 10   We have agreed that the most venerable Hierarchy of the Intelligences,[1] which is close to God, is consecrated by His first and highest Ray, and uplifting itself directly to It, is purified, illuminated and perfected by the Light of the Godhead which is both more hidden and more revealed. It is more hidden because It is more intelligible, more simplifying, and more unitive; It is more revealed because It is the First Gift and the First Light, and more universal and more infused with the Godhead, as though transparent. And by this again the second[2] in its own degree, and by the second the third,[3] and by the third our hierarchy,[4] according to the same law of the regular principle of order, in divine harmony and proportion, are hierarchically led up to the super-primal Source and End of all good orders, according to that divinely established law.

Each Order is the interpreter and herald of those above it, the most venerable being the interpreter of God who inspires them, and the others in turn of those inspired by God. For that superessential harmony of all things has provided most completely for the holy regulation and the sure guidance of rational and intellectual beings by the establishment of the beautiful choirs of each Hierarchy; and we see that every Hierarchy possesses first, middle and last powers.

But to speak rightly, He also divided each rank in the same divine harmonies, and on this account the Scriptures say that the most divine Seraphim cry one to another,[5] by which, as I think, it is clear that the first impart to the second their knowledge of divine things.[6]

This may fittingly be added, that each Celestial and human intelligence contains in itself its own first, middle and last powers, which are manifested in a way analogous to the aforesaid ordination belonging to each of the Hierarchical illuminations; and accordingly each intelligence, as far as is right and attainable to it, participates in the most spotless purity, the most abundant light, and the most complete perfection. For nothing is self-perfect nor absolutely unindigent of perfection, save only That which is truly self-perfect and above all perfection.

21

AURELIAN OF RÉÔME

flourished 840-850

Aurelian of Réôme (now Moutiers-Saint-Jean) dedicated his treatise
for the use of ecclesiastical singers to the Benedictine abbot
Bernardus (locum tenens 840-9), a grandson of Charlemagne. *Musica
disciplina* is the oldest surviving medieval music treatise, and the first
to describe the eight church modes. Aurelian says that the modes
seem to imitate the eightfoldness of the cosmic motions, but declines
to judge whether the reverse is true, the celestial music following
modal rules, as so many other philosophers believed. He gives a
succinct account of the progression of subjects within the
Quadrivium, and mentions the possible connection of modes to
Muses. Nothing here is original[1] or even very interesting except in
showing the cosmic and classical associations that came naturally to
a Carolingian scholar. But at the very end of the work, after a survey
of the sung parts of the Mass, Aurelian adds, as if beginning anew,
some instances of the hearing of angelic music in modern times that
are without parallel in the musical literature and quite fascinating.
The idea of plainsong melodies being corrected by the angels, in
particular, reminds one of the Medieval pictures of St Gregory the
Great composing at the dictation of the Holy Spirit, represented as a
dove perched upon his shoulder.

Source *Musica Disciplina*, ed. Lawrence Gushee, n.p., American Institute of
Musicology, 1975, ch. 20.

Hearing Angels Sing

Know that among the ancients, ignorance of music was held as
shameful as illiteracy. For indeed the very world and the heaven
above us are said by the philosophers to circulate with a harmonious
sound. Music moves the affections of men, provoking sensations of
various characters. In war or combat it restores strength, and the
louder the trumpet's sound, the more ready is the soul for battle. It

also arouses beasts, serpents, birds and dolphins to listen to it, as we have said above to the best of our ability in praise of the discipline of music. And what more? The art of music surpasses every other art. None who reads the Apocalypse will doubt that the angels in the sidereal sphere also praise God by means of this discipline.

Many instances demonstrate to us that the voices of angels are also heard on earth, and of these we will cite two here.[2] If my memory of the past does not fail me, there was a certain monk of the monastery of Saint Victor, near the city of the Cinnamanni, who by the grace of prayer arrived at the basilica of the Archangel Michael on Mount Gargano.[3] Holding vigil by night before the porch of the church, he heard a choir of angels singing the responsory which is sung at the Nativity of Apostles: the respond *Cives Apostolorum et domestici Dei advenerunt hodie portantes, etc.* as far as the verse *Emitte Domine spiritum.* When he came to Rome he repeated it to the clerics of the Roman Church, and left a record of it as he had heard it. They changed the verse *In omnem terram exivit sonus eorum, etc.,* and thus it is now sung not only by them but by the whole church.

In the city of Auxerre, there was once a very pious priest who among other religious observances used to say of himself that if the very banner of the church should stir he would forthwith arise and immediately hasten into the church. While he was flourishing in this and other such acts, one night, coming out of his own house adjoining the wall of Saint Alban's basilica, he heard a harmonious choir of angels singing the word *Alleluia* with Psalm 148 up to the end of the Psalter. Listening astounded, he followed it to the door of the church. It was the Alleluia that is usually sung with the above psalm on Sundays, repeated once within the first verse, twice with the second, thrice with the third, and with the fourth repeated from the beginning (in honor, I believe, of the holy and co-equal Trinity). The veracity of this became clearly apparent to all when he bore witness to the clerics, assembled after the celebration of matins, and then retired from the center to the crowd so as not to receive a word of praise for himself. And worthily so, for he to whom celestial things are revealed and passes them on to others, although led by a love of the good, should then remain with the others rendering praise to God, and be himself forgotten.

Saint Gregory accords with this, when in his book of dialogues[4] he refers to some boy who recognized celestial speech and knew the properties of many languages. When he came to himself he began to reveal who was in that place, and who would go there and when. Whereupon he tore off his privy parts and gave up the ghost. Fearing this, the Apostle Paul says of himself: "I heard secret words which it is not lawful for a man to speak." [II Corinthians 12.4] And John was warned not to write the words of the seven thunders. [Apocalypse 10.4]

22

ANONYMOUS OF THE SCHOOL OF CHARTRES

twelfth century

This passage is part of a series of notes on Martianus Capella which Peter Dronke identifies[1] as being based on the teaching of William of Conches (*c.* 1080–*c.* 1154), a philosophical encyclopedist of the Cathedral School of Chartres. This school was responsible for the first systematic revival of Platonism on the basis of the Latin Neoplatonic legacy: Calcidius, Apuleius, Macrobius, Martianus, and Boethius. As Bernard of Chartres (d. between 1124 and 1130) said, he and his colleagues were dwarves standing on the shoulders of giants[2] – at two removes, one might add, because the same could also be said of these sources in relation to Plato himself.

William of Conches wrote a commentary on Plato's *Timaeus* – the part preserved by Calcidius – in which he interpreted the work as if every incidental detail were deliberately planned to conceal philosophical and scientific mysteries. This is the kind of exegesis we first meet in Philo (see no. 12), and which Sufis and Kabbalists were simultaneously applying to their own sacred texts. Thus the World-Soul of the *Timaeus* is for the Chartrians a personification of natural forces, subordinate, dependent, and modelled on the image of an Idea of God. The numbers of which it is constituted are a living mathematical form-principle, which harmony is the one bond between body and soul.

With this type of interpretation in mind, the present text approaches the opening lines of Martianus[3] in a bold effort to draw from them a variety of historical, anatomical, cosmological and theological truths. The musical harmony of Plato's World-Soul serves here to articulate creation on the cosmic, elemental, and embryological levels: a harmony also known to us as Love. In Dronke's words, "The theophanies of this Spirit are not exclusively 'spiritual': they can be experienced not only through the theological virtue charity, but by couples through their sexual love and procreation – as well as by the scientist contemplating the cosmic harmonies" (ed. cit., p. 106).

97

Source MS. Commentary on Martianus Capella, translated by Peter Dronke in his *Fabula: explorations into the uses of myth in Medieval Platonism*, Leiden, Brill, 1974, pp. 102-4. Reprinted by kind permission of E.J. Brill Ltd.

Hymen and Harmony

There are three ways of reading about Hymenaeus: the narrative, whether realistic or fabulous, the scientific, and the philosophical. According to the (realistic) story Hymenaeus, a young Athenian, rivalled a girl in beauty, and burned with love for a girl who was his equal in looks but of higher birth. Though rejected because of the social inequality, he put on a girl's dress and kept company with the girls; along with them he was captured by pirates but, being seen to be a man, was sent back to his people. He promised he would get the girls freed if he were allowed to marry the one he desired. This was granted and she was freed, and he likewise enjoyed his love. Thus among others a custom arose of invoking him at weddings for the marriage's sake, as if he were a god. According to the fabled account, however, he is the son of Bacchus and of Cypris or Camena, that is, of Venus, and he is the god of weddings, whose function it is to play at weddings, to sing at the bridal chamber, and to deck the doors with garlands. . . .

Hymenaeus is the little membrane beneath which children are conceived, (in) the womb, that is, which contains seven little cells marked with the impress of the human form,[4] in which the semen that is retained is, as if impressed by a seal, transmitted into the human form.[5] So Hymenaeus is the name for that power which retains the semen. For the ancients called certain innate powers of things gods, as they called the power of producing the harvest Ceres, and the power of bringing forth grapes Bacchus.

Hymenaeus, therefore, because he is present before childbearing, is aptly called god of weddings, for the lawful sexual union of man and woman always looks forward to this goal, inasmuch as it is desired for the procreation of children. That is why he plays in the bridal chamber and garlands the door, for these tasks, which precede the sexual union of the couple, augur the joy of progeny. His father is aptly called Bacchus, for with Ceres and Bacchus [i.e. food and wine] Venus grows hot: the motion Hymenaeus most delights in is aroused. So too Camena, that is voluptuousness or delectation, is his mother, or Cypris, that is commingling, for the human body is produced from the particles of seed proportionately commingled, and the four elements are adjusted proportionately, as in the ordering of the world – for the human body is a microcosm.

But the philosophical interpretation is as follows. Take Hymenaeus as the natural power of propagation, that is to say the loves which they (who love) cherish mutually in glory; and these loves are regarded as reciprocal where Philosophia says:

> This order of things is bound
> by the love ruling earth and sea
> and dominating heaven.
> If this love relaxed its reins,
> all things that now love each other
> would at once wage war.[6]

This is the Holy Spirit, who infuses an ardent charity in all things. He is called god of weddings, that is, he composes the holy conjunction of elements. So the name Camena is said as if it were *canens amena* (singing lovely things),[7] in the delight of musical harmonies. For even as there are nine Muses, and Camena is the one made out of eight,[8] so is it in the composition of the world: there are nine sounds, one in the firmament, seven in the planets, but the ninth on earth. Eight of them – the sounds of the firmament and the planets – have harmonized all that heaven contains, and thereby all the world's bodies are maintained in due proportion. So too he is the son of Cypris, or commingling, for the Spirit can be perceived in the conjunction of diverse things. And his father is Bacchus, for by Bacchus the world-soul is meant, which is the Spirit of the Lord that filled the universe and generated divine love in each thing.

23

ADAM SCOT

d. 1212?

Adam Scot (Scotus) or Adam of Dryburgh was a member of the Premonstratensian Order in Dryburgh, Scotland, subsequently spent time in France, and returned to the Carthusian monastery of Witham, Somerset. The mystical work *De triplici genere contemplationis* probably dates from the 1180s.

In this extract the contemplative experience of sound is described in a hierarchy that rises from natural noises, the cries of animals, and instrumental music of every kind to the human voice; thence to the Divine Word, envisaged both as the archetype of all sound and as the source of the virtues experienced as a harmony in the soul. Adam's description, deeply imbued with Logos theology and Platonic doctrines, is vastly different from the later, more emotional accounts of Rolle and Suso.

Source *De triplici genere contemplationis*, in *Patrologia Latina*, vol. 198, cols 801-2.

The Music of God's Word

I, x. *Both noises and pleasant voices teach us the euphony of the sound of that Word which is God*

After all these things (O Lord God, Creator of all!) which appear to my bodily senses, and these magnificent beauties that amaze my eyes – yet however many and great and beautiful they may be, they are by no means the whole – they come to my ears intending to enter therein, and thus they address me: "Say, how many different voices do we seem to be?" I open my ears, O my God, and into them pour manifold voices and divers sounds. I hear the violent breath of winds, the horrid noise of thunders, the swelling waves of the sea. I hear various cries resembling those of birds and brute beasts; the tones of all manner of musical instruments, both concordant and discordant; harmonies that are in some strange way inharmonious, and dissonances that sound consonant. And foremost among them, Lord God, man, intelligible to man's ears! By the moving tongue, the sounding lips, the listening ear and the understanding mind, one man knows another as a being with wants and aversions, knowledge and powers, just like himself. Through this we gain comfort in adversity, counsel in perplexity, learning in our ignorance; secret things are revealed, things occult laid bare; our ignorance turns to searching, our questions find an answer. Evil things are forbidden, good things enjoined, the indifferent allowed, the perfect urged on us. We are given memories of the past, consciousness of the present, presages of the future. And I address all these things and say to them: "What can you tell me of my God?" And they answer me with a loud voice: "Nothing in us is like unto that Word, the highest and greatest which was in the beginning with God, and was God; the uncreated Word, creating all things; the unmoved mover of all; the Word not made in time, but begotten from eternity; the timeless and spaceless Word, disposing time, spaces and all things temporal and spatial; the Word that nothing precedes or follows, but to which all things are present; the Word which comes forth from the mouth of the Most High, which the heart or the Father gave forth, which without the motion of the tongue of the noise of lips teaches knowledge to angels and men; the Word which is not transient but permanent; which instils sweet sounds in the faithful soul; which fills the inner ear with a spiritual symphony of love for God and one's neighbour; of faith, hope and charity. It sounds the *diatessaron*[1] of prudence, fortitude, justice and temperance, and the *diapason*[2] of the five senses, that the eye may not be tainted with vanity, nor the ear with curiosity, the nose with voluptuousness, the taste with gluttony, the touch with impurity. At its extreme, encompassing both the inner and the outer man, this word sings the sweet melody of a *diapason* in the ear of the heart: the four cardinal virtues mentioned above operate through the five senses, as the *diatessaron* is joined to the *diapente*[3] to make a *diapason*. Beauteous, therefore, is our melody, and wholly beautiful; yet far more so is the euphony of this Word by which we ourselves have our being, and which is verily your God. But you will not find it unless you search above us; because it made us, too."

24

JACQUES DE LIÈGE

c. 1260–after 1330

Jacques de Liège (Jacobus Leodiensis) was the author of the musical *summa* of the high Middle Ages: the vast encyclopedia in 7 books and 521 chapters whose title, *The Mirror of Music*, announces his universal approach.[1] Writing in old age, he says that he himself is still "as it were seized and possessed" by music. But what he means is very broad: "Music extends itself to all things," he says in Chapter 2, comprising not only the Boethian categories of *musica mundana* and *humana* (see no. 10) but one higher still, *musica coelestis* or *divina*: an addition necessitated by the Christian cosmology, with its intelligible heavens beyond the visible ones. Actually, Jacques regards all of these divisions of music as intelligible rather than sensible. His exposition of them stands unequalled as a monument of the medieval achievement in speculative music, but it stands alone. The theorists of the Ars Nova period who succeeded him were not concerned with these matters, and there was no living tradition of musical esotericism comparable to the Islamic *samā'* from which such speculative enterprises could draw their lifeblood. Jacques himself was not happy with the state of music. His final book is a defense of the Ars Antiqua style of polyphony against the current Ars Nova: a defense which has brought him an unfavorable reputation among historians who value innovation above all. But in this rejection we can see a symptom of the peculiar destiny of the arts in the West. In place of concentration on the "vertical" spiritual possibilities inherent in every artistic tradition, Western culture has witnessed a "horizontal" flux of ever-changing styles, fascinating in themselves but quite irrelevant to the higher purposes of art. Believing as he did, Jacques was right to fear the incursion of musical secularism, the cultivation of variety for its own sake, and the devaluation of the speculative in favor of the practical.

Source   Speculum musicae, ed. R. Bragard, vol. I, Rome, American Institute of Musicology, 1955, pp. 50-4.

The Music of the Human Being

Ch. 14   What musica humana treats of

1.   *Musica humana*, in accordance with its name, treats those things which concern man; who, as was mentioned, is as it were a lesser world in whom, according to Blessed Gregory,[2] every created thing shines forth in another way. For man has being, like stones; life, like plants and trees; feeling, like irrational animals; intelligence, like celestial angels; and is himself, according to others, the end of every creature. Hence on the sixth day he, of all creatures, was formed after the image of God. 2. And since there are three parts in man – soul, body, and the union of these two – *musica humana* is principally a matter of these three: for it concerns the powers in him which are called parts of the soul or virtues, in order to compare them to each other, to the soul, and to his acts; to investigate the proportion of elements which come together to make the human body; and to consider the union of body with soul. And since Boethius[3] appears to treat this last matter first, we too will treat it first, though it will be well to make mention of other things which are connected to it.

The soul, whatever it may be, in order to be united with the body it is to inform, requires the body to be of such a kind that it can do its work therein. Hence it requires a body suitably adapted and disposed for itself. 3. For the acts of active things are upon something passive and disposed. But the soul is the first act of the physical body, the power of an organism to have life; and, in consequence, the more any soul is perfect and the principle of many and perfect operations, the more it requires a well-disposed and organized body. 4. But the human soul is considered the most perfect of the forms which can be united with a body. Therefore it requires a better disposed and organized body than other living things, which is why the embryo is said to live first the life of a plant, then that of an animal. The proper disposition of human life, however, is such that the disposition which suffices for the life of a plant or an animal does not suffice for the life of man, which is through the intellective soul, by which we have our being, move, live, feel and understand. 5. Therefore a marvelous proportion is required between the soul of man and the body which it has to inform; and the union of the soul with a body is marvelous, because the soul itself, existing incorruptibly, is not led either by the active power of any natural agent, nor by the passive power of the matter itself, but is induced from outside, namely by God himself creating directly and instilling it into a corruptible body. 6. Boethius spoke of

103

this as follows: "For what is it that mingles that incorporeal life of reason with the body, if not some harmony [*coaptatio*] and, as it were, tuning, making low and high notes like a single consonance?",[4] in which the body serves as an image of the low notes and the soul of the high ones. 7. And although man is thus mixed from disparate parts, the union of a soul to its own body, and its love for it, are such that as far as possible it never naturally wishes to be separated from it, and remains in it so long as it can fulfil its operations through it; and even if the body is rendered wholly useless, it cannot be separated from it without great pain; and this separation is called death. For excluding or excepting the pain which a soul incurs through mortal sin which separates it from God, the greatest pain is caused by being separated from the body. Hence the Philosopher said that "death is a terrible end":[5] most of all that which is through mortal sin, and secondly that which is through the separation of the soul from the material body. For if matter can receive no more perfect form than the human soul, it is no wonder that it grieves, as one might say, on losing it. 8. Even when the soul is separated from the body, though it may live and remain without it, it desires so much to reunite with it that, according to Blessed Augustine,[6] it is said to be detained from its perfect bliss until it is reunited with it, unless it be made otherwise by dispensation (which I say because Christ's soul was separated from His body for those three days, but was not detained thereafter from its perfect bliss).

Yet *musica humana* does not only look into the union and proportions of the body and soul, but also those of the soul and its powers; the first union, however, is essential, the other accidental. 9. For the powers flow from the soul like accidents from their own subject. They are called powers, then, because by means of them the soul performs its operations. By means of the intellect, for example, it goes forth into action by understanding, when an object is present and an act of will concurs with it (because it lies in us to understand as we wish). And since the human soul is the principle of many operations, such as understanding, willing, feeling, growing and moving, and since it does not exercise them directly, but by means of powers, it requires many of these: some rational, which are not essentially tied to the organs, others irrational, tied to the corporeal organs. This type of music will have to compare these powers or parts of the soul with one another, and observe the connections which they have among themselves, to the soul, and to its objects: how so many distinct powers are connected within one single soul. 10. Thus Boethius says: "What is it that unites the parts of the soul, which, according to Aristotle, is a compound of the rational and the irrational?"[7] Music must also investigate the organization of the powers of the soul (which Boethius calls the parts): which are superior and nobler, which rational, and which are parts of the image by which man is capable of acts of blessedness (such as memory, which corresponds to the Father; intelligence, to the Son; will, to the Holy Spirit); how these should dominate the others, and how man should chiefly be ruled by them. Through this type of music one may observe these and many other things about the soul and its powers.

By this means one may even descend to man's body and see how it should best be disposed towards the reception of the soul, as was said above; how it is best constituted for exercising the operations of the organism's powers; and, since it is made from the four elements, how these are mutually connected and, thus joined, how they may persist. 11. Thus Boethius says: "What is it, in truth, that mingles the elements of the body or connects the parts together in an established order?"[8] Now there are in the human body, among other mixed elements, four that are best proportioned, best disposed for moderation, concord and temperament; and this is why man has a better sense of touch than other animals, a stronger constitution, and better sense-organs. For this furthers it. Man is thus the most prudent of animals. 12. Even the soul, so long as it is joined to the body, depends for the works of intellect on the sensitive virtues which minister to it: for as far as the natural intellect of the conjoined soul is concerned, whatever is in the intellect was previously in the senses, and the intelligence is obliged to look at appearances [fantasmata]. When these are disturbed, the intellect is also disturbed, as we see in those who are raging, drunk, insane, or excessively angry.

13. And that will suffice as a summary of these types of music. If anyone were able and willing to pursue them in detail, he could fill many pages. But even Boethius promised to discuss *musica mundana* and *humana* at a later time, and did not do so. Even his *musica instrumentalis* is not complete, perhaps because he was prevented by death. 14. It was a great loss that he did not complete what he proposed to do, because after he had finished treating these matters relating to music (but in the three types named), perhaps he would have given us geometry and astronomy. The types of music we have touched on seem to be concerned purely with theoretical music. But *instrumentalis*, which we will now pursue, is divided into theoretical, as it is called, and practical.

25

RICHARD ROLLE

d. 1349

Richard Rolle of Hampole (near Doncaster) was an educated and well-connected man who chose to live for the most part as a hermit, unattached to any community or religious order. He calls the forms taken by his mystical experiences by three terms: *calor* (heat), *dulcor* (sweetness), and *canor.* (song), of which the latter is described here. First, it seems, he heard supernatural voices singing, then the song welled up in him of its own accord, gradually becoming a continuous state which made earthly music seem redundant.

Rolle is quite naïve and matter-of-fact in describing his gift. His nature, and consequently what he gained from his experience of supernatural song, seems to have been strongly emotional: he is very different from a mystic such as Pythagoras who brought back mathematical revelations from his musical voyages. Rolle writes without any display of learning or intellectual curiosity, but with a fair sense of his own worth and of the special favor shown to him in this gift. Like many mystics, he had difficulty adjusting to the expectations of ordinary believers. I have retained Misyn's translation, made in 1435, because it seems to reflect the qualities of Rolle's character better than modern versions.

Source *The Fire of Love*, translated by Richard Misyn (spelling modernized), London, Early English Text Society, 1896 (Orig. Ser., no. 106), pp. 35-6, 68-73.

A Mystic's Inner Song

from Bk I, ch. 16

From the beginning forsooth of my life-changing and of my mind to the opening of the heavenly door, that, the face cast down, the eye of heart heavenly things might behold and see what way my love it might seek and to him busily desire, three years are run except three months or four. The door forsooth yet biding open, unto the time in which in heart verily was felt heat of love everlasting, a year near-hand is passed.

I sat forsooth in a chapel and whilst with sweetness of prayer or meditation much I was delighted, suddenly in me I felt a merry heart and unknown. But when first I wondered doubting of whom it should be, by long time, I am expert not of creature but of my maker it was, for more hot and gladder I found it. That heat truly sensibly sweet smelling unhopingly, I was busy unto the inshedding and taking of heavenly sound or ghostly, the which to songs long of loving everlasting and sweetness of melody unseen – for known or heard may it not be but of him that it takes; whom it behoves clean to be and from the earth departed – half a year, three months and some weeks are overrun. Whilst truly in the same chapel I sat, and in the night before supper as I might psalms I sung, as were the noise of readers or rather singers above me I beheld. Whilst also praying to heaven with all desire I took heed, on what manner I wot not suddenly in me noise of song I felt, and likingest melody heavenly I took, with me dwelling in mind. Forsooth my thought continually to mirth of song was changed, and as were loving I had [when] thinking, and in prayers and psalms saying the same sound I set down, and so forth to sing that before I said for plenty of inward sweetness I burst out, forsooth privily, for alone before my maker. I was not known of them that me saw, as peradventure, if they had known, above measure they would have worshipped me, and so part of the flower fairest I should have lost, and into forsaking I should have fallen.

from Bk II, ch. 1

Because that in the church of God are singers, ordained in their degrees, set to love God, and the people to stir to devotion, some have come to me asking why I would not sing as other men when they have oft-times seen me in solemn masses. They weened forsooth I had done wrong, for any man they say is bound to sing bodily before his maker and music yield of his outward voice. Therefore I answered not, for how to my maker I gave melody and sweet voice they knew not. They weened truly that ghostly song no man might have, for by what way they could not understand. A fondness truly it is to trow that a man, and namely he that to God's service is perfectly given, of his love no special gift should have that many others have not; but many this trow for in themselves none such they found. Therefore I have sought some manner of answer to show, and to reproofs fully not give stead.

What belongs it to them of other men's life, whose manners in many things surpass their life as they wot, and are far higher in things that are unseen? Whether it is lawful to God that he will do, or their sight is wicked and God is good, or will not they God's will bring under their measure? Are not all men God's, and whom he will he takes, and whom he will he forsakes, and when he will he gives that him pleases to show the greatness of his goodness? I trow therefore the grumblers and backbiters for they would that others, higher in devotion, to them come down and them conformed in all things to their laws; they ween they be higher when they are far lower.

Therefore my soul boldness has found a little to open my music that to me is come by burning love, in which I sing before Jesu, and notice sounds of the greatest sweetness. The more also against me they have stood for outward songs that in churches are wont and organs' sweetness that gladly of the people are heard, I fled, alone amongst these biding or else when need of mass hearing it asked, the which else I might not hear, or solemnity of the day for wrong biting of the people. Alone truly I have desired to fit that to Christ alone I might take heed, that to me had given ghostly song in the which to him loving and prayers I should offer.

from Bk II, ch. 2

Continually, when Christ will, not of his deserving but Christ's goodness, a sound holy thought he shall take from heaven sent, and meditation into song shall be changed, and the mind shall bide in marvelous melody. It is soothly angels' sweetness that he has taken in soul, and the same loving, though it be not in the same words, to God he shall sing. Such song as is of angels, so is the voice [of] his true lover, though it be not so great or perfect for frailty of flesh that yet cumbers [the soul]. He that this knows, angels' song also he knows, for both are of a kind here and in heaven. Tune to song pertains, not to the ditty that is sung. This praising and song is angels' meat, in which also men living hottest in love singing in Jesu are glad, now when they have taken the doom of endless praising that of angels to God is sung, in psalm 78 is written *Panem angelorum manducavit homo*, that is to say, "Angels' bread man has eaten: and so nature is renewed and now shall pass into a godly joy and happy likeness, so that it shall be happy, sweet, godly and soundly and in themself, shall feel lust of everlasting love and with great sweetness continually it shall sing." To such a lover soothly happens in doctors' writings that I have not found expressed, that is: these songs shall swell to his mouth, and his prayers he shall sing with a ghostly symphony, and of his tongue he shall be slow, for be great plenty of inward joy and singular sounds tarrying by songs that he in an hour was wont to say, scarcely in half an hour he may fulfil. Alone soothly shall he sit whilst he it takes, with others not singing, nor psalms read. I say not every man thus should do, but he to whom it is given, and what him likes let him fulfil, for of the Holy Ghost he is led, nor for men's words from his life he shall not turn. In a clear heat certain he shall dwell, and in full sweet melody he shall be lifted; person of man he shall not accept, and therefore a fool or churl of some he shall be called, for God in joyful songs he shall praise, loving of God of his whole heart shall up burst, and his sweet voice shall come to height, the which God's majesty likes to hear.

A fair visage he has whose fairness God desires. Wisdom unmade in the self it keeps. Wisdom truly is drawn of privities, and the liking thereof is with lovers of everlasting, for it is not found in their souls that likingly live. He dwells in him of whom I spake, for all holy in Christ's love he melts. And all his inward members to God cry. This cry is love and song, that a great voice raises to God's ears. It is also a good desire affection of virtue. His crying is out of this world, for his mind nothing but Christ desires. His soul within is all burned with fire of love, so that his heart is light and burning, and nothing outward he does but that to good may be expounded. God he loves in song, but that in silence, not to men's ears but in God's sight and in a marvellous sweetness praising he yields.

from Ch. 3

But every man in holiness raised, in this may know that he this song has of which I speak, if he may not sustain cry of singers, but if his inward songs to mind be brought, and outward to say he be erring. That some truly among singers and readers are distracted is not of perfection, but of unstableness of mind, for other men's words their prayers break and destroy; and foorsooth to perfects this happens not, they truly are so stable that with no cry or noise or any other thing from prayer they may be distracted, or thought, but only from song. For sweet ghostly song truly and full special it is given, with outward songs accords not the which in churches and elsewhere are used. It discords much, for all that the man's voice outward is formed with bodily ears to be heard, but among angels' tones it has an acceptable melody and with marvels it is commended of them that have known it. See and understand and be not beguiled, for to you I have showed, to the worship of almighty God and to your profit, why that I fled singers in churches and by what cause I loved not with them to mingle, and organ players I desired not to hear.

26

HENRY SUSO

c. 1295–1366

Blessed Henry Suso (Heinrich Seuse) was a German mystic, a follower of the great Meister Eckhart, who lived as a monk and wandering preacher. His autobiography, in which he writes of himself in the third person as the "Servitor," shows him as a deeply romantic soul, visited by glorious visions and witness of strange phenomena. He was also something of a fanatic, inflicting gruesome physical tortures on himself.[1]

Suso's inner music, as described in these chapters, seems to have been an experience closely akin to Rolle's (no. 25): it was both the hearing of angelic voices, and a responding melody in his own soul. The angels' telling him that they also hear his song recalls the reciprocal listening of angels and men in the Jewish tradition, while the transition from music to active dance – though here it transpires only in the Imaginal World – occurs also in the celebration of *samāʿ* (see the Islamic texts, especially Majd al-Dīn al-Ghazālī (no. 17)). It also recalls the visions of Dante's *Paradiso*, in which dance, rather than music alone, figures as the expression of angelic worship.[2]

Source *The Life of Blessed H. Suso, by Himself*, translated by T.F. Knox, London, 1865, pp. 23-9.

Singing and Dancing with the Angels

Ch. 6 Of the foretaste of divine consolations, with which God sometimes allures beginners

It was his custom to go into his chapel after matins, and sitting down upon his chair to take a little rest. He sat there but a short time, until the watchman announced the break of day; when, opening his eyes, he used to fall at once on his knees, and salute the rising morning star, heaven's gentle queen, with this intention that, as the little birds in summer greet the daylight, and receive it joyously, even so did he mean to greet with joyful longings her, who brings the light of the everlasting day; and he did not merely say these words, but he accompanied them with a sweet still melody in his soul.

Once at this time, while he sat thus at rest, he heard within him something which rang so tenderly, that his whole heart was stirred by it. The voice sang in tones sweet and loud, as the morning star uprose, these words: – "*Stella maris Maria hodie processit ad ortum*: Mary the morning star has risen today." This strain resounded in him with such unearthly sweetness, that it filled his whole soul with gladness, and he sang with it joyously. After they had thus sung together, he was embraced in a way ineffable, and it was said to him at the time: – The more lovingly thou embracest me, and the more spiritually thou kissest me, so much the more ravishingly and lovingly shalt thou be embraced by my glory. Upon this he opened his eyes, and, the tears rolling down his cheeks, he saluted the rising morning star according to his custom. When this first salutation was ended, he next saluted with a *venia* the gentle Eternal Wisdom in the words of the prayer, beginning "*Anima mea desideravit te*," etc. This was followed by a third salutation, with another *venia*, which he addressed to the highest and most fervent of the Seraphim, even to the one who flames upwards in hottest and fieriest love towards the Eternal Wisdom, and this he did with the intention that the spirit should so inflame his heart with divine love, that he might both be on fire himself and enkindle the hearts of all men with his loving words and teaching. These were the salutations which he made every morning.

One night in the carnival time, when he had prolonged his prayer until the watchman's horn announced the daybreak, the thought came to him: – Sit a little longer, before thou greetest the bright morning star. Thereupon, his senses being thus for a short time lulled to rest, it seems to him that the heavenly spirits began with loud voice to intone the beautiful responsory, "*Surge et illuminare, Jerusalem* (Isaiah 60.1): Arise, and be illuminated, Jerusalem", and it rang with exceeding sweetness in his soul. They had scarcely sung a little, when his soul became so full of the heavenly strain, that his frail body could bear no more, and opening his eyes, his heart overflowed, and the burning tears streamed down his cheeks.

Once at this time, as he was sitting thus, it seemed to him in a vision that he was carried into another land, and that his angel stood there before him full tenderly at his right hand. The Servitor sprang up at once, and, embracing his dear angel, clung round him, and pressed him to his soul as lovingly as he could, so that there was naught between them, as it appeared to him. Then in sorrowful accents and with weeping eyes he exclaimed out of the fulness of his heart: – O my angel, whom the faithful God has given me for my consolation and guard, I pray thee, by the love thou hast for God, not to leave me. The angel answered him and said: – Canst thou not trust God? Behold, God has so lovingly embraced thee in His eternity, that He will never leave thee.

It came to pass once, after the time of his sufferings was over, that early one morning he was surrounded in a vision by the heavenly spirits. Whereupon he besought one of the bright princes of heaven to show him the manner of God's secret dwelling in his soul. The angel answered thus: – Cast, then, a joyous glance into thyself, and see how God plays His play of love with thy loving soul. He looked immediately, and saw that his body over his heart was clear as crystal, and that in the centre of his heart was sitting tranquilly, in lovely form, the Eternal Wisdom; beside whom there sat, full of heavenly longing, the Servitor's soul, which, leaning lovingly towards God's side, and encircled by God's arms, and pressed close to His divine heart, lay thus entranced and drowned in love in the arms of the beloved God.

Ch. 7   How one, who had begun well, was drawn onward in his search after divine consolation

He had made anew for himself certain bands, with which he was accustomed to chastise his body. Now, on the night before the feast of All Angels, it seemed to him in a vision that he heard angelic strains and sweet heavenly melody; and this filled him with such gladness that he forgot all his sufferings. Then one of the angels said to him: – Behold, with what joy thou dost hear us sing the song of eternity; even so, with like joy, do we hear thee sing the song of the venerable Eternal Wisdom. He added further: – This is a portion of the song which the dear elect saints will sing joyously at the last day, when they shall see themselves confirmed in the everlasting bliss of eternity. At another time, on the same festival, after he had spent many hours in contemplating the joys of the angels, and daybreak was at hand, there came to him a youth, who bore himself as though he were a heavenly musician sent to him by God; and with the youth there came many other noble youths, in manner and bearing like the first, save only that he seemed to have some preeminence above the rest, as if he were a prince-angel. Now this same angel came up to the Servitor right blithely, and said that God had sent him down to him, to bring him heavenly joys amid his sufferings; adding that he must cast off all his sorrows from his mind and bear them company, and that he must also dance with them in heavenly fashion. Then they drew the Servitor by the hand into the dance, and the youth began a joyous ditty about the infant Jesus, which runs thus: "*In dulci jubilo*," etc. When the Servitor heard the dear Name of Jesus sounding thus sweetly, he became so blithesome in heart and feeling, that the very memory of his sufferings vanished. It was a joy to him to see how exceeding loftily and freely they bounded in the dance. The leader of the song knew right well how to guide them, and he sang first, and they sang after him in the jubilee of their hearts. Thrice the leader repeated the burden of the song, "*Ergo merito*," etc. This dance was not of a kind like those which are danced in this world; but it was a heavenly movement, swelling up and falling back again into the wild abyss of God's hiddenness. These and the like heavenly consolations were granted to him innumerable times during these years, but especially at the times when he was encompassed with great sufferings, and they made it all the easier for him to bear them.

IV

RENAISSANCE

27

MARSILIO FICINO
1433–99

Ficino is one of the main links in our chain of musical philosophers because of his role in translating the works of Plato and the Neoplatonists, as well as the *Corpus Hermeticum*, from Greek into Latin. This he did at the behest of Cosimo de' Medici, patron of the revived Platonic Academy in Florence of which Ficino was the head and Pico della Mirandola the brightest young star.

Ficino's own life was spent in single-minded devotion to the philosophy of Antiquity and to its reconciliation with the Christian religion, but his interest in Platonism and Hermetism was a practical as well as a theoretical one. Respecting these philosophies for their insights into the intermediate world, above the realm of earthly corruption but below the spiritual realm which theology treats, he deduced from them principles for calling down the influences of the heavenly bodies and their guiding souls. In Plotinus and Iamblichus (both of whom he translated) he would have read the extracts we have given on the power of harmony as a bridge between the worlds. Words and music, appropriately chosen, joined Ficino's repertory of sigils, incenses, colors and metals as generators of these harmonies or correspondences.

De vita coelitus comparanda (1489), whose title could mean, as D.P. Walker has pointed out,[1] both "On life led in a heavenly manner" and "On obtaining life from the heavens," is a manual on the conduct of the contemplative and "magical" life. In the light of Ficino's suggestions, the marvelous psychological effects of music described by the writers of Antiquity now take on a new meaning: they are not records so much of music as of ceremonial magic, of precisely the kind Ficino was trying to revive. He had to be extremely cautious in writing about this: he could easily have been executed as a sorcerer. Twice in this chapter alone he explains that in following his principles one is not *adoring* the stars or their daemons, only imitating them in order to bring about purely natural results. He gives no usable examples of ceremonies, only vague directions for performing them oneself on a basis of celestial similarities and correspondences. Behind all this is the desire for the Hermetic ascent through the spheres to the intelligible heavens beyond the stars. The sevenfold ladder of ceremonies here described as corresponding to the planets is a method of purification (cf. *Poimandres*, no. 4), not a quest for powers that might be used on earth.

Source *De Vita Coelitus Comparanda*, from John Clark and Carol Kaske, eds, Carol Kaske, translator: Marsilio Ficino, *De Vita Libri Tres*. Medieval and Renaissance Texts, Binghamton, New York, 1986. Reprinted by permission.

The Magical Use of Music

Bk III, ch. 21   On the power of words and song for capturing celestial benefits and on the seven steps that lead to celestial things

In addition, they hold that certain words pronounced with a quite strong emotion[2] have great force to aim the effect of images precisely where the emotions and words are directed. And so, in order to bring two people together in passionate love, they used to fashion an image[3] when the Moon was above the horizon and was coming together with Venus in Pisces or Taurus, and they followed many precise directions involving stars and words which I will not tell you, for we are not teaching philters but medicine. It is however more likely that an effect of this sort is achieved either by Venereal daemons who rejoice in such deeds and words or by daemons who are simply deceivers. For they say Apollonius of Tyana often caught and unmasked Lamiae, that is, lascivious and Venereal daemons who take the shape of beautiful girls and entice beautiful men; as the serpent with its mouth sucks the elephant, so they likewise suck those men using the genital opening as a mouth and drain them dry. But I leave this to Apollonius.[4]

That a specific and great power exists in specific words, is the claim of Origen in *Contra Celsum*, of Synesius and Al-Kindi where they argue about magic, and likewise of Zoroaster where he forbids the alteration of barbarous words, and also of Iamblichus in the course of the same argument. The Pythagoreans also make this claim, who used to perform wonders by words, songs, and sounds in the Phoebean and Orphic manner. The Hebrew doctors of old practiced this more than anyone else; and all poets sing of the wondrous things that are brought about by songs. And even the famous and venerable Cato in his *De re rustica* sometimes uses barbarous incantations to cure the diseases of his farm animals. But it is better to skip incantations. Nevertheless that singing through which the young David used to relieve Saul's insanity – unless the sacred text demands that it be attributed to divine agency – one might attribute to nature.

Now since the planets are seven in number, there are also seven steps through which something from on high can be attracted to the lower things.[5] Sounds occupy the middle position and are dedicated to Apollo. Harder materials, stones and metals, hold the lowest rank and thus seem to resemble the Moon. Second in ascending order are things composed of plants, fruits of trees, their gums, and the members of animals, and all these correspond to Mercury – if we follow in the heavens the order of the Chaldeans. Third are very fine powders and their vapors selected from among the materials I have already mentioned and the odors of plants and flowers used as simples and of ointments; they pertain to Venus. Fourth are words, song, and sounds, all of which are rightly dedicated to Apollo whose greatest invention is music. Fifth are the strong concepts of the imagination – forms, motions, passions – which suggest the force of Mars. Sixth are the sequential arguments and deliberations of the human reason which pertain designedly to Jupiter. Seventh are the more remote and simple operations of the understanding, almost now disjoined from motion and conjoined to the divine; they are meant for Saturn, whom deservedly the Hebrews call "Sabbath" from the word for "rest."

Why all of this? To teach you that even as a certain compound of plants and vapors made through both medical and astronomical science yields a common form [of a medicine], like a harmony endowed with gifts from the stars; so tones first chosen by the rule of the stars and then combined according to the congruity of these stars with each other make a sort of common form [presumably a melody or a chord], and in it a celestial power arises.[6] It is indeed very difficult to judge exactly what kinds of tones are suitable for what sorts of stars, what combinations of tones especially accord with what sorts of constellations and aspects. But we can attain this, partly through our own efforts, partly by some divine destiny; for Andromachus wore himself out for ages compounding theriac, and finally, after all that effort, he found the power of theriac by divine destiny. Both Galen and Avicenna confirm that this happened by divine aid. Indeed, Iamblichus and Apollonius of Tyana testify that all medicine had its origin in inspired prophecy; and therefore they make Phoebus the seer preside over medicine.

We will apply three principal rules for this undertaking, provided you be warned beforehand not to think we are speaking here of worshipping the stars, but rather of imitating them and thereby trying to capture them. And do not believe that we are dealing with gifts which the stars are going to give by their own election but rather by a natural influence. We strive to adapt ourselves to this multifarious and occult influence by the same studied methods we use every day to make ourselves fit to receive in a healthy manner the perceivable light and heat of the Sun. But it is the wise man alone who adapts himself to the occult and wonderful gifts of this influence. Now, however, let us go on to the rules that are going to accommodate our songs to the stars. The first is to inquire diligently what powers in itself or what effects from itself a given star, constellaton, or aspect has – what do they remove, what do they bring? – and to insert these into the meaning of our words, so as to detest what they remove and to approve what they bring. The second rule is to take note of what special star rules what place or person and then to observe what sorts of tones and songs these regions and persons generally use, so that you may supply similar ones, together with the meanings I have just mentioned, to the words which you are trying to expose to the same stars. Thirdly, observe the daily positions and aspects of the stars and discover to what principal speeches, songs, motions, dances, moral behavior, and actions most people are usually incited by these, so that you may imitate such things as far as possible in your song, which aims to please the particular part of heaven that resembles them and to catch an influence that resembles them.

But remember that song is a most powerful imitator of all things. It imitates the intentions and passions of the soul as well as words; it represents also people's physical gestures, motions, and actions as well as their characters and imitates all these and acts them out so forcibly that it immediately provokes both the singer and the audience to imitate and act out the same things. By the same power, when it imitates the celestials, it also wonderfully arouses our spirit[7] upwards to the celestial influence and the celestial influence downwards to our spirit. Now the very matter of song, indeed, is altogether purer and more similar to the heavens than is the matter of medicine. For this too is air, hot or warm, still breathing and somehow living; like an animal, it is composed of certain parts and limbs of its own and not only possesses motion and displays passion but even carries meaning like a mind, so that it can be said to be a kind of airy and rational animal. Song, therefore, which is full of spirit and meaning – if it corresponds to this or that constellation not only in the things it signifies, its parts, and the form that results from those parts, but also in the disposition of the imagination – has as much power as does any other combination of things [e.g., a medicine] and casts it into the singer and from him into the nearby listener. It has this power as long as it keeps the vigor and the spirit of the singer, especially if the singer himself be Phoebean by nature and have in his heart a powerful vital and animal spirit. For just as the natural power and spirit, when it is strongest, not only immediately softens and dissolves the hardest food and soon renders harsh food sweet but also generates offspring outside of itself by the emission of the seminal spirit, so the vital and animal power, when it is most efficacious, not only acts powerfully on its own body when its spirit undergoes a very intense conception and agitation through song but soon also moves a neighboring body by emanation. This power influences both its own and the other body by a certain stellar property which it drew both from its own form and from the election of a suitable astrological hour. For this reason in particular many dwellers in the East and South, especially Indians, are said to have an admirable power in their words, as these peoples are for the most part Solar. I say that they are the most powerful of all, not in their natural, but in their vital and animal forces; and the same goes for all persons in other areas who are especially Phoebean.

Now song which arises from this power, timeliness, and intention is undoubtedly nothing else but another spirit recently conceived in you in the power of your spirit – a spirit made Solar and acting both in you and in the bystander by the power of the Sun. For if a certain vapor and spirit directed outwards through the rays of the eyes or by other means can sometimes fascinate, infect, or otherwise influence a bystander, much more can a spirit do this, when it pours out from both the imagination and heart at the same time, more abundant, more fervent, and more apt to motion. Hence it is no wonder at all that by means of song certain diseases both mental and physical can sometimes be cured or brought on, especially since a musical spirit of this kind properly touches and acts on the spirit which is the mean between body and soul, and immediately affects both the one and the other with its influence. You will allow that there is a wondrous power in an aroused and singing spirit, if you allow to the Pythagoreans and Platonists that the heavens are a spirit and that they order all things through their motions and tones.

Remember that all music proceeds from Apollo; that Jupiter is musical to the extent that he is consonant with Apollo; and that Venus and Mercury claim music by their proximity to Apollo [i.e., to the Sun]. Likewise remember that song pertains to only those four; the other three planets have voices but not songs.[8] Now we attribute to Saturn voices that are slow, deep, harsh, and plaintive; to Mars voices that are the opposite – quick, sharp, fierce, and menacing; the Moon has the voices in between. The music, however, of Jupiter is deep, earnest, sweet, and joyful with stability. To Venus, on the contrary, we ascribe songs voluptuous with wantonness and softness. The songs between these two extremes we ascribe to the Sun and Mercury: if with their grace and smoothness they are reverential, simple, and earnest, the songs are judged to be Apollo's; if they are somewhat more relaxed [than Apollo's or Jupiter's], along with their gaiety, but vigorous and complex, they are Mercury's. Accordingly, you will win over one of these four to yourself by using their songs, especially if you supply musical notes that fit their songs. When at the right astrological hour you declaim aloud by singing and playing in the manners we have specified for the four gods, they seem to be just about to answer you like an echo or like a string in a lute trembling to the vibration of another which has been similarly tuned. And this will happen to you from heaven as naturally, say Plotinus and Iamblichus,[9] as a tremor re-echoes from a lute or an echo arises from an opposite wall. Assuredly, whenever your spirit – by frequent use of Jovial, Mercurial, or Venereal harmony, a harmony performed while these planets are dignified – singing at the same time most intently and conforming itself to the harmony becomes Jovial, Mercurial, or Venereal, it will meanwhile become Phoebean as well, since the power of Phoebus himself, the ruler of music, flourishes in every consonance. And conversely when you become Phoebean from Phoebean song and notes, you at the same time lay claim to the power of Jupiter, Venus, and Mercury. And again, from your spirit influenced within, you have a similar influence on your soul and body.

Remember, moreover, that a prayer when it has been suitably and seasonably composed and is full of emotion and forceful has a power similar to a song. There is no use in reporting what great power Damis and Philostratus tell us certain Indian priests have in their prayers, nor in mentioning the words they say that Apollonius employed to call up the shade of Achilles. For we are not now speaking of worshipping divinities but of a natural power in speech, song, and words. That there is indeed in certain sounds a Phoebean and medical power, is clear from the fact that in Puglia everyone who is stung by the phalangium [= one of various kinds of venomous spider] becomes stunned and lies half-dead until each hears a certain sound proper to him.[10] For then he dances along with the sound, works up a sweat, and gets well. And if ten years later he hears a similar sound, he feels a sudden urge to dance. I gather from the evidence that this sound is Solar and Jovial.

28

MATTHAUS HERBENUS
1451–1538

Herbenus was one of the first Renaissance humanists in the Netherlands. After a youth spent studying in Italy, he took orders and returned to become the Rector of St Servatius in his home town of Maastricht. Among his correspondents were the scholar Conrad Celtis and the Christian Kabbalist Johannes Reuchlin; among his close friends Abbot Trithemius of Spondheim, an adept in occult studies. Most of Herbenus' work was in theology and philology, and these studies inform the incomplete *De Natura Cantis*, of which Books 1-3 were dedicated in 1496 to Johann von Dalberg, Bishop of Worms. The treatise dwells on the meaning of *vox*, the expressive powers and physiology of the human voice, and the mystical voices of the heavens and of God.

In general, this text belongs with that of Jacques de Liège (no. 24) as part of a continuing attempt to prove rationally the existence of higher forms of music: using the Aristotelian method, in fact, to disprove Aristotle's denials on this subject. Herbenus is applying a version of the "First Cause" or cosmological argument for the existence of God, in raising his conception of music as high as it can possibly go. But he is not a mere logician: towards the end of this extract he looks within himself and speaks from intuitive certainty.

Source   Herbeni Traiectensis de Natura Cantus ac Miraculis Vocis, ed. Joseph Smits van Waesberghe, Cologne, Arno, 1957, pp. 34-7.

Human, Angelic and Divine Song

Ch. VIII   That the Angels also sing in the Empyrean heaven; and on the song of the most blessed Trinity in the Deity

Now that our discourse has proceeded to the point at which we must treat the voices of the heavens, it may be asked what reasons can be given for believing that those holy Spirits make music in the

123

Empyrean heaven. For this heaven beneath which we live and which is distinguished by different planets gives forth no note. Quite the contrary, whatever Macrobius on the Dream of Scipio, Cicero in the same, or the ancient philosophers say: it makes no sound. I will forbear from this matter, since it pertains little to the proposed question. At most I will say this: those who fancied the contrary are known to have been even more clearly in error than in the assignation of the *phthongoi*,[1] without which no music can be made, for they disagree most violently. The Pythagoreans attribute the lowest sound to Saturn, but the Ciceronians give it the highest. Nothing in the nature of things could differ more than these things called highest and lowest, which sound *mese* and *proslambanomenos*. Wherefore Pliny calls that idea "more entertaining than true,"[2] agreeing with the opinion of Averroes on Aristotle.

Having therefore taken up the question of whether there is a music of heavenly things, I will satisfy it better if we consider God, the chief maker of all things in this admirable cosmic work [*opere mundano*] – a name given it, so the Ancients assert, on account of its absolute beauty;[3] thus by definite steps all creatures may be displayed in the incredible scheme, whereby some excel others in nobility of form. To some, then, he has given the faculty of mere existence; to others that they should not only exist, but also rejoice in the nobler gift of life. And since things are said to live in many ways – for some live only a vegetative life, others a sensitive, others an intelligent one – the more noble the life with which they are endowed, the more excellent the actions which result.

Song belongs to life's nobler actions, for those with voices are easily proved superior to mute and inanimate beings. On which account, both vegetables and inanimate objects are easily surpassed by those which enjoy a sensitive life. For the latter are called vociferous because they silence the other, inferior ones. But since Man stands out from the sensitive creatures on account of his dignity and excellence,[4] he must necessarily surpass them by his nobler acts. Thus he is not merely vociferous, like other creatures, but uses discourse and speaks with his voice, and by art and divine skill is able to sing. Since, therefore, there is nothing beneath heaven which can be compared to Man in its vital actions, much less excel him, it follows that other immortal creatures must exist, inhabiting not this dingy [*fumidum*] world but the celestial homeland and the brighter regions, who excel us by the incredible majesty of their vital actions, and surpass us in the beauty of their song, as much as we do the other creatures. And since the greatest happiness is caused by song, it is in Spring, the most joyful season of the year, that the woods resound with birdsong and the cattle fill the broad meadows with their lowing. Men oppressed by sorrow are dumb: released by joy they become happy and begin to sing together. In the Empyrean heaven,[5] where there is no sorrow but only perpetual joy and what I might call a perennial mildness, we can guess that the most exquisite kind of singing is practiced by the holy Angels. Since joy almost never comes except from love, and since the highest love is the divine sort, there must also exist among the Angels that which serves to show the supreme love: which certainly cannot be better done than by heavenly music. Otherwise the proof of love would be greater in Man than in the Angels, which would be flatly absurd and contradictory. And since they hover eternally in the blessed light of the Deity, they cannot be ignorant of that which best suits his excellence. Since, therefore, the Angels perceive all his knowledge, love, and joy illuminated by divine radiance, they break out in untiring melody, singing to God. Who can still doubt that all these things were in the Creator from eternity before the Creation was made from nothing; in the exemplar before the example; in his infinite and intrinsic work before it was finished and separated from his nature? Therefore, since in God is joy unbounded, utter love of himself, the peak of wisdom, incomprehensible power, who would ever deny that these actions of singing exist eternally in God?[6] Who but one man, the universally censured Epicurus, would ever say that God was idle? The most blessed Trinity sings so divine a song by the production of Persons that its angelic creatures, loved and ordained, rejoice utterly in God with unanimous singing throughout all ages.

Ch. IX   The different ways in which Angels, Men, and other beings praise God with their voices; and the excellence of the musical art

Moreover, since God has established all works for his praise and glory, he desired most of all the actions of his creatures those of song and benediction, that they might in every way show forth his praise. I would guess that this would none the less include, besides the song of Angels and men, the voices of the other creatures: for those which are beneath Man give voice, indeed, naturally following a single "tenor" according to the condition of their species, but cannot be said to sing because they lack art. They lack art because they have no mind by which they can artificially join their notes. Hence God has ordained the actions of all animals for his praise in a different manner; he wished to be honored by them with simple cries, so that he might be honored more excellently by those of a nobler condition. On this account, since man is one degree higher than all the animals, and is endowed with mind and intelligence – in fact conforming marvelously to the divine Image – it suited his more excellent gifts to praise his Maker more honorably. He is therefore gifted with a voice, not that he might bellow like cattle or chatter like birds, but so that he can honor his Creator by song and by artistic partnership with his fellows. No one should suppose that divine

Music is bestowed on the human mind in vain: it was, on the contrary, so that God might be more excellently honored that he chose to give his divine creature the divine art of Music and the supreme gift of a voice.

From human voices joined skilfully together arises that consonance which is rightly called a "symphony": for as it surpasses all living beings in nobility of nature, so it does in musical excellence. It ascends above the human condition with a truly angelic nature, and God has counted it no less among his perpetual praises. Who could doubt that God would wish to be honored by a more excellent creature in a more excellent way? Thus the angelic Spirits hymn their Maker not with birdsongs, nor with human symphonies composed of arithmetical numbers, but with suitably heavenly and angelic harmonies. With the human mind we cannot attain to these, because of their sublime nature, just as those beneath the human condition cannot understand our music. But just as we can tell that the songs of birds are produced artlessly, so the celestial musicians know that all our music is made by human art and skill. And should the Angels praise God in perpetual song any the less, because I cannot explain the modes in which this takes place? Should pepper grow the less in India, or balsam in Egypt, because I have never seen these trees or their native lands? Certainly not: for the things which I cannot grasp with my senses exceed those which I can experience through them. I do not even know myself as constituted of such diverse things as body and soul: how something so divine and so secret as these two can make a man, I am quite ignorant. From various thoughts I can understand that there is something which has potential, which lives, understands, and desires to coincide with God and be one and the same: yet the senses can obviously not comprehend how this happens. We can therefore believe that God, wisest of all, desires to be praised by his noblest creature in the most excellent way, known only to his Divinity: not by any fragile or corruptible organs, but by immortal and spiritual instruments; not by arithmetical numbers but by intellectual modes suitable to such a nature;[7] not laboriously but with the greatest constancy, love, joy, and perpetual free will. Such is the music by which I believe God is honored in heaven by the angelic Choristers, with supreme concord, by creatures most like his own nature; so that the divine praise in the heavens is no less than the worship paid by mortal men on Earth.

29

HENRY CORNELIUS AGRIPPA VON NETTESHEIM

1486–1535

Agrippa was the author of three famous works: *The Vanity of all Sciences*, *The Superiority of Women*, and *Occult Philosophy*. He was a perpetual wanderer, a friend of Erasmus and of Trithemius, of Platonists and Kabbalists, with his personal convictions deeply rooted in Evangelical Christianity.

As early as 1510 he had completed in outline three books of *De Occulta Philosophia*, which was published in Antwerp in 1533 and has remained a primary source for occultists ever since. Its books deal respectively with Natural, Celestial, and Angelic Magic, covering the three realms of the Hermetic universe. A fourth book on Kabbalistic Magic, published in English in 1655, is accepted by some as Agrippa's own work.

While musical theory was evidently of little interest to Agrippa, the power of sound, word, and tone was so. In these extracts we have the fullest development of Plotinus' and Iamblichus' hints on the role of the spoken word in magic. Words, for him, inhabit a subtle realm and have an existence which is in a way superior to that of the elemental world, where everything is in flux and decay. The Name of God; the Word of the Lord; the true names of things: all these will endure, while the things themselves pass away. The human gift of speech is a divine one, which marks man as an intellectual or rational being (in the Platonic sense), hence as resembling God. The magus, in naming God and the Angels (aided by the appropriate physical and astrological circumstances), activates a part of their power on earth. And so it is with music too: the Dorian mode as it were "names" the Sun, hence fills the spirits of its listeners with solar force; and when the right words are joined to the right music, the effect will naturally be redoubled – as composers were beginning to discover during Agrippa's own lifetime, when reflection of the text in the music became a serious issue.

Source *Three Books of Occult Philosophy*, translated by "J.F.," London, 1651. Spelling modernized.

The Magic of Words

Bk I, ch. 69   Of Speech, and the Occult Virtue of Words

It being shown that there is a great power in the affections of the soul, you must know, moreover, that there is no less virtue in words and the names of things, and greatest of all in speeches and motions; by which we chiefly differ from the brutes, and are called rational; not from reason, which is taken for that part of the soul which contains the affections (which Galen saith is also common to brutes, although in a less degree), but we are called rational from that reason which is, according to the voice, understood in words and speech, which is called Declarative Reason; by which part we do chiefly excel all other animals. For logos, in Greek, signifies reason, speech, and a word. Now, a word is two-fold, viz., internal and uttered. An internal word is a conception of the mind and motion of the soul, which is made without a voice; as in dreams we seem to speak and dispute with ourselves, and whilst we are awake, we run over a whole speech silently. But an uttered word hath a certain act in the voice, and properties of locution, and is brought forth with the breath of a man, with opening of his mouth and with the speech of his tongue; in which nature hath coupled the corporeal voice and speech to the mind and understanding, making that a declarer and interpreter of the conception of our intellect to the hearers; and of this we now speak. Words, therefore, are the fittest medium betwixt the speaker and the hearer, carrying with them not only the conception of the mind, but also the virtue of the speaker, with a certain efficacy, unto the hearers; and this oftentimes with so great a power, that often they change not only the hearers but also other bodies and things that have no life. Now those words are of greater efficacy than others which represent greater things – as intellectual, celestial, and supernatural; as more expressly, so more mysteriously. Also those that come from a more worthy tongue,[1] or from any of a more holy order; for these (as it were certain signs and representations) receive a power of celestial and supercelestial things, as from the virtue of things explained, of which they are the vehicle, and from a power put into them by the virtue of the speaker.

Ch. 70   Of the Virtue of Proper Names

That the proper names of things are very necessary in Magical Operations, almost all men testify. For the natural power of things proceeds, first, from the objects to the senses, and then from these to the imagination, and from this to the mind, in which it is first conceived, and then is expressed by voices and words. The Platonists, therefore, say that in this very voice, or word, or name framed, with its articles, that the power of the thing, as it were some kind of life, lies under the form of the signification. First conceived in the mind, as it were through certain seeds of things, then by voices or words, as a birth brought forth; and lastly, kept in writings. Hence magicians say, that the proper names of things are certain rays of things, everywhere present at all times, keeping the power of things, as the essence of the thing signified rules, and is discerned in them, and know the things by them, as by proper and living images. For, as the great operator doth provide diverse species and particular things by the influences of the Heavens, and by the elements, together with the virtues of planets, so, according to the properties of the influences, proper names result to things and are put upon them by him who numbers the multitude of the stars, calling them all by their names; of which names Christ in another place speaks, saying, "Your names are written in Heaven."[2] Adam, therefore, that gave the first names to things, knowing the influences of the Heavens and properties of all things, gave them all names according to their natures, as it is written in Genesis, where God brought all things that he had created before Adam, that he should name them; and as he named any thing, so the name of it was; which names, indeed, contain in them wonderful powers of the things signified. Every voice, therefore, that is significative, first of all signifies by the influence of the celestial harmony; secondly, by the imposition of man, although oftentimes otherwise by this than by that. But when both significations meet in any voice or name, which are put upon them by the said harmony, or men, then that name is with a double virtue, viz., natural and arbitrary, made most efficacious to act as often as it shall be uttered in due place and time, and seriously, with an intention exercised upon the matter rightly disposed, and that can naturally be acted upon by it. So we read in Philostratus,[3] that when a maid at Rome died the same day she was married, and was presented to Apollonius, he accurately inquired into her name, which being known, he pronounced some occult thing, by which she revived. It was an observation amongst the Romans, in their holy rites, that when they did diligently enquire into the proper and true name of it, and the name of that God under whose protection it was; which being known, they did then with some verse call forth the Gods that were the protectors of that city, and did curse the inhabitants of that city, so at length, their Gods being absent, did overcome them, as Virgil sings:

– That kept this realm, our Gods
Their Altars have forsook, and blest abodes.[4]

Now the verse with which the Gods were called out and the enemies were cursed, when the city was assaulted round about, let him that would know find it out in Livy and Macrobius; but also many of these Serenus Samonicus, in his book of secret things,[5] makes mention of.

Ch. 71 Of many Words joined together, as in Sentences and Verses; and of the Virtues and Astrictions of Charms

Besides the virtues of words and names, there is also a greater virtue found in sentences, from the truth contained in them, which hath a very great power of impressing, changing, binding, and establishing, so that being used it doth shine the more, and being resisted is more confirmed and consolidated; which virtue is not in simple words, but in sentences, by which anything is affirmed or denied; of which sort are verses, enchantments, imprecations, deprecations, orations, invocations, obtestations, adjurations, conjurations, and such like. Therefore, in composing verses and orations for attracting the virtue of any star or deity, you must diligently consider what virtue any star contains, as, also, what effects and operations, and to infer them in verses, by praising, extolling, amplifying, and setting forth those things which such a kind of star is wont to cause by way of its influence, and by vilifying and dispraising those things which it is wont to destroy and hinder, and by supplicating and begging for that which we desire to get, and by condemning and detesting that which we would have destroyed and hindered; and duly distinct, by articles, with competent numbers and proportions. Moreover, magicians command that we call upon and pray by the names of the same star, or name to them to whom such a verse belongs, by their wonderful things, or miracles, by their courses and ways in their sphere, by their light, by the dignity of their kingdom, by the beauty and brightness that is in it, by their strong and powerful virtues, and by such like things as these. As Psyche, in Apuleius, prays to Ceres, saying, "I beseech thee by thy fruitful right hand, I entreat thee by the joyful ceremonies of harvests, by the quiet silence of thy chests, by the winged chariots of dragons, thy servants, by the furrows of the Sicilian earth, the devouring wagon, the clammy earth, by the place of going down into cellars at the dark nuptials of Prosperina, and returns at the light inventions of her daughter, and other things which are concealed in her temple in the city of Eleusis, in Attica."[6] Besides, with the diverse sorts of the names of the stars, they command us to call upon them by the names of the Intelligences ruling over the stars themselves, of which we shall speak more at large in their proper place. They that desire further examples of these, let them search into the hymns of Orpheus, than which nothing is more efficacious in Natural Magic, if they, together with their circumstances, which wise men know, be used according to a due harmony with all attention. But to return to our purpose. Such like verses, being aptly and duly made, according to the Rule of the Stars, and being full of signification and meaning, and opportunely pronounced with vehement affection (as according to the number and the proportion of their articles, so according to the form resulting from the articles) and, by the violence of imagination, do confer a very great power in the enchanter, and sometimes transfer it upon the thing enchanted, to bind and direct it to the same purpose for which the affections and speeches of the enchanter are intended. Now, the instrument of enchanters is a most pure, harmonical spirit[7] – warm, breathing, living, bringing with it motion, and signification; composed of its parts, endued with sense, and conceived by reason. By the quality, therefore, of this spirit, and by the celestial similitude thereof (besides those things which have already been spoken of) verses, also, from the opportunity of time, receive from above most excellent virtues; and, indeed, are more sublime and efficacious than spirits, and vapors exhaling out of the vegetable life, such as herbs, roots, gums, aromatical things, and fumes and such like. And, therefore, magicians enchanting things, are wont to blow and breathe upon them the words of the verse, or to breathe in the virtue with the spirit, that so the whole virtue of the soul be directed to the thing enchanted, being disposed for the receiving of said virtue. And here it is to be noted that every oration, writing, and words, as they induce accustomed motions by their accustomed numbers, proportions, and form, so (besides their usual order) being pronounced, or wrote backwards, move unto unusual effects.

The Magic of Tone

Bk II, ch. 25   Of Sound, and Harmony, and whence their wonderfulness in operation

Moreover we shall not deny, that there is in Sounds a virtue to receive the heavenly gifts; if with *Pythagoras* and *Plato* we thought the heavens to consist of an Harmonial composition, and to rule and cause all things by Harmonial tones and motions: Singing can do more than the sound of an Instrument, in as much as it arising by an Harmonial consent, from the conceit of the mind, and imperious affection of the phantasy and heart, easily penetrateth by motion, with the refracted and well tempered Air, the aerious spirit of the hearer, which is the bond of soul and body; and transferring the affection and mind of the Singer with it, It moveth the affection of the hearer by his affection, and the hearer's phantasy by his

131

phantasy, and mind by his mind, and striketh the mind, and striketh the heart, and pierceth even to the inwards of the soul, and by little and little, infuseth even dispositions: moreover it moveth and stoppeth the members and the humors of the body. From hence in moving the affections harmony conferreth so much, that not only natural, but also artificial and vocal Harmony doth yield a certain power both to the souls and bodies: but it is necessary that all Consorts proceed from fit foundations, both in stringed instruments, in pipes, and vocal singings, if you would have them agree well together: for no man can make the roaring of Lions, the lowing of Oxen, the neighing of Horses, the braying of Asses, the grunting of Hogs to be harmonious: neither can the strings made of Sheep's and Wolves' guts, be brought to any agreement, because their foundations are dissonant; but the many and divers voices of men agree together, because they have one foundation in the species or kind: so many birds agree, because they have one nigh genus or kind, and a resemblance from above; also artificial instruments agree with natural voices, because the similitude that is betwixt them, is either true and manifest, or hath a certain analogy. But every harmony is either of sounds or voices. Sound is a breath, voice is a sound and animate breath; speech is a breath pronounced with sound, and a voice signifying something: the spirit of which proceedeth out of the mouth with sound and voice: *Chalcidius* saith that a voice is sent forth out of the inward cavity of the breast and heart, by the assistance of the spirit. By which, together with the tongue, forming, and striking the narrow passages of the mouth, and by the other vocal organs, are delivered forth articulate sounds; the elements of speech, by which Interpreter the secret motions of the mind are laid open: but *Lactantius* saith, that the nature of the voice is very obscure, and cannot be comprehended how it is made, or what it is. To conclude, All Music consisteth in voice, in sound, and hearing: sound without Air cannot be Audible, which though it is necessary for hearing, yet as Air, it is not of it self audible, nor to be perceived by any sense, unless by accident; for the Sight seeth it not, unless it be colored, nor the Ears unless sounding, nor the Smell unless odoriferous, nor the Taste unless it be sapid, nor the Touch unless it be cold or hot, and so forth: Therefore though sound cannot be made without Air, yet is not sound of the nature of Air, nor air of the nature of sound, but air is the body of the life of our sensitive spirit, and is not of the nature of any sensible object, but of a more simple and higher virtue; but it is meet that the sensitive soul should vivify the air joined to it; and in the vivificated air, which is joined to the spirit, perceive the species of objects put forth into act, and this is done in the living air, but in a subtle and Diaphonous the visible species, in an ordinary air the audible, in a more gross air the species of other senses are perceived.[8]

30

GIOSEFFO ZARLINO

1517–90

Zarlino, "easily the most influential personality in the history of music theory from Aristoxenus to Rameau,"[1] was a member of the Franciscan Order, and from 1565 until his death *maestro di cappella* (director of music) at St Mark's in Venice. His theoretical works show enormous learning, intelligence, and insight into the fundamental nature of music, formulating for the first time many concepts such as major and minor, or the triad, which are now taken for granted.

By Zarlino's time it was evident that the task of the encyclopedic music theorist had broken irrevocably beyond the Boethian mould: in addition to the traditional topics of the nature and power of music, interval and modal theory, it was now imperative to add principles and rules for the composition of polyphonic music in the modern idiom. The main historical interest of Renaissance treatises lies, of course, in the latter field; but it is no less remarkable and instructive that the foremost theorists of the age, such as Ramis de Pareja, Gaffurius, Glarean, and Zarlino, pay their respects, one and all, to the speculative divisions of music. And it is more than mere respect. They seem to have entertained no more doubts concerning the cosmic background against which their practical expositions unfold than they did about the dogmas of Christianity. The concepts of *musica mundana* and *musica humana* are as basic a part of Zarlino's assumptions as is his reverence for Classical theory and for his teacher Willaert. When he comes to discuss the four voices of polyphonic music, for example, he compares their qualities in detail to those of the four elements.[2] The motives and methods of both theorists and composers in the Golden Age of polyphony could not help but be affected by metaphysical preconceptions such as we meet here, and it is not hard to hear in the music of the period the purest exemplification of these theories.[3]

Source Institutioni harmoniche (first published 1558), edition of Venice, 1573, reprinted Gregg Press, 1966, pp. 16-23.

The Music of the Human Being

Pt I, ch. 7 On musica humana

Human music is the harmony which may be known by any person who turns to contemplation of himself. It is that which mingles the incorporeal energy of reason with the body; it is nothing other than a certain adaptation or temperament as of low and high voices, making a kind of consonance. It is this that joins together the parts of the soul, and keeps the rational part united with the irrational. It mixes with reasonable proportion the elements, or their qualities in the human body.

The principal thing to observe, as I have said, is that it may be known by any person who turns to contemplation of himself. One should not, therefore, call "human music" that process which Nature observes in the generation of our bodies, as the physicians say, and as St Augustine agrees.[4] According to them, the human seed within the female womb breaks down in the space of six days and is converted into milk; in nine more days it is transformed into blood; after twelve days a formless mass of flesh develops, which little by little takes on form until in eighteen days it becomes human. Then, after forty-five days when generation is completed, the Omnipotent God instils the intellectual soul. Hence the saying:

> Six days make milk, thrice three blood,
> Twice six flesh, and thrice six shape the members.

This miraculous process certainly contains concord and harmony, considering the distance from one number to another: between the first and second is plainly the interval of a fifth; from the second to the third, the interval of a fourth; from the third to the fourth stage another fifth. From the first to the third, moreover, and from the second to the last, there are octaves; from the first to the last we perceive the interval of a twelfth, as one can easily see from the figure.

But this I do not call human music. That, I maintain, can be known from three things: the body, the soul, and the conjunction of one with the other. In the case of the body it is as in things that grow: in its humors and human behavior [*operationi*]. As to its growth, we see each living thing changing its state with a certain harmony: children become old men, growing from small to large; plants turn from moist, green, and tender to arid, dry, and hard. And although we see them each day, having them before our eyes, we still cannot perceive this change. Even so in music one cannot

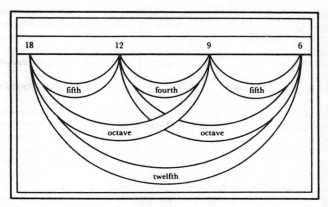

hear the space which lies between a high and a low voice when they sing; one can conceive of it, but not hear it. As to humors, we can see the tempering of all four elements in the human body. And in human behavior we recognize the rational soul within man, for in this way he is directed and governed by reason. Passing in its operation through the proper means, it conducts his affairs with a certain harmony to a perfect conclusion.

This harmony can again be recognized in the divisions of the soul: the intellect, the senses, and the autonomous functions [*habito*]. According to Ptolemy,[5] these correspond to the ratios of three consonances: the octave, fifth, and fourth. The intellectual part corresponds to the octave because it has seven intervals and its species are seven. So there are found therein seven members: mind, imagination, memory, cogitation, opinion, reason, and knowledge. To the fifth, with its four species and four intervals, correspond the four divisions of the senses: vision, hearing, smell, and taste (touch being common to all of them, particularly to taste). To the fourth, which is made up of three intervals and has three species, correspond the autonomous functions of growth, maturity, and decline. Similarly, if we want the parts of the soul to be the seats of reason, anger, and desire, we will find seven divisions of the first, corresponding to the intervals and species of the octave: subtlety, skill, diligence, judgment, wisdom, prudence, and experience. Of the second we will find four divisions, corresponding to the species and intervals of the fifth: gentleness or temperance of the soul, animosity, fortitude, and tolerance. In the third are three divisions, corresponding to the intervals and species of the fourth: sobriety or temperance, continence, and respect.

One can also observe this harmony between the powers of the soul, as between anger, reason, and virtue, or as one might say

135

between justice and fortitude. For these things will temper each other in the same way as a consonance will make high and low notes agree. Finally, this harmony can be known from the conjunction of body and soul through the natural friendship by which they are joined: not of course by corporeal bonds, but (as the Platonists believe) by the spirit which is incorporeal, as we saw above.[6] This is the bond from which all human harmony results: which joins the diverse qualities of the elements in one compound. This occurs in the human body, according to the Philosophers, who all agree that human bodies are composed of earth, water, air, and fire. Flesh, they say, is generated by the tempering of all four elements together; sinews by earth and fire; lastly bones by water and earth. But if this seems strange, we cannot reasonably deny that we are composed, at least, of elemental qualities, through the four humors found in every body: melancholy, phlegm, blood, and choler. They are contrary one to another, but none the less in their mixture and composition, as we may say, they are harmonically united. Thus if one suffers cold, or overwhelming heat, or eats too much, or from any other cause does violence to one of the humors, there will instantly follow a distemper and infirmity of the body. And it will not recover until they return to their pristine proportion and concord. This could not be so unless a bond such as we mentioned above existed between the spiritual and corporeal nature, between the rational and the irrational.

It is therefore this harmonic concord of the spiritual and corporeal natures, of the rational and the irrational, that constitutes human music. For while the soul persists in remaining united with the body as if by reason of numbers, the body can be called a living being, and if not prevented by any accident it has the power to do what it will. But when the harmony is undone it decays and, no longer a living being, it remains in darkness and the soul flies to immortality. Well may this be said to occur by reason of numbers, for the Ancients had a strange opinion: that if someone drowned or were killed, the soul could not go to its appointed place until the musical number was completed by which it had been joined to the body at birth. And because they firmly believed that one could not violate such a number, these accidents were called fate, or a fatal period. Hence the poet, introducing Deiphobus, who was killed by the Greeks, touches on this belief in the following words:[7]

I will fulfil the number, and return to the dark.

All this, however, belongs more to the arguments of philosophy than to those of music. We will speak of it no more, content to have said this much and to have shown the variety of the soul's music. Since it is of little or no concern to our subject, we will make no further mention of it.

31

LUIS DE LEÓN
1528–91

Fray (Friar) Luis de León is recognized as one of the greatest Spanish poets. He was very much a man of his golden but terrible century – the century of the Inquisition – and spent the period 1572-6 imprisoned on charges trumped up by rival religious orders in the midst of academic rivalries at the University of Salamanca. His crimes were those of being of Jewish ancestry, knowing Hebrew too well, and applying his scholarship to the Song of Songs. When eventually he was released and returned to his professorial chair, he is reputed to have begun his first lecture: "As we were saying yesterday . . .," and the rest of his life was spent in full and courageous public activity and controversy.

Fray Luis's poetic vein is a lyric mysticism of great beauty and concentrated meaning. He was a contemporary of St John of the Cross, and of St Teresa of Avila (whose works he edited), and like them celebrates the mystical encounter with God. But his imagery is not so much erotic, as theirs, but Platonic, full of astral and musical references. The *Ode to Salinas* (between 1577 and 1580), probably his best known poem, is the fullest statement of his type of mystical experience. It contains the ascent through the aether, the vision of Christ as Demiurge harmonizing the cosmos, and the transport of the soul in supersensual bliss. Fray Luis was well aware that the poetic form he was using here was called *lira* (lyre), and that *salinas* are salt-beds in which the salt is extracted from sea-water by sublimation: an alchemical symbol of the soul's ascent from the earth.

Francisco de Salinas (1514?-90) would have appreciated this tribute. A blind organist, composer and theorist, he wrote a most comprehensive treatise (*De Musica*, Salamanca, 1577) in which the music of soul and spheres is paid its due, drawing on all the available Latin and Greek sources. No doubt Fray Luis gave his friend the benefit of his own enormous learning while they were colleagues on the university faculty, Salinas occupying the chair of music.

The Renaissance philosophy of music enjoyed an extraordinarily long life in Spain. As late as the 1720s, Fray Pablo Nassarre, another blind organist, could publish *Escuela Musica* (Zaragoza, 1723-4), a long treatise very similar to Salinas's in which the old doctrines of cosmic harmony, planet-mode correspondences and the marvelous effects of music on mind and body are recounted at length, with Francesco Giorgi's *Harmonia Mundi* (1525) as the authority most frequently cited. The so-called Enlightenment never happened in Spain, where medical doctors were required to know astrology right up to the end of the eighteenth century. Nassarre's work is not suitable to be excerpted here, but it is important to know that such a late survival exists.

Source *A Francisco de Salinas*, in *La Poesía de Fray Luis da León*, ed. Oreste Marcí, Salamanca, Anaya, 1970, pp. 225-6.

On Francisco de Salinas' Organ Playing

The air becomes serene[1]
And takes on unusual beauty and light,
Salinas, when the supreme music sounds forth,
Governed by your knowing hand.

At its divine sound
The soul, usually plunged in forgetfulness,
Regains its senses, and the lost memory
Of its primal origin shines forth.

And as it recognizes itself,
Then its fate and thoughts are bettered;
It spurns the gold which the vulgar crowd worships,
That temporal, deceiving beauty.

It traverses the entire realm of air
To pass to the highest sphere,
And there listens in another way
To imperishable music, which is the source of first [music].

It sees how the great Maestro,
Playing this immense lyre with skilful motions,
Produces the sacred sound
By which this eternal temple is sustained.[2]

And as the latter is composed
Of concordant numbers, it sends out
A consonant response; and both in rivalry
Mingle with the sweetest harmony.[3]

There the soul sails
On an ocean of bliss, and finally
Drowns in it, so that it neither hears nor feels
Any strange or passing accident.[4]

O happy swoon! O death that gives life!
O sweet oblivion! Let me stay, reposing in you,
Without ever being sent back
To those base and vile senses!

I call you to this treasure,
Glory of Apollo's sacred choir,
Friends[5] (whom I love above all riches):
For all that is visible is but sorrowful tears.

O Salinas, may your music sound
Unceasing in my ears, by which the senses
Which at other times are asleep
May awaken to the divine treasure!

32

GUY LEFÈVRE DE
LA BODERIE
1541–98

Guy Lefèvre was one of the most gifted linguists of his day, an orientalist, and the translator of Francesco Giorgi's *Harmonia Mundi*. He worked as interpreter and secretary to the Duc d'Alençon, the French King's brother and heir, and unsuccessful suitor of Queen Elizabeth I. He belongs within the circle of French humanists whose efforts to recreate the marvelous effects of the Ancients led to the foundation of Jean-Antoine Baïf's Academy of Poetry and Music, with its brilliant constellation of poets, musicians and philosophers, and its important political dimensions which Frances Yates has revealed in her books.

Like Athanasius Kircher (see no. 35) and Fabre d'Olivet (see no. 47), Guy Lefèvre combined an interest in ancient languages and in speculative music with an ambition to reconstruct the prehistoric past. *La Galliade* – a Gallic *Aeneid*, as the name suggests – is the spiritual history of the French nation. It claims that the bards of ancient Gaul, under their King Bardus, were the fountainhead of all arts and philosophy, and especially of the knowledge of cosmic harmony which only later flowed from them to Orpheus and Plato. D.P. Walker, one of the few who have discussed it, felt obliged to write that "The *Galliade* is an entirely serious poem in spite of the preposterous history of culture which is its main theme."[1] But perhaps it is not so absurd when one considers the extraordinary astronomical and mathematical knowledge shown by the Megalithic civilizations of France and Britain, and the legend of a Hyperborean origin for the arts of Apollo.[2] The poem is in five "circles," which treat (1) the 72 descendants of Noah, (2) Architecture, (3) Druidic knowledge, especially of natural magic and prediction (of which Lefèvre makes a dutiful disavowal), (4) Music of macrocosm and microcosm and its effects, (5) Poetry and the divine fury, etc. Later in part 4 Lefèvre gives an immense scheme of cosmic, musical and Kabbalistic correspondences, analogous to that of Kircher's "Enneachord of Nature."

Source   La Galliade, Paris, 1578, fols 85v-87r.

The Lyre of Man

The inner man and the outer man, with his four elements and discordant concord, even he is restored to blessed grace. Adonaii has placed in him, concealed, four vestures of golden hue to cover and hide his shame and his sins. These four vestures are whiter than the finest linen of Malta or Holland, and they enclose him as a veil or a pavilion; and this is the gift of Jehovah, to whom be all praise.

The Natural Soul[3] is his earth and shadow; his night and winter, his cold and somber humor. It is his slackest string with the deepest pitch, a heavy tone, gross, obscure, and very low.

The Vital Soul is his water; his evening and autumn, his phlegm. With this second string the next register sounds.

The Spirit is his air, his morning and springtime; his sanguine humor, his third string with silvery resonance.

High Intellect, or transparent Thought, is his fire, his noontime and summer, throbbing with heat; his enflamed choler, and the tightest string which sounds the highest note.

It is this well-tuned lute whose fertile notes resound above in the lute of the round spheres, and make their solemn chord to echo on the vault of Time, and in the eternal Temple. There twice twelve Elders in orderly ranks have tuned harmoniously the strings of the harps slung at their sides, and as one chorus they sound the hymns of God.[4] It is the well-strung Bow which thrusts and springs back,[5] and hurls many an arrow into Eternity from the heart-strings tensed in prayer, which makes its echo heard as far as the Bow in Heaven – that Rainbow, coloured red, blue and green, its hues shifting and variegated, which as a semicircular vault surrounds the Throne whereon sits the lofty Majesty of God. His most high Name, four-lettered,[6] accords with the quatrain of our Soul, or with its tetrachord which makes in us the fourfold connection of Sense, Phantasy, Intellect, and Reason.

Sense sounds the lowest, with a gloomy voice. Pure Intellect with a high and pure voice sounds and re-echoes. Phantasy attunes its accents to Sense, or else to Reason. Reason, in the midst, goes both high and low, now united to Intellect, now to Sense. The Intellect is divine, simple, pure, immortal; Sense is elemental, obscure, adulterated, mortal; Imagination, more limpid, is ethereal; but celestial Reason is sometimes illuminated by the great Intellect, the supermundane Sun, its light and life, the object of its eye; and sometimes it is more or less obscured, seized either by gross Sense or else by Phantasy.

If then the *mese* or mean, Reason, should attune its thought in unison to *nete*, and the Phantasy to the Sense, then their parts are

141

matched with one another in sonorous concords.

If the loving Spirit of the Saints prevails, then just as it sounds in the rose[7] [of a lute], so it sounds in the heart of the lyre of man; in his holy hymns he praises the great Harper of Heaven with a tongue which plays and moulds its anthems with a more finely-drawn tone than bow ever made upon violin. The Intellect above, like the *chanterelle*,[8] adds the sweet ringing of its immortal voice, and draws Reason in the middle to its *nete*, the Moon to its Sun, the Two to Unity.

If the four Worlds are in tune together – the human, elemental, and lowest spheres[9] with the Archetype – then the Universe sounds a single harmony from its four different lutes.

33

ROBERT FLUDD
1574–1637

Born in Bearsted, Kent, Fludd spent most of his life working as a physician in London, following the principles of Paracelsus which he had learnt during his wanderings on the continent of Europe. He was also a Hermetist, something of an alchemist, and a man of universal knowledge whose major legacy is his *Utriusque Cosmi Historia* (History of the Two Worlds, 1617-26). The "two worlds" are the greater one of the Cosmos, with its creation, structure, and inhabitants, and the lesser one of Man, which, as Fludd describes it, reflects the first in every detail.[1]

Fludd was involved with the Rosicrucian movement which announced itself with two manifestos, the *Fama Fraternitatis* (Fame of the Brotherhood) of 1614 and the *Confessio Fraternitatis* (Confession of the Brotherhood) of 1615. In the latter, the anonymous brethren set forth their ambitions for the renovation of the whole world, the downfall of the Roman Church and the end of sectarian strife among Christians. Fludd's first publication was a defense of this controversial movement, coupled with a request for admission to the Brotherhood. Although there is no evidence that he was ever a member, his ideals were perfectly in harmony with theirs. In a second, revised version of his defense, from which this is excerpted, Fludd reviews and approves the Rosicrucian claims to be capable of performing musical marvels: of recapturing the legendary powers of Orpheus and Arion and the marvelous effects of ancient music which had so obsessed music theorists for the fifty years preceding him, and would do so for another century. The "Text" which he discusses here is taken from the *Confessio*.[2]

Fludd's works are full of musical references, actually including several entire treatises on music both human and divine. With his contemporaries Johannes Kepler (no. 34), Athanasius Kircher (no. 35) and Marin Mersenne (not included here), he belongs to the last great flowering of speculative music, in which ideas of universal harmony were still generally thought viable as a means for understanding the universe. None of these four, significantly enough, was a professional musician: respectively a physician, an astronomer, a Jesuit and a Friar, they each used music in a different way to help them read the mind of the Creator, the intellectual plan behind the manifested universe.

Source   *Tractatus Apologeticus Integritatem Societatis de Rosea Crucis defendens*, Leiden, 1617, pp. 177-83.

Rosicrucian Music

Ch. 6   *On the occult and wondrous effects of the secret Music*

Text: Whosoever can sing with the voice or play on an instrument so as to attract not the rocks of Amphion, but pearls and gemstones; not the beasts of Orpheus, but the spirit; not Pluto from Tartarus, but the mighty princes of the world: he shall enter the Brotherhood.[3]

If we accord any credence to the opinions of Plato and Cardan,[4] the best of harmonies is generated by the conglomeration of the spheres. This cannot be perceived by our ears because of the great distance; but it can be known from the effects on these lower regions not only of this music's symphonious concords, but also of its discords. The former excite in things love, harmony and pleasant desire: the latter hatred, discord and destructive scorn. From the symphonious influence of the heavens, then, it arises that the magnet attracts iron, amber silver, the sea-crab (*carabe*), hairs and straw, and the magnetic salve the nature of a wounded man,[5] each holding the other in extraordinary affection. Their dissonant influence also produces the antipathy and discord of things, such as between lamb and wolf, dormouse and cat, the cock's crow and the lion, the sight of basilisk or *catoblepas* and man, and many others.[6] Now the concords of divine music draw similar things to them for their protection, and the discords of the same drive away and put to flight dissimilar and contrary things for the same purpose. There are certain stars which complete their more perfect consonances in discordant places (as we have explained clearly with an infallible proof elsewhere, in our *Harmonia mundana*):[7] Saturn, by nature cold and dry, concludes its octave[8] in the element of fire which is hot, and Mars, which is hot and dry, ends its octave in the element of water which is cold and humid. Thus these planets, although by accident malevolent and unfortunate, may in themselves be as good as the other planets, the Sun excepted. But Jupiter, conversely, which is hot and humid, ends its octave in the element of its own nature, namely air, with which Venus accords with a fifth which is modified in combination with it. Hence it is that sublunary creatures, receiving the combinations of these good planets, love each other and combine with natural symphonious love, and hate those creatures which are produced by the contrary impressions of malevolent stars. The wolf, for instance, is known to have a martial and ferocious disposition, the lamb a jovial and tender one, the toad a saturnine one, and the catoblepas a martial and fiery eye; just as man is assigned a jovial, woman a venereal [character].

Thus, too, the Sun or Apollo, who is the prince and governor of the celestial music (whence some have called him Mind and World-soul) every year freely and benevolently showers down the notes and harmonious sounds of his lyre into the aethereal matter concealed in earth and sea;[9] and these symphonious concords occultly modulate the secret music of lives whose audible sounds lie hid in creatures just as fire does in wood, flint or turpentine: their hidden fires become visible and are brought from potency to act either by the blow of steel or by any other actual fire similar to themselves. He, therefore, to whom it is given to know the true Phoebic tones, will not find it an impossible matter to produce them in sensible action, and with their harmony to attract and draw to himself all those things originally assembled therefrom.[10] We can see that pearls are full of aethereal nature, and that other precious gems are distinguished as much by aethereal as by solar harmony; and it is very likely that if there were a unison of celestial harmony in note and voice, there might occur that consonance, by virtue of the middle or airy spirit, by which the bodies of pearls and gems would be moved; and the following experiment shows this. Place two lutes on the same table, and put a straw on the string of one of them. If you sound the string of the other which is in unison with the string carrying the straw, the string holding the straw will forthwith vibrate and move and throw off the straw with a sudden motion. From this we can learn the marvelous relationship of one creature to another by virtue of this harmony.

If we examine carefully the fables of the poets, we will find prodigious secrets in them. Why should Pan (by whom is signified Universal Nature) have made his pipe of seven syringes or reeds, by which hue evoked a sweet harmony, if not because the intellectual spirit which moves the heavens makes a corresponding music in these inferior parts? For by the composition out of seven pipes is meant the assembly of seven planetary spheres, with their wondrous harmony in Heaven and Earth, i.e. wherever that universal nature extends. Similarly, we may seek the reason why Mercury gave Apollo the lyre, and Apollo in turn gave Mercury the caduceus staff.[11] If we examine all things succinctly in this way, we will find that it is no more outside nature's power that a wise man should cause to move by his music (*harmonia*) the essentializing (*essentificam*) substance of the aethereal heaven concealed in lower bodies, than that the soul situated in an animal should urge its body hither or thither at will. For music moves a body by setting in motion the airy nature, and by purified air arouses the spirit and the airy bond of soul and body. And music by its virtue renders evil spirits more kindly, as the Holy Scriptures tell us in the story of Saul, possessed by an evil spirit, which, raging in the body of Saul, was pacified by the virtue of David's music.

This surely appertains to the remarkable operation of music in man, according to Plato's doctrine in the third Book of the *Republic* [398d *et seq.*]. For by the motion of the subtle air it penetrates the inner parts of the soul, which it vehemently strikes and imprints with a suitable figure; and this affects the senses by its mood, acts on the mind by its meaning, and gives sweet delight in contemplation. By its similar quality it causes both the spiritual and material nature to flow with a wondrous pleasure; it seizes and takes possession of the whole man at once, making him liberal, joyous and lovable. There is therefore no doubt that music can have the miraculous power of moving not only common people but even the very princes, especially when the new, secret and astonishing harmony of music is heard.

For what is more conformable to the celestial music than man? In his wonderful constitution there is an image of the whole *musica mundana*, thanks to the double consonance of octave and fifth.[12] Certainly the spiritual and material [consonances] are infused by Jupiter in his aethereal spirit, and the double diapason of the Sun, spiritual and material, in the elements of his body; and the whole composition as much spiritual as material. So it will not be surprising if the Brothers are adept in knowledge of this music, since they are able to attract powerful princes to themselves by its virtue. We conclude, therefore, that as the idea of truth which is impressed on our intellect and thought remains there, so it is with the miraculous effects of divine works and the secrets of nature; thus we may understand with our minds that such things may be accomplished without the craft of spirits[13] (although we may be ignorant of the means of operation). And I think we may say that it ill becomes a true Christian (who should be burning with the fire of love) not only openly to call these unknown men magicians, but also to trumpet to the world that their operations are magical and the effects of necromancy; even though in the courts of their philosophy, where such secrets flourish, he will never achieve anything – or nothing good. Wherefore they do wickedly and wrongfully who condemn unjustly, with minds veiled in darkness, those things which they do not understand. For there are infinite secrets hidden in nature's casket, shut away so as not to be revealed to the multitude; which, however, once revealed, disclose to us infinite mysteries in themselves. Of these we will make mention of one little box of nature which to the senses is very insignificant, but under whose lid I have found hid marvelous secrets of things most high, as I will explain more fully in the next chapter.[14]

34

JOHANNES KEPLER
1571–1630

The period which we enter with Kepler's works is a watershed in the history of our ideas. Kepler, a man of stupendous genius, patience and spirituality, shows how the vision human beings have of their universe may be widened, corrected and made ever more wonderful, awe-inspiring, exalting ·and humbling through the alliance of mystical insight with objective observation. When he was 24 he had an epiphany of the laws of the solar system as deriving from the Five Regular Solids. Placed between the planetary spheres, these forms both determine the number of planets, confirming the heliocentric system of Copernicus, and govern the distances between their orbits. *Mysterium cosmographicum* (The Cosmographical Mystery, 1596) was the result of this revelation of divine law, interpreted not only as a geometrical but also as a musical harmony, and Kepler was never to lose sight of it.

In *Harmonices Mundi Libri V* (Five Books on Cosmic Harmony, 1619) he returned to interpret it in the light of twenty-five years of painstaking calculation and concentrated questioning of his Creator. His mathematical studies of planetary motion had not only led to the discovery of the three laws for which he is most celebrated, and which provided the starting-point for Isaac Newton's further work: they now called for a refinement of the harmonic laws which were only adumbrated in his earlier book. By 1619 he was able to give a rational notation of the planets' songs, confirming that their real music is polyphonic, and not some static scale of distances or periods such as previous writers had struggled with in their efforts to pin down their intuitions of cosmic harmony. Advances in astronomy since the seventeenth century have only served to confirm and amplify Kepler's findings.[1]

This extract is a concise account of his beliefs about cosmogony, acoustics and the psychology of perception. In a short space he expounds his Neopythagorean theory of the mathematics behind the manifested universe; his physical explanation of the workings of sympathetic vibration, hence, by implication, of universal harmony; and his firm conviction that the source of the human response to music is to be sought in the soul and intellect, not in physical matter.

Kepler was able to keep in balance the twin claims of the head and the heart, of calculation and intuition, analysis and awe. That is why his work is a watershed. After him, from the point of view of secular history, the currents of thought flowed with the assumption that the irrational can and must be excluded from science, leading ultimately to an age of deadly technocracy. Our subsequent extracts, however, demonstrate that there was another stream – at times an underground one, it is true – and that the spiritual impulse which informed Kepler was never to be completely extinguished.

Source Harmonices Mundi Libri V, first published Linz, 1619, in Kepler's *Gesammelte Werke*, ed. Max Caspar, vol. VI, Munich, 1940, pp. 104-7. Also consulted: Caspar's German translation, *Harmonice Mundi: Weltharmonik*, Munich and Berlin, Oldenbourg, 1939.

The Metaphysics of Harmony

Book III, Ch. 1 On the causes of consonances. *Section on "The metaphysical cause of harmonics"*

The reflections that can be made on these axioms,[2] particularly on the first five, are lofty, comparable to those of Platonism and the Christian faith, for they concern metaphysics and the doctrine of the Soul. For Geometry, whose relevant part was contained in our first two books, is coeternal with God and shines within the divine Mind. As was said in the preamble to this book, it has been amply endowed by God with examples for the world's beautification, in order that the latter might be the best and most beautiful, in fact most like its Creator. For all these things – Spirits, Souls, Intellects[3] – are images of God the Creator, set in charge of their bodies to govern, move, increase, preserve and also propagate them.

Since, therefore, their functions include a certain type of creation, they observe the same laws as their Creator: laws derived from geometry. They rejoice in the same proportions as God uses wherever they find them, whether in pure speculation, or through the mediation of the senses in matters subject thereto, or even without the discourse of the Intellect, through a hidden and inborn instinct. Perhaps God himself has invariably expressed these proportions in bodies and motions. Or perhaps, following a certain geometrical necessity governing infinitely divisible matter and the motions corresponding to its quantity, there occur at the appropriate times amongst the infinite non-harmonic proportions those which are harmonic; and thus they do not exist in Being but in Becoming.

But it is not only delight that these proportions afford to the Intellects, the images of God: they also serve as laws for the execution of their functions and proportions, expressed as far as possible in the motions of their bodies. The following books will offer two shining examples: that of God the Creator himself, who has distributed the motions of the heavens in harmonic proportions; another of that soul which we call sublunary Nature, which controls meteorological phenomena according to the rules of proportions which occur in the radiations of the stars.[4] A third example, also relevant to this book, is that of the human soul, and to an extent also that of beasts. For these are glad when hearing the harmonic proportions of voices, and sad at inharmonic ones. Owing to these affects of the soul the harmonic ones are named consonances, the inharmonic ones dissonances. And if one were to add yet another harmonic proportion, that of voices or tones longer or shorter in respect to time, then they are the ones that move bodies to dancing and tongues to speaking according to the same laws: thus workmen regulate their hammering, soldiers their marching. All things live while harmonies last, and fall unconscious when they are disturbed.

These and similar things are the work of intention or of instinct, i.e. of the mind. The philosophers have debated variously whether it is a necessary consequence of the nature of the elements and of matter that there can be no well-being in the senses except that which consists in the harmonic proportions of figures. They have examined everything to find where the sweetness resides that flows into the ear from the proportion of tones by which consonances are defined. Those who lean toward matter and the motion of the elements cite the example, certainly a very remarkable one, of how a plucked string will transfer its sound to another unplucked one if they are consonant with one another, but leave it immobile if they are dissonant. Since this cannot be the work of any mind, because a sound thus caused has neither mind nor intellect, it follows that we must say that it is caused by a simultaneity of motions. For the sound of a string owes its high or low pitch to the speed or slowness of the vibration which runs along its whole free length. These differences of sounds do not reside primarily in the length or shortness themselves, but secondarily, because we know that a lesser length diminishes the slowness of vibration and increases its speed. Hence it happens that in the same free length of a string, stretching raises the pitch since it makes the string tighter and reduces the space in which it can vibrate with its to-and-fro motion.

When the tension of two strings is the same, so that they sound in unison, then the sound of one, i.e. the immaterial species[5] of the body of the string caused by the vibration, leaves its own string and moves the other one. It is the same when one shouts near a lute or any other hollow body: the shout shakes the cavity and makes all its strings vibrate. This species of vibration moves the second string in the same rhythm of speed as the latter would move in, because it is tuned alike, in the following way. The single impulses (into which we must understand that a vibration is divided) arouse in the other, struck string single rebounds [*cessiunculas*]. Thus the string that will be moved most of all is the one which is tuned in unison to the first; but the string of double or half speed will also be moved, because two impulses of vibration will be resolved in one rebound of the string, and thus every third impulse[6] will coincide with the end of a rebound. Finally, the string will not remain unmoved when the speeds are as 3:2, for then three impulses will go with every two rebounds; but now these impulses and those rebounds begin to interfere with and impede each other more frequently, since two impulses are contrary to the end of a rebound, while only one coincides. When this happens, the motion of the other strings is stopped just as if one had touched a finger to the vibrating one. This seems to me to be the cause of this remarkable experiment, but I will give the palm to anyone who is better endowed with mental penetration than myself.

[7]What follows from this? If the speed of one string can serve to move the other one tuned to it, though it be untouched as far as the eye can see, will not the same speeds of both strings serve for the pleasant stimulation of the ear, because the latter is in some way moved uniformly by the two strings, and two impulses from the two sounds or vibrations meet at the same moment? I think, however, that one cannot deal with this matter so easily, and I am surprised that Porphyry in his Commentary on the *Harmonics* of Ptolemy could be satisfied with something like this as an explanation of the phenomenon, for he was a philosopher of the deepest insight. It is probable that he was prevented by the difficulty of researching the cause from penetrating into it as far as he would have liked; and that he thought it better to produce something than to be altogether silent, which they say is shameful for a philosopher. For what proportion, I ask, can there be between the stimulation of the hearing, a corporeal thing, and that incredible pleasure which harmonic consonances cause us to perceive deep in our innermost selves [*animo*]?[8] If the pleasure arises from the stimulation, does not the organ which sustains the stimulation play the primary rôle in this pleasure? In dioptrics I have come to define every sense such that the sensible perception which gives pleasure or pain is absolutely closed off as soon as the species of the organ, which serves this perception in so far as it is affected from outside, comes into the tribunal of the common sense, led by the life-spirits. Now, in the hearing of consonances of voices or sounds, what parts of pleasure belong in the ears? Do we not often feel pain in our ears, when we listen to music and hold our hand up against the clangour, in order

to hear the consonances, and our heart leaps up?[9] Moreover, this argument, deduced from motion, is most valid for the unison; yet sweetness is not principally in the unison, but in the other consonances, and in their combination. Much more could be adduced to demolish the above argument for the sweetness of consonances, but I will omit its fuller exposition for the moment. I will stress only one thing, which I have touched on above, which may stand for all of these: the functions and motions of bodies in which harmonic proportions are imitated arise from the soul and mind, showing that they are the cause why consonances give pleasure. The authority of the Ancients does not disagree. For in defining the soul now as motion, now as harmony, they have not so much spoken absurdly as been ineptly understood: since in difficult matters a mystical sense often lies hidden beneath the surface of the words. The philosophy of Timaeus the Locrian,[10] according to which the soul is assembled in harmonic proportions (treated in the preamble) was refuted by Aristotle in the literal sense of the words. But I would not dare to assert that nothing is hidden in those pages but what the words say. I believe that no one would deny that this author believes at least what I posit here: that the sense of hearing discriminates between pleasant proportions, i.e. consonant ones, and unpleasant and dissonant ones. Let him consider diligently that proportions are entities of reason, perceptible by reason alone, not by sense, and that to distinguish the proportions, i.e. the form, from the thing proportioned, i.e. from matter, is a function of the Intellect.

35

ATHANASIUS KIRCHER
1602–80

At the mid-point of the seventeenth century, the Jesuit polymath Athanasius Kircher wrote the last great work of speculative music in the traditional sense. It was not only the last work but also the longest, with the exception of Jacques de Liège's *Speculum Musicae*; and like Jacques's it summed up the collected wisdom of an era that was already closing. The *Musurgia Universalis* of 1650 is awesome in its size, its scope and its strangeness, beside the fact that it was just an incidental work of this formidable author: a diversion between his major works on astronomy and optics, *Ars magna lucis et umbrae* (1646) and Egyptology (*Oedipus Aegyptiacus*, 3 vols, 1652-4).[1]

Kircher was a Hermetist at heart,[2] but he had to steer a careful course between Church dogma and esotericism. He is equally careful in his balance of magic with science. He respected and utilized experimental science, which he called the Empirical Art, but subordinated it to the higher purpose of demonstrating the *a priori* truths of religion or of mystical intuition. Like Kepler, he was a philosopher of the watershed period in Western culture, though by his later life the waters were well and truly flowing in a direction which left him far behind. *Musurgia* is a magnificent monument to the entire period which precedes it: after it there were only a few stragglers like Werckmeister, Nassarre and Tartini[3] before the impulses with which we are concerned took flight and migrated from the world of learning and science to that of imaginative literature.

Kircher's "Enneachord of Nature" is founded on the Hermetic doctrine of correspondences, here envisioned as an instrument on which every string, when plucked, resounds through all the levels of being in the universe. In the conclusion to the whole work he completes the image by expanding his metaphorical instrument from nine to ten strings, as mentioned in Psalm 33.2. Ten is the number of perfection; the number of the Tetraktys of the Pythagoreans (see notes to Plato, no. 1); the number of the Sephiroth of the Kabbalistic Tree of Life.[4] The tenth string is therefore the One from which, in all these systems, the other nine hypostases emanate; or, alternatively, the One in which they all seek and find their perfection.

Source Musurgia Universalis, Rome, 1650, reprinted Hildesheim, Olms, 1970, vol. II, pp. 390-4, 461-2.

The Nine-Stringed Instrument of Nature

The Symphony of Stones, Plants, and Animals with the Heavens

In the preceding register GOD, best and greatest, showed us the admirable harmony of the heavenly bodies. In this one he offers to mortals another stupendous symphony, entirely consonant with the first: that of sublunary things, both with each other and with regard to the stars and planets. This harmony is as it were reflected from the heavenly ones: for Iamblichus says truly that the harmonies of inferior things are nothing but echoes of the lofty notes of the heavens, reverberating in this inferior world in accordance with their nature.

Although in *Ars Anacamptica* and *Gnomica Physico-Astrologica*[5] we gave out much information on the remarkable effects of the Sun and on the secrets of the heavenly artificer, we see fit to touch again on their harmonic qualities, so that nothing in this great art should be omitted. The Sun is the chief, prince, and choragus of all heavenly bodies. Proceeding on his oblique circuit of the world, he gladdens, fecundates, brightens, and makes all things to grow whenever he approaches; but when he is distant he leaves them filthy, foul, rough, foggy, dark, and imperfect. Through his departure and absence he supplies a period for the conceptions of the Earth, then by his return and proximity he cares for them and silently builds up their strength. He withdraws just sufficiently for the Earth to fill with appropriate and opportune humors, and thus become fit for intercourse with her powerful friend. At last he returns by the same route, and dries up her high places. At his appearance the accumulated energies first generate the fibres within the stem, then they entice the green leaves forth, and finally lead all things to full growth. For this there is no lack of assistance and support in the igneous and starry heavens: the planets especially, like a second force working with the Sun upon the Earth, will sometimes assemble as one and direct their influences from a single quarter, reaching out to incite inferior natures to strife. At another time they will be widely scattered in different places and from their various seats on high will declare peace on Earth.

Now just as one may be lacking in energy, yet when worldly affairs demand its instant presence it will quickly descend for them, even so these [celestial forces] are sometimes long absent, rising aloft and forbearing from things below; then, since service to a loved one is no burden, they will stop wherever they are, and since delays can be inconvenient they will hasten together almost as if summoned to the place; or as if interrupted by prayers for help will turn backwards in their courses.[6] All these things are most wisely ordered by GOD for producing corresponding effects in the world. Whence Proclus tells us that the harmony proceeding from the concord of the heavens and the elegance of their movements is first shared by the divinities [Numina] superior to us, and then by the man who disposes his life rightly, consonant in his behavior and harmonious in his actions. He believed that the same gift of heavenly harmony could descend even to animals, plants, and stones. For all things above are maintained and perfected in harmonic ratios, and adapt themselves mutually for the order of the world. The ancient Egyptians considered the harmony of earthly things with celestial; they observed the sympathy, agreement, and relationships that sublunary things have with one another, and those that connect the manifest world with occult forces. They founded a sacred and mystical philosophy in which these matters were given out under various symbols designed to veil them, called hieroglyphs; and it is this science, lost to our day, which we will restore by God's grace in *Oedipus Aegyptiacus*.

The higher things they perceived hidden in the lower, and lower things concealed in the higher; earthly things in heaven, but in celestial form, and heavenly things in an earthly mode on earth. For how else are we to consider those plants called heliotropes or "sun-followers" (treated at length in our *Ars Magnetica*)[7] which point towards the sunrise? Or the selenotropes, "moon-followers," which face the Moon? Surely it is none other than the longing for harmony latent everywhere that causes each living being to pray and address hymns to the Lords of its order; but some do this intellectually, others rationally; some naturally and others sensibly. You will find that plants forcibly bent down will try with all their strength to rise and face the sky again; and that the shoots of trees, forced through an oblique aperture, as soon as they meet the light of day will avidly and impatiently raise their heads for love of the sky. So things solar tend toward the Sun in whatever way they can, to the extent that if anyone could hear the vibration which a plant causes to circulate in the air, he would certainly find the sound composed as much in accordance with its laws as were possible to the plant or other thing in question. On Earth we can contemplate the Sun, the Moon, and the stars, but in an earthly condition; and in heaven we will find plants, animals, and stones in heavenly form, according to the same analogy. Some of these stones, plants, and animals are Solar, others Saturnine, Jovial, Martial, Venereal, Mercurial, or Lunar. The secret Kabbalists maintain, in fact, that there is no herb on earth that does not have its star in the firmament to order its growth.

Beginning with stones, who does not know of their great appetite for higher bodies and for all things that naturally correspond to them in any way? Proculus [sic] says that the stone Helites imitates the golden rays and the motion of the Sun, not unlike the gem on the finger of Clement VII mentioned by Cardanus, which had a bright spot that moved each day from East to West, following the Sun. There are solar stones, like all Carbuncles and Garnets; lunar ones, called Selenites, of which it is written that Gregory X had one that copied the metamorphoses of the Moon, changing from a bluish to a whitish color according to the variation in the Moon's light. The Magnet is connected with Mars, the Sapphire with Jupiter, the Agate with Mercury, and all are imbued with the appropriate virtues.

The various movements of herbs, plants, and trees are sufficient to show that the vegetable nature also agrees with the heavens. Some plants follow the diurnal motion of the Sun, like the sunflower described in *Ars Magnetica*; others his proper movement, like the leaves of willows, white poplars, elms, lindens, olives – called for that reason solstitial. Experience has shown them completely turned over on the day [of the solstice]. Some flowers open at dawn, at noon gape as wide as they can, and close at sunset. Such is their love of the Sun that they will turn about, following in his train, until their very stems are twisted; then at night they will shrink and pine with desire for him. Some such as the licorice and acacia lift their leaves or branches in the presence of the Sun as if to embrace their star. In his absence they drop them as if to seek him below the horizon, and draw them together for the night. Many lunar plants there are, aroused by love for the Moon, which move erratically according to the Moon's various forms, and themselves assume different shapes. In the same way the other planets have their corresponding plants: to Saturn they assign the cypress, hellebore, and aconite; to Jupiter the rosemary, lemon, betony, and valerian; to Mars the oak, verbena, and wormwood; to Venus the myrtle, vine, olive, and orchid; lastly to Mercury the pomegranate, hyacinth, and narcissus.

Finally in the animal kingdom there is found an even greater consensus of this sort. Some manifest their love for their governing star by song, others by aspect or gesture. We will not dwell long on this here, having treated part of it in *Ars Magnetica* and part in our forthcoming *Oedipus Aegyptiacus*. But what does the lion or the cock evoke if not a kind of terrestrial Sun? Likewise the cat could not be otherwise than lunar, the wolf, martial. And the dog, horse, stag and ass must surely bear witness respectively to a terrestrial Mercury, Venus, and Saturn. Its voice, movement, and vivacity all declare that the cock belongs to the Sun. Proculus tells of a remarkable thing: that the solar daemons appear with the faces of lions, and leave with the crowing of a white cock. He explains that those things which are constituted lower in their order always revere the higher, and willingly obey and yield to them. All these things present a marvelous and delightful pageant and bear witness to the covenant between heaven and earth; in an harmonious concord they freely bless mankind, and urge them to revere, worship and venerate the Author of so much good, the Artist of so many miracles, and the most sage Architect of these supreme beauties. If indeed the whole Earth together with the mass of waters and all that dwell therein are thus matched with the superior elements, and the latter explained by the sky and stars, and each, moreover, regulated, ordered, and constituted hierarchically by decree of the inscrutable divine wisdom and foresight so that everything we call Nature is connected by mutual embraces, bonds, duties, and services, then there must dwell in this multitude of dissimilar and contrary things a wondrous harmony of one with all, and all with one. And now, so that this harmony may more clearly appear, we have drawn up here a chart of the whole symphony.[8] (See pp. 158-9.)

The better to show the sympathies and antipathies, or, which is the same, the concord and discord in Nature, let us now imagine ten enneachords [nine-stringed instruments] all tuned in unison. That is, first tune nine strings to the harmonic steps of one octave, and then tune all the rest to them. So all the strings which give the proslambanomenos [A] will sound in unison, and likewise every hypate [B], parhypate [c], lichanos mese [d], etc., as shown in this chart.[9]

Placing all these enneachords next to one another, we know from what was explained in the first part of the book that if one proslambanomenos [A] is struck, every other enneachord, even though untouched, will sound its corresponding note; likewise the mese [e] of the first will excite the meses of all the other monochords, and so on. Therefore if one were to play the four strings proslambanomenos [A], parhypate [c], mese [e], and nete [a] simultaneously, all the others would respond in kind, though untouched, and there would be heard a beautiful harmony of fourth, third, and octave. No other strings would resonate except those tuned in unison. This harmony would be all the more perceptible if other strings or resonators were tuned to the octave above. If, on the other hand, one were to pluck simultaneously the dissonant strings of proslambanomenos [A], hypate [B], lichanos [d], and hyponete [sic – g?] in the first octave, a most powerful dissonance would be aroused in the others. It is certainly a remarkable thing that the corresponding strings tuned to the unison also vibrate, but that those tuned to intervals contradictory to the harmonic laws of sound do not. If the numbers of the intervals are unequal, partaking of properties that are mutually unsatisfying and incompatible, they

The Sympathetic Harmony of the World, showing the whole Symphony of Nature in Ten Enneachords

	Enneachord I	Enn. II	Enn. III	Enn. IV
Tenth	*Archetypal World* GOD	*Sidereal World* Empyrean	*Mineral World*	*Stones*
Ninth	Seraphim	Firmament [b]	Salt, Mineral stars	Astrites
Octave	Cherubim	Saturn Nete [a]	Lead	Topaz
Seventh	Thrones	Jupiter Paranete [g]	Copper [sic]	Amethyst
Sixth	Dominations	Mars Parameson [f]	Iron	Adamant
Fifth	Virtues	Sun Mese . [e]	Gold	Garnet
Fourth	Powers	Venus Lichanos [d]	Tin [sic]	Beryl
Third	Principalities	Mercury Parhypate [c]	Quicksilver	Agate Jasper
Tone	Archangels	Moon Hypate [B]	Silver	Selenite Crystal
	Angels	Earth & Elements Proslambanomenos [A]	Sulphur	Lodestone

Enn. V	Enn. VI	Enn. VII	Enn. VIII	Enn. IX	Enn. X
Plants	*Trees*	*Aquatic Creatures*	*Birds*	*Quadrupeds*	*Colors*
Stellar herbs & flowers	Fruits & Berries	Stellar fish	Egyptian vulture	Panther	Different colors
Hellebore	Cypress	Tunny	Owl	Ass Bear	Dark
Betony	Lemon	Sturgeon	Eagle	Elephant	Rose
Absinthe	Oak	Psyphias	Falcon Vulture	Wolf	Flaming
Sunflower	Lotus Laurel	Dolphin	Cock	Lion	Gold
Orchid	Myrtle	Trout	Swan Dove	Stag	Green
Peony	Apple	Beaver	Parrot	Dog	Blue
Honesty	Pod-bearers	Oyster	Ducks Geese	Cat	White
Wheat	Fruits	Eel	Ostrich	Insects	Black

cannot sound in a single harmony unless coerced by a musician's skill into syncopations or suspensions. But by this artifice they will not only observe harmonic laws, but also manifest the beauty of the greatest harmony, as we shall show.

Nature thus arranges the various enneachords in the world so that all are in tune with the celestial enneachord; and when one is set going, all the rest will resonate. Thus in the preceding chart Enneachord I is that of the angelic world, II of the heavenly bodies, III of metals, IV of stones, V of plants, VI of trees, VII of aquatic creatures, VIII of flying ones, IX of quadrupeds, and X of colors. To these could be added scales of tastes and odors, and so on stepwise through every order of natural phenomena. Turning to the individual strings, we find one string of each enneachord tuned to nete, said to symbolize Saturn and to assume a certain Saturnine quality; and these all mutually linked so that if any one is struck, all the rest will vibrate with it in unison. Then again, all things which correspond to the paranete string in every enneachord, since they symbolize Jupiter, will affect wholly Jovian characteristics. Now just as proslambanomenos [A] and hypate [B] strings are not concordant with each other, because their tones make a dissonant interval, even so the things of Jupiter are quite out of tune with those of Saturn on account of their dissonant interval, unless they are corrected by syncopation as shown below.[10] Then on the other hand, just as proslambanomenos [A] makes the imperfect consonance of a third with parhypate [c], so the things of Mars are imperfectly concordant with those of Saturn; and as the fourth, fifth, and octave make perfect consonances, so there are species of things corresponding thereto. In a word, if you combine concordant strings in nature you will produce concordant effects: if discordant ones, discords will result.

The Ultimate Music

I will say nothing here of the inner peace of blessed minds, or of the tranquility of souls in their dance; nothing of the incomprehensible symphony of angels and men in the eternal Odeon of the Arch-muse. Surely the appearance or the enjoyment of even the most beautiful things of this world, compared to it, are no more than vile dross, rotten chaff, and a little sand, the dregs of the earth. Everything imaginable which could ever be invented by the skill of human genius, all harmony and music, every conceivable beauty and allure of musical instruments, every excellence and perfection of human voices: what are these, compared to that supreme music, but the cacophonous bellowing of cattle, the howling of wolves, the grunting of pigs? What are the harmonious fragrance, sweetness, and tenderness of odor, taste, and touch, but stink, bitterness, and sheer filth? Its all-orderly and supereminent form "eye has not seen, nor ear heard, neither has it entered into the heart of man." [I Corinthians 2.9.] No one can explain this symphony in verbal concepts, none declare it with however felicitous or eloquent a pen, none can penetrate it with the profoundest scrutiny of mind. Compounded not of three, four, or five voices, but of the utterly ineffable chorus of Saints, all disposed in their different classes, it resonates for all eternity in the supramundane palace of the Heavenly King. There the choirs of Virgins, of Confessors, of Martyrs, Apostles, and Patriarchs all interweave with the triple hierarchy of Angels, singing to the fount of the water of eternal life, enjoying eternal rest as they tirelessly sing the eternal Alleluia in praise of GOD, who like a supreme conductor directs the symphony by his wisdom, and animates the organ by the breath of his mouth. There they sing a new song to the Lamb of GOD, who in this eternal home is the musician, the instrument, and the music: the wondrous epithalamium and marriage-song of the Word of GOD who was wedded to human nature in the womb of an immaculate Virgin. There the remembrance of this world's labors, of torments endured to the end for love of GOD, is like a dissonance mingled with the consonance of blessed life everlasting, and a syncopation coalescing with the ecstatic and perfect harmony of all things. O unhappy is the fate of those who, deafened by the transitory goods of this calamitous life, by the noise of worldly ambition, by the discordant cataracts of impure affections and pleasures, have lost their hope of ever attaining or hearing the music we have described.

O great Harmost, who has disposed all things in number, and weight, and measure, may it please thee to tune the enneachord of my soul to thy divine will; play upon all the strings of my soul to the praise and glory of thy name, that I may love thee with Seraphic ardor, and seek thee constantly with a Cherubic mind; let my soul be a Throne where thou wilt rest and lay thee down at noon. May the Dominations, Virtues, and Powers be present for my defense. Establish a Principality over the whole untamed and rebellious host of my soul's affections, that I may serve thee for ever in Angelic purity. Let thy voice sound in my ears, for thy voice is sweet and thy visage fair; dispose in me that same harmony of virtues as thou hast stablished in thyself from the beginning, that progressing from virtue to virtue as from one tone to another I may attain the octave of all virtues and the fullness of perfection, and, armed with these, may sing to thee with an instrument of ten strings, praising and glorifying thee for ever and ever. Amen.

36

JOHN HEYDON
1629–after 1667

John Heydon was a prolific writer on esoteric matters, a professional
astrologer and attorney, an adventurer and self-proclaimed expert on
the Rosicrucians. He was often in and out of prison, and Ashmole
called him "an ignoramus and a cheat."[1] Nevertheless, his books are
a fair representation of the popular occult revival that took place in
England during the Protectorate and continued after the Restora-
tion, bringing about the publication in English of works that had
formerly been available only in Latin, German, or in manuscript.
Agrippa's *Occult Philosophy* (1651), Ashmole's *Theatrum Chemicum
Brittanicum* (1652), and Fludd's *Mosaicall Philosophy* (1659), are some
of the most important. This extract shows how Kepler's ideas of
cosmic geometry and harmony filtered down to the general public,
wrongly attributed to Descartes, combined with allusions to the
Hermetic doctrine of the descent of the soul, and peppered with the
names of authorities on philosophy and astrology. Elsewhere in the
same book, Heydon makes an elegant précis of another important
doctrine:

> What the ignorant call evil in this Universe, is but as the shadowy
> strokes in a fair picture; or the mournful notes in Music, by which the
> beauty of the one is more lively and express, and the melody of the other
> more pleasing and melting. (p. 239)

Source   *The Harmony of the World*, London, 1662, pp. 69-70, 75-6.

The Harmonious Influences of the Planets

These speculations [about the powers of the astrological aspects of
opposition, trine and square] therefore considered, it were senseless
to imagine, that Nature hath so many ways honoured these
irradiations of the Stars in vain, and admonished us to a special
regard of them by so many and secret observations both in the

motions of the Planets (as you heard before) and also in their effects and proportions; if they were not indued with more virtue than the others; wherefore it hath no less exercised the learned Dr. *Ward*, Mr. *Tho. Heydon*, Mr. *More*, and *Eugenius Theodidactus*,[2] to find out the reason, why these few Configurations, selected out of an infinite number, should be indued with such eminent efficacy. Neither as yet hath any reason been invented, with more applause for the probability thereof, than these proportions; *The Learned Knight*, Sir *Christopher Heydon*,[3] demonstrates whereof, the Aspects are before showed to consist, and they are the same which are found in *Harmonical Concords*.

For which cause, it is also thought no less probable, that the light of the Stars in these proportional distances, should powerfully affect the matter of sublunary things, then that the like Geometrical Symmetry in sounds and voices should passionately stir up the sense of the hearer. For to confess the truth, so hath the admired providence of Nature ordained, throughout all her works, that where due proportion is not wanting, there she never faileth to endue all her effects with such height of perfection, that the same becomes evident to the eye of every man: And from hence it is even in Artificial compositions also, as in Medicines; we know those only to be most kind and sovereign which observe a competent symmetry or temperature of the Active and passive qualities; with good likelihood therefore, and appearance of truth do most of the learned with *Hobbes*, Dr. *Barlow of Queens*, Master *More*, and Mr. *Fisk*,[4] resolve the only cause of this efficacy from *Harmonical proportion*.

I shall next lay down some Reasons, why the aforesaid *Harmonical* proportions are so effectual, drawn from the Symmetry of the world, being the same that is found between the five regular bodies inscribed one within another, why in the infinite variety of sounds and lights, these only should consent most sweetly in music, sending down souls so merrily to the *Moon*,[5] and from thence they come down sadly to the belly and Matrix of the *Earth* in prolific spirited *Winds* and *Waters*, and be effectual in the operations of nature. Neither hath any man herein endeavoured with more probability to give satisfaction unto the learned than *Des Cartes*, who having wittily laboured to demonstrate, that God in the creation of the world hath observed the same proportion in the magnitude and distance of the *heavenly spheres*, which is found in the regular *Solids*, which (as *Geometry* teacheth) have their original from the ordinate planes: In the end concludeth with good probability, that the Heavenly motions shall then consent sweetly, and co-operate strongly together, when the nature of these sublunary things, indued (as he supposeth) with a sensitive or knowing faculty, apprehendeth the beams of the

Stars at the Center of the *Earth*, which answereth unto the ordinate Planes, from whence the Regularity of these proportions is derived, as the impressed Characters of that *Symmetry*, which God is said to have used in the Creation of the world itself.

So supposing, that as often as the nature of anything meeteth with these proportions, it exerciseth itself as it were by *The Idea*, which it always retaineth, and that in such sort, as what it doth but ordinarily and slackly at other times, it performeth now much more effectually, and as it were with extraordinary diligence: Nor (saith Sr. *Christopher Heydon*) that these proportions work anything of their own virtue, but of their *Idea's*; for in music it is neither the sounds, neither the proportions of the concords, that work anything of themselves, or beget any delightful humour in a man, but the *Genius* approaching to the Instruments of sense first carrieth the sounds inwardly and entertaining it, there valueth their proportions: and (finding the same good and *Geometrical*[6]) lastly exhibiteth itself, and moveth the body, wherein it is as with an Object, wherein it taketh delight.

37

ANDREAS WERCKMEISTER

1645–1706

Werckmeister stands as a representative of the Renaissance culture which persisted in the most remote parts of Europe (Spain, Bohemia, the small principalities of Germany) long after it was extinct in the major centers. Like J.S. Bach, Werckmeister was a Lutheran provincial organist, his intellect nourished by Protestant piety, humanistic learning and the musical Platonism of Kepler and Kircher. Music, in his view, had one origin – the Divine Mind – and one purpose: the returning of the gift to God, to His greater glory and the increase of human piety.

Werckmeister was familiar with all the available Classical and Renaissance music theory, as well as with the German writers Calvisius, Lippius, Baryphonus, Printz and Bartholus; also with Praetorius, some of whose manuscripts he owned.[1] But this wide reading did not make him broad-minded in his musical sympathies: it confirmed his opinion that the modern style in music, especially when used in the theatre, was the Devil's own work.

In the *Paradoxal-Discourse* he takes a purely Keplerian view of astronomy and goes back to Cornelius Agrippa for his physiology. Here the Cosmos still works harmonically, in a literal sense, and Man's place in it is as a literal microcosm. But soon these ideas were to become poetic properties merely, except among those esoteric circles which persisted in allegiance to the Hermetic world-view while accepting the relatively small-scale alterations brought about by scientific progress.

Source   Musicalische Paradoxal-Discourse oder Allgemeine Vorstellungen Wie Die Musica einen Hohen und Gottlichen Uhrsprung habe, Quedlinburg, 1710, reprinted Hildesheim, Olms, 1970, pp. 16-17.

Musical Astrology

Ch. III   How man's body and soul are harmonically created, and on the influence of the stars

Next we see that Man's members are also fashioned and created through musical proportions, as has been remarked upon by many curious philosophers, particularly Cornelius Agrippa in *Philosophia Occulta*, Book 2, ch. 27,[2] and Escholzius in *Anthrometria*,[3] and as can be found and measured in a well-proportioned body. A certain poet also testifies to this when he writes:

> Not only your form but all your members will charm
>   If they are composed of harmonious numbers.
> Charm resides in the whole compound of the members,
>   Harmony comes from viewing of the whole.[4]

Since the outward parts, which have their origin and creation in the inward ones, are harmonious, it must follow that God himself, the almighty Creator, is a harmonious and beautiful being. For the exterior arises from the inward and spiritual, which always creates and engenders a similar being, having a kinship and resemblance to itself, and rejoices in its own kind as in its own image. Now if every being brings forth its own likeness, and if almighty God has breathed into Man a living soul after his own image, it follows, since God's being is harmonious, that the soul of Man is a harmony as many Christian philosophers have told us, such as Arias Montanus, *De Homine*, ch. I, Cornelius Agrippa, *lib. cit.*, ch. 28, and A. Bartholus in his *Musica Mathematica*.[5] The ancient philosophers such as Pythagoras, Plato, and others also had the same insight. So Man and music stem from a single principle and origin, namely God himself, and music must therefore contain something divine. The objection might be raised here that since God has also created beasts and all the insects, there must be something divine in them, too. I answer that one must certainly admire these manifold miracles as God's creations: a miserable worm can guide itself and move and have understanding to a certain degree, yet if the whole world were full of artists, they could not make such a worm in the natural way, no, not even a grass seed. (Magically, however, it is a different matter and must happen through the medium of nature.)[6] It is a different matter that any one of God's creations is always nobler and finer than another: for the stars, harmoniously made by God, are so magnificent that they are called God's Ministers: for they are arranged as specific instruments to accomplish God's ministry, and to give signs, time, and days (Genesis 1.14). Would not everything decay and moulder and grow cold if the light and warmth of the Sun did not irradiate our earth? Would not everything wither and languish if we did not sometimes receive a fruitful rain, which the constellations control (Deuteronomy 28.12; Leviticus 26.4)? Blessed Johann Arndt[7] writes in Book 4, chapter 4: "God the true Creator has ordered all things so that the lower must receive their power and influences from the higher," etc. The Prophet Hosea describes it very clearly in chapter 2: "(I, saith the Lord) will hear the heavens, and the heavens will hear the earth, and the earth will hear the wine and corn, and these will hear Israel." These natural processes all come from the stars and the command of God, as the above-mentioned 4th book of Johann Arndt explains exhaustively. And King David sings in Psalm 104, verse 19, "Thou makest the Moon to divide the year, and the Sun knows his setting." I will not now touch on what Theophrastus Paracelsus and innumerable other philosophers have written on the wonderful effects of the stars, for this is already well known to us from Holy Scriptures.

Now if the harmony of the stars is established by God so that they can have control on earth, they must be far more glorious than the beasts and insects, since they give life to the beasts through God's ordinance, yea, even to the worms. Must not the one who bestows the power of sustenance be more precious and glorious than the one which receives its life and power therefrom? Are not the holy Angels far more glorious and powerful in their actions and works than Mankind? Is not Man so much higher than the beasts, since God has made him in his own image and breathed into him the breath of life and an intelligent soul? And thus is Man distinguished from the other creatures: he is *rational*, as Aristides Quintilianus so well distinguishes it in his *Musica*, Book 2. For by this he understands nothing other than *prudence*, which is only concerned with the soul and with a blissful departure from this world. Therefore Man is a "rational animal." Irrationality is a concern which only cares for the body and desires its comfort, with which all beasts are imbued. Therefore it is my belief that if all philosophers were to make this distinction, they would soon rest content with this definition and dispense with the conflicts which often occur over it, such as whether horses or dogs and other intelligent beasts are gifted with reason. But returning to our subject, we assume that God has invested so great a power in the stars that all of Nature on the surface of the Earth is sustained and governed thereby. One can see, therefore, that they are far nobler and more glorious than beasts without understanding: particularly since the efficacious power of God comes forth from the stars so gloriously and manifestly that it is written even of certain dumb beasts that they love music; so the birds, too, must derive their instinct for music from the stars.

Now since musical proportions are arranged in the same way as the stars, should they not also have their own efficacy; especially if Man, into whom God has breathed an intelligent soul, and thereby prepared him, can wisely control Music (this lower realm of stars, as it were) to the honour of his Creator? On this account the ancient musicians say (cf. Macrobius *In somnio Scipionis*, Book 2, ch. 3): "Music possesses all that lives, because it is the soul of Heaven."

Man, Music and the Constellations

Ch. IV   Why Man enjoys music, and whence musical composers and performers arise

Now that we see how God has created and ordered all things harmonically, we may know and discover to a certain extent why Man enjoys music. In the first place, all consonances are nothing but the proportional numbers closest to unity and equality, as is also the motion of rhythm and beasts. Whatever is closest to unity is clearer, more regular, and more pleasant than whatever tends to multiplicity and irrationality and gives rise to confusion. Now since music is an orderly and intelligible matter, such as could only be formed and ordered by the wisdom of God, so man, if he is not like a brute beast, must also be freely moved to joy whenever the order and wisdom of his blessed Creator are borne through such sonorous numbers into his ear and thence into his heart and feelings. Moreover, since Man bears in himself the image of God, he can become all the more aware of God's wisdom through such wondrous union: for like cleaves readily to like. Boethius says this, too, in the preface of his *Musica*: he writes that "Similarity is pleasing, whereas dissimilarity is displeasing and contrary." Thus Man also has the proportions of music in his soul and outward members, as we have heard. When Man perceives this through sounds, his own image is thereby presented to him for his enjoyment. And these musical proportions have the power which St Augustine mentions in his *De Musica*, Book I, Ch. 13: "For even those who would change these numbers experience them in clapping and dancing," etc. That gives rise to the good order of which blessed Herr Luther also speaks: "He who loves music is good-hearted and adept at all things; he who disdains it is an uncouth lout." Such disdain comes from a confused disposition which is not fashioned in harmonious proportions according to the wise Creator's order. Now if a well-disposed man hears some music, his spirit feels the beauty which his Creater has ordained, but he does not know the cause thereof, unless it be that the numbers induced it in him and showed him the harmonic proportions which are ordered by God.

So now we know that God is a harmonious being, and that a living soul after God's image was breathed into Man by the Almighty Creator, who also arranged the stars in a beautiful harmony and thereby ordered their courses, motion, and influences. We may also know how music was discovered and cultivated by man: for there is no doubt that God himself has imparted this power and science to his own image, just as he endowed Bezabeel and Ahaliab[8] with his gifts in Exodus 31, to reveal his marvels that his Name might be honored and glorified. For if Man were not harmoniously made, he could not be endowed with this art and these gifts, nor comprehend them. And regenerated Man has these gifts directly from God. I will not deny, moreover, that Man is also ruled by the order of the proportions of the stars, and their movements which cause manifold figures, conjunctions, and harmonious aspects, and stimulated thereby to the art of music.

So God is the author, both immediately and indirectly, of our music in this temporal state, and Man is not the inventor so much as the tool which God uses for it. But since lower things are ruled by higher ones or by the stars, so is the natural man, as so many philosophers have long maintained and as no one will deny who is endowed by Nature with a good intellect. Now just as the constellations are not the same from one moment to the next, but are always in a state of change, one completing its orbit more slowly, another faster, so I believe that men or artists are impelled and ruled by such constellations, and that this is how new inventions come to light. Consider the inspiration and composition of music as it has been practiced for about 2000 years; how the styles and compositions change markedly from one period to another, even altering considerably from one twenty-year period to the next; how the compositions of about 100 years ago are now unknown to anybody, perhaps having become disagreeable through much use and too artificial for our taste. The cause, one will agree, is that we are ruled by the constellations above, which are now quite different from that time: hence the old style and melodies do not seem so pleasant to us. One could say much about this, but I leave each to his own opinion.

V
ROMANTICISM

38

GIOVANNI MARCAZI

eighteenth century

This poem is, in one respect, a learned classical ode, typical of its century in its use of Greek references for poetic atmosphere. But it is more than that. The author (of whom nothing is known) is not merely exploiting classicism for poetic purposes: he is speaking from his own deeply held convictions. Ficinian Platonism, it seems, was still alive in the Arcadian academies of Italy in the second half of the eighteenth century. If one had to classify Marcazi, it would probably be as a very late Renaissance Platonist, virtually overlapping in time with the very early Romantic Platonists in other countries such as Dalberg and Novalis (see nos 39, 42). There seems, in fact, to have been an unbroken Platonic and Pythagorean tradition in the eighteenth century, preserving such doctrines as metempsychosis and the metaphysical primacy of number, within the esoteric orders of Freemasonry, Rosicrucians, Illuminati, etc.

In this context it is interesting to consider the source of this poem, discovered by John Allitt among the notebooks of Johann Simon Mayr (1763-1845) in Bergamo.[1] Mayr was one of the founders of Romantic opera: the reconciler of German and Italian elements, the teacher of Donizetti, and an originator of the *bel canto* style. In his earlier years he was initiated into the esoteric order of Adam Weishaupt, the "Illuminati of Bavaria," and, although a devoted Catholic, was steeped in the Hermetic world-view. Mayr belonged to the reforming branch of the Illuminati of von Knigge and his patron von Bassus. He adhered to the Pythagorean and Platonic doctrines of the primacy of number and the spiritual power of tone, a knowledge which he passed on, as John Allitt has shown, to his illustrious pupil.

Source   The *Zibaldone* or notebooks of Johann Simon Mayr, preserved in the Bibliotèca Civica, Bergamo, translated by John Allitt in his forthcoming article "Jacob's Ladder, or Music as Knowledge in the Thought of Simon Mayr." Reprinted by kind permission of Mr Allitt.

The Origins and Powers of Music

If beside this verdant spacious bank
you could hear Orpheus' melody divine
which frequently arrests the beat of wings
and liberates the river's rapid flow;
silent you may watch trees loose themselves
from their deep roots, rugged mountains move,
flocks of birds take wing, the wild beasts stir,
the river pause, hearing this joyful note.

O soul[2] who animates these earthly shapes,
bestow their form, rejoice in harmony –
who are indeed yourself, true harmony,
behold your contours, known to you alone
radiant though as yet you dwell in sleep,
oppressed, imprisoned by the miry clay;
if with frail tongue you can utter your first origin,
speak out, that I may declare on paper
the value, order, out of music's modes.

Throughout the work proceeding from God's hand,
formed by his majesty,
nothing created equals you in beauty –
not only since you come forth from his mouth[3]
to vivify this terrain of cold clay, as the undying spirit
to hold dominion over heaven's footstool –
but by the sign which still controls your gestures,
apart from which, you would regret your deeds,
vainly oppose his work, which you cannot disturb.
Therefore live, rejoice in your virtues, containing the harmony from
    which you were formed
by him who wills that you excel all living forms.

Since I compose
reveal your inspiration,
your rich inebriation.
Should my song fail
to free you from your dungeon,
yet shall you still return
to beauty,
your first habitation,

where each true melody is freely born,
compared to which
our earth is but a shadow.

If truth was uttered by Pythagoras
in the sovereign intellect, Number was the prime idea,
when he fused his First idea with ice,
thus tempering his heat,
Number was foremost in his thought.
Desirous to form man content and just,
he grounded him in Number,
from which he had created this great mass,
of stars, moon, sun –
Number was to be his first example
granting the Spirit wings to rise to the divine temple.

Since thus the soul is touched by Number's concord
as a well-tempered harp,
utters divine and ardent ecstasy,
what were the soul to hear
the various sounds concert among themselves,
as spheres, now slow, now fast, which travel the heavens?
Why does not Style, lying sick within,
beg strength from you, O Muses,
who, on the banks of Aganippe,[4] tune
not merely golden harps –
but even the stars in their celestial cycles?

That sonorous shell, echoing the heaven's harmony –
ineffable concert –
what tongue can define?
Since world is Soul,
tunes the heavens, plays now fast now slow
– she alone is leader and inspirer:
this is the eternal arena
through which resounds
glory in lightning flash, in thunder.
No living creature could describe that sound
divine, even if he could hear it.

In part we hear it
on the golden chords of the Pelasgian or Thracian lyre;
people said it was the song of birds
when Orpheus played –
and that melting anger into pity
he restored from Dis his life's beauty.
When Amphion – sometimes called Aerius
danced to the Lydian note,

moved even stones by his lyrical paces,
Thus nature played a superb symphony,
rustled willows, stilled the water's ripples, yet the winds contained.

When the hearts of a primaeval people
were dwelling in cave and forest,
this harmonious, appealing voice
impressed a certain virtue and tradition,
attracted them away from their rough manger.
Thus it is the wise
succeed in taming the Spartans
– desiring that they should be trained by music.
The conqueror of Neptune's gates[5]
was first taught by the Centaur
how another lovely laurel fled through song.

Surely it was this sound that moved
the heavenly messengers to Sacred verse
– which in turn the Hebrew people by the Jordan sung?
Thus, O harmony, by pouring strength and sweetness
you stimulate, attract
to where abides your origin divine.
But here my verse must cease –
too clear to me I speak too wretchedly
concerning vibrant Number's Sound –
that original sublime idea with which the Eternal Craftsman
gave the created world both weight and measure.

Song – you are rough and indistinct –
remain amid the oaks, the beeches in the dark cold wood.
You may travel clothed, but insecure
amongst a crude people who remain in darkness,
who reject and hate, through habit,
what they do not understand.

39

JOHANN FRIEDRICH HUGO FREIHERR VON DALBERG

1760–1812

Friz Dalberg (as he styles himself in the dedication of this essay to Phillip Hacke) was a true dilettante, in the best sense of the term. He was a nobleman and churchman, holding the post of Dom-kapitular at Trier Cathedral; a composer whose works include several piano sonatas, a melodrama with piano, *Jesus auf Golgotha* and settings of Indian songs; a Pythagorean music theorist; a writer of short prose sketches anticipating E.T.A. Hoffmann's style;[1] and a scholar and translator who wrote on the Meteor cult of Antiquity, the Parsees, and Islamic and Indian subjects.

This essay soon turns from a vision of cosmic music and a meeting with the Spirit of Harmony to reflections on the symbolism of the monochord and musical ethics. As an experimenter who had investigated the overtones up to the 64th partial (sounding them on a Stein piano with the help of a glass bar),[2] Dalberg was familiar with the mathematical basis of his symbolism. But he is cautious to keep the creature distinct from the Creator, and has a more optimistic view of the multiplicity of creation, finding the fall from unity a necessary education of the soul. In this, as in other respects, he resembles his contemporary Novalis (no. 42).

Blikke eines Tonkünstlers is written in an informal, spontaneous style with many italics (here omitted). It is a concise summation of almost all the doctrines with which our authors are concerned, but Dalberg presents them not as scholarly facts but as a living revelation, like those of Plato's Er or Cicero's Scipio.

Source *Blikke eines Tonkünstlers in die Musik der Geister*, n.p., n.d. [Mannheim, 1787]. This is the entire work.

A Composer's Glimpses of the Music of Spirits

> And those most eminent in Philosophy, such as Plato,
> say that the wise man is like a musician, having his
> soul well tuned and harmoniously put together.
>
> Sextus Empiricus, *adv. Math.*, ch. 22

Never have I experienced more powerfully the magic of music as yesterday evening, when illness and dark melancholy had taken hold of me; I tried everything to dispel them, but in vain: they returned in myriad forms. I went to the piano and improvised in tones of wild grief. Suddenly Pergolesi's *Salve Regina* lay before me, as if sent by an angel: I sang it, and the heavenly "O dulcis o" pia filled my soul with such a feeling of devotion and tender sadness that I dissolved in tears; I felt lighter, the intensity of my fever eased, and a refreshing calmness enveloped me. Happy I was not – but it was well with me. I left the keyboard, lay down on my couch, and thought of the manifold and rapidly changing states of my soul.

Then the Genius of Harmony hovered around my bed and whispered to me secrets of the higher mysteries of spiritual music (*Tonkunst*).[3]

Never have I felt a more heavenly bliss! He stood there like the glitter when bright silver is melted – and vanished. It was a dream: but the remembrance of it still looms forth as through a mist.

The earthly veil fell from my eyes, I left the Earth behind, and was suddenly floating in the measureless spaces of the universe. Suns, planets and stars innumerable all around me, in indescribable beauty; and what magic filled my ears! The spheres turned with the most magnificent song, often suspected by men but too pure for their hearing: the greatest unity in the richest variety, audible only to spiritual ears. True, the divine Pythagoras calculated the laws of their numbers and developed earthly from heavenly harmony, but his numbers are only the vestures of the spiritual tones: they give no euphony to the ear, and the spirit in its earthly prison cannot hear them.

But it is not only the material world and that contained in space that moves according to the laws of heavenly harmony – so the Genius said – but the realm of spirits also makes a perfect music whose true tone and unison is God himself. All souls are parts of this eternal symphony; all move according to an appropriate melody prescribed for them; each is a whole, yet each also a part of a greater whole, and all the endless parts make up the great chorus of Creation which worships the Godhead in eternal songs of praise.

Could we but view the realm of spirits with our limited senses, we would marvel at how exactly they follow harmonic laws, and would see that our earthly music is only an image, a vesture, an emblem of the eternal and spiritual.

In all man's relationships to the Universe, to God, to Society and to himself or to his inner nature, he acts according to the laws of music.

The relationship and hierarchy of spirits to the being who includes them all, out of which they flow, into whose bosom they return – though without becoming it, since they are never capable of its simplicity and purity – all this is perfectly pictured in the Monochord, out of which all tones are derived.

As the tones are only modifications of a single one, the first fundamental (*Grundton*), yet are not itself but proceed and derive from it, so are the souls in respect to God, the first, eternal and only pure fundamental.

Each single species, each family, each individual of the spiritual world is a tone of this one string, more or less resembling its fundamental.

You know how the variety of tones arises: from the heaviness of a weight hung on a string, and the faster or slower vibrations of the strings; the slighter the oscillation in a given time, the lower and milder (*weicher*) the tone; the greater oscillation, the more piercing (*schärfer*) the tone. So there arise by degrees the second, third, fourth, fifth, etc.

The farther from the fundamental, the more piercing; the nearer it, the milder: that is to say the more restfulness in the string, in the physical vibration of hearing, in the emotion of the soul; true peace is only in the fundamental and its harmonizing triad.

Let the strings be for us a picture of the created spirits, and let us imagine in their vibrations the passions which keep souls in incessant melody. The souls will be purest (or, physically speaking, the least piercing and keen) which, least disturbed by passions, come closest to the original tone, the place of peace and its harmonious triad, i.e. to moral harmony.

Just as the triad is the highest perfection in music, so in man are equanimity and the right relationship to his soul-powers.

As all tones return to their source, the fundamental, so spirits return to the Godhead – yet they only approach it, never become it.

This approach takes place through inner purification, i.e. through lessening the earthly weight which causes excessive vibrations in us (the storm of passions).

The single tone will be an image of the fundamental, the soul an image of its Creator, only when it becomes a pure echo of unity in the triad; when it approaches the heavenly peace of the fundamental.

As the tuning of single tones makes chords pure, and the purity of chords brings about the perfection of the whole tonal family (*Klanggeschlecht*), so purification takes place through gradual individual advancement and through the progress of species, genera, and races of spirits, until they are all sufficiently ripe for that higher purity that they can escape from their earthly vestures, return to the Intellectual World, and there become strings of the heavenly lyre on which God alone plays.

Each being has its own tone assigned to it. But single tones make neither melody nor chords, and without rhythm and harmony there is no real music.

The object of spirits should not be to make single, isolated notes, but to flow into one another as tones related (though independent) and to create a harmonious whole, a society.

Harmony is as old as song; society arose with the Creation.

Harmony consists of consonances and dissonances. The former are pleasant to the ear; from the latter it shrinks, finding satisfaction only when they are resolved into consonances.

No light without shadows; no charm of consonances without discords.

Consonances are love, dissonances hatred. An old poem says that the Creation was made from love and hatred.[4] They struggle still, but hatred will eventually be resolved into love. It is the fable of Isis and Osiris, Typhon and Ahriman.

Thirds and triads are the loveliest to the ear, as the emotion of love is to the spirit; but sixths and fourths, the origin of dissonances or painful emotions, are needful to increase the value of thirds, to bring about excitement, to avoid the disgust of monotony; pain and displeasure are as necessary to creation as joy.

This is so true that too long a sequence of perfect consonances – thirds, fifths, sixths – even offends the ear, and is contrary to harmonic rules; and the harshest dissonances cause the sweetness of their resolution into consonances to be felt most strongly.

In order to bring about perfect harmony and pure music in friendly association, each must sound purely the tone assigned to him, and follow his own melody without dominating, or trying to subdue the other voices; he is assigned the part of sacrificing himself as far as possible to the whole, to overflow into other tones with and through love.

Desires are to the animal condition as the strings are to an instrument: even when they have the correct relations to one another, if the instrument is tuned too high it will break or give forth only noise.

If some tones are in tune and others not, no pure melody can arise.

The various systems and species of being are like instruments: each has its own tuning, each its own strings. The tuning that is appropriate to one would deprive another of many strings – perhaps ruin the whole instrument; the tone which on one is as gentle as a zephyr's breath would be too piercing and screeching on another.

Nothing is more difficult than the tuning of manifold instruments: how deeply must one have delved into their nature! Who possesses the key to every single instrument? Whose ear is pure enough to measure all the necessary temperaments and vibrations? Is there an accurate tonometer for souls?

Many are so out of tune that the most skilled hand cannot help them! Often there is only one wrong note, which puts the whole instrument in discord. If you are fortunate enough to find it and give it another direction, harmony will be restored.

Each should know best his own instrument, but how few trouble themselves about it! Most want to sound in foreign tones, and lose their own in the process.

Do not try to tune other instruments as long as your own is not purely tuned, or else you will share your discord with them.

Do not force your own temperament on anyone else: each has his own. The art is to know them and direct them.

Soft instruments need soft tones; harsh ones produce piercing sounds.

So it is with moral beings; those who are more inclined to love and mild desires need tones or emotions that concord therewith.

Such gentle melodies are not suitable for beings of stronger constitution: they do not feel them.

If we could determine and view the manifold tones and modes of the passions, what a fascinating and instructive knowledge that would be!

We are truly instruments, and the passions are our tones. Only equal temperament (*gleichmässige Stimmung*) is salutary on an instrument.

In madmen the tone is tuned too high, and shrieks; in idiots it is too low, the instrument is dumb, the melody senseless.

Inspired (*genialische*) souls give forth tones which the others cannot find in their tonal systems; hence they fit so little into the common music of life: they have their own gamut, and it is foolish to judge them according to the common measure of tones.

If a well-tuned tone is sounded, it makes the strings of the adjacent instrument vibrate, if they are in tune with it, and these [set in motion] all the others which harmonize with them.

A fair picture, this, of the relationship of moral inclinations and their magical influence on souls, especially of beautiful and tender emotions which communicate themselves far more quickly, and are far more beneficial to the soul than discords; through them it is conceivable how Love works like the electrical spark, how one beautiful action can bring about a complete conversion in so many souls.

The inner state and regulation of the soul is also truly music, and founded on harmonic laws.

The object of music is the tone; its purpose, the pleasure of the ear.

So the object of soul-music, of each being's own tone, is to tune it rightly, to purify it more and more, and to mingle it with the most related keys.

The object of soul-music is the pure pleasure of the spiritual organ of hearing. The highest wisdom can best call to the soul: "Seek happiness," and "in the most perfect agreement of the part with the whole" you will find it.

Socrates, Plato, Epicurus prescribed this ethical rhythm for the soul, while Pythagoras and Aristoxenus found the laws of music in relationship and euphony.

Order, symmetry, agreement is the goal (*Sele*) of the spirit, whereby it feels the greatest happiness. It is the pleasure of music, it is the flower of the beautiful and pleasing, it is the charm of the morally beautiful.

The soul is a tone which must be tuned ever more purely. Each tone has something of the fundamental in it, and the more it approaches the latter, the more pure and spiritual it becomes. The soul must first run its course, as the tone of the monochord the octave, before it achieves completion. For this it has a two-fold duty of activity and rest, of lethargy and movement, both essential to it.

The vibrations of the string (the passions of the soul) are therefore not harmful: it is rather these that lead the spirit ever onwards in the melody of its existence.

Therefore it is given its own counterbalance: will and self-control.

This is the likeness, the true echo of the fundamental tone: that by which it comes to resemble it.

But Creation decreed not melody alone, but harmony, too; it told similar tones to seek out and join with one another!

Thus the soul searches around itself for the most related, homogeneous tones; not to make a unison with them, but to bring forth a sweet concord, to purify itself with and through them. Tender love, sweet friendship, gentle companionship: who does not suspect, recognize, feel here your magical power?

There are some souls, as there are tones, which can mingle with many others; there are some which mix with few. Each should behave here according to the laws of its being, not seeking to join what Nature has put asunder.

Music varies between two modes: the one a child of joy, the other the image of sorrow. So, too, in the eternal concert of life: and this mixture speaks for the wisdom of its inventor, now in major, now in minor keys; now in faster, moderate or slow tempo, the pulse of Nature beats in ever new, ever changing variations.

One person is allotted more of this mode, another more of that.

Fate allots the voices of this concert.

If many notes of sorrow have fallen to your lot, poor mortal, try to accustom your hearing to them: it will depend largely on your pure will whether many minor tones will change into joyful vibrations.

The soul is eager to discover relationships and to order them; the purer and simpler they are, the more they please it. Owing to its nature, which loathes all spatial and temporal limitation, it is also eager to behold many relationships in the shortest possible time.

What delights the soul in music is precisely the contemplation and comparison of relationships. What attracts it to the enrapturing Pergolesi, the seraphic Händel, the noble Gluck, more than to one of the many other composers who luxuriate in harmony, is the simple, grand nobility which inspires the former and transports the soul to a larger sphere.

What makes for the soul's delight in composed pieces is also the wealth of ideas offered in a short space of time.

It is the special gift of so few men, artists and composers, only to point out to the soul the way it should go, and to leave the rest to the free impulse of the imagination. So too in the music of life.

The great and unique delight of the soul is to discover relationships, and to make order.

The simplest relationships are the most lovable, the most beautiful, the most profitable to it; and so it always seeks them.

It strives after a great wealth of ideas in the shortest possible space of time; that is to say, it becomes ever more spiritual, its melody purer, and its harmony more concordant with other tones.

40

FRANÇOIS RENÉ CHATEAUBRIAND
1768–1848

The Vicomte de Chateaubriand was the foremost literary figure of Napoleonic France: a politician, traveler and opportunist to whom fell the role of apologist for Christianity (in *Génie du Christianisme*, 1802), when Napoleon and Talleyrand reinstated it as the national religion. During the turbulent period of his post-Revolutionary exile, Chateaubriand had spent seven months in America, which supplied him with the material and local colour for a novel of Indian life, *Les Natchez*, written in 1794-9 but published entire only in his Complete Works of 1826-31. It has few readers today. The novel vacillates between an earthly adventure-story of crime and passion, and the heavenly episodes which act on the earthly events. In the chapters preceding this extract, Satan has taken up residence in "Nouvelle France" (Canada) and is causing untold misery. The Angel of America has petitioned St Geneviève, patron saint of France, and St Catherine des Bois, patron of Canada, for aid, and they now embark on a journey to ask the Blessed Virgin herself for intercession on behalf of the suffering young nation. Plato and Dante are the main inspiration of the majestic flow of purple prose in which the ascent of the saints through the spheres is described. They hear the Harmony of the Spheres, the song of the three Fates, the ubiquitous music of heaven and the playing and singing of the angels in which the souls of the blessed join. Despite occasional lapses into banality, it is a magniloquent recasting of these themes in Romantic dress.

Source Les Natchez, Book IV, in *Oeuvres Complètes*, vol. 2, Paris, 1834, pp. 491-3.

Two Saints Ascend through the Spheres

Thus the two saints traveled together: the one who saved Paris from Attila, Geneviève who preceded the first of the Most Christian Kings,[1] who for many centuries opposed the obscurity and the virtue

184

of her ashes to all the ceremonial and all the calamities of the monarchy of Clovis; the other who preceded on earth by only a few years the last of the Most Christian Kings,[2] Catherine who knew only the history of a few apostles of New France, similar to those whom the shepherdess of Nanterre saw when the gospel reached ancient Gaul.

The brides of the Lord undertook the message of the Angel of America, who plunged straightway down to earth while they continued on their way towards the firmament.[3]

In a meadow of the Sun, in prairies whose soil seems to be of chalcedony, onyx and sapphire, there stand in rank the subtle chariots of the soul: chariots which move by themselves, made after the same manner as the stars. The two saints took their places one behind the other in one of these chariots. They left the star of light, rising with a movement more rapid than thought, and soon they saw the Sun suspended beneath them in space, like an imperceptible star.

They followed the way traced in a diamond-shape of light by the spirits of the righteous who, released from their bodily chains, wing to the realm of eternal joys. On this route there passed and repassed the souls of the saved, as well as a multitude of angels descending to the worlds to carry out the order of the Most High, or reascending to him bearing the prayers and vows of mortals.

Soon the saints arrived at the world which extends above the region of the stars, from which one can behold the Sun, the Moon and the planets as they are in reality, without the gross medium of air which disguises them from the eyes of men. Twelve bands of different colors[4] compose this pure world of which ours is the material sediment: one of these bands is a glittering purple, another a bright azure, a third snow-white: colours surpassing in brilliance those of our painting, which are but shadows of them.

Catherine and Geneviève passed through this zone without halting, and soon they heard that harmony of the spheres which the ear cannot grasp and which only reaches the interior sense of the soul.[5] They entered into the region of the stars, which they saw as many suns with their systems of dependent planets. O grandeur of God, who can comprehend thee? The saints were already approaching the first of those worlds which are so far apart that a bullet shot by gunpowder would take millions of years to pass from one to another, and yet the two virgins were only at the furthest frontiers of Jehovah's realm. Suns upon suns emerged from the immensity, and unknown creations gave way to still more unknown ones!

A man who attempted to comprehend the infinite by placing himself in imagination in the middle of space might try to imagine expanse upon expanse, regions which neither begin nor end anywhere. Such a man, seized by vertigo, would turn his brain by so futile an enterprise: and such would be my useless efforts if I tried to trace the route along which Geneviève and Catherine passed. Now they cleave a path across stars thick as sand; now they cut across the unknown orbits where comets pursue their wandering steps. The two saints thought they had made progress, yet still they only touched the axis common to all created universes.

This golden axis, living and immortal, beholds all the worlds turning around it in rhythmical rotations.[6] At equal distances along this axis are seated three grave Spirits: the first is the angel of the past, the second the angel of the present, the third the angel of the future. They are the three powers who let time fall upon the earth, for time does not enter into heaven nor descend from thence. Three lower angels, similar to the fabulous Sirens in the beauty of their voices, sit at the feet of these first three angels, and sing with all their strength, while the sound which the golden axis of the world makes by turning about itself accompanies their hymns. This concert forms that triple voice of time which tells of past, present and future, which the wise have sometimes heard on earth by pressing their ear to a tomb in the silence of night.

The subtle chariot of the soul flies on: the brides of Jesus Christ approach the globes where throng the human souls whom the Eternal created by his second idea, after having thought of the angels.[7] God formed all the human souls at once, and distributed them in different dwellings where they await the moment which will unite them with earthly bodies. The creation was once and for all. God allows no succession in his productions.

The chaste pilgrims were stirred by the spectacle of these souls, equal in innocence, who would become unequal through sin, some remaining immaculate, others bearing the marks of the nails by which the passions would one day attach them to flesh and blood.[8]

Beyond these globes where sleep the souls who have not yet undergone mortal life is delved the valley to which they must return to be judged after their passage upon earth.[9] The saints perceive in the terrible Josaphat the pale horse ridden by Death, the locusts with the faces of men, the teeth of lions and wings sounding like a war-chariot. There appear the seven angels having the seven vials filled with the wrath of God; there is the woman seated on the scarlet-colored beast, on whose forehead is the name *Mystery*. The pit of the Abyss smokes at one end of the valley, and the Angel of Judgment, gradually raising the trumpet to his lips, seems ready to fill it with the last which will tell the dead: "*Awake!*"

On coming out of the mystic valley, Geneviève and Catherine finally entered those regions where the joys of Heaven begin. Unlike our joys, these are not such as will tire or satiate the heart: on the contrary, they feed in those who taste of them an insatiable thirst to taste them again.

As the patronesses of France approach the realm of the Divine, the brightness and bliss redouble. As soon as they perceive the walls of the heavenly Jerusalem they descend from the chariot and prostrate themselves, like pilgrims in the fields of Judaea when Sion in southern splendor suddenly appears before their ardent faith. Geneviève and Catherine arise and, gliding in air that is no air at all, but which one must call by this name in order to be understood, enter by the eastern gate. At the same moment the Blessed Las-Casas and the Canadian martyrs Bréboeuf and Jogues hurry on Catherine's footsteps.[10] Ever burning with love for the Indians, they never cease to care for their salvation. It is an effect of God's glory that the more these confessors have suffered from their ungrateful neophytes, the more they cherish them. Las-Casas, addressing the patroness of New France, says:

"Handmaid of the Lord, what peril is threatening our brethren of the Americans lands? The sorrow in your face, and that which shows on the brow of Geneviève, make me fear misfortune. We have been busy singing of the world's creation, and I have not been able to descend to the sublunary regions."

"Protector of the cabins," replied Catherine, "your concern is not aroused for nothing. Satan has unleashed Hell upon America: the French and their native brethren are threatened. The guardian angel of the New World has been forced to go up to Uriel to tell him of the attacks of evil spirits. I have come with the Virgin of the Seine, charged with his message, to implore Mary to intercede before the Redeemer. O Prelate, and you confessors of the faith, join with us and entreat the divine mercy!"

While the daughter of the torrents was speaking thus, the saints, angels, archangels, seraphim and cherubim gathered around them felt a holy sorrow. Las-Casas and the Canadian missionaries, all glorious with their wounds, join with the two illustrious women. And now the royal Saint Louis comes, a palm in his hand, stands at the head of the children of France and leads the suppliants towards the tabernacles of Mary. They proceed amidst the celestial choirs, across fields in which those who have practiced virtue dwell for ever.

The waters, trees and flowers of these unknown fields have nothing resembling our own but their names; it is the charm of verdure, of solitude, of the freshness of our woods, and yet it is not that; it is something whose existence cannot be grasped.

Music never ceases in these places: music which one hears everywhere, but which is nowhere; sometimes it is a murmuring like that of an Aeolian harp which the soft breath of Zephyr strokes on a night in springtime; sometimes the ear of a mortal believes it hears the plaint of a divine harmonica,[11] those vibrations which have nothing terrestrial about them and which swim in the middle region of the air. Voices, brilliant modulations, suddenly break from the depths of the celestial forests, then dispersed by the breath of the Spirits these strains seem to have expired. But soon a confused melody revives afar off, and one distinguishes perhaps the velvet sounds of a horn wound by an angel, or the hymn of a seraph who sings the splendours of God on the banks of the River of Life.

A gross daylight like our own never lights these regions, but a soft brightness falls noiselessly on the mystic lands, almost as it were snow; it enters into everything and makes it lambent with the loveliest light, giving it a perfect beauty to the eye. The ether, so subtle, would still be too material for this place: the air one breathes is divine love itself: air which is like a sort of visible melody which fills all the white plains of souls with splendor and harmony alike.[12]

41

LUDWIG THEOBALD KOSEGARTEN

1758–1818

Gotthard Ludwig Theobald (or Theobul) Kosegarten was an Evangelical pastor in Wolgast, Pomerania and later Rector of Greifswald University. He was a prolific poet who invested his local land- and seascape with mythological associations of a heroic Teutonic past, inspired especially from the example of Ossian and Scottish legend. Among his many writings are a Neoplatonic treatise *Über die wesentliche Schönheit* (On Essential Beauty, 1798), a translation of the mystic Madame Guyon, and a poem (1800) on "Alexander's Feast," inspired by John Dryden's ode of the same name which records a famous legend of the power of music.[1] Kosegarten also has the distinction of having been the friend and mentor of two of Germany's first Romantic painters, Philipp Otto Runge and Caspar David Friedrich, and one of the first collectors of Friedrich's paintings.[2]

For the Romantic writers, the Harmony of the Spheres belonged not so much to the planets as to the stars. Perhaps eighteenth-century astronomy had made the planets too familiar, too small and insignificant, in comparison with the unbounded universe of countless suns, each perhaps with its own planetary system. Kosegarten's poem is written in classicizing couplets (which I have attempted to reproduce) and belongs partly to the unbroken tradition of musical imagery that had kept *musica mundana* and *musica coelestis* alive since the Renaissance as convenient poetic fictions, partly also to the new, Romantic acceptance of them as witnesses to a real feeling of cosmic and transcendent harmony. Here are also references to *musica humana*, to the music of Nature, the Divine Musician, and the dissolution of self in harmony with the universe.

Die Harmonie der Sphaeren (1797) was set to music for soloists, chorus and orchestra by Andreas Romberg (1767-1821) and enjoyed several reprints in an English version, made in 1839 by Lowell Mason and John L. Dwight.

Source *Die Harmonie der Sphaeren*, in score of setting by A.J. Romberg, Bonn, n.d.

The Harmony of the Spheres

O holy night, you banish the daytime's irreverent tumult.
  Stillness reigns, from which a nobler song may arise.
Round me I hear many voices intoning the hymn of the cosmos.
  Softly at first, then louder swells the resounding sea.
Sacred LYRA, your air lends wings to the festival dances.
  Singing she mounts, and again singing CYGNUS descends.
Melodies render benign the beating wings of AQUILA.
  Along the Olympian road the CHARIOTS noisily roll.
Sounds like harmonious bells ring forth from the scales of the
      BALANCE.
  Out of AQUARIUS' urn starry cataracts pour.
Heaven's ORELLANA flies in a vortex of lightning and thunder.
  Angrily rising, ORION grimly seizes his shield,
Rattles the crystalline vault, all studded with myriad lanterns,
  Sending melodious storms through the ambrosial night.

O familiar Earth, you too move in the round-dance of planets,
  Softly and smoothly you go, yet neither silent nor dead.
Trees have voices, and breath is in every leaf of the forest,
  Chattering springs give tongue, rippling brooks have their speech.
Crazed with love, Bardale[3] greets every reddening morning;
  To the ambrosial night Aödi[4] sings her lament.
Stirred by the chords which engulf it, also the human heart
  Gently attunes its strings under the vault of the breast.
See! its motions become a sound, and the sound has a meaning!
  Hear how its discourse turns into the sweetness of song.

Whose is the finger that plays on creation's musical glasses?[5]
  Whose is the soul that breathes over the strings of the world?[6]
To this harper sublime the hymn of the cosmos is singing;
  Life-giving breath, to thee rises and kindles the heart.
Let my life be a song that joins in the heavenly paean;
  Let it dissolve therein, a pure and melodious chord.

42

NOVALIS
(FRIEDRICH VON
HARDENBERG)
1772–1801

In his short life, Novalis mastered literature and mythology, philosophy and natural science, and wrote some of the very greatest German poetry. By religious upbringing he was a Moravian Brother, by profession a competent geologist; but his soul was free. He lived in the world of the Creative Imagination, and his stories relate events whose location is not the earth but the Imaginal World that intervenes between sensible reality and the radiant Darkness to which he dedicated his *Hymns to the Night*.

The novel *Heinrich von Ofterdingen* (1801), his longest work, was left unfinished at Novalis's death. It has no plot in the usual sense, but describes the initiations of its hero (exemplifying mankind) through dreams, poems and stories. The first two stories, told by merchants, depict the power of music, which for Novalis also meant poetry. The first (not given here[1]) is the legend of Arion, already accepted in Antiquity as an allegory of the well-tuned soul's passage across the hazards of death to immortal life. The second tale, in Chapter 3, is a longer one, from which we give only the setting for the song of the hero, a wise man's son who is the lover of the king's lost daughter. With his songs he will reconcile the king to their union. Our second extract comes from the earlier part of a still longer tale in Chapter 9, told by Klingsohr, Ofterdingen's teacher and father of his lover Mathilde. The scene is set in the northern, astral realm of King Arktur, deserted by his Queen Sophie who has descended to earth. Although Arktur's kingdom is bereft of Wisdom and is sterile and cold, the description of the Star Game is of extraordinary beauty.

Novalis shows how the old ideas of the power of music over the soul and the music of the spheres could take on new life, when emancipated from mathematical, psychological, or astronomical theory and approached purely through the poetic imagination. And although for some Romantic writers these ideas may have been served as picturesque fictions, for Novalis they were absolutely real.

Source Heinrich von Ofterdingen, Stuttgart, Reclam, 1976, pp. 45-6, 124-7.

The Song of the Wise Man's Son

Suddenly the stillness was broken by the soft tones of an unbelievably beautiful voice which seemed to come from an ancient oak tree. All eyes turned to it, and saw there a young man, clad in simple but foreign clothes, holding a lute in his hands and quietly going on with his song. Only when the king turned his glance on him did he respond with a low bow. His voice was extraordinarily beautiful, and the song had a strange, fabulous quality. It told of the world's beginnings; of the birth of stars, plants, beasts and men; of the all-powerful sympathy of Nature; of the archaic Golden Age and its ruling queens; of love and poetry; of the appearance of hatred and barbarism and their strife with those benign goddesses; and lastly of the eventual triumph of the latter, the end of suffering, the rejuvenation of Nature and the return of a Golden Age without end.[2] The old poets themselves, overcome with fascination, moved during the song closer to the uncanny stranger. A delight never felt before gripped the onlookers, and the king himself felt as if he were being borne away on a current from heaven. Such a song had never before been heard, and everyone thought that a heavenly being must have appeared among them, especially as the youth seemed in the course of his song to grow ever more handsome and noble, and to sing with a voice of increasing power. The breeze played with his golden locks. Beneath his hands the lute seemed a thing ensouled, and his gaze seemed intoxicated by the sight of an invisible world. Even the childlike innocence and simplicity of his face seemed supernatural.

Now the beauteous song was over. The hoary bards pressed towards the youth with tears of joy on their breasts. A silent, inward sigh went through the company. The king, deeply moved, approached him, and the youth threw himself modestly at the monarch's feet. The king raised him up, embraced him warmly, and bade him name a gift. But with blushing cheeks he asked the king to hear one more song, and then to judge his request. The king stepped back a few paces, and the youth began again: [a song follows].

The Star-Game[3]

In the great square before the palace there was a garden of metal trees and crystal plants, heavy with fruits and bright flowers of precious stones. The variety and elegance of the figures and the lively lights and colors made for the most delightful entertainment, and the crowning splendour was a tall fountain in the midst of the garden which was turned entirely to ice. The aged hero went slowly past the palace gates. A voice within called his name. He leaned on the door, which opened with a gentle sound, and stepped into the hall. He held his shield before his eyes. "Have you still found nothing?" plaintively asked the fair daughter of Arktur. She lay on a silken cushion on a throne cunningly fashioned from a great sulphur crystal, and a few maidens busily rubbed her soft limbs which seemed mingled of milk and crimson. Beneath the hands of the maids there streamed from her in all directions the alluring light by which the palace was so wonderfully illuminated. A fragrant breeze wafted in the hall. The hero was silent. "Let me touch your shield," she said softly. He walked up to the throne and trod its rare carpeting. She grasped his hand, pressed it tenderly to her heavenly bosom, and touched his shield. His armour clanged, and a penetrating force enlivened his body. His eyes blazed, and his heart beat audibly against his breastplate. The beautiful Freya seemed more glad, and the light that streamed out from her became more fiery. "The King is coming," cried a splendid bird which was seated behind the throne. The servants spread a sky-blue coverlet over the Princess, covering her up to the breasts. The hero let sink his shield and looked up to the dome, to which two broad staircases led from either side of the hall. A soft music preceded the king, who shortly appeared in the dome with a large entourage and came down.

The beautiful bird unfolded its bright wings, moved gently and sang to the king as with a myriad voices:

> The beauteous stranger will not tarry long.
> The warmth is near, eternity begins.
> The Queen awakens out of her long dreams,
> When sea and land are both dissolved in love.
> The frozen night will empty out this town,
> When fairytales shall win their ancient right.
> In Freya's breast the world will catch on fire
> And each desire will find its own desire.

The king embraced his daughter with tenderness. The spirits of the stars arranged themselves around the throne, and the hero took his place in the row. Innumerable stars, ornately grouped, filled the hall. The serving maids brought a table and a small chest in which were a mass of cards bearing sacred signs, deep in meaning, composed of the pure figures of the constellations. The king placed a reverent kiss on these cards, mixed them carefully and passed some to his daughter. The others he himself retained. The princess drew out a number of her cards from her hand and laid them on the table, then the king examined his own hand and pondered long before he laid down a single card. At times he seemed compelled to play this card or that: but often one would see that he was pleased when he was able with a well-chosen card to create a beautiful harmony of

193

signs and figures. As the game began, one was aware of signs of the liveliest participation and the strangest expressions and gestures on the part of all the onlookers, just as if they were each working busily with an invisible instrument in their hands. Simultaneously there was heard in the air a soft but deeply moving music that seemed to stem from the stars in the hall which wove in and out so marvelously, and from the other strange motions. The stars moved around now slowly, now faster, in ever varied lines, and as the music proceeded they copied most exactly the figures on the cards. The music changed continuously with the configurations on the table, and although often the transitions were quite surprising and abrupt, still it seemed that one simple theme bound the whole together.[4] With incredible agility the stars flew as the cards dictated. Now they were all in one great labyrinth, now neatly separated into distinct groups; sometimes the whole company dispersed like a beam in countless sparks, then it would form little circles and patterns which would gradually enlarge until, to one's astonishment, a single design would emerge. The colored figures in the windows meanwhile remained stationary. The bird ceaselessly moved its vesture of magnificent feathers in the most varied ways.

Up till now the aged hero had also dutifully pursued his invisible business, when suddenly the king cried out joyously: "All shall be well! Iron, cast thy sword into the world, that they may know where peace dwells." The hero drew his sword from its sheath, held it with its point to the sky, then seized it and hurled it out of the open window, over the town and the frozen sea. Like a comet it flew through the air until at the encircling mountains it seemed to explode with a loud noise, and fall to earth in a mass of sparks.

43

ERNST THEODOR
AMADEUS HOFFMANN
1776–1822

This strange, mercurial figure – dissolute Bohemian, conscientious lawyer, caricaturist, composer and novelist – embodied the Romantic ideal in his life as well as his stories. The fantastic, the gruesome, the humorous and above all the supernatural which fill Hoffmann's world had never before been described with such realism, albeit at times the realism of the victim of hallucination or *delirium tremens*. In this short story of 1809 the narrator is visited by the ghost of the composer Christoph Willibald von Gluck, who becomes Hoffmann's device for recounting a synaesthetic, perhaps even a psychedelic experience. As so often in Romantic fiction, the visionary account is full of symbols which root it firmly in the collective experience of mankind: symbols of the soul's journey, in particular, through both the hellish and heavenly regions of the Imaginal World, where everything, including musical tones, takes on a living personality. Thus the third, that harmonic interval which above all others carries emotion in Western music, is described as a "tender youth" between two giants, Tonic and Dominant. In the enigmatic last paragraph, Gluck relates, in the spirit of Goethe's botanizing, how a long contemplation of the hidden harmonies of nature – the music of flowers – culminates in a dissolution of subject and object as he himself becomes both flower and sun, the source alike of light and tone.

Source   *Ritter Gluck*, translated by R. Murray Schafer in *E.T.A. Hoffmann and Music*, Toronto University Press, 1975, pp. 34-5. Reprinted by kind permission of University of Toronto Press. © University of Toronto Press 1975.

The Ghost of Gluck

He stood up and strode about boldly, then he went to the window where he began to sing the chorus of the priestesses from *Iphigenia in Tauris* in scarcely audible tones, striking the windowpane now and then with the entrances of the tuttis. I noticed with amazement that he took certain original turns of melody which were strikingly unique and powerful. I let him be. He concluded and returned to his seat. Quite shaken by the man's peculiar behaviour and the fantastic expression of his odd musical talent, I was silent. After a while he began:

"Have you ever composed?"

"I've given it a try, but I found that everything I wrote down in what I thought were moments of inspiration later proved to be feeble and insipid, so I let it go."

"You made a mistake. Just because a few attempts should not win your favour is no bad sign for your talent. One learns music as a boy because Mama and Papa wish it, and one hacks and strums away; but the mind is imperceptibly being initiated to melody. Perhaps that half-forgotten theme of a song which affected one so indifferently then was the first true thought, and this embryo was slowly nourished by strange powers until it grew to gigantic proportions and consumed everything about it, transforming it completely. Ah! how is it possible to indicate the thousand ways in which one can be led to composition? It is like a broad highway full of people bustling about rejoicing and crying 'We are the chosen; we have reached the goal!' Through the Ivory Gate one enters the land of dreams.[1] Few even notice the Gate; fewer still pass through! What an adventure! Behind the Gate intoxicating shapes sway back and forth. Some more rapidly, others slowly; all are oblivious of the highway. They exist only behind the Ivory Gate. Once entered it is difficult to leave this realm, for just as monsters blocked the way to Alzinen's castle, the shapes whirl about threatingly. Many are those who dream away the dream of this dream-world – dissolving into dreams. No longer do they cast a shadow, or they would be aware of it by the ray that passes through this realm. Only a few awake from this dream to pass through the dream-world and advance on high to the moment of truth, the highest moment there is, contact with the eternal, the inexpressible! Look at the sun![2] It is the triad from which the chords of the stars shower down at our feet to wrap us in their threads of crystallized fire! A chrysalis in flames, we await Psyche to carry us on high to the sun!"

With the last words he sprang up and threw his arms and his eyes heavenwards. Then he sat down again and quickly emptied his glass. A stillness arose that I did not dare break in order not to throw this unique man off the track. At length he began again more calmly:

"As I was in the realm of dreams a thousand fears and pains tormented me. It was night and I was terrified of the leering masks of the monsters who dragged me one moment into the abyss of the sea and the next raised me on high. Rays of light came through the night, and the rays of light were tones which surrounded me with their serene purity. I awoke from my pains and saw a great, clear eye which stared into an organ; and as it stared, tones arose and wound themselves into more shimmering and majestical chords than I had ever thought possible. Melodies poured up and down and I swam in their current and wanted to drown. Then the eye looked at me and raised me up over the raging waves. It was night again. At length two giants stepped up to me in shining armour; the Tonic and the Dominant. They bore me on high with them and the giant eye smiled. 'I know the reason for the longing which fills thy breast. It is the longing for the Third, that tender youth, who now steps up between the two giants. May you hear his sweet voice and until we meet again, may all my melodies be thine.' "

He paused.

"And you saw the eye again?"

"Yes, I saw it again! For years I lingered on in the world of dreams. Yes, I lingered – lingered! I sat in a magnificent valley and listened to the flowers singing to one another. But one sunflower was silent and bent its unopened petals sadly to the earth. An invisible force drew me to it. It raised its head, its bloom opened, and from it the eye beamed towards me. Now tones, like beams of light, flowed from my head to the flowers which eagerly absorbed them. The sunflower's leaves grew larger and larger, liquid fire poured from them, they flooded me; the eye had disappeared and I was the bloom!"

With the last words he sprang up and rushed out of the room.

44

BETTINA BRENTANO VON ARNIM

1785–1859

The letters published anonymously as *Goethes Briefwechsel mit einem Kind* (Goethe's Correspondence with a Child) are a remarkable document of Romantic feminine sensibility. The Brentano family was friendly with Goethe's mother, but the goal of the young woman (not exactly a "child," for she was in her twenties) was Goethe himself, for whom she conceived a chaste passion of astonishing power. In numerous letters she poured out to him her thoughts, feelings, observations and protestations of devotion; he replied more laconically. But the delight was not altogether one-sided. Bettina was later to write (in her Preamble to the English edition) of "that paternal relation of Goethe's delicious hearty affection to the child, from whose ecstasy he explored a sweet nurture for his immortality."

One sometimes has the impression that romantic women like Bettina and Rahel Varnhagen (see no. 46) worshipped two gods: one was Goethe, the other Music. In other letters Bettina describes her ecstasies as a young girl, lying on the grass and listening to her uncle's orchestra. There music is the vehicle for an ascent which, while one hesitates to call it altogether mystical, leads her into the realms of the Imaginal World, the *Paradies der Phantasie* as she calls it, peopled by nature-spirits and adorned with fantastic architecture: the world to which inspired artists have ever penetrated. And she would go further than this. She was only joking in manner, not in substance, when she told Goethe's mother: "Be careful that the Angels don't hit you over the head with their fiddlesticks until you realize that Heaven *is* music!"[1]

Bettina's book reveals little of Goethe himself, but it is precious for its account, in a letter of May 28, 1810, of her friendship with Beethoven, in which the composer speaks more freely than at any other recorded time about the spiritual nature of his creative genius. Even if the elegant mode of expression of this reported statement is Bettina's own,[2] it reveals Beethoven unambiguously as one of those elect, like Pythagoras, for whom music was the gateway to higher knowledge. Read in isolation or in the context of Beethoven's biography, it may seem like a typically extravagant Romantic effusion, perhaps of no more moment than Bettina's own fantasies. But in the present context it can be recognized as a precise definition of the musical experience as the veritable nourishment of the soul through vibrations akin to its own organism, affording a gnosis of orders of being which cannot be grasped through word or logic. There is nothing metaphorical about it: it is a statement of fact, and belongs (as Beethoven well knew) within an ancient and unbroken tradition.

Source *Goethe's Correspondence with a Child*, London, 1839, vol. II, pp. 206-16.

Beethoven speaks of his Genius

It is Beethoven of whom I will now speak to you, and with whom I have forgotten the world and you: true, I am not ripe for speaking, but I am nevertheless not mistaken when I say (what no one now perhaps understands and believes) that he far surpasses all in mind, and whether we shall ever overtake him? – I doubt it! may he only live till that mighty and sublime enigma, which lies within his spirit, be matured to its highest perfection! yes, may he reach his highest aim, then will he surely leave a key to heavenly knowledge in our hands, which will bring us one step nearer to true happiness.

To you I may confess, that I believe in a divine magic, which is the element of mental nature; this magic does Beethoven exercise in his art; all relating to it which he can teach you, is pure magic; each combination is the organisation of a higher existence, and thus too does Beethoven feel himself to be the founder of a new sensual basis in spiritual life. You will understand what I mean to say by this, and what is true. Who could replace this spirit? from whom could we expect an equivalent? The whole business of mankind passes to and fro before him like clock-work: he alone produces freely from out himself the unforeseen, the uncreated: what is intercourse with the world to him, who, ere the sun rise is already at his sacred work, and who after sun-set, scarcely looks around him, who forgets to nourish his body, and is borne in his flight on the stream of inspiration, far beyond the shores of flat every-day life? He says himself, "When I open my eyes, I cannot but sigh, for what I see is against my religion, and I am compelled to despise the world, which has no presentiment, that music is a higher Revelation than all their wisdom and philosophy: – music is the wine, which inspires new creations, and I am the Bacchus, who presses out this noble wine for mankind and makes them spirit-drunk; and then when they are sober again – what have they not fished up to bring with them to dry land. – I have no friend: I must live with myself alone, but I well know that God is nearer to me in my art than to others; I commune with Him without dread, I have ever acknowledged and understood him; neither have I any fear for my music, it can meet no evil fate; he to whom it makes itself intelligible, must become freed from all the wretchedness which others drag about with them." – All this did Beethoven say to me the·first time I saw him: a feeling of reverence penetrated me, as, with such friendly openness he uttered his mind to me, who could have been only very unimportant to him. I was surprized too, because I had been told, he was very shy and conversed with no one. They were afraid to introduce me to him, and I was forced to find him out alone; he has three dwellings, in which he alternately secretes himself, one in the country, one in the town, and the third upon the bulwarks; here I found him upon the third floor; unannounced I entered – he was seated at the piano: I mentioned my name; he was very friendly and asked, if I would hear a song that he had just composed? – then he sung shrill and piercing, so that the plaintiveness reacted upon the hearer, "Know'st thou the land," – "It's beautiful, is it not," said he inspired, "most beautiful! I will sing it again"; he was delighted at my cheerful praise. "Most men," said he, "are touched by something good, but they are no *artist-natures*; artists are ardent, they do not weep." Then he sung another of your songs, to which he had a few days ago composed music, "Dry not the tears of eternal love." He accompanied me home and it was upon the way that he said so many beautiful things upon Art; withal he spoke so loud, stood still so often upon the street, that some courage was necessary to listen: he spoke passionately and much too startlingly, for me not also to forget that we were in the street: – they were much surprised to see me enter with him in a large company assembled to dine with us. After dinner he placed himself, unasked at the instrument and played long and wonderfully: his pride and genius were both in ferment; under such excitement his spirit creates the inconceivable, and his fingers perform the impossible. – Since this he comes every day or I go to him. For this, I neglect parties, picture-galleries, theatres and even St Stephen's tower itself. Beethoven says, "Ah! what should you see there? I will fetch you, and towards evening we will go through the Schönbrunn alley." Yesterday, I walked with him in a splendid garden, in full blossom, all the hot-houses open, the scent was overpowering; Beethoven stood still in the burning sun, and said, "Goethe's poems maintain a powerful sway over me, not only by their matter but also their rhythm; I am disposed and excited to compose by this language, which ever forms itself as through Spirits to more exalted order, already carrying within itself the mystery of harmonies. Then, from the focus of inspiration I feel myself compelled to let the melody stream forth on all sides – I follow it – passionately overtake it again – I see it escape me, vanish amidst the crowd of varied excitements – soon I seize upon it again with renewed passion; I cannot part from it, – with quick rapture I multiply it in every form of modulation – and at the last moment I triumph over the first musical thought, – see now – that's a Symphony; – yes, Music is indeed the mediator between the spiritual and sensual life. I should like to speak with Goethe upon this: if he would understand me? – Melody is the sensual life of poetry. Do not the spiritual contents of a poem become sensual feeling through melody? – do we not in Mignon's song perceive its entire sensual frame of mind through melody? and does not this perception excite again to new productions? – There, the spirit extends itself to unbounded universality, where, all in all forms itself into a bed for the stream of feelings, which take their rise in the simple musical thought, and which else would die unperceived away: *this* is harmony, this is expressed in my symphonies, the blending of various forms rolls on as in a bed to its goal. Then one feels, that an Eternal, an Infinite, never quite to be embraced, lies in all that is spiritual; and although in my works I have always a feeling of success, yet I have an eternal hunger, – that what seemed exhausted with the last stroke of the drum with which I drive my enjoyment, my musical convictions into the hearers – to begin again like a child. Speak to Goethe of me, tell him, he should hear my symphonies; he would then allow me to be right in saying that Music is the only unembodied entrance into a higher sphere of knowledge, which possesses man, but he will never be able to possess it. – One must have rhythm in the mind, to comprehend music in its essential being; music gives presentiment, inspiration of heavenly knowledge, and that which the spirit feels sensual in it, is the embodying of spiritual knowledge. – Although the Spirits live upon music, as one lives upon air, yet it is something else spiritually to understand it – but the more the soul draws out of it its sensual nourishment, the more ripe, does the spirit become for a happy intelligence with it. – But few attain to this, for as thousands engage themselves for love's sake, and among these thousands, love does not once reveal itself, although they all occupy themselves of love, in like manner do thousands hold communion with music, and do not possess its revelation: signs of an elevated moral sense form too the groundwork of music as of every art. All genuine invention is a moral progress. – To subject oneself to music's unsearchable laws; by virtue of these laws to curb and guide the spirit, so that it pours forth these revelations, this is the isolating principle of Art; to be dissolved in its revelations, this is abandonment to Genius, which tranquilly exercises its authority over the delirium of unbridled powers; and thus grants to fancy the highest efficacy. Thus does art ever represent Divinity, and that which stands in human relation to it is Religion; what we acquire through art is from God, a divine suggestion which sets up a goal for human capacities which the spirit attains.

"We do not know what grants us Knowledge; the firmly enclosed seed needs the moist, warm, electric[3] soil to grow, think, express itself. Music is the electric soil, in which the spirit lives, thinks, invents. Philosophy is the precipitation of its electric spirit, and its necessity, which will ground every thing upon a first principle, is supplied by music; and although the spirit be not master of that which it creates through music, yet is it blessed in this creation; in this manner too is every creation of art, independent, mightier than the artist himself, and returns by its appearance, back to the divine, and is only connected with men, in so much as it bears witness to the divine mediation in him.

"Music gives to the spirit relation to harmony. A thought abstracted, has still the feeling of communion, of affinity in the Spirit: thus each thought in Music is in the most intimate, inseparable affinity with the communion of Harmony, which is Unity.

"The electric excites the spirit to musical, fluent, streaming production.

"I am of electric nature. – I must break off with my unwitnessed wisdom, else I shall miss the rehearsal; write to Goethe about me, if you understand me; but I can answer nothing, and I will willingly let myself be instructed by him." – I promised him, to write to you all, as well as I could understand it. – He took me to a grand rehearsal, with full orchestra – there I sat in the wide, unlighted space, in a box quite alone; single gleams stole through the crevices and knot-holes, in which a stream of bright-sparks were dancing, like so many streets of light, peopled by happy spirits.

There then I saw this mighty spirit exercise his rule. O Goethe! no Emperor and no King feels such entire consciousness of his power, and that all power proceeds from him, as this Beethoven, who just now in the garden, in vain sought out the source, from which he receives it all: did I understand him as I feel him, then I should know everything. There he stood so firmly resolved – his gestures, his countenance, expressed the completion of his creation; he prevented each error, each misconception; not a breath was voluntary, all, by the genial presence of his Spirit set in the most regulated activity.– One could prophesy that such a spirit, in its later perfection, would step forth again as ruler of the earth.

Yesterday evening I wrote every thing down, this morning I read it to him: he asked, "*Did I say that?* – well then I have had a rapture";[4] he read it once more attentively, and made the erasures, writing between the lines, for he is interested that you should understand him.

202

45

HEINRICH VON KLEIST
1777–1811

Alas, Kleist was to take his own life[1] before he had the opportunity to put into practice the intentions which he describes here. His whole life was a tragedy of psychological disharmony: the price which he, not alone among artists, was to pay for his creative genius as manifested in the comedy *Der zerbrochene Krug*, the tragedy *Penthesilea*, and short stories such as *Michel Kohlhaas* and *Die Marquise von O*. What he meant by the last sentence of this extract, he never seems to have explained. It probably had to do with an analysis of number and rhythm in poetry, associated with the numerical foundations of the most basic chords and progressions.

Kleist had already incorporated into his story *Die heilige Cäcilie, oder die Gewalt der Musik* (St Cecilia, or the Power of Music) the idea of music's transforming effects on the psyche. In that tragi-comic story four Calvinist brothers, fanatic iconoclasts, set out to violate a convent church, but are bewitched by the performance of an ancient Italian Mass, apparently under the direction of St Cecilia herself, and spend the rest of their days in a state of psychopathic devotion, daily howling the Gloria Patri.

Source Letter to Marie von Kleist, summer 1811, in Kleist's *Sämtliche Werke und Briefe*, vol. 2, Munich, Hanser, 1965, pp. 874-5.

Dissonances in the Psyche

I feel that there may be many dissonances in my psyche which are becoming more and more out of tune under the pressure of the hateful circumstances in which I live, and which a properly cheerful enjoyment of life, if I could only achieve it, might quite easily resolve into harmony. In this situation I may let my creative work rest altogether for a year or more, and, apart from a few studies which I still have to finish up, devote myself to nothing but music. For I regard this art as the root, or – to express myself pedantically – as the algebraic formula of all the others; and just as we already have a poet[2] (with whom I wouldn't care to compare myself in any other way) who has related all his thoughts on his own art to color, so I, from my earlier youth, have related everything I've thought about poetry to music. I believe that the most important elucidations of the poetic art are contained in the figured bass (*Generalbass*).

46

RAHEL VARNHAGEN
1771–1833

Like a sensitive nerve-ending, Rahel Varnhagen was exposed to all the spiritual currents of her time. She was not a creative woman, but a recorder and commentator on a life which she invited to pour down on her "like a storm without an umbrella"; most of all, she was gifted with the ability to draw forth the best from all whom she met, and exercised this talent for ten years in her garret flat in Berlin, which by all accounts was one of the most brilliant salons, and certainly the most *gemütlich*, of its time. As a Jewess she felt the finest nuances of social acceptance and rejection in a period of changing fortunes for the Jews of Prussia. She knew the fall from inherited wealth into comparative penury and the slow climb up again in the company of a husband fourteen years her junior. She knew the artistic elite who transcended all these distinctions. And she was a reader not only of literature but also of theosophy and mysticism, familiar with Louis-Claude de Saint-Martin's works and an admirer of the seventeenth-century mystical poet Angelus Silesius, whom she loved second only to her idol Goethe.

Rahel recorded her dreams, some of them of great psychological interest. (There is a remarkable one in which she was accompanied by her friend Bettina von Arnim and the Mother of God.)[1] Although her outward associations were largely with people in the literary and visual arts, this brief but intense account shows her unconsciously assenting, like so many Romantics, to the special nature of music as the royal road to a world beyond form and image.

Source Diary entry for December 25, 1815, in *Lebensläüfe*, vol. 14: *Rahel Varnhagen und ihre Zeit (Briefe 1800-1833)*, Munich, Kösel, 1968, pp. 91-2.

A Musical Dream

Last night I dreamed I heard such a beautiful prelude, coming from on high – or wherever it came from, for I saw nothing – which developed into so grand a harmony that I had to sink to my knees. I wept, prayed, and cried out again and again: "Have I not said that Music is God; that the *true* Music" (by which I meant harmonies, not melodies) "is God?" The music became ever more beautiful; I prayed, wept, and cried out more and more. As if in a radiance, and without thought-forms, everything – the whole being in my breast – became lambent and clear. My heart broke in two from my ecstatic weeping: and I awoke.

47

ANTOINE FABRE D'OLIVET
1767–1825

Fabre d'Olivet was born into a comfortable Protestant family, and worked until 1805 as a poet and prose writer, composer and civil servant. In this year he married and underwent a conversion to theosophy, thereafter writing a series of unparalleled works on universal history (*Histoire philosophique du genre humain*), philology (*La Langue hébraïque restituée*) and Pythagoreanism (*Les Vers dorés de Pythagore expliqués*). In later life he founded an esoteric sect, while outwardly advocating a universal theocracy as the most favorable climate for the control and nurture of the masses of mankind who could not, like Fabre, comprehend the transcendent unity of all faiths and the reconciliation of polytheism with the One God.

Music for Fabre was not just another mode of expression but a pillar of his whole system. Musical and acoustical questions occupied him throughout his life. In 1804 he composed a cantata for the Protestant church's celebration of Napoleon's coronation. In 1811 he cured a young deaf-mute by applying mysterious acoustical principles he had learnt in his arcane studies, proving thereby that he had rediscovered the lost secrets of Moses. His magnum opus on music was written in 1813-15 but was never published and only partially survives in the form of posthumously published articles collected as *La Musique expliquée comme science et comme art* (Music, explained as science and art). Fabre is, in short, the truest Pythagorean of his epoch. He sees music as a primary and formative force in the world, playing its part in the grand cosmic drama of fall and redemption to which Man is summoned both as spectator and as chief protagonist.

Source *La Musique expliquée comme science et comme art*, new ed. by Jean Pinasseau, Paris, Dorbon Aîné, 1928, pp. 17-22. This essay first published in *France Musicale*, October 23, 1842.

Music's Powers, Ancient and Modern

The true cause of the moral effects of music

Without attempting to deny something as firmly proven as the moral power of music among the Ancients, let us rather try to discover the causes of this power, and lose, if we can, the bad habit that through ignorance and laziness tends to make us flatly deny whatever is outside the sphere of our knowledge, and treat as visionaries or impostors those who have seen in the nature of things that which we do not see. Let us try to persuade ourselves that the intellectual vision of man can extend or contract itself just like his physical vision; it can penetrate with more or less accuracy and force into the essence of things just as into space, and embrace in either sphere a considerable number of relationships according to whether the circumstances are favorable or whether one strives to grasp them. Let us recognize that there are considerable differences from person to person and from one race to another; let us take note of times and places, political revolutions and the vicissitudes of nature, and remember that in a thick fog for example, a man distinguishes objects less well, however acute his vision, than someone endowed with inferior vision who observes in the calmness of pure air. Thus Europe, long enveloped in a spiritual fog, has lost the foreign illumination that she received from Africa and Asia; the invasion of the northern hordes brought upon her a dense and cimmerian shadow. Although her inhabitants are generally blessed with a firm enough moral outlook, and are even better endowed than the Asiatic nations with a penetrating and lively spirit of investigation, they have none the less been unable to acquire the same intellectual knowledge on account of the profound darkness which surrounds them.

The physical sciences, whose torches the Europeans kindled, have served them well, it is true, to guide them in this long night; but however brilliant their light has been, it has only been able to show them the exterior form of things. It is true that they have known this exterior form far better than the ancient peoples, owing to these same physical sciences with which need has forced them to enlighten themselves, and which they have brought to a pitch of perfection never attained in any previous era. One can also be certain that at the moment when the intellectual light, shining on them in all its force, has dissipated the remainder of the darkness which prejudice, ignorance and systematic pride still retains, the peoples of modern

Europe will see things that could never have been seen by those of ancient Europe, nor by their instructors, the Asiatics or Africans.

While waiting for the irresistible course of the universe[1] to bring about that happy moment and carry modern man to the pinnacle of science, let us examine impartially the roads which the Ancients trod, and learn by the waxing rays of intelligence to follow them at first, that we may eventually surpass them.

Music, whose principles I have undertaken to explain, does not – I reiterate – consist in external forms. If the forms were all there were in this science, I would certainly not write on this subject, for what are my qualifications? Regarded as dependent on composition, they would be best expounded by the great masters[2] – Pergolesi, Gluck, Durante, Léo, Sacchini, Cimarosa, Handel, Haydn, Boccherini; considered as things intimately connected with performance, the proper people to discuss them would be the celebrated virtuosi: singers such as Balthazar Ferri, Posi, Faustina Bordoni, or instrumentalists such as Zarnovich, Balbastre, Gavinies, Viotti, Duport. But the forms are transitory things, and less able than in any other art to resist the passage of time: scarcely a century passes without three or four compositions which music-lovers judge to be immortal being usurped, destroyed, and buried in their turn. An intelligent composer or an able symphonist, without knowing in any way the intimate principles of these elements – without even investigating them in themselves, but inspired by genius or guided by his talent – can fashion them according to the rules or the taste of his century, and produce or make heard a music which appeals to the senses; his success, however brilliant at first, will be brief. Because such composers only considered the forms without worrying in the least about the basis for their use, and because their listeners, knowing nothing beyond it, looked only for pleasure, their glory has vanished along with the edifice they built, while new forms have arisen and met with a welcome by the senses, always friends to novelty.[3] The pleasure which caused their triumph also brought about their fall: as soon as they begin to bore, they are dead.

It is never by its external forms that music exercises its true power; it is not even by the elements which serve to develop these forms: it is by means of the principles which constitute them. Whenever one imagines that the Ancients caused the marvels which they attributed to music by means of some special melody or harmony, an abstraction from everything else, one is in error. This melody, this harmony, was but the physical envelope of a known intellectual principle whose presence awoke in the soul an analogous thought, and by its means produced not only the sensual pleasure dependent on the form but the moral feeling dependent on the principle. This moral feeling could never fail in its effect because the thought that gave it birth was connected, through education, to the musical principle, and pleasure itself always followed it, because the form given by a man of genius recalled the principle and inhered inseparably therein. It was thus that in Egypt one could listen with the same pleasure to songs whose origins were lost in the mists of time. Herodotus speaks of a certain song called Linos[4] which had passed from Egypt to Phoenicia, Cyprus, Ionia and the whole of Greece; it is believed to have been the same as the Latins later called Noenia. Plato, as we have seen, holds that its principle goes back more than ten thousand years.[5]

I know well that it is difficult enough to understand things so distant from what our own experience shows us; but, once more, let us try to believe that we have not attained the zenith of science, and that the sphere of our knowledge is very far from having encircled that of nature.

Let us cease from turning our strength against ourselves by denying the existence of that which we do not know. The obstacle most to be feared in the path of wisdom is the belief of knowing what one does not know. Whatever the difficulty that I foresee in presenting clearly such novel ideas, with nothing to serve me as a thread in passing from the known to the unknown, I will nevertheless try to complete the task I have set myself, and ask the reader to give me the necessary attention.

Music can be envisaged from several standpoints: among the Moderns it is known merely as theoretical or practical; by the Ancients it was considered as speculative, intellectual or celestial. Practical music belongs to the composer or the symphonist, and does not go beyond the boundaries of art. The man who composes and the one who performs compositions receive the musical elements as they find them, without examining or discussing them; they use or develop them according to known rules, in conformity with the taste of the people whom they aim to please – with more or less success, according as they are endowed with more or less genius or talent. Theoretical music, aside from the composer or symphonist to whom it can also belong, also occupies the philosopher who, without himself composing anything or playing any instrument, attempts none the less to examine with them the elements which they put to works, i.e. the manner in which the musical system is adopted, the sound in itself as a resultant of the sounding body, and the voice and instruments which modify it. Music thus becomes a sort of science which, inasmuch as it is enclosed in the physical sphere, can only be considered a science of the second order.

It is at this point, as I have said, that the Moderns have generally stopped; they have scarcely glimpsed the speculative music which the Ancients studied so assiduously and regarded with good reason as the only kind worthy of the name of science. This part of music served as a sort of link or passage between the physical and the moral, and treated in particular the principles, which it distinguished from the forms and elements. But as, after the dogmatic way of the Egyptians,[6] the principles of all sciences were unveiled only to initiates in the secrecy of the sanctuaries, it followed that the principles on which the musical system of the ancient nations reposed remained hidden from the profane, and were never exposed to the public except under cover of symbols and veiled in allegory.

Intellectual and celestial music, finally, was the application of the principles given by speculative music, no longer to the theory or the practice of the art pure and simple, but to that sublime part of the science which had as its object the contemplation of nature and the knowledge of nature and the knowledge of the immutable laws of the universe. Having then reached its highest degree of perfection, it formed a sort of analogical bond between the sensible and the intelligible, and thus afforded a simple means of communication between the two worlds. It was an intellectual language which was applied to metaphysical abstractions and made known their harmonic laws, in the way that algebra, as the scientific part of mathematics, is applied by us to physical abstractions, and serves to calculate relationships. This, I know, is none too easy to understand in our present state of enlightenment, but we will return to it.

48

ARTHUR
SCHOPENHAUER
1788–1860

This philosopher, famous for his pessimism, his debt to Buddhism and Vedanta, and his influence on Richard Wagner, published his major work, *Die Welt als Wille und Vorstellung* (The World as Will and Representation), at the age of 30. It is a survey of the whole of human activity and knowledge in the light of a philosophical attitude that regards the manifested universe, for all its wonder and variety, as something eventually to be transcended. The universe is, to use the Hindu term, *Maya*: the cosmic illusion brought about by what Schopenhauer calls the Will, and Hinduism knows as Ishwara, Lord of created beings. This illusory manifestation, developed inexhaustibly according to definite archetypal Ideas, is reflected in the consciousness of the witnessing subject. But if it can be extinguished from consciousness, there will follow the release from bondage to the Will and its productions: a release which by its very nature escapes philosophical definition, since, like "the Good" of Plato, it is beyond even Being itself. Hence readers of Schopenhauer (and of his oriental inspirations) have often interpreted it falsely as extinction in Nothingness; which is only true in the limited sense of its being "no *thing*-ness."

Schopenhauer's universe, like the Hermetic one, is a hierarchy ranging from the pure Will to its most unconscious productions, and the human being, as in Hermetism, has the potential to know it all. The arts, in particular, give a closer idea of what the Will itself is like than does everyday life, for their object is the Platonic Ideas on which the world is molded. The "aesthetic attitude" which they serve to bring about is one in which thought is stilled, self is forgotten, subject and object no longer distinguished, and the human condition, which is fundamentally one of suffering, transcended in a temporary denial of the insatiable Will.

Music is an important element in Schopenhauer's philosophy because he considers it superior to all other arts. To simplify his terminology, his claim is that music accurately represents the very

212

process of the Will at work – the process of cosmic manifestation – whereas the other arts represent it at second or third hand by depicting only its productions. What is this but a Romantic reincarnation of the old Western doctrine of universal harmony? In that, the whole universe of angels, cosmos, elements and human souls was said to be a kind of superior music (*divina, mundana, humana,* etc.): in Schopenhauer, *musica instrumentalis* (which is all he speaks about) is honored as a true representation of this universe. Elsewhere he actually calls purely instrumental music – specifically the Symphonies of Beethoven – "*rerum concordia discors* [a discordant concord of things], a true and perfect picture of the nature of the world which rolls on in the boundless maze of innumerable forms, and through constant destruction supports itself" (ed. cit., vol. III, p. 237). Schopenhauer's recasting of the traditional philosophy of music could be taken with or without his metaphysical pessimism. In the subsequent selections from Wagner and Steiner (nos 54, 55) we will meet two minds of even more universal scope to whom Schopenhauer was an essential stimulus. Wagner, being in a sense a Buddhist at heart, was able to embrace Schopenhauer's philosophy in its entirety, at least while writing the poems for *Tristan und Isolde* and *Der Ring des Nibelungen*. Steiner, on the other hand, was less sympathetic to oriental metaphysics, and too faithful a follower of Goethe to depreciate the manifested universe. Wagner and Steiner develop, each in his own way, what must be the most original impulse in musical philosophy to have appeared in the nineteenth century.

Source *The World as Will and Idea*, translated by R.B. Haldane and J. Kemp, Boston, Osgood, 1883, vol. I, pp. 339-42.

Music as the Cosmic Will Revealed

We may regard the phenomenal world, or nature, and music as two different expressions of the same thing, which is therefore itself the only medium of their analogy, so that a knowledge of it is demanded in order to understand that analogy. Music, therefore, if regarded as an expression of the world, is in the highest degree a universal language, which is related indeed to the universality of concepts, much as they are related to the particular things. Its universality, however, is by no means that empty universality of abstraction, but quite of a different kind, and is united with thorough and distinct definiteness. In this respect it resembles geometrical figures and numbers, which are the universal forms of all possible objects of experience and applicable to them all *a priori*, and yet are not abstract but perceptible and thoroughly determined. All possible efforts, excitements, and manifestations of will, all that goes on in the heart of man and that reason includes in the wide, negative concept of feeling, may be expressed by the infinite number of possible melodies, but always in the universal, in the mere form, without the material, always according to the thing-in-itself, not the phenomenon, the inmost soul, as it were, of the phenomenon, without the body. This deep relation which music has to the true nature of all things also explains the fact that suitable music played to any scene, action, event, or surrounding seems to disclose to us its most secret meaning, and appears as the most accurate and distinct commentary upon it. This is so truly the case, that whoever gives himself up entirely to the impression of a symphony, seems to see all the possible events of life and the world take place in himself, yet if he reflects, he can find no likeness between the music and the things that passed before his mind. For, as we have said, music is distinguished from all the other arts by the fact that it is not a copy of the phenomenon, or, more accurately, the adequate objectivity of will, but is the direct copy of the will itself, and therefore exhibits itself as the metaphysical to everything physical in the world, and as the thing-in-itself to every phenomenon. We might, therefore, just as well call the world embodied music as embodied will; and this is the reason why music makes every picture, and indeed every scene of real life and of the world, at once appear with higher significance, certainly all the more in proportion as its melody[1] is analogous to the inner spirit of the given phenomenon.

The unutterable depth of all music by virtue of which it floats through our consciousness as the vision of a paradise firmly believed in yet ever distant from us, and by which also it is so fully understood and yet so inexplicable, rests on the fact that it restores to us all the emotions of our inmost nature, but entirely without reality and far removed from their pain. So also the seriousness which is essential to it, which excludes the absurd from its direct and peculiar province, is to be explained by the fact that its object is not the idea, with reference to which alone deception and absurdity are possible; but its object is directly the will, and this is essentially the most serious of all things, for it is that on which all depends. How rich in content and full of significance the language of music is, we see from the repetitions, as well as the *Da capo*, the like of which would be unbearable in works composed in a language of words, but in music are very appropriate and beneficial, for, in order to comprehend it fully, we must hear it twice.

The pleasure we receive from all beauty, the consolation which art affords, the enthusiasm of the artist, which enables him to forget the cares of life, – the latter an advantage of the man of genius over other men, which alone repays him for the suffering that increases in proportion to the clearness of consciousness, and for the desert loneliness among men of a different race, – all this rests on the fact that the in-itself of life, the will, existence itself, is, as we shall see farther on, a constant sorrow, partly miserable, partly terrible; while, on the contrary, as idea alone, purely contemplated, or copied by art, free from pain, it presents to us a drama full of significance. This purely knowable side of the world, and the copy of it in any art, is the element of the artist. He is chained to the contemplation of the play, the objectification of will; he remains beside it, does not get tired of contemplating it and representing it in copies; and meanwhile he bears himself the cost of the production of that play, *i.e.*, he himself is the will which objectifies itself, and remains in constant suffering. That pure, true, and deep knowledge of the inner nature of the world becomes now for him an end in itself: he stops there. Therefore it does not become to him a quieter of the will, as, we shall see in the next book, it does in the case of the saint who has attained to resignation; it does not deliver him for ever from life, but only at moments, and is therefore not for him a path out of life, but only an occasional consolation in it, till his power, increased by this contemplation and at last tired of the play, lays hold on the real. The St Cecilia of Raphael may be regarded as a representation of this transition.

49

CHARLES FOURIER
1772–1837

This item is included, not without some misgiving, because it is the only instance I have found of the incorporation of musical notes into a practical recipe for ritual magic.

My misgivings are due to the incongruity of the ritual and of the talisman that results from it, with the character of the man to whom it is attributed. Charles Fourier, best remembered today as a pioneer socialist and prophet of the commune movement, certainly had some very strange ideas about planets, colors and musical notes: they are all part of his vast system of correspondences, of the scheme of Universal Harmony which mankind is destined, sooner or later, to realize. But no one was more suspicious of tradition, or more skeptical about the value of religious observances. Yet this talisman seems to belong firmly in the tradition of Western ritual magic: it might have been designed by Cornelius Agrippa, or by Eliphas Lévi.[1]

The source itself is not entirely satisfactory. Paul Piobb, the editor of the review in which it appeared, will only say that it was communicated to him by a Russian collector, "Madame A.M.", who modestly desires to guard her anonymity. It may be, in fact, that the Talisman itself is a later invention, attributed to Fourier in the manner that alchemical texts often claim the authorship of famous men (Raymond Lull, etc.) who almost certainly did not write them. But if this is the case, the recipe should still take its place in this anthology, only perhaps somewhat later, perhaps as part of the French occult revival of the second half of the nineteenth century.

In the Notes, the correspondences are given as they are found in Fourier's works, although he acknowledges only four "cardinal" planets, and never showed any reverence either for the number seven or for the Zodiac.

Source   Paul Piobb, "Le Talisman protecteur de Charles Fourier," in *L'Année Occultiste et Psychique*, vol. I (1907), pp. 143-5.

The Making of a Talisman

1.   Take a piece of virgin parchment, made from the skin of a stillborn lamb.

2.   Trace on this parchment two concentric circles, one in red ink and the other with an ink made from powdered silver.

3.   Divide the crown, that is to say the space contained between the two circles, into twelve equal parts by means of double lines drawn with the same silver ink.

4.   In the spaces thus obtained, draw the twelve signs of the Zodiac.

5.   In the central part of the circles, draw a star with seven points.

[6., 7. lacking]

8.   Paint each of the points of the star with one of the seven colours of the solar spectrum.

9.   In each point of the star, write the name of the planet, the name of the metal, and the name of the musical note corresponding to the colour of the point.[2]

10.   At the centre of the star, trace the image of the Sun in red ink and paint its centre with gold.

11.   These operations should be made at night; the colours and the various names of the metals, planets and notes should be filled in during the hours corresponding to their respective planets, the work thus lasting for seven unequal hours.

12.   Next, take a plate of pure silver large enough for one to glue the parchment on without the figure being folded.

13.   The parchment should be stuck on with glue of mistletoe, and the figure applied with its face to the metal.

14.   Lastly, make a sachet of green satin, put the talisman in it, and wear it around the neck on a cord of green silk.

Charles Fourier added that, since the day he constructed this pantacle and began to wear it, he never again had an accident or an annoyance of any sort.

50

HONORÉ DE BALZAC

1799–1850

For all his earthly realism, the author of the *Comédie humaine* – of *Père Goriot* and the *Contes drolatiques* – was an adherent of the mystical philosophy which, in its various forms, has given rise to the ideas assembled in this collection. When Balzac describes the ascent through the heavens it is not a mere literary device, as it was in the hands of Chateaubriand (no. 40): it is the explicit statement of his own belief. Balzac was a convinced Swedenborgian, and probably a Martinist initiate as well.[1]

Those novels and stories of the *Comédie humaine* which he entitled *Études philosophiques* are "divine" comedies, rather, which give an undiluted exposition of the esoteric world-view. Although literary history has shifted its emphasis today, it should be realized that Balzac was only one of the many French Romantic writers for whom the spiritual world was a reality and its attainment the goal of man, first as an individual but eventually as a race.[2] These tendencies were willingly embraced by the writers of the later Symbolist school, and continue to the present day, giving to French literature a secret agenda and a spiritual unity which is lacking in that of other nations.

Séraphîta (1833-5) is set in the exotic realm of the Norwegian fiords – exotic to Balzac the Parisian, who had never been there, and perhaps adopted in homage to Swedenborg's own part of the world. The characters Wilfrid and Minna have both fallen in love with a mysterious being whom they perceive respectively as the woman Séraphîta and the man Séraphîtus. The death of this figure at the book's conclusion affords Wilfrid and Minna the vision of the realm which she/he inhabited even while incarnate on earth, and to which she/he is now fully translated. It is the journey through the spheres to the world above the stars, such as has been traced so often in these pages.

Music is heard a dozen times in this chapter: the sound of the Creative Word; the solitary hymn of the spirit yearning for the

218

release of death; the apocalyptic trumpets of the angels; the living melody of cosmic cycles; the music which is identical to color, number, perfume and thought; the voices of angels and of the seven worlds; and the reminiscence of the harmonies of heaven, still vaguely audible on earth.

Source *Séraphîta*, translated by Clara Bell and R.S. Scott, Philadelphia, Gebbie, 1899, pp. 145-55.

Séraphîta's Assumption

Ch. VII *The assumption*

This last hymn was not uttered in words, nor expressed by gestures, nor by any of the signs which serve men as a means of communicating their thoughts, but as the soul speaks to itself; for, at the moment when Séraphîta was revealed in her true nature, her ideas were no longer enslaved to human language. The vehemence of her last prayer had broken the bonds. Like a white dove, the soul hovered for a moment above this body, of which the exhausted materials were about to dissever.

The aspiration of this soul to heaven was so infectious that Wilfrid and Minna failed to discern death as they saw the radiant spark of life.

They had fallen on their knees when Séraphîtus had turned to the dawn, and they were inspired by his ecstasy.

The fear of the Lord, who creates man anew and purges him of his dross, consumed their hearts. Their eyes were closed to the things of the earth, and opened to the glories of heaven.

Though surprised by the trembling before God which overcame some of those seers known to men as prophets, they still trembled, like them, when they found themselves within the circle where the glory of the Spirit was shining.

Then the veil of the flesh, which had hitherto hidden him from them, insensibly faded away, revealing the divine substance. They were left in the twilight of the dawn, whose pale light prepared them to see the true light, and to hear the living word without dying of it.

In this condition they both began to understand the immeasurable distances that divide the things of earth from the things of heaven.

The life on whose brink they stood, trembling and dazzled in a close embrace, as two children take refuge side by side to gaze at a conflagration – that Life gave no hold to the senses. The Spirit was above them; it shed fragrance without odor, and melody without the help of sound; here, where they knelt, there were neither surfaces, nor angles, nor atmosphere. They dared no longer question him nor gaze on him, but remained under his shadow, as under the burning rays of the tropical sun we dare not raise our eyes for fear of being blinded.

They felt themselves near to him, though they could not tell by what means they thus found themselves, as in a dream, on the border-line of the visible and the invisible, nor how they had ceased to see the visible and perceived the invisible.

They said to themselves, "If he should touch us, we shall die!" But the Spirit was in the infinite, and they did not know that in the infinite time and space are not, that they were divided from him by gulfs, though apparently so near. Their souls not being prepared to receive a complete knowledge of the faculties of that life, they only perceived it darkly, apprehending it according to their weakness.

Otherwise, when the Living Word rang forth,[3] of which the distant sound fell on their ear, its meaning entered into their soul as life enters into a body, a single tone of that Word would have swept them away, as a whirl of fire seizes a straw.

Thus they beheld only what their nature, upheld by the power of the Spirit, allowed them to see; they heard only so much as they were able to hear.

Still, in spite of these mitigations, they shuddered as they heard the voice of the suffering soul, the hymn of the spirit awaiting life, and crying out for it. That cry froze the very marrow in their bones.

The Spirit knocked at the sacred gate.

"What wilt thou?" asked a choir, whose voice rang through all the worlds.

"To go to God."

"Hast thou conquered?"

"I have conquered the flesh by abstinence; I have vanquished false speech by silence; I have vanquished false knowledge by humility; I have vanquished pride by charity; I have vanquished the earth by love; I have paid my tribute of suffering; I am purified by the fires of faith; I have striven for life by prayer; I wait in adoration, and I am resigned."

But no reply came.

"The Lord be praised!" said the Spirit, believing himself rejected. His tears flowed, and fell in dew on the kneeling witnesses, who shuddered at the judgments of God.

On a sudden, the trumpets sounded for the victory of the Angel in this last test; their music filled space, like a sound met by an echo; it rang through it, making the universe tremble. Wilfrid and Minna felt the world shrink under their feet. They shivered, shaken by the terrors of apprehending the mystery that was to be accomplished.

There was, in fact, a vast stir, as though the eternal legions were forming to march, and gathering in spiral order. The worlds spun round, like clouds swept away by a mad whirlwind. It was all in a moment. The veils were rent; they saw far above them, as it were, a star immeasurably brighter than the brightest star in the skies; it fell from its place like a thunderbolt, still flashing like the lightning, paling in its flight all that they had ever hitherto thought to be light.

This was the messenger bearing the good-tidings, and the plume in his helmet was a flame of life. He left behind him a wake, filled up at once by the waves of the luminous flood he passed through.

He bore a palm and a sword; with the palm he touched the Spirit, and it was transfigured; its white wings spread without a sound.

At the communication of the Light, which changed the Spirit into a seraph, the garb of heavenly armor that clothed its glorious form, shed such radiance that the two seers were blinded. And, like the three apostles to whose sight Jesus appeared, Wilfrid and Minna were conscious of the burden of their bodies, which hindered them from complete and unclouded intuition of the Word and the True Life.

They saw the nakedness of their souls, and could measure their lack of brightness by comparison with the halo of the seraph, in which they stood as a shameful spot. They felt an ardent desire to rush back into the mire of the universe, to endure trial there, so as to be able some day to utter at the sacred gate the answer spoken by the glorified Spirit.

That seraph knelt down at the gate of the sanctuary, which he could at last see face to face, and said, pointing to them –

"Grant them to see more clearly. They will love the Lord, and proclaim His Word."

In answer to this prayer, a veil fell. Whether the unknown power that laid a hand on the two seers did for a moment annihilate their physical bodies, or whether it released their spirit to soar free, they were aware of a separation in themselves of the pure from the impure.

Then the seraph's tears rose round them in the form of a vapor which hid the lower worlds from their eyes, and wrapped them round and carried them away, and gave them oblivion of earthly meanings, and the power of understanding the sense of divine things. The True Light appeared; it shed light on all creation, which, to them, looked barren indeed when they saw the source whence the world – earthly, spiritual, and divine – derive motion.

Each world had a centre to which tended every atom of the sphere; these worlds were themselves each an atom tending to the centre of their species. Each species had its centre in the vast celestial region that is in communion with the inexhaustible and flaming *motor power of all that exists*. Thus, from the most vast to the smallest of the worlds, and from the smallest sphere to the minutest atom of the creation that constitutes it, each thing was an individual, and yet all was one.

What, then, was the purpose of the Being, immutable in Essence and Faculty, but able to communicate them without loss, able to manifest them as phenomena without separating them from Himself, and causing everything outside Himself to be a creation immutable in its essence and mutable in its form? The two guests bidden to this high festival could only see the order and arrangement of beings, and wonder at their immediate ends. None but angels could go beyond that, and know the means and understand the purpose.

But that which those two chosen ones could contemplate, and of which they carried away the evidence to be a light to their souls for ever after, was the certainty of the action of worlds and beings, and a knowledge of the effort with which they all tend to a final result. They heard the various parts of the infinite forming a living melody; and at each beat, when the concord made itself felt as a deep expiration, the world, carried on by this unanimous motion, bowed to the Omnipotent One, who in His unapproachable centre made all things issue from Him and return to Him. This ceaseless alternation of voices and silence seemed to be the rhythm of the holy hymn that was echoed and sustained from age to age.

Wilfrid and Minna now understood some of the mysterious words of the being who on earth had appeared to them under the form which was intelligible to each – Séraphîtus to one, Séraphîta to the other – seeing that here all was homogeneous. Light gave birth to melody, and melody to light; colors were both light and melody; motion was number endowed by the Word; in short, everything was at once sonorous, diaphanous, and mobile; so that, everything existing in everything else, extension knew no limits, and the angels could traverse it everywhere to the utmost depths of the infinite.[4]

They saw then how puerile were the human sciences of which they had heard. Before them lay a view without any horizon, an abyss into which ardent craving invited them to plunge; but burdened with their hapless bodies, they had the desire without the power.

The seraph lightly spread his wings to take his flight, and did not look back at them – he had nothing now in common with the earth.

He sprang upward; the vast span of his dazzling pinions covered the two seers like a beneficent shade, allowing them to raise their eyes and see him borne away in his glory escorted by the rejoicing archangel. He mounted like a beaming sun rising from the bosom of the waters; but, more happy he than the day-star and destined to more glorious ends, he was not bound, like inferior creatures, to a circular orbit; he followed the direct line of the infinite, tending undeviatingly to the central one, to be lost there in life eternal, and to absorb into his faculties and into this essence the power of rejoicing through love and the gift of comprehending through wisdom.

The spectacle that was then suddenly unveiled to the eyes of the two seers overpowered them by its vastness, for they felt like atoms whose smallness was comparable only to the minutest fraction which infinite divisibility allows man to conceive of, brought face to face with the infinitely numerous which God alone can contemplate as He contemplates Himself.

What humiliation and what greatness in those two points, strength and love, which the seraph's first desire had placed as two links uniting the immensity of the inferior universe to the immensity of the superior universe! They understood the invisible bonds by which material worlds are attached to the spiritual worlds. As they recalled the stupendous efforts of the greatest human minds, they discerned the principle of melody as they heard the songs of heaven which gave them all the sensations of color, perfume, and thought,[5] and reminded them of the innumerable details of all the creations, as an earthly song can revive the slenderest memories of love.

Strung by the excessive exaltation of their faculties to a pitch for which there is no word in any language, for a moment they were suffered to glance into the divine sphere. There all was gladness. Myriads of angels winged their way with one consent and without confusion, all alike but all different, as simple as the wild rose, as vast as worlds.

Wilfrid and Minna did not see them come nor go; they suddenly pervaded the infinite with their presence, as stars appear in the unfathomable ether. The blaze of all their diadems flashed into light in space, as the heavenly fire is lighted when the day rises among mountains. Waves of light fell from their hair, and their movements gave rise to undulating throbs like the dancing waves of a phosphorescent sea.

The two seers could discern the seraph as a darker object amid deathless legions, whose wings were as the mighty plumage of a forest swept by the breeze. And then, as though all the arrows of a quiver were shot off at once, the spirits dispelled with a breath every vestige of his former shape; as the seraph mounted higher he was purified, and ere long he was no more than a filmy image of what they had seen when he was first transfigured – lines of fire with no shadow. Up and up, receiving a fresh gift at each circle, while the sign of his election was transmitted to the highest heaven, whither he mounted purer and purer.

None of the voices ceased; the hymn spread in all its modes –

"Hail to him who rises to life! Come, flower of the worlds, diamond passed through the fire of affliction, pearl without spot, desire without flesh, new link between earth and heaven, be thou Light! Conquering spirit, queen of the world, fly to take thy crown; victorious over the earth, receive thy diadem! Thou art one with us!"

The angel's virtues reappeared in all their beauty. His first longing for heaven was seen in the grace of tender infancy. His deeds

223

adorned him with brightness like constellations; his acts of faith blazed like the hyacinth of the skies, the hue of the stars. Charity decked him with oriental pearls, treasured tears. Divine love bowered him in roses, and his pious resignation by its whiteness divested him of every trace of earthliness.

Soon, to their eyes, he was no more than a speck of flame, growing more and more intense, its motion lost in the melodious acclamations that hailed his arrival in heaven.

The celestial voices made the two exiles weep.

Suddenly the silence of death spread like a solemn veil from the highest to the lowest sphere, throwing Wilfrid and Minna into unutterable expectancy. At that instant the seraph was lost in the heart of the sanctuary, where he received the gift of eternal life.

Then they were aware of an impulse of intense adoration, which filled them with rapture mingled with awe. They felt that every being had fallen prostrate in the divine spheres, in the spiritual spheres, and in the world of darkness. The angels bent the knee to do honor to his glory, the spirits bent the knee to testify to their eagerness, and in the abyss all knelt, shuddering with awe.

A mighty shout of joy broke out, as a choked spring breaks forth again, tossing up its thousands of flower-like jets, mirroring the sun which turns the sparkling drops to diamond and pearl, at the instant when the seraph emerged, a blaze of light, crying:

"Eternal! Eternal! Eternal!"

The worlds heard him and acknowledged him; he became one with them as God is, and entered into possession of the infinite.

The seven divine worlds were aroused by his voice and answered him.

At this instant there was a great rush, as if whole stars were purified and went up in dazzling glory to be eternal. Perhaps the seraph's first duty was to call all creations filled with the Word to come to God.

But the hallelujah was already dying away in the ears of Wilfrid and Minna, like the last waves of dying music. The glories of heaven were already vanishing, like the hues of a setting sun amid curtains of purple and gold.

Death and impurity were repossessing themselves of their prey.

As they resumed the bondage of the flesh from which their spirit had for a moment been released by a sublime trance, the two mortals felt as on awaking in the morning from a night of splendid dreams, of which reminiscences float in the brain, though the senses have no knowledge of them, and human language would fail to express them. The blackness of the limbo into which they fell was the sphere where the sun of visible worlds shines.

"We must go down again," said Wilfrid to Minna.

"We will do as he bade us," replied she. "Having seen the worlds moving on toward God, we know the right way. Our starry diadems are above!"

They fell into the abyss, into the dust of the lower worlds, and suddenly saw the earth as it were a crypt, of which the prospect was made clear to them by the light they brought back in their souls, for it still wrapped them in a halo, and through it they still vaguely heard the vanishing harmonies of heaven. This was the spectacle which of old fell on the mind's eye of the prophets. Ministers of all religions, calling themselves true, kings consecrated by force and fear, warriors and conquerors sharing the nations, learned men and rich lording it over a refractory and suffering populace whom they trampled under foot – these were all attended by their followers and their women, all were clad in robes of gold, silver, and azure, covered with pearls and gems torn from the bowels of the earth or from the depths of the sea by the perennial toil of sweating and blaspheming humanity. But in the eyes of the exiles this wealth and splendor, harvested with blood, were but filthy rags.

"What do ye here in motionless ranks?" asked Wilfrid.

They made no answer.

"What do ye here in motionless ranks?"

But they made no answer.

Wilfrid laid his hands on them and shouted –

"What do ye here in motionless ranks?"

By a common impulse they all opened their robes and showed him their bodies, dried up, eaten by worms, corrupt, putrid, crumbling to dust, and rotten with horrible diseases.

"Ye lead the nations to death," said Wilfrid; "ye have defiled the earth, perverted the Word, prostituted justice. Ye have eaten the herb of the field, and now ye would kill the lambs! Do ye think that there is justification in showing your wounds? I shall warn those of my brethren who still can hear the Voice, that they may slake their thirst at the springs that you have hidden."

"Let us save our strength for prayer," said Minna. "It is not your mission to be a prophet, nor a redeemer, nor an evangelist. We are as yet only on the margin of the lowest sphere; let us strive to cleave through space on the pinions of prayer."

"You are my sole love!"

"You are my sole strength!"

"We have had a glimpse of the higher mysteries; we are, each to the other, the only creatures here below with whom joy and grief are conceivable. Come then, we will pray; we know the road, we will walk in it."

"Give me your hand," said the girl. "If we always walk together, the path will seem less rough and not so long."

"Only with you," said the young man, "could I traverse that vast desert without allowing myself to repine."

' "And we will go to heaven together!" said she.

The clouds fell, forming a dark canopy. Suddenly the lovers found themselves kneeling by a dead body, which old David was protecting from prying curiosity, and insisted on burying with his own hands.

Outside, the first summer of the nineteenth century was in all its glory; the lovers fancied they could hear a voice in the sunbeams. They breathed heavenly perfume from the new-born flowers, and said as they took each other by the hand –

"The vast ocean that gleams out there is an image of that we saw above!"

"Whither are you going?" asked Pastor Becker.

"We mean to go to God," said they. "Come with us, father."

51

GEORGE SAND
1804–76

The fiction of George Sand (pen-name of the Baroness Aurore Dudevant), like that of Balzac, covers a vast canvas of human existence and bears witness to a superabundant creative energy. Sand also came under the initiatic influences of Romanticism. In her case they were for the most part political ones, leading her to a vision of Christian social renovation after the pattern of Saint-Simon and Pierre Leroux. In her schoolgirl convent days, however, she had had a mystical awakening, and her whole life, for all its ups and downs, was lived in the ultimate conviction of the truths which she expressed most overtly in the drama *The Seven Strings of the Lyre* (1839).

George Sand wrote this philosophical and fantastic drama in two months, as she was beginning her love-affair with Frédéric Chopin. François Buloz, who at this period published all her work in the *Revue des Deux Mondes*, was uncomfortable about the piece, finding it incomprehensible and far too mystical for his readers' liking. George Sand's friends were equally discouraging, and she seems to have taken the hint and refrained in subsequent works from laying her convictions quite so bare. Here, and here only, she writes not of the earthly realm which she knew and described so well, but of the world of the pure Imagination. René Bourgeois, the modern editor of the work, has traced its spiritual ancestry and interpreted its many-layered intentions in a most perceptive prefatory essay, mentioning the "secret thread [that] united Goethe, Quinet, Ballanche, Nodier, Balzac and George Sand" (ed. cit., p. 39), and tracing the characters' resonances in the author's own circle of friends.

Les Sept Cordes de la Lyre is a play to be read and imagined, not acted. Much of it is didactic prose-poetry, but there is also humor in the depiction of "connoisseurs," and cosmic sound effects which no producer would dare attempt to realize. It presents the spiritual education of the philosopher Albertus through the naïve and beautiful young mystic Hélène, who is ultimately freed to return to

Heaven as the strings of the Lyre, made from the planetary metals, break one by one. As in Goethe's *Faust*, Mephistopheles also has a necessary part to play in the divine plan. The Spirit of the Lyre has been plausibly interpreted as the genius of Chopin; the twin themes of the power of music and the even greater power of love certainly reflect George Sand's brief period of fulfilment before the lovers' unfortunate trip to Majorca. These extracts – two of many that could have been chosen from this most musical of plays – show the optimistic mysticism which is the brightest side of the Romantic movement, confident in the ultimate unity and goodness of the Universe, and in the inevitable progress of all beings towards reintegration.

Source   *Les Sept cordes de la lyre*, with introduction by René Bourgeois, Paris, Flammarion, 1973, pp. 110-11, 121-2.

The Universal Lyre

from Act II, scene 1

(*The Lyre resounds magnificently*)

The Spirit of the Lyre:
Awaken, daughter of men! Behold your sun coming forth from the earth's horizon. Bow your spirit before this fragment of the infinite light! This sun is in no wise God, but it is divine. It is one of the diamonds innumerable with which God's vesture is sown. The Creation is the body or vesture of God; it is infinite as the Spirit of God. The Creation is divine; the Spirit is God.

Daughter of men, I am a fragment of the Spirit of God. This lyre is my body; sound is divine, harmony is God. Daughter of men, your being is divine, your love is God.

God is within you, like a ray that penetrates you; but you cannot see the fire from which this ray emanates, for this Sun of intelligence and love swims in the Infinite. Like one of the atoms of gold which you see glittering and rising in this ray from the East, O virgin, it must shine and rise towards the Sun which never sets for the pure Spirits called to contemplate it.[1]

Daughter of men, purify your heart, fashion it as the jeweller purifies a rock crystal by cutting it, so that the lustre of the prism plays upon it. Make of yourself a surface so limpid that the ray of the Infinite can pass through you and embrace you, and reduce your being to dust, so as to assimilate you to him and dissolve you in divine fluid in his burning breast, ever devouring, ever fecund.

(*The Lyre is silent*)

Choir of Celestial Spirits:

Hark, hark, O daughter of the Lyre, to the divine chords of the Universal Lyre! All this infinitude which weighs upon your being and which crushes it with its immensity may open up before you and let you rise like a pure flame, like a subtle spirit! May your ears hear and your eyes see! All is harmony, sound and color. Seven tones and seven colors intertwine and move around you in eternal nuptials. There is no silent color. The universe is a lyre. There is no invisible sound. The universe is a prism. The rainbow is the reflection of a drop of water. The rainbow is the reflection of the Infinite; it raises to the heavens seven shining voices which sing unceasingly the glory and beauty of the Eternal. Repeat the hymn, O daughter of the Lyre! Unite your voice with the Sun's. Every golden speck of dust poised in the solar ray sings the glory and beauty of the Eternal; every drop of dew which sparkles on every blade of grass sings the glory and beauty of the Eternal; every wave on the shore, every rock, every thread of moss, every insect sings the glory and beauty of the Eternal!

And the earth's Sun, and the pale Moon, and the vast planets, and all the suns of the Infinite with the innumerable worlds which they illuminate, and the splendors of the glittering aether, and the immeasurable depths of the Empyrean, hear the voice of the grain of sand which rolls on the mountain slope, the voice which the insect makes, unfolding its mottled wing, the voice of the flower which dries and bursts as it drops its seed, the voice of the moss as it flowers, the voice of the leaf which swells as it drinks the dewdrop and the Eternal hears all the voices of the Universal Lyre.[2] He hears your voice, O daughter of men, as well as those of the constellations; for nothing is too small for him for whom nothing is too great, and nothing is despicable to him who created all!

Color is the manifestation of beauty; sound is the manifestation of glory. Beauty is sung incessantly on all the strings of the infinite Lyre; harmony is incessantly vivified by all the rays of the infinite Sun. All the voices and all the rays of the Infinite tremble and vibrate incessantly before the glory and beauty of the Eternal!   ·

The Prophecy of the Lyre

from Scene 4

Mephistopheles: [*reads the magic parchment of Adelsfreit, the maker of the Lyre*]

"A time will come when men will all have the knowledge and the feeling of the Infinite, and then they will all speak the language of the Infinite: the word will be no more than the language of sense; the other will be that of the Spirit."

Albertus:
What does he mean by the other? . . . Music?

Mephistopheles: (*aside*)
Ah! we're beginning to listen.

(*Aloud, continuing to read*)

"Every intelligent being will be a lyre, and this lyre will sing only for God. The language of orators and dialecticians will be the vulgar tongue.

"And the intelligent beings will hear [and understand – *entendront*] the songs of the higher world. Just as the eye will grasp the magnificent spectacle of the heavens and discover the marvels hidden in the infinite order, the ear will grasp the sublime concert of the stars and discover the mysteries of infinite harmony.

"This will not be a conquest of the senses, but a conquest of the Spirit. It is the Spirit which will see the movement of the stars; it is the Spirit which will hear the voice of the stars. The Spirit will have senses as the body has senses. It will transport itself into the worlds of the Infinite and pass through the depths of the Infinite. This labor is begun on Earth. Man raises himself, each century, a hundred thousand and a hundred million cubits above the slime from which he emerged. It is a long way from the Corybantes whom the clash of brazen shields aroused to fury, to the Christians who bow themselves on hearing the sighs of the organ.

"In the end, Man will comprehend that if metal has a voice, if wood, if the guts and throats of animals, if the wind, if the thunder, if the wave has a voice, if he himself has in his material organs a powerful voice, his soul, and the Universe which is the homeland of his soul, have voices to call and to respond. He will comprehend that the power of harmony is not in the sound produced by the wood or the metal, still less in the puerile exercise of the fingers or the throat, any more than there is perpetual movement in the machines of wood or metal which an industrious hand can create. The senses are only the servants of the Spirit, and what the Spirit does not comprehend, the hand cannot create.

"I will create a Lyre which will have no equal. The densest ivory, the purest gold, the most resonant wood, shall be used in it. I will bring to it all the science of music, all the art of the instrument-maker. The most skilled and experienced hands will draw no more from it than vulgar songs if the Spirit does not guide them, nor the Divine Breath embrace the Spirit.

"O Lyre! The Spirit is within you as it is within the Universe; but you will be dumb if the Spirit does not speak to you!"

Well, master, do you begin to understand?

52

GÉRARD DE NERVAL
1808–55

Nerval's life was spent exploring, or being forced through, the full range of supernatural experiences which most other Romantic writers knew only through faith or from brief glimpses. Although periodically institutionalized as insane, he was always able to write about his states of mind with perfect honesty and clarity: the states were simply such as to make normal behavior irrelevant or temporarily impossible. Even his suicide by hanging seems to have been a natural conclusion to his self-identification with the twelfth Tarot Trump, the "Hanged Man."

The fantastic novella *Aurélia* (1841-54) was the last work finished by Nerval before his suicide. It relates the initiatory experiences – a veritable descent into Hell – of a man deeply involved in practical occultism and with a more than literary interest in oriental religion, Neoplatonism both Alexandrian and Renaissance, Swedenborg, Christian Martinism, and the German Romantic movement.[1] This extract comes from the appendix, whose title, "Memorabilia," is borrowed from Swedenborg's term for his visions of the other world.

At the beginning of this extract appears Nerval's feminine soul-guide, an archetypal personification of Divine Wisdom (Sophia) who was reflected on the biographical level as his human beloved Jenny Colon. The vision of the word "Pardon" probably concerns his ambivalent and heterodox attitude to Christianity. The octave is the type of cyclic development, the motive force of the universe, later taking form as the choir of stars which in turn shed a harmonious and loving influence upon the earth. Here is a fresh statement of the ancient description of Creation as arising from the primal numbers 1 (the Same) and 2 (the Different).[2] The last paragraph knowingly echoes the Blue Flower whose attainment is the quest of Novalis's *Heinrich von Ofterdingen*.

Source *Aurélia, ou le rêve et la vie*, ed. Jean Richer, Paris, Minard, 1965, pp. 116-18. This has very informed critical and explanatory material by the editor and others.

A Vision

I came out of a most sweet dream: I beheld her whom I had loved, transfigured and radiant. The heavens opened in all their glory – and I read there the word "Pardon" written in the blood of Jesus Christ.

A star suddenly blazed out and revealed to me the secret of the world and of the worlds. Hosanna! Peace on Earth and glory in the Heavens.

(Know, my children, the secret of the world and of all the worlds: it is Harmony, wife of Cadmus, who will teach it to you.)

From the bosom of the silent darkness, two notes sounded forth – one low, the other high – and the eternal globe began forthwith to turn. Blessed be thou, O first octave which begins the divine hymn! From Sunday to Sunday, weave each day into your magic web: the mountains sing it to the valleys, the springs to the streams, the streams to the rivers, the rivers to the Ocean. Hosanna on Earth! Hosanna in Heaven! The air vibrates, and the light harmoniously opens the nascent flowers. A sigh, a shiver of love, comes from the swollen bosom of the earth, and the choir of stars unfolds into infinity; it swerves and turns back on itself, contracts and expands, and sows far and wide the germs of new creations.

On the peak of a blue mountain a little flower is born. "Forget me not!" The shimmering glance of a star rests for an instant upon it, and an answer is heard in a sweet, strange tongue: "*Myosotis.*"[3]

53

ROBERT SCHUMANN
1810–56

The tragic circumstances of this report do nothing to diminish its value as a witness to the world of supernatural music. This is from the diary entries of Robert's wife Clara, recording the culminating phase of her husband's mental disturbances which made it necessary for him to be confined for the rest of his life to a private asylum. From her diary we learn that his consuming interest in the preceding months had not been in composing but in researching materials to be included in his *Dichtergarten* (Poet's Garden), a collection of writings about music by poets and authors. He began with the Bible, brushed up his Latin and Greek to read the classics in the Düsseldorf city library, and searched the fertile field of German Romanticism. Perhaps this reading had some effect on the form which his insanity was to take; but he was not unprepared for it philosophically if he could say in his youth: "For me, music is always the language which permits one to converse with the Beyond."[1] The musical hallucinations described here are so close to those of our visionary and mystical writers that one wonders whether Schumann had not penetrated, against his will, to realms with which he was not psychologically equipped to deal. Such experiences are quite common under the influence of hallucinogenic drugs, but to enter them without artificial assistance is the mark either of "a certain ineffable divinity" such as Pythagoras is said to have possessed (see no. 7), or of a loosening of the doors of perception which keep most people safely shut up in the world of the senses.[2] A few days later Robert was to throw himself into the Rhine, and Clara would not see him again until his last hours.

Source Berthold Litzmann, *Clara Schumann, ein Künstlerleben nach Tagebüchern und Briefen*, 2nd ed., Leipzig, 1906, vol. II, pp. 295-9, partially translated by Grace E. Hadow in *Clara Schumann, an Artist's Life*, London, Macmillan, 1913, vol. II, pp. 55-7.

The Advent of Insanity

From the night of Friday the 10th February, 1854 until Saturday the 11th, Robert suffered from so violent an affection of the hearing that he did not close his eyes all night. He kept on hearing the same note over and over again, and at times also another interval. By day it was covered up by other sounds. On the night of Sunday the 12th, it was just as bad again, and on the following day also, for the pain ceased only for two hours in the morning, and at 10 o'clock it began again. My poor Robert suffers terribly! Every noise, he says, sounds to him like music, a music more wonderful and played by more exquisite instruments than was ever heard on earth! But naturally he is frightfully upset by it. The doctor says he can do absolutely nothing.

The following nights were very bad – we hardly slept at all. . . . He tried to work by day, but he could do so only at the cost of the most terrible effort. He said frequently that if this did not cease, it would destroy his mind [*Geist*]. . . . The affection of his hearing had so increased that he heard whole pieces as if played by a full orchestra, from beginning to end, and the last chord went on sounding until Robert fastened his thoughts on another piece. Ah! and one could do nothing to ease him!

[Written in April, 1854] The aural hallucinations increased markedly from the 10th to the 17th of February. We consulted another doctor, Regimental Physician Dr Böger, and Hasenclever also came daily, but only as an advising friend.

On the night of Friday the 17th, after we had been in bed for some time, Robert suddenly got up and wrote down a theme, which, as he said, an angel had sung to him. When he had finished it he lay down again and all night long he was picturing things to himself, gazing towards heaven with wide-open eyes; he was firmly convinced that angels hovered round him revealing glories to him in wonderful music. They bade us welcome, and before a year had passed we should be united and with them. . . . Morning came and with it a terrible change. The angel voices turned to those of demons and in hideous music they told him he was a sinner and they would cast him into hell. In short, his condition increased to an actual nervous paroxysm; he cried out with pain (for as he said to me afterwards, they pounced on him in the forms of tigers and hyaenas, to seize him), and two doctors, who luckily came quickly enough, could scarcely hold him. I will never forget this sight, I actually suffered the pains of torture in it. After about half an hour he was calmer, and said that he again heard friendlier voices which gave him courage. The doctors got him into bed, and for some hours he stayed there contentedly, but then he got up again and made corrections to his 'Cello Concerto; he thought that by this he would be somewhat relieved from the ceaseless sound of the voices. On Sunday the 19th, he spent the day in bed, dreadfully tormented by evil spirits! He could not be persuaded that heavenly and infernal beings were not swarming around him; he certainly believed it when I told him that he was very ill, his cerebral nerves frightfully strained, but I never broke him for a moment from belief in the spirits: on the contrary, he said to me several times in a piteous voice, "Clara dear, you will believe me, I'm not telling you lies!" I could do no more than quietly to agree with him, since I upset him still more by arguing. In the evening at 11 he was suddenly quiet again, the angels promised him that he should sleep. . . .

On the 20th, Robert spent the whole day at his writing desk, with paper, pen and ink before him, and listened to the angel-voices, then would often write a few words, but very little, and then listen again. He had a look full of rapture that I can never forget; yet this unnatural rapture wounded my heart as much as when he was suffering from the evil spirits. Ah! all this filled my heart with the most dreadful worry about how it would end; I saw his mind ever more unsettled, yet had no idea of what still awaited him and me. On Tuesday the 21st of February, we again did not sleep the whole night; he kept talking about how he was a sinner and ought to read the Bible constantly, etc. I noticed that his condition was always more agitated when he read the Bible, and therefore concluded that perhaps by reading it while collecting items for his *Dichtergarten* he had delved too deeply into things that confused his mind, for his suffering was then almost consistently of a religious nature, a genuine overexcitement.

During the days that followed, things remained much the same. He felt himself surrounded alternately by good and evil spirits, but no longer did he hear them only in music, often they spoke. At the same time his mind was so clear that he wrote touching, peaceful variations on the wonderfully peaceful, holy theme[3] which he had written down on the night of the 10th; and he also wrote two letters, a business letter to Arnold in Elberfeld, and another to Holl in Amsterdam.

At night there were often moments in which he begged me to leave him, as he might do me an injury. Then I would go away for a few minutes in order to quiet him, and when I came back, it was all right again. . . . He often complained that his head was spinning, and then he would assert that it would soon be all over with him, and he would take leave of me, and make all sorts of arrangements about his money and his compositions etc. . . . On Sunday, the 26th, he felt a little better, and in the evening he played a sonata by a young musician, Martin Cohn, to Herr Dietrich, with the greatest interest, but worked himself into such a state of joyous exaltation that the perspiration poured down from his brow. Afterwards he ate a large supper very hastily. Then suddenly, at 9:30, he stood up and said he must have his clothes, he must go into the asylum as he no longer had his mind under control and did not know what he might not end by doing in the night. . . . Herr Aschenberg, our landlord, at once came down to quiet him, and I sent for Dr Böger. Robert laid out all the things that he wished to take with him, watch, money, note-paper, pens, cigars, everything in short, with perfectly clear mind; and when I said to him: "Robert, will you leave your wife and children?" he answered, "It will not be for long. I shall soon come back, cured."

54

RICHARD WAGNER

1813–83

As W.A. Ellis, the translator, remarks (note 2), Wagner developed Schopenhauer's theories of music far beyond anything their originator could have imagined. He carried them, in fact, from the realm of philosophical theory into that of creative practice. Schopenhauer's misnamed "pessimism" is the philosophy behind the mythological poems of *Tristan und Isolde* and *Die Götterdämmerung*: dramas which culminate respectively in the extinction of ego-consciousness and in the closing of a world-cycle. Are these operas tragedies? Certainly not, if one can accept the Schopenhauerian and Buddhist view that such extinction, such a closure, is but the birth into a state beyond the limitations of individuality and free from the wearisome cosmic circuit.

Wagner's subject here, a digression from his encomium on Beethoven (1870), the only other composer he fully recognized as a brother, is not the endless Night but a step on the path that eventually leads thither: a turning of consciousness from outward to inward things. While Schopenhauer's approach is from *musica mundana*, as it were, Wagner's is from *musica humana*, concentrating on the subjective experience of the arts through inner faculties. Wagner proposes the equation: Experience of tone differs from Experience of sight, as Dream world from Waking world. Far from being a depreciation of it, this is a way of expressing the insight that tone, whatever its external cause, is an entirely inner experience (compare Fabre d'Olivet, no. 47), and that it is inner experience alone that furnishes us with a direct link to Nature and to the timeless Essences of things. Not for nothing does Wagner refer here to telepathy and clairvoyance: music for him is the royal road to the supersensible universe whose "events" no words can describe.

Wagner is reported in a conversation of 1880, towards the end of his life, as having been even more explicit on this subject, revealing the degree to which his beliefs had come to resemble those that were being publicized at the same time by the Theosophical Society:[1]

I am convinced that there are universal currents of Divine Thought vibrating the ether everywhere and that anyone who can feel those vibrations is inspired, provided he is conscious of the process. . . . I believe, first of all, that it is this universal vibrating energy that binds the soul of man to the Almighty Central Power from which emanates the life principle to which we all owe our existence. This energy links us to the Supreme Force of the universe, of which we are all a part . . . in that trance-like condition, which is the prerequisite of all true creative effort, I feel that I am one with this vibrating Force, that it is omniscient, and that I can draw upon it to an extent that is limited only by my own capacity to do so. Why did Beethoven appropriate it to a far greater degree than Dittersdorf, to name only one of the many minor composers of that period? Because Beethoven was much more aware of his oneness with Divinity than was Dittersdorf.

Imagination is the creative force, and this is true, I find, not only of musical creations but also of external circumstances. For instance [after 1850] I commenced work on the *Ring* and while composing the four music dramas, I conjured up distinct visions of a special Wagner Theater, where they could be produced, and lo and behold, it became a reality! Believe me . . . , imagination creates the reality [*die Fantasie schafft die Wirklichkeit*]. This is a great cosmic law.

Source Beethoven, trans. William Ashton Ellis in *Richard Wagner's Prose Works*, vol. 5, London, 1896, pp. 65-81.

On Inspiration

But it was *Schopenhauer* who first defined the position of Music among the fine arts with philosophic clearness, ascribing to it a totally different nature from that of either plastic or poetic art. He starts from wonder at Music's speaking a language immediately intelligible by everyone, since it needs no whit of intermediation through abstract concepts (*Begriffe*); which completely distinguishes it from Poetry, in the first place, whose sole material consists of concepts, employed by it to visualise the *Idea*. For according to this philosopher's so luminous definition it is the Ideas of the world and of its essential phenomena, in the sense of Plato, that constitute the "object" of the fine arts; whereas, however, the Poet interprets these Ideas to the visual consciousness (*dem anschauenden Bewusstsein*) through an employment of strictly rationalistic concepts in a manner quite peculiar to his art, Schopenhauer believes he must recognise *in Music itself an Idea of the world*, since he who could entirely translate it into abstract concepts would have found withal a philosophy to explain the world itself. Though Schopenhauer propounds this theory of Music as a paradox, since it cannot strictly be set forth in logical terms, he also furnishes us with the only serviceable material for a further demonstration of the justice of his profound hypothesis; a demonstration which he himself did not pursue more closely, perhaps for simple reason that as layman he was not conversant enough with music, and moreover was unable to base his knowledge thereof sufficiently definitely on an understanding of the very musician whose works have first laid open to the world that deepest mystery of Music; for *Beethoven*, of all others, is not to be judged exhaustively until that pregnant paradox of Schopenhauer's has been solved and made right clear to philosophic apprehension. –

In making use of this material supplied us by the philosopher I fancy I shall do best to begin with a remark in which Schopenhauer declines to accept the Idea derived from a knowledge of "relations" as the essence of the Thing-in-itself, but regards it merely as expressing the objective character of things, and therefore as still concerned with their phenomenal appearance. "And we should not understand this character itself" – so Schopenhauer goes on to say – "were not the inner essence of things confessed to us elsewise, dimly at least and in our Feeling. For that essence cannot be gathered from the Ideas, nor understood through any mere *objective* knowledge; wherefore it would ever remain a mystery, had we not access to it from quite another side. Only inasmuch as every observer [lit. knower, or perceiver – *Erkenner*] is an Individual withal, and thereby part of Nature, stands there open to him in his own self-consciousness the adit to Nature's innermost; and there forthwith, and most immediately, it makes itself known to him as *Will*."

If we couple with this what Schopenhauer postulates as the condition for entry of an Idea into our consciousness, namely "a temporary preponderance of intellect over will, or to put it physiologically, a strong excitation of the sensory faculty of the brain (*der anschauenden Gehirnthätigkeit*) without the smallest excitation of the passions or desires," we have only further to pay close heed to the elucidation which directly follows it, namely that our consciousness has two sides: in part it is a consciousness of *one's own self*, which is the will; in part a consciousness of *other things*, and chiefly then a *visual* knowledge of the outer world, the apprehension of objects. "The more the one side of the aggregate consciousness comes to the front, the more does the other retreat."

After well weighing these extracts from Schopenhauer's principal work it must be obvious to us that musical conception, as it has nothing in common with the seizure of an Idea (for the latter is absolutely bound to physical perception of the world), can have its origin nowhere but upon that side of the consciousness which Schopenhauer defines as facing inwards. Though this side may temporarily retire completely, to make way for entry of the purely apprehending "subject" on its function (i.e. the seizure of Ideas), on the other hand it transpires that only from this inward-facing side of

239

consciousness can the intellect derive its ability to seize the Character of things. If this consciousness, however, is the consciousness of one's own self, i.e. of the Will, we must take it that its repression is indispensable indeed for purity of the outward-facing consciousness, but that the nature of the Thing-in-itself – inconceivable by that physical [or "visual"] mode of knowledge – would only be revealed to this inward-facing consciousness when it had attained the faculty of seeing within as clearly as that other side of consciousness is able in its seizure of Ideas to see without.

For a further pursuit of this path Schopenhauer has also given us the best of guides, through his profound hypothesis[2] concerning the physiologic phenomenon of Clairvoyance, and the Dream-theory he has based thereon. For as in that phenomenon the inward-facing consciousness attains the actual power of sight where our waking daylight consciousness feels nothing but a vague impression of the midnight background of our will's emotions, so from out this night *Tone* bursts upon the world of waking, a direct utterance of the Will. As dreams must have brought to everyone's experience, beside the world envisaged by the functions of the waking brain there dwells a second, distinct as is itself, no less a world displayed to vision; since this second world can in no case be an object lying outside us, it therefore must be brought to our cognisance by an *inward* function of the brain; and this form of the brain's perception Schopenhauer here calls the Dream-organ. Now a no less positive experience is this: besides the world that presents itself to sight, in waking as in dreams, we are conscious of the existence of a second world, perceptible only through the ear, manifesting itself through sound; literally a *sound-world* beside the *light-world*, a world of which we may say that it bears the same relation to the visible world as dreaming to waking: for it is quite as plain to us as is the other, though we must recognise it as being entirely different. As the world of dreams can only come to vision through a special operation of the brain, so Music enters our consciousness through a kindred operation; only, the latter differs exactly as much from the operation consequent on *sight*, as that Dream-organ from the function of the waking brain under the stimulus of outer impressions.

As the Dream-organ cannot be roused into action by outer impressions, against which the brain is now fast locked, this must take place through happenings' in the inner organism that our waking consciousness merely feels as vague sensations. But it is this inner life through which we are directly allied with the whole of Nature, and thus are brought into a relation with the Essence of things that eludes the forms of outer knowledge, Time and Space; whereby Schopenhauer so convincingly explains the genesis of prophetic or telepathic (*das Fernste wahrnehmbar machenden*), fatidical dreams, ay, in rare and extreme cases the occurrence of somnambulistic clairvoyance. From the most terrifying of such dreams we wake with a *scream*, the immediate expression of the anguished will, which thus makes definite entrance into the Sound-world first of all, to manifest itself without. Now if we take the Scream in all the diminutions of its vehemence, down to the gentler cry of longing, as the root-element of every human message to the ear; and if we cannot but find in it the most immediate utterance of the will, through which the latter turns the swiftest and the surest toward Without, then we have less cause to wonder at its immediate intelligibility than at an *art* arising from this element: for it is evident, upon the other hand, that neither artistic beholding nor artistic fashioning can result from aught but a diversion of the consciousness from the agitations of the will.

To explain this wonder, let us first recall our philosopher's profound remark adduced above, that we should never understand even the Ideas that by their very nature are only seizable through will-freed, i.e. objective contemplation, had we not another approach to the Essence-of-things which lies beneath them, namely our direct consciousness of our own self. By this consciousness alone we are enabled to understand withal the inner nature of things outside us, inasmuch as we recognise in them the selfsame basic essence that our self-consciousness declares to be our very own. Our each illusion hereanent had sprung from the mere *sight* of a world around us, a world that in the show of daylight we took for something quite apart from us[3]: first through (intellectual) perception of the Ideas, and thus upon a circuitous path, do we reach an initial stage of undeception, in which we no longer see things parcelled off in time and space, but apprehend their generic character; and this character speaks out the plainest to us from the works of Plastic art, whose true province it therefore is to take the illusive surface (*Schein*) of the light-shewn world and, in virtue of a most ingenious playing with that semblance, lay bare the Idea concealed beneath. In daily life the mere sight of an object leaves us cold and unconcerned and only when we become aware of that object's bearings on our will, does it call forth an emotion; in harmony wherewith it very properly ranks as the first æsthetic principle of Plastic art, that its imaginings shall entirely avoid such references to our individual will, and prepare for our sight that calm which alone makes possible a pure Beholding of the object according to its own character. Yet the effector of this æsthetic, will-freed contemplation, into which we momentarily plunge, here remains nothing but the *show* of things. And it is this principle of tranquillisation by sheer pleasure in the semblance, that has been extended from Plastic art to all the arts, and made a postulate for every manner of æsthetic pleasing. Whence, too, has come our term for *beauty* (*Schönheit*); the root of which word in our German language is plainly connected with Show (*Schein*) as object, with Seeing (*Schauen*) as subject. –

But that consciousness which alone enabled us to grasp the Idea transmitted by the Show we looked on, must feel compelled at last to cry with Faust: "A spectacle superb! But still, alas! a spectacle. Where seize I thee, o Nature infinite?"

This cry is answered in the most positive manner by *Music*. Here the world outside us speaks to us in terms intelligible beyond compare, since its sounding message to our ear is of the selfsame nature as the cry sent forth to it from the depths of our own inner heart. The Object of the tone perceived is brought into immediate rapport with the Subject of the tone emitted: without any reasoning go-between we understand the cry for help, the wail, the shout of joy, and straightway answer it in its own tongue. If the scream, the moan, the murmured happiness in our own mouth is the most direct utterance of the will's emotion, so when brought us by our ear we understand it past denial as utterance of the same emotion; no illusion is possible here, as in the daylight Show, to make us deem the essence of the world outside us not wholly identical with our own; and thus that gulf which seems to sight is closed forthwith.

Now if we see an art arise from this immediate consciousness of the oneness of our inner essence with that of the outer world, our most obvious inference is that this art must be subject to æsthetic laws quite distinct from those of every other. All Æsthetes hitherto have rebelled against the notion of deducing a veritable art from what appears to them a purely pathologic element, and have consequently refused to Music any recognition until its products shew themselves in a light as cold as that peculiar to the fashionings of plastic art. Yet that its very rudiment (*ihr blosses Element*) is felt, not seen, by our deepest consciousness as a world's Idea, we have learnt to recognise forthwith through Schopenhauer's eventful aid, and we understand that Idea as a direct revelation of the oneness of the Will; starting with the oneness of all human being, our consciousness is thereby shewn beyond dispute our unity with Nature, whom equally we recognise through Sound.

Difficult as is the task of eliciting Music's nature as an art, we believe we may best accomplish it by considering the inspired musician's modus operandi. In many respects this must radically differ from that of other artists. As to the latter we have had to acknowledge that it must be preceded by a will-freed, pure beholding of the object, an act of like nature with the effect to be produced by the artwork itself in the mind of the spectator. Such an object, however, to be raised to an Idea by means of pure Beholding, does not present itself to the musician at all; for his music is itself a world's-Idea, an Idea in which the world immediately displays its essence, whereas in those other arts this essence has to pass through the medium of the understanding (*das Erkenntniss*) before it can *become* displayed. We can but take it that the *individual will*, silenced in the plastic artist through pure beholding, awakes in the musician as the *universal Will*, and – above and beyond all power of vision – now recognises itself as such in full selfconsciousness. Hence the great difference in the mental state of the concipient musician and the designing artist; hence the radically diverse effects of music and of painting: here profoundest stilling, there utmost excitation of the will. In other words we here have the will in the Individual as such, the will imprisoned by the fancy (*Wahn*) of its difference from the essence of things outside, and unable to lift itself above its barriers save in the purely disinterested beholding of objects; whilst there, in the musician's case, the will feels *one* forthwith, above all bounds of individuality: for Hearing has opened it the gate through which the world thrusts home to it, it to the world. This prodigious breaking-down the floodgates of Appearance must necessarily call forth in the inspired musician a state of ecstasy wherewith no other can compare: in it the will perceives itself the almighty Will of all things: it has not mutely to yield place to contemplation, but proclaims itself aloud as conscious World-Idea. One state surpasses his, and one alone, – the Saint's, and chiefly through its permanence and imperturbability; whereas the clairvoyant ecstasy of the musician has to alternate with a perpetually recurrent state of individual consciousness, which we must account the more distressful the higher has his inspiration carried him above all bounds of individuality. And this suffering again, allotted him as penalty for the state of inspiration in which he so unutterably entrances us, might make us hold the musician in higher reverence than other artists, ay, wellnigh give him claim to rank as holy. For his art, in truth, compares with the communion of all the other arts as *Religion* with the *Church*.

We have seen that in the other arts the Will is longing to become pure Knowledge (*gänzlich Erkenntniss zu werden verlangt*), but that this is possible only in so far as it stays stock-still in its deepest inner chamber: 'tis as if it were awaiting tidings of redemption from there outside; content they it not, it sets itself in that state of clairvoyance; and here, beyond the bounds of time and space, it knows itself the world's both One and All. What it here has seen, no tongue can impart:[4] as the dream of deepest sleep can only be conveyed to the waking consciousness through translation into the language of a second, an allegoric dream which immediately precedes our wakening, so for the direct vision of its self the Will creates a second organ of transmission, – an organ whose one side faces toward that inner vision, whilst the other thrusts into the reappearing outer world with the sole direct and sympathetic message, that of Tone. The Will cries out; and in the countercry it knows itself once more: thus cry and countercry become for it a comforting, at last an

243

entrancing play with its own self.

Sleepless one night in Venice, I stepped upon the balcony of my window overlooking the Grand Canal: like a deep dream the fairy city of lagoons lay stretched in shade before me. From out the breathless silence rose the strident cry of a gondolier just woken on his barque; again and again his voice went forth into the night, till from remotest distance its fellow-cry came answering down the midnight length of the Canal: I recognised the drear melodic phrase to which the well-known lines of Tasso were also wedded in his day, but which in itself is certainly as old as Venice's canals and people. After many a solemn pause the ringing dialogue took quicker life, and seemed at last to melt in unison; till finally the sounds from far and near died softly back to new-won slumber. Whate'er could sun-steeped, colour-swarming Venice of the daylight tell me of itself, that that sounding dream of night had not brought infinitely deeper, closer, to my consciousness? – Another time I wandered through the lofty solitude of an upland vale in Uri. In broad daylight from a hanging pasture-land came shouting the shrill jodel of a cowherd, sent forth across the broadening valley; from the other side anon there answered it, athwart the monstrous silence, a like exultant herd-call: the echo of the towering mountain walls here mingled in; the brooding valley leapt into the merry lists of sound. – So wakes the child from the night of the mother-womb, and answer it the mother's crooning kisses; so understands the yearning youth the woodbird's mate-call, so speaks to the musing man the moan of beasts, the whistling wind, the howling hurricane, till over him there comes that dreamlike state in which the ear reveals to him the inmost essence of all his eye had held suspended in the cheat of scattered show, and tells him that his inmost being is one therewith, that only in *this* wise can the Essence of things without be learnt in truth.

The dreamlike nature of the state into which we thus are plunged through sympathetic hearing – and wherein there dawns on us that other world, that world from whence the musician speaks to us – we recognise at once from an experience at the door of every man: namely that our eyesight is paralysed to such a degree by the effect of music upon us, that with eyes wide open we no longer intensively see. We experience this in every concert-room while listening to any tone-piece that really touches us, where the most hideous and distracting things are passing before our eye, things that assuredly would quite divert us from the music, and even move us to laughter, if we actively saw them; I mean, besides the highly trivial aspect of the audience itself, the mechanical movements of the band, the whole peculiar working apparatus of an orchestral production. That this spectacle – which preoccupies the man untouched by the music – at last ceases to disturb the spellbound listener, plainly shews us that we no longer are really conscious of it, but, for all our open eyes, have fallen into a state essentially akin to that of hypnotic clairvoyance. And in truth it is in this state alone that we immediately belong to the musician's world. From out that world, which nothing else can picture, the musician casts the meshwork of his tones to net us, so to speak; or, with his wonder-drops of sound he dews our brain as if by magic, and robs it of the power of seeing aught save our own inner world.

To gain a glimpse of his procedure, we again can do no better than return to its analogy with that inner process whereby – according to Schopenhauer's so luminous assumption – the dream of deepest sleep, entirely remote from the waking cerebral consciousness, as it were translates itself into the lighter, allegoric dream which immediately precedes our wakening. We have seen that the musician's kindred glossary extends from the scream of horror to the suave play of soothing murmurs. In the employment of the ample range that lies between, the musician is controlled, as it were, by an urgent impulse to impart the vision of his inmost dream; like the second, allegoric dream, he therefore approaches the notions (*Vorstellungen*) of the waking brain – those notions whereby it is at last enabled to preserve a record, chiefly for itself, of the inner vision. The extreme limit of this approach, however, is marked by the notions of *Time*: those of Space he leaves behind an impenetrable veil, whose lifting needs must make his dream invisible forthwith. Whilst *harmony*, belonging to neither Space nor Time, remains the most inalienable element of Music, through the *rhythmic* sequence of his tones in point of time the musician reaches forth a plastic hand, so to speak, to strike a compact with the waking world of semblances; just as the allegoric dream so far makes contact with the Individual's wonted notions that the waking consciousness, albeit at once detecting the great difference of even this dream-picture from the outer incidents of actual life, yet is able to retain its image. So the musician makes contact with the plastic world through the *rhythmic* ordering of his tones, and that in virtue of a resemblance to the laws whereby the motion of visible bodies is brought to our intelligence.[5] Human Gesture, which seeks to make itself intelligible in Dance through an expressive regularity of changeful motion, thus seems to play the same part toward Music as bodies, in their turn, toward Light: without refraction and reflection, Light would not shine; and so we may say that without rhythm, Music would not be observable. But, at this very point of contact between Plastique and Harmony, the nature of Music is plainly shewn to be entirely distinct from that of Plastic art in particular; whereas the latter fixes Gesture in respect of space, but leaves its motion to be supplied by our reflective thought, Music speaks out Gesture's inmost essence in a language so direct that, once we are saturated with the music, our

245

eyesight is positively incapacitated for intensive observation of the gesture, so that finally we understand it without our really seeing it. Thus, though Music draws her nearest affinities in the phenomenal world into her dream-realm, as we have called it, this is only in order to turn our visual faculties inwards through a wondrous transformation, so to speak, enabling them to grasp the Essence-of-things in its most immediate manifestment, as it were to read the vision which the musician had himself beheld in deepest sleep. –

As for Music's standing toward the plastic forms of the phenomenal world, and toward abstractions derived from things themselves, nothing can possibly be more lucid than what we read under this heading in Schopenhauer's work; so that it would be quite superfluous for us to dwell thereon, and we may turn to our principal object, namely an inquiry into the nature of the Musician himself.

However, we first must dwell on a crucial point in the æsthetic judgment (*Urtheil*) of Music as an art. For we find that from the forms wherein Music seems to join hands with the outer world of Appearance there has been deduced an utterly preposterous demand upon the character of her utterances. As already mentioned, axioms founded simply on a scrutiny of Plastic art have been transferred to Music. That such a solecism could have been committed, we have at any rate to attribute to the aforesaid "nearest approach" of Music to the visual side of the world and its phenomena. In this direction indeed the art of Music has taken a development which has exposed her to so great a misapprehension of her veritable character that folk have claimed from her a function similar to that of plastic works of art, namely the susciting of our *pleasure in beautiful forms*. As this was synchronous with a progressive decline in the judgment of plastic art itself, it may easily be imagined how deeply Music was thus degraded; at bottom, she was asked to wholly repress her ownest nature for mere sake of turning her outmost side to our delectation.

Music, who speaks to us solely through quickening into articulate life the most universal concept of the inherently speechless Feeling, in all imaginable gradations, can once and for all be judged by nothing but the category of the *sublime*; for, as soon as she engrosses us, she transports us to the highest ecstasy of consciousness of our infinitude.[6] On the other hand what enters only *as a sequel* to our plunging into contemplation of a work of plastic art, namely the (temporary) liberation of the intellect from service to the individual will through our discarding all relations of the object contemplated to that will – the required effect of *beauty* on the mind, – is brought about by Music at her very *first entry*; inasmuch as she withdraws us at once from any concern with the relation of things outside us, and – as pure Form set free from Matter – shuts us off from the outer world, as it were, to let us gaze into the inmost Essence of ourselves and all things. Consequently our verdict on any piece of music should be based upon a knowledge of those laws whereby the effect of Beauty, the very first effect of Music's mere appearance, advances the most directly to a revelation of her truest character through the agency of the Sublime. It would be the stamp of an absolutely empty piece of music, on the contrary, that it never got beyond a mere prismatic toying with the effect of its first entry, and consequently kept us bound to the relations presented by Music's outermost side to the world of vision.

Upon this side alone, indeed, has Music been given any lasting development; and that by a systematising of her rhythmic structure (*Periodenbau*) which on the one hand has brought her into comparison with Architecture, on the other has made her so much a matter of superficies (*ihr eine Ueberschaulichkeit gegeben hat*) as to expose her to the said false judgment by analogy with Plastic art. Here, in her outermost restriction to banal forms and conventions, she seemed e.g. to Goethe so admirably suited for a standard of poetical proportion (*zur Normirung dichterischer Konzeptionen*). To be able in these conventional forms so to toy with Music's stupendous powers that her own peculiar function, the making known the inner essence of all things, should be avoided like a deluge, for long was deemed by æsthetes the true and only acceptable issue of maturing the art of Tone. But to have pierced through these forms to the innermost essence of Music in such a way that from that inner side he could cast the light of the Clairvoyant on the outer world, and shew us these forms themselves again in nothing but their inner meaning, – this was the work of our great *Beethoven*, whom we therefore have to regard as the true archetype of the Musician.

VI

TWENTIETH
CENTURY

55

RUDOLF STEINER

1861–1925

Rudolf Steiner was an Austrian scholar, lecturer, seer, and the founder of Anthroposophy, now a worldwide movement devoted to the spiritual development of mankind. A truly universal genius, Steiner gave out enough information in his 6000 lectures to found entirely new schools of thought in many disciplines, including music, movement (Eurythmy), education (the Waldorf Schools), the treatment of the handicapped, agriculture (the Bio-Dynamic method), practical occultism, psychology, social philosophy (the Threefold Social Order), architecture (the two Goetheanums in Dornach, Switzerland), and liturgy (the Christian Community).

Steiner was gifted with clairvoyance to an extraordinary degree, but unlike many such people he embarked on the difficult task of submitting his visions to the thinking process, thus becoming a purely conscious and intelligent medium for what he called "knowledge of higher worlds." For a time he was a prominent member of the Theosophical Society (founded in 1875 by H.P. Blavatsky[1] and Henry Olcott), but broke away from it for many reasons, notably his conviction of the pivotal importance of Christianity, as opposed to the Eastern religions to which the Theosophists were more sympathetic. He named his own movement, in contrast to theirs, after the "Wisdom of Man" (*anthropos*) which was for him the indispensable prelude to the "Wisdom of God" (*theos*). This orientation led him to be very practical in his application of Spiritual Science, with the results mentioned above.

In this lecture, Steiner moves, as he did in his life's work as a whole, from nineteenth-century German philosophy to a plain and direct account of what he has learnt for himself of higher worlds.[2] Goethe, Schopenhauer,[3] Nietzsche and Wagner were among his philosophical forebears; his spiritual mentor and initiator was a man of humble station whose identity remains unknown to this day. Steiner said that he never spoke or wrote of anything he had not seen personally with his own inner faculties. But for all his originality –

and he would have been the first to acknowledge this – he was as much in the tradition of Christian Hermeticism as Paracelsus, Boehme, Fludd or Saint-Martin, who likewise accepted the whole phenomenal world as something to be valued and recast through spiritual vision.

In plain language Steiner provides here a key to certain mysteries of music which other authors have only fumbled or hinted at: he shows where it comes from, and how (a modern version of *musica mundana*), and how it affects us (*musica humana*). With his lectures esoteric music theory finally becomes exoteric, for they provide a context in which many of the older ideas at last become comprehensible.

Lecture given Berlin, November 12, 1906,[4] translated by Marie St Goar in Rudolf Steiner, *The Inner Nature of Music and the Experience of Tone*, Spring Valley, N.Y., Anthroposophic Press, 1983, pp. 10-21. Copyright. Used by permission of Anthroposophic Press.

Music, the Astral World, and Devachan

Through spiritual scientific investigation, we see how the world and all nature surrounding us becomes intelligible. It also becomes increasingly clear to us how the outer facts of our surroundings can have a more-or-less profound significance for the inner being of man. Today we will develop further the theme of why music affects the human soul in such a definite, unique way. In doing this, we will cast light on the very foundations of the soul.

To begin with we must ask how a remarkable hereditary line such as we see in the Bach family, for example, can be explained. Within a period of 250 years, nearly thirty members of this family exhibited marked musical talent. Another case is the Bernouilli family, in which a mathematical gift was inherited in a similar way through several generations, and eight of the family members were mathematicians of some renown. Here are two phenomena that can be understood by heredity, yet they are totally different situations.[5]

To those who have sought to penetrate deeply into the nature of things, music appears to be something quite special. Music has always occupied a special place among the arts. Consider this from Schopenhauer's viewpoint. In his book, *The World as Will and Idea*, he speaks of art as a kind of knowledge that leads more directly to the divine than is possible for intellectual knowledge. This opinion of Schopenhauer's is connected with his world-view, which held that everything surrounding us is only a reflection of the human mental image or idea. This reflection arises only because outer things call forth mental images in the human senses, enabling man to relate to the things themselves. Man can know nothing of that which is unable to make an impression on the senses. Schopenhauer speaks physiologically of specific sense impressions. The eye can receive only light impressions; it is insensitive to all other impressions; it can sense only something that is light. Likewise, the ear can sense only tone impressions, and so on. According to Schopenhauer's view, everything observed by man as the world around him reflects itself like a Fata Morgana within him; it is a kind of reflection called forth by the human soul itself.

According to Schopenhauer, there is one possibility of bypassing the mental image. There is one thing perceptible to man for which no outer impression is needed, and this is man himself. All outer things are an eternally changing, eternally shifting Fata Morgana for man. We experience only one thing within ourselves in an immutable manner: ourselves. We experience ourselves in our will, and no detour from outside is required to perceive its effects on us. When we exercise any influence on the outer world, we experience will, we ourselves are this will, and we therefore know what the will is. We know it from our own inner experience, and by analogy we can conclude that this will working within us must exist and be active outside us as well. There must exist forces outside us that are the same as the force active within us as will. These forces Schopenhauer calls "the world will."

Now let us pose the question of how art originates. In line with Schopenhauer's reasoning, the answer would be that art originates through a combination of the Fata Morgana outside us and that within us, through a uniting of both. When an artist, a sculptor, for example, wishes to create an ideal figure, say, of Zeus, and he searches for an archetype, he does not focus on a single human being in order to find the archetype in him; instead, he looks around among many men. He gathers a little from one man, a little from another, and so on. He takes note of everything that represents strength and is noble and outstanding, and from this he forms an archetypal picture of Zeus that corresponds to the thought of Zeus he carries. This is the idea in man, which can be acquired only if the particulars the world offers us are combined within man's mind.

Let us place Schopenhauer's thought alongside one of Goethe's, which finds expression in the words, "In nature, it is the intentions that are significant."[6] We find Schopenhauer and Goethe in complete agreement with one another. Both thinkers believe that there are intentions in nature that she can neither bring completely to expression nor attain in her creations, at least not with the details. The creative artist tries to recognize these intentions in nature; he tries to combine them and represent them in a picture. One now comprehends Goethe, who says that art is a revelation of nature's secret intentions and that the creative artist reveals the continuation of nature.[7] The artist takes nature into himself; he causes it to arise in him again and then lets it go forth from him. It is as if nature

253

were not complete and in man found the possibility of guiding her work to an end. In man, nature finds her completion, her fulfillment, and she rejoices, as it were, in man and his works.[8]

In the human heart lies the capability of thinking things through to the end and of pouring forth what has been the intention of nature. Goethe sees nature as the great, creative artist that cannot completely attain her intentions, presenting us with something of a riddle. The artist, however, solves these riddles; he thinks the intentions of nature through to the end and expresses them in his works.

Schopenhauer says that this holds true of all the arts except music. Music stands on a higher level than all the other arts. Why? Schopenhauer finds the answer, saying that in all the other creative arts, such as sculpture and painting, the mental images must be combined before the hidden intentions of nature are discovered. Music, on the other hand, the melodies and harmonies of tones, is nature's direct expression. The musician hears the pulse of the divine will that flows through the world; he hears how this will expresses itself in tones. The musician thus stands closer to the heart of the world than all other artists; in him lives the faculty of representing the world will. Music is the expression of the will of nature, while all the other arts are expressions of the idea of nature. Since music flows nearer the heart of the world and is a direct expression of its surging and swelling, it also directly affects the human soul. It streams into the soul like the divine in its different forms. Hence, it is understandable that the effects of music on the human soul are so direct, so powerful, so elemental.

Let us turn from the standpoint of significant individuals such as Schopenhauer and Goethe concerning the sublime art of music to the standpoint of spiritual science, allowing it to cast its light on this question. If we do this, we find that what man *is* makes comprehensible why harmonies and melodies affect him. Again, we return to the three states of consciousness that are possible for the human being and to his relationship to the three worlds to which he belongs during any one of these three states of consciousness.

Of these three states of consciousness, there is only one fully known to the ordinary human being, since he is unaware of himself while in either of the other two. From them, he brings no conscious recollection or impression back into his familiar state of consciousness, that is, the one we characterized as waking day-consciousness. The second state of consciousness is familiar to an extent to the ordinary human being. It is dream-filled sleep, which presents simple daily experiences to man in symbols. The third state of consciousness is dreamless sleep, a state of a certain emptiness for the ordinary human being.

Initiation, however, transforms the three states of consciousness.

First, man's dream-life changes. It is no longer chaotic, no longer a reproduction of daily experiences often rendered in tangled symbols. Instead, a new world unfolds before man in dream-filled sleep. A world filled with flowing colors and radiant light-being surrounds him, the astral world.[9] This is no newly created world. It is new only for a person who, until now, had not advanced beyond the lower state of day-consciousness. Actually, this astral world is always present and continuously surrounds the human being. It is a real world, as real as the world surrounding us that appears to us as reality. Once a person has been initiated, has undergone initiation, he becomes acquainted with this wonderful world. He learns to be conscious in it with a consciousness as clear – no even clearer – than his ordinary day-consciousness. He also becomes familiar with his own astral body and learns to live in it consciously. The basic experience in this new world that unfolds before man is one of living and weaving in a world of colors and light. After his initiation, man begins to awaken during his ordinary dream-filled sleep; it is as though he feels himself borne upward on a surging sea of flowing light and colors. This glimmering light and these flowing colors are living beings. This experience of conscious dream-filled sleep then transmits itself into man's entire life in waking day-consciousness, and he learns to see these beings in everyday life as well.

Man attains the third state of consciousness when he is capable of transforming dreamless sleep into a conscious state. This world that man learns to enter shows itself to him at first only partially, but in due time more and more is revealed. Man lives in this world for increasingly longer periods. He is conscious in it and experiences something very significant there.

Man can arrive at perception of the second world, the astral world, only if he undergoes the discipline of so-called "great stillness."[10] He must become still, utterly still, within himself. The great peace must precede the awakening in the astral world. This deep stillness becomes more and more pronounced when man approaches the third state of consciousness, the state in which he begins to have sensations in dreamless sleep. The colors of the astral world become increasingly transparent, and the light becomes ever clearer and at the same time spiritualized. Man has the sensation that he himself lives in this color and this light, as if they do not surround him but rather he himself is color and light. He feels himself astrally within this astral world, and he feels afloat in a great, deep peace. Gradually, this deep stillness begins to resound spiritually, softly at first, then louder and louder. The world of colors and light is permeated with resounding tones. In this third state of consciousness that man now approaches, the colorful world of the astral realm in which he dwelt up to now becomes suffused with sound. This new dimension that opens to man is Devachan,[11] the so-

255

called mental world, and he enters this wondrous world through the portals of the "great stillness." Through the great stillness, the tone of this other world rings out to him. This is how the Devachanic world truly appears.

Many theosophical books contain other descriptions of Devachan, but they are not based on personal experience of the reality of the world. Leadbeater,[12] for example, gives an accurate description of the astral plane and of experiences there, but his description of Devachan is inaccurate. It is merely a construction modeled on the astral plane and is not experienced personally by him. All descriptions that do not describe how a tone rings out from the other side are incorrect and are not based on actual perception. Resounding tone is the particular characteristic of Devachan, at least essentially. Of course, one must not imagine that the Devachanic world does not radiate colors as well. It is penetrated by light emanating from the astral world, for the two worlds are not separated; the astral world penetrates the Devachanic world. The essence of the Devachanic realm, however, lies in tone. That which was light in the great stillness now begins to resound.

On a still higher plane of Devachan, tone becomes something akin to words. All true inspiration originates on this plane, and in this region dwell inspired authors. Here they experience a real permeation with the truths of the higher worlds. This phenomenon is entirely possible.

We must bear in mind that not only the initiate lives in these worlds. The only difference between the ordinary human being and the initiate is that an initiate undergoes these various altered conditions consciously. The states that ordinary man undergoes unconsciously again and again merely change into conscious ones for him. The ordinary human being passes through these three worlds time after time, but he knows nothing about it, because he is conscious neither of himself nor of his experiences there. Nevertheless, he returns with some of the effects that these experiences called forth in him. When he awakens in the morning, not only is he physically rejuvenated by the sleep, but he also brings back art from those worlds. When a painter, for example, goes far beyond the reality of colors in the physical world in his choice of the tones and color harmonies that he paints on his canvas, it is none other than a recollection, albeit an unconscious one, of experiences in the astral world. Where has he seen these tones, these shining colors? Where has he experienced them? They are the after-effects of the astral experiences he has had during the night. Only this flowing ocean of light and colors, of beauty and radiating, glimmering depths, where he has dwelt during sleep, gives him the possibility of using these colors among which he existed. With the dense, earthy colors of our physical world, however, he is unable to reproduce anything close to the ideal that he has experienced and that lives in him. We thus see in painting a shadow-image, a precipitation of the astral world in the physical world, and we see how the effects of the astral realm bear magnificent, marvelous fruits in man.

In great art there are wonderful things that are much more comprehensible to a spiritual scientist, because he discerns their origin. I am thinking, for instance, of two paintings by Leonardo da Vinci that hang in the Louvre in Paris. One portrays Bacchus, the other St John. Both paintings show the same face; evidently the same model was employed for both. It is not their outward narrative effect, therefore, that makes them totally different from each other. The artistic mysteries of light contained in the paintings are based more purely on their effects of color and light. The painting of Bacchus displays an unusual glistening reddish light that is poured over the body's surface. It speaks of voluptuousness concealed beneath the skin and thus characterizes Bacchus's nature. It is as if the body were imbibing the light and, permeated with its own voluptuous nature, exuded it again. The painting of John, on the other hand, displays a chaste, yellowish hue. It seems as if the color is only playing about the body. The body allows the light only to surround its forms; it does not wish to absorb anything from outside into itself. An utterly unselfish corporeality, fully pure and chaste, addresses the viewer from this painting.

A spiritual scientist understands all this. One must not believe, however, that an artist is always intellectually aware of what is concealed in his work. The precipitations of his astral vision need not penetrate as far as physical consciousness in order to live in his works. Leonardo da Vinci perhaps did not know the occult laws by which he created his paintings – that is not what matters – but he followed them out of his instinctive feeling. We thus see in painting the shadow, the precipitation, of the astral world in our physical realm.

The composer conjures a still higher world; he conjures the Devachanic world into the physical world. The melodies and harmonies that speak to us from the compositions of our great masters are actually faithful copies of the Devachanic world. If we are at all capable of experiencing a foretaste of the spiritual world, this would be found in the melodies and harmonies of music and the effects it has on the human soul.

We return once again to the nature of the human being. We find first of all the physical world, then the etheric body, then the astral body, and finally the "I," of which man first became conscious at the end of the Atlantean age.[13]

When man sleeps, the astral body and the sentient soul release themselves from the lower nature of man. Physical man lies in bed connected with his etheric body. All his other members loosen and dwell in the astral and Devachanic worlds. In these worlds, specifically in the Devachanic world, the soul absorbs into itself the world of tones. When he awakens each morning, man actually has passed through an element of music, an ocean of tones. A musical person is one whose physical nature is such that it follows these impressions, though he need not know this. A sense of musical pleasure is based on nothing other than the right accord between the harmonies brought from beyond and the tones and melodies here. We experience musical pleasure when outer tones correspond with those within.[14]

Regarding the musical element, the cooperation of sentient soul and sentient body[15] is of special significance. One must understand that all consciousness arises through a kind of overcoming of the outer world. What comes to consciousness in man as pleasure or joy signifies victory of the spiritual over merely animated corporeality [*Körperlich-Lebendige*], the victory of the sentient soul over the sentient body. It is possible for one who returns from sleep with the inner vibrations to intensify these tones and to perceive the victory of the sentient soul over the sentient body, so that the soul feels itself stronger than the body. In the effects of a minor key man can always perceive how the vibrations of the sentient body grow stronger, while in a major key the sentient soul vibrates more intensely and predominates over the sentient body. When the minor third is played, one feels pain in the soul, the predominance of the sentient body, but when the major third resounds, it announces the victory of the soul.

Now we can grasp the basis of the profound significance of music. We understand why music has been elevated throughout the ages to the highest position among the arts by those who know the relationships of the inner life, why even those who do not know these relationships grant music a special place, and why music stirs the deepest strings of our soul, causing them to resound.

Alternating between sleeping and waking, man continuously passes from the physical to the astral and from these worlds to the Devachanic world, a reflection of his overall course of incarnations.[16] When in death he leaves the physical body, he rises through the astral world up into Devachan. There he finds his true home; there he finds his place of rest. This solemn repose is followed by his re-entry into the physical world, and in this way man passes continuously from one world to another.

The human being, however, experiences the elements of the Devachanic world as his own innermost nature, because they are his primeval home. The vibrations flowing through the spiritual world are felt in the innermost depths of his being. In a sense, man experiences the astral and physical as mere sheaths. His primeval home is in Devachan, and the echoes from this homeland, the spiritual world, resound in him in the harmonies and melodies of the physical world. These echoes pervade the lower world with inklings of a glorious and wonderful existence; they churn up man's innermost being and thrill it with vibrations of purest joy and sublime spirituality, something that this world cannot provide. Painting speaks to the astral corporeality, but the world of tone speaks to the innermost being of man. As long as a person is not yet initiated, his homeland, the Devachanic world, is given to him in music. This is why music is held in such high esteem by all who sense such a relationship. Schopenhauer also senses this in a kind of instinctive intuition and expresses it in his philosophical formulations.

Through esoteric knowledge the world, and above all the arts, become comprehensible to us. As it is above so it is below, and as below so above.[17] One who understands this expression in its higher sense learns to recognize increasingly the preciousness in the things of this world, and gradually he experiences as precious recognition the imprints of ever higher and higher worlds. In music, too, he experiences the image of a higher world.

The work of an architect, built in stone to withstand centuries, is something that originates in man's inner being and is then transformed into matter. The same is true of the works of sculptors and painters. These works are present externally and have taken on form.

Musical creations, however, must be generated anew again and again. They flow onward in the surge and swell of their harmonies and melodies, a reflection of the soul, which in its incarnations must always experience itself in the onward-flowing stream of time. Just as the human soul is an evolving entity, so its reflection here on earth is a flowing one. The deep effect of music is due to this kinship. Just as the human soul flows downward from its home in Devachan and flows back to it again, so do its shadows, the tones, the harmonies.[18] Hence the intimate effect of music on the soul. Out of music the most primordial kinship speaks to the soul; in the most inwardly deep sense, sounds of home rebound from it. From the soul's primeval home, the spiritual world, the sounds of music are borne across to us and speak comfortingly and encouragingly to us in surging melodies and harmonies.

56

HAZRAT INAYAT KHAN
1882–1927

Inayat Khan, born to an old musical family in Baroda (NW India),
was an eminent singer and vina player in the North Indian tradition.
He had a successful career as a performer and lecturer at courts and
concert halls throughout India, and in 1910 began tours of Russia,
Europe and the United States. The West remained his destined field
of activity. In Paris from 1911 to 1914 he was befriended by Edmond
Bailly whose bookshop, "L'Art Indépendant,"[1] had been a center for
the symbolists and esotericists of the 1880s and 1890s. He was also
in contact, briefly, with Claude Debussy, but he certainly did not
inspire the *Prélude à l'Après-midi d'un Faune* (1892-4) as has been
claimed! Later in his comparatively short life he gave up practical
music to devote himself entirely to Sufism, of which he felt himself to
be the mouthpiece for the West, founding the Sufi Movement which
continues today, headed by his son Pir Vilayat Khan.

Inayat Khan, in his ecumenical acceptance of the truth in all
religions and in his devotional style of spirituality, seems closer in
spirit to those Hindu apostles of the "bhaktic" path such as
Ramakrishna and Vivekananda than to the modern movements
within his own religion of Islam. No doubt his Indian background
was partly responsible for this. But since Christianity in its universal
and public dimension is essentially a religion of love, any effective
revival of Western spirituality has to take this form, whether its
devotion be to Jesus, to Krishna, to the Mother, or to Allah.

Inayat Khan's published works, like Rudolf Steiner's, are largely
transcripts of his lectures. These chapters come from a series given
in 1921, called simply *Music*.[2] They have been chosen to show his
ideas on the effects of music at two extremes: on physical matter,
where he joins the widespread consensus on its magical powers, also
found here in Plotinus (no. 6), Iamblichus (no. 7), the Brethren of
Purity (no. 15), Ficino (no. 27), Agrippa (no. 29) and Fludd
(no. 33); and on the soul's development. Inayat Khan is an
evolutionist: he believes, like many Sufis, in the progressive

development of life-forms from mineral, vegetable and animal to human, and thence to consciousness, spiritual striving, and finally union with God. As Beethoven called music "a higher wisdom than philosophy" (see no. 44), and Schopenhauer "the direct copy of the will itself . . . the metaphysical to everything physical in the world" (no. 48), so Inayat Khan calls it "the bridge over the gulf between form and the formless," which enables man himself to cross that gulf.

Source   *The Sufi Message of Hazrat Inayat Khan*, vol. II, *The Mysticism of Sound; Music; the Power of the Word; the Cosmic Language*, Geneva, Wassenaar, 1962, pp. 106-9, 147-52. Reprinted by kind permission of the Sufi Movement.

Chapter VII   The manifestation of sound on the physical plane

Modern science has discovered recently, that on certain plates the impression of sound can be made clearly visible.[3] In reality the impression of sound falls clearly on all objects, only it is not always visible. It remains for a certain time on an object and then it disappears. Those who have scientifically studied the different impressions that are made by sound, have found the clear forms of leaves and flowers and other things of nature, which is proof of the belief held by the ancient people, that the creative source in its first step towards manifestation was audible, and in its next step visible.[4] It also shows that all we see in this objective world, every form, has been constructed by sound and is the phenomenon of sound.

When we look further into this subject from a mystical point of view, we see that every syllable has a certain effect. As the form of every sound is different, so every syllable has a special effect; and therefore every sound made or word spoken before an object has charged that object with a certain magnetism. This explains to us the method of the healers, teachers and mystics, who by the power of sound charged an object with their healing power, with their power of thought. And when this object was given as a drink or as food, it brought about the desired result. Besides that, many masters of occult sciences, who have communicated with the unseen beings by the power of sound, have done still greater things. By the power of sound they have created beings; in other words by the power of sound they gave a body to a soul, to a spirit, making it into a kind of being which is not yet a physical being but a being of a higher kind. They called such beings Muwakkals; and they worked through these beings, using them in any direction of life for a certain purpose.

The physical effect of sound has also a great influence upon the human body. The whole mechanism, the muscles, the blood circulation, the nerves, are all moved by the power of vibration. As

261

there is resonance for every sound, so the human body is a living resonator for sound. Although by sound one can easily produce a resonance in all such substances as brass and copper, yet there is no greater and more living resonator of sound than the human body. Sound has an effect on each atom of the body, for each atom resounds; on all glands, on the circulation of the blood and on pulsation, sound has an effect.

In India a feast is celebrated every year where the people commemorate the great heroes of the past and mourn over their life's tragedy; and certain instruments are played, certain drums, sometimes very badly and sometimes better. And there are some who on hearing those drums instantly fall into ecstasy; because the sound of the drum goes directly into their whole system, bringing it to a certain pitch where they feel ecstasy. And when they are in ecstasy they can jump into the fire and come out without being burned; they can cut themselves with a sword and they are instantly healed; they can eat fire and they are not burned. One can see it every year at that particular time.

They call such a condition *Hál*. Hál means the same as condition; it is an appropriate term for it, because by hearing the drum they think of that condition and then they enter into it. They need not be very educated to go into that trance, nor very evolved; sometimes they are very ordinary people; but sound can have such effect upon them that they are moved to a higher ecstasy.

The question was raised by a physician in San Francisco, Dr Abrams, of how the sudden healing of a sword-cut in ecstasy is brought about. Although all other doctors disagreed with him, he intuitively thought that by the help of vibrations illnesses could be cured. But instead of looking for the power of vibrations in the word, he wanted to find it in electricity. Yet the principle is the same: he took the rate of vibrations of the body, and by the same rate of electrical vibrations he treated the elements of the body. He began to get some good results, but it is a subject which will need at least a century to develop fully. It is a vast subject and this is just a beginning; therefore there is still no end to the errors; but at the same time, if people could bear with it, after many years something might come out of it which could be of great use to the medical world.

This example shows that when a man can cut himself and be healed at the same time, he has created such a condition in his body that its vibrations are able to heal any wound immediately. But when that same person is not in that condition, then if there is a cut, he cannot be healed; he must be in that particular condition; the vibrations must be working at that particular rate.

There is a school of Sufis in the East which is called the Rafai school. Their main object is to increase the power of spirit over matter. Experiments such as eating fire or jumping into the fire or cutting the body are made in order to get power and control over matter. The secret of the whole phenomenon is that by the power of words they try to tune their body to that pitch of vibration where no fire, no cut, nothing, can touch it. Because the vibrations of their body are equal to fire, therefore the fire has no effect.

Now coming to the question of music, why has music an effect upon a person, why does someone naturally like music? It is not because he is trained in it or because it is a habit, but because attraction is a natural effect of sound. One may ask why it is that some people have no feeling for music. It is because that feeling has not yet been created in them. The day when they begin to feel life, they will begin to enjoy music also.

It is on this account that the wise considered the science of sound to be the most important science in every condition of life: in healing, in teaching, in evolving, and in accomplishing all things in life. It is on this foundation that the science of Zikr was developed by the Sufis, and that the Yogis made Mantra Shastra. By Zikr is not meant here one particular phrase, but a science of words. In the spoken word finer vibrations act. The vibrations of the air are nothing; but because every word has a breath behind it, and breath has a spiritual vibration, the action of breath works physically while at the same time breath itself is an electric current. The breath is not only the air, but an electric current; therefore it is an inner vibration.

Apart from the meaning a word has, even the sound of the syllables can bring about a good result or a disastrous result. Those who know about this can recall several instances in history when, through the mistake of a poet who did not use the proper words in the praise of a king, his kingdom was destroyed. And yet how little one thinks about this! In saying, "Well, I may have said it, but I did not mean it," people believe that by saying something they have done nothing as long as they did not mean it. But even saying something without meaning has a great effect upon life.

The science of sound can be used in education, in business, in industry, in commerce, in politics, in order to bring about a desired result. But the best use of it is made in spiritual evolution; by the power of sound or word one can evolve spiritually and experience all the different stages of spiritual perfection. Music is the best medium for awakening the soul; there is nothing better. Music is the shortest, the most direct way to God; but one must know what music and how to use it.

Chapter XIV Spiritual development by the aid of music

The word "spiritual" does not apply to goodness, or to wonder-working, the power of producing miracles, or to great intellectual power. The whole of life in all its aspects is one single music; and the real spiritual attainment is to tune one's self to the harmony of this perfect music.

What is it that keeps man back from spiritual attainment? It is the denseness of this material existence, and the fact that he is unconscious of his spiritual being. His limitations prevent the free flow and movement which is the nature and character of life. Take for instance this denseness. There is a rock, and you want to produce sound from it, but it does not give any resonance;[5] it does not answer your desire to produce sound. String or wire on the contrary will give an answer to the tone you want. You strike them and they answer. There are objects which give resonance; you wish to produce a sound in them, and they respond; they make your music complete. And so it is with human nature. One person is heavy and dull; you tell him something, but he cannot understand; you speak to him, but he will not hear. He will not respond to music, to beauty, or to art. What is it? It is denseness.

There is another person who is ready to appreciate and understand music and poetry, or beauty in any form, in character or in manner. Beauty is appreciated in every form by such a person; and it is this which is the awakening of the soul, which is the living condition of the heart. It is this which is the real spiritual attainment. Spiritual attainment is making the spirit alive, becoming conscious. When man is not conscious of soul and spirit, but only of his material being, he is dense; he is far removed from spirit.

What is spirit and what is matter? The difference between spirit and matter is like the difference between water and ice: frozen water is ice, and melted ice is water. It is spirit in its denseness which we call matter; it is matter in its fineness which may be called spirit. Once a materialist said to me, "I do not believe in any spirit or soul or hereafter. I believe in eternal matter." I said to him, "Your belief is not very different from mine, only that which you call eternal matter I call spirit; it is a difference in terms. There is nothing to dispute about, because we both believe in eternity; and so long as we meet in eternity, what difference does it make, if the one calls it matter, and the other calls it spirit? It is one life from beginning to end."

Beauty is born of harmony. What is harmony? Harmony is right proportion, in other words, right rhythm. And what is life? Life is the outcome of harmony. At the back of the whole creation is harmony, and the whole creation is harmony. Intelligence longs to attain to the perfection of harmony. What man calls happiness, comfort, profit or gain, all he longs for and wishes to attain is harmony; in a smaller or greater degree he is longing for harmony. Even in attaining the most mundane things, he always wishes for harmony. But very often he does not adopt the right methods. Very often his methods are wrong. The object attained by both good and bad methods is the same, but the way one tries to attain it makes it right or wrong. It is not the object which is wrong, it is the method one adopts to attain it.

No one, whatever his station in life, wishes for disharmony, for all suffering, pain and trouble is lack of harmony.

To obtain spirituality is to realize that the whole universe is one symphony; in this every individual is one note, and his happiness lies in becoming perfectly attuned to the harmony of the universe. It is not following a certain religion that makes one spiritual, or having a certain belief, or being a fanatic in regard to one idea, or even by becoming too good to live in this world. There are many good people who do not even understand what spirituality means. They are very good, but they do not yet know what ultimate good is. Ultimate good is harmony itself. For instance all the different principles and beliefs of the religions of the world, taught and proclaimed by priests and teachers but which man is not always able to follow and express, come naturally from the heart of someone who attunes himself to the rhythm of the universe. Every action, every word he speaks, every feeling he has, every sentiment he expresses, is harmonious; they are all virtues, they are all religion. It is not following a religion, it is living a religion, making one's life a religion, which is necessary.

Music is a miniature of the harmony of the whole universe, for the harmony of the universe is life itself, and man, being a miniature of the universe, shows harmonious and inharmonious chords in his pulsation, in the beat of his heart, in his vibration, rhythm and tone. His health or illness, his joy or discomfort, all show the music or lack of music in his life.

And what does music teach us? Music helps us to train ourselves in harmony, and it is this which is the magic or the secret behind music. When you hear music that you enjoy, it tunes you and puts you in harmony with life. Therefore man needs music; he longs for music. Many say that they do not care for music, but these have not heard music. If they really heard music, it would touch their souls, and then certainly they could not help loving it. If not, it would only mean that they had not heard music sufficiently, and had not made their heart calm and quiet in order to listen to it, and to enjoy and appreciate it. Besides music develops that faculty by which one learns to appreciate all that is good and beautiful in the form of art and science, and in the form of music and poetry one can then appreciate every aspect of beauty.

What deprives man of all the beauty around him is his heaviness of body or heaviness of heart. He is pulled down to earth, and by that everything becomes limited; but when he shakes off that heaviness and joy comes, he feels light. All good tendencies such as gentleness and tolerance, forgiveness, love and appreciation, all these beautiful qualities, come by being light; light in the mind, in the soul and in the body.

Where does music come from? Where does the dance come from? It all comes from that natural and spiritual life which is within. When that spiritual life springs forth, it lightens all the burdens that man has. It makes his life smooth, as though floating on the ocean of life. The faculty of appreciation makes one light. Life is just like the ocean. When there is no appreciation, no receptivity, man sinks like a piece of iron or stone to the bottom of the sea. He cannot float like a boat, which is hollow and which is receptive.

The difficulty in the spiritual path is always what comes from ourselves. Man does not like to be a pupil, he likes to be a teacher. If man only knew that the greatness and perfection of the great ones who have come from time to time to this world, was in their being pupils and not in teaching! The greater the teacher, the better pupil he was. He learned from everyone, the great and the lowly, the wise and the foolish, the old and the young. He learned from their lives, and studied human nature in all its spheres.

Someone learning to tread the spiritual path must become like an empty cup, in order that the wine of music and harmony may be poured into his heart. When a person comes to me and says, "Here I am, can you help me spiritually," and I answer, "Yes," very often he says, "I want to know first of all what you think about life or death, or the beginning and the end." And then I wonder what his attitude will be if his previously conceived opinion does not agree with mine. He wants to learn, and yet he does not want to be empty. That means going to the stream of water with a covered cup; wanting the water, and yet the cup is covered, covered with preconceived ideas. But where have the preconceived ideas come from? No idea can be called one's own. All ideas have been learned from one source or another; yet in time one comes to think they are one's own. And for those ideas a person will argue and dispute, although they do not satisfy him fully; but at the same time they are his battleground, and they will continue to keep his cup covered. Mystics therefore have adopted a different way. They have learned a different course, and that course is self-effacement, or in other words, unlearning what one has learned; and this is how one can become an empty cup.

In the East it is said that the first thing to be learned is how to become a pupil. One may think that in this way one loses one's individuality; but what is individuality? Is it not what is collected? What are one's ideas and opinions? They are just collected knowledge, and this knowledge should be unlearned.

One would think that the character of the mind is such that what one learns is engraved upon it; how then can one unlearn it? Unlearning is completing this knowledge. To see a person and say, "That person is wicked, I dislike him" that is learning. To see further and recognize something good in that person, to begin to like him or to pity him, that is unlearning. When you see the goodness in someone whom you have called wicked, you have unlearned. You have unravelled that knot. First one learns by seeing with one eye; then one learns by seeing with two eyes, and that makes one's sight complete.

All that we have learned in this world is partial knowledge, but when this is uprooted by another point of view, then we have knowledge in its completed form. This is what is called mysticism. Why is it called mysticism? Because it cannot be put into words. Words will show us one side of it, but the other side is beyond words.

The whole manifestation is duality, the duality which makes us intelligent; and behind the duality is unity. If we do not rise beyond duality and move towards unity, we do not attain perfection, we do not attain spirituality

This does not mean that our learning is of no use. It is of great use. It gives us the power of discrimination and of discerning differences. This makes the intelligence sharp and the sight keen, so that we understand the value of things and their use. It is all part of human evolution and all useful. So we must learn first, and unlearn afterwards. One does not look at the sky first when one is standing on the earth. First one must look at the earth and see what it offers to learn and to observe; but at the same time one should not think that one's life's purpose is fulfilled by looking only at the earth. The fulfilment of life's purpose is in looking at the sky.

What is wonderful about music is that it helps man to concentrate or mediate independently of thought; and therefore music seems to be the bridge over the gulf between form and the formless. If there is anything intelligent, effective and at the same time formless, it is music. Poetry suggets form, line and colour suggest form, but music suggests no form. It creates also that resonance which vibrates through the whole being, lifting the thought above the denseness of matter; it almost turns matter into spirit, into its original condition, through the harmony of vibrations touching every atom of one's whole being.

Beauty of line and colour can go so far and no further; the joy of fragrance can go a little further; but music touches our innermost being and in that way produces new life, a life that gives exaltation to the whole being, raising it to that perfection in which lies the fulfilment of man's life.

57

PIERRE JEAN JOUVE
1887–1976

This French poet grew up as an avid music-lover and amateur pianist. The adherent, for a time, of an almost nihilistic philosophy, he underwent a dual conversion in the 1920s, to Roman Catholicism and to the Freudian view of the psyche. His poetry consequently reflects an involvement with issues of sex, death and redemption. Jouve was a man of broad interests and sympathies, an intellectual in the best modern sense. As a translator, he made French versions of several of Shakespeare's plays. As an art critic, he was one of the first to appreciate the painter Balthus. His musical interests led him to write studies of Mozart's *Don Giovanni* and of Berg's *Wozzeck*.

The first part of this essay treats music from a viewpoint shared with many, if not most of our writers: that the nature of music is unchanging, and consequently that what it could do in ancient Greece or India, it can do today, because the laws of harmony that rule both macrocosm and microcosm do not alter. But in the second part he acknowledges that twentieth-century music, like all the arts, has taken a new turn that separates it completely – he mentions a "fracture" – from the past. Those who regard the arts from a deeper viewpoint tend to react to this in one of three ways. Some reject modernism outright: this is the response of the traditionalists for whom all progress, in the arts or elsewhere, is an unnecessary and probably a perilous excursion down a blind alley. For them the deviation began in the Renaissance, if not actually in Greece. Next, some accept it as a necessary evil, like a painful operation: that is Cyril Scott's view of the "ultra-discordant" music of Schoenberg and others (see no. 60). Thirdly, there are those who try to understand what is happening in the arts not as a phase to be outgrown, not as something to be judged by the criteria of a restrictive education, but as something to be entered into just as its creators have felt themselves compelled to enter into it. This essay exemplifies the last approach. With prophetic insight, Jouve recognizes in Bartók's *Music for Strings, Percussion and Celesta* the very conception of sonority – he calls it "blocks of sound" – that was to become, after World War II, one of the starting points for a new music, of which Pierre Boulez and Karlheinz Stockhausen (see no. 61) were the acknowledged pioneers, and which made no secret of its transcendent intentions.

Source "La Musique et l'état mystique," in *La Nouvelle Revue Française*, vol. 51 (July, 1938), pp. 135-9. Reprinted by kind permission of Dr Catherine Jouve.

Music and the Mystic State

We are completely ignorant of the essence of Music. To say that it is rhythm and consequently active magic does not explain the power of melody, nor on the other hand the force of counterpoint. To say that by means of sound, like a canal, it causes the affective mass of our unconscious (perhaps previously captivated) to rise, is to state a truism without arriving at a single substantial detail. To say that Music makes our spirits rejoice with sonorous number[1] is no less true a proposition, but how much good is that to describe a world at once integral and closed, a world of desire, nostalgia, memory, energy – all the living powers of Destiny? The living powers of Destiny, I wrote: that is to say the powers of a being that are fettered by the laws of proportion and repetition, which themselves comprise the fate of a being. As though in a magnificent hysteria common to all mankind, the secrets of the most ardent love were buried, though able to be liberated, invisible to ordinary life, ungraspable even by thought, they appear with all their force, simple and naked, as soon as three notes of music are heard, and their immense vapors, all the more formidable because long confined, vapors of memory, of time past and of time future intuitively known, forthwith envelop the clear consciousness which they exalt, while also disarming it of its principal defenses; in this manner it seems that the eternal, subjectively colored by passion and expectation, comes to be present at each instant, and that which escapes into the past, immediately replaced without even having been able to become memory, is not lost by any means because it is placed, or replaced, in the eternal whence it came. All in all, Music makes us plunge into the eternal with the most personal part of our being, because with our most fervent pleasure, and makes of the instant a state of passionate expectation of the eternal. Through Music, the least able person is transported into his own abilities. Through Music, time is absorbed into religious expectation, since the instant is immediately open to eternity.

Within this relation there move the infinitely varied values of Music, and then it is true that instinct is disciplined there by numbers, vague energy by precise energy, and the unconscious is shattered by transcendence beyond form. Music would offer an epitome and an illustration of the whole spirit, if it also had the power to express clear ideas – if it could name, – a supreme illumination that it can never achieve. It would describe the whole tableau of the deeper instincts, if it were not as it were tied to the fundamental radiation of sympathy, which prevents it from knowing the forces of destruction in their entirety. Music does not touch on death, on destruction, except through forms that are too human, still too charged with life; or else it distances itself from them, as one might say, metaphysically, to the degree that it considers them, to the extent of making us "happy" to consider them as if we were beyond them. In Music, death can only be like the death of Don Giovanni: sublime; and Hell can only be the Hell of Orpheus. Thus it is possible to speak of the reconciling qualities of Music, but it is an error to speak of its ethical values; Music preserves everything from its own transcendence if it possesses the genuine quality of music (but only then), and would lead the listener to a certain dangerous level of the erotic, if it were not actually the occasion of scandal.

In the supreme works of Music (those of Palestrina, Monteverdi, J.S. Bach, Mozart, Beethoven, Schubert), the religious expectation signified by the instant plunged in the eternal is raised, by way of suffering and far beyond suffering, to its maximum efficacy. We are carried forward, we are thrown into a high and luminous region, or again (the division of the spirits' operations into high and low being more and more difficult to justify) into a region detached from all the objective zones that we can ascertain and name, either in ourselves or outside. Hence the poverty of the descriptions of Music: one cannot describe a mental abyss, nor even find any words to say that there is an abyss. But in the seduction of the concert a continual abyss is produced in which one can *see*, by a perspicacious observation of the listeners, the human personality dissolving.

One comes to think that the higher states of Music have a relationship, or at least a resemblance, with the states of the soul's second life, where by refusal and annihilation of itself and by absorption in the real divine Substance it obtains the knowledge and the joys that have been called by the term "ecstasy." Mystical existence, religious in tendency and representation, is always an effective perdition, at the level of the object as much interior as exterior, and a simultaneous submersal in a current of being of a different nature; and this double movement seems to stem at once from the point where the psyche is most attached to the body, and from a reality revealed to the soul, the two actions being on a certain threshold. All the same, one must admit that there is an antinomy between mysticism and art, because the mystic begins by denying what is most important for art: the supremely sensual order which clothes the object with beauty. And yet all "great" art, paradoxically, must contain a mystical intention. The works with which we live – Gregorian chant, the cathedral, French sculpture of the thirteenth century, Giotto's frescoes, Bach's chorales, Mozart's symphonies, the paintings of Goya and the poetry of Shakespeare or Baudelaire – prove this mystical appetite, completely unassuageable because it is in the bosom of the most powerful sensuality, some would say the most infernal. Music approaches closest to the goal which cannot be attained. Music, which has no need for representations, which makes use of no language, established in fact on the *Nada*, on negation, is placed before every other art on the road of perfect accomplishment within the Promise.

I had just re-read these notes when I heard, for the second time, the *Music for Strings, Percussion and Celesta* of Béla Bartók.[2]

No work of modern music, with the exception of Alban Berg's, can support so well the title of this essay; just as no work of music is more modern. It is here that one measures the distance, and the fracture, that separates our musical understanding from that which the people of the nineteenth century still had; here that one sees forming, as in a gigantic mold, the powers, the proportions, the *substances* of which older music certainly could not conceive that they might ever exist as materials of art. That is what one must describe first of all: everything is unusual, everything is necessary, and the discipline of it all is formidable. As a consequence, the greatest imaginable quantity of energy is gathered under a strict discipline, to such an extent that the form, one might say, disappears: it is no longer on the listener's level. From this point of view Bartók, coming from Bach and Schoenberg, becomes anti-Bach by the play of complexity. The very structures at the foundations are renewed, as if tonal and atonal ceased to oppose one another; through ambiguity, atonality is capable of carrying certain tonal illusions. The extraordinary polyvalence of sounds, of contrapuntal lines, of rhythms and of general movements, is forged into a unity through the extraordinary discipline which we mention: a unity that is not simple, indiscernable; a unity that is mysterious and lucid, and irresistible.

The enterprise of a child who would be an old man, this sound-construction makes of the unconscious the definitive actor of the drama: the unconscious of the cosmic darkness, of the desires, the anguish, the inordinate power of Creation. In certain places (the Adagio) it is a matter of a kind of "sound-block," an enormous quantity of organized sound whose organization escapes us, which reabsorbs both counterpoint and melody, but is equally contrary to the notion of harmony, whose nature is a sort of active texture. The sound-block – for example, in the Allegro, that panting cadenza of the piano, a gauche, overhanging cadenza with a dull sound one might call off-white – the block advances, retreats, evolves, as if a vast superhuman being were presenting itself to our eyes, a little ponderously but with a demonic power; were shining forth, beginning to feel out the world in order to reveal its truth. For this sound-block, the endpoint of all music, is so to speak the beginning of another music: it *opens* something. The opening, the vista, is being formed; the substance in which we are has no longer anything human about it, in the terribly empty sense that the society from which we come has given to this term; the ugliness of the world in which we were living just now becomes fantasmagoria, error; the real world is the one that this mass of incandescent sound points out to us, and leads us into. "I predict a fabulous opera," writes Rimbaud. Or again, also Rimbaud, "the reasonable song of the angels." One cannot overemphasize the importance of seeing the "fabulous opera" projected and brought out of the subjectivity of the dream in which it still rested in Rimbaud's time.

The *Music* of Béla Bartók, coming at the peak of a musician's magnificent career, gives new strength to every modern artist in so far as it is concerned with strength, but it is even more admirable in being altogether *creation*, and accepting this destiny with a formidable gravity. To recreate the world within the world is not a simple operation; it is an operation which always grimly opposes itself to all that is facile. If only from the mission which it takes upon itself, it assumes a sacred character. The universe into which one ventures is necessarily a mystic universe in a real sense, that is to say a universe in communication with the Invisible. Without losing its contacts with the earth, with the popular level that is immediately superseded, which the spirit loves and disperses, the *Music* of Béla Bartók translates the most profound need of contemporary man, who desires ardently, in a time desiccated by concepts and impoverished as much by pleasure as by hatred, to rediscover the *state*, the situation of the interior man, which alone does not alter and alone permits one to create.

58

WARNER ALLEN
before 1887–after 1946[1]

A man who calls himself "neither an advanced mystic nor a profound philosopher,"[2] who nevertheless had an experience which reoriented his life and led him to write one of the most lucid and unpretentious modern books on mysticism, describes how he came to discover another dimension of being, at first in a dream and then in the waking state, between two notes of a Beethoven symphony. His book looks to both East and West for elucidation of his experiences, and he finds parallels especially in Plotinus, Dante, St Teresa, and the Tibetan Book of the Dead. One of the pioneers in the movement of East-West philosophic reconciliation, his is one of the many remarkable books published while T.S. Eliot was a director of Faber & Faber, and he acknowledges the poet's own mystical insight in his title. This extract could serve as an illustration of Pierre Jean Jouve's words (see no. 57): "Through Music, time is absorbed into religious expectation, since the instant is immediately open to eternity."

Source *The Timeless Moment*, London, Faber & Faber, 1946, pp. 30-1, 33. Reprinted by kind permission of the Estate of H. Warner Allen.

The Timeless Moment

When the writer was on the threshold of fifty, it occurred to him, as it must have occurred to many another ordinary journalist, no less hostile to the apparent sloppiness of fashionable mysticism than he was, that he had lived for nearly half a century without discerning in life any pattern or rational purpose. His views on the matter might have been roughly summed up in a vague notion that the meaning of the universe was shrouded in impenetrable darkness by the Powers of Life and Death, for fear that life should lose its savour as a brave adventure, if the mystery of death and suffering was solved and uncertainty was exchanged for the assurance of future beatitude. A curiously vivid dream shook his faith in this tentative explanation of human ignorance, though he could not possibly have said what the appearance in his sleep of a light brighter than the sun had to do with the matter. Almost before he knew it, he found himself involved in the task of recalling everything he could remember of his past life in the hope of tracing some pattern and design that underlay its outward incoherence and fitting the disjointed episodes of his thoughts, feelings and actions into the unity of a rational purpose. This quest of truth led through paths of unforeseen darkness and danger, but within a year of clock-time an answer came.

It flashed up lightning-wise during a performance of Beethoven's Seventh Symphony at the Queen's Hall, in that triumphant fast movement when "the morning stars sang together and all the sons of God shouted for joy".[3] The swiftly flowing continuity of the music was not interrupted, so that what Mr T.S. Eliot calls "the intersection of the timeless moment"[4] must have slipped into the interval between two demi-semi-quavers. When, long after, I analysed the happening in the cold light of retrospect, it seemed to fall into three parts: first the mysterious event itself which occurred in an infinitesimal fraction of a split second; this I learned afterwards from Santa Teresa to call the Union with God; then Illumination, a *wordless* stream of complex feelings in which the experience of Union combined with the rhythmic emotion of the music like a sunbeam striking with iridescence the spray above a waterfall – a stream that was continually swollen by tributaries of associated Experience; lastly, Enlightenment, the recollection in tranquillity of the whole complex of Experience as it were embalmed in thought-forms and words. . . .

Rapt in Beethoven's music, I closed my eyes and watched a silver glow which shaped itself into a circle with a central focus brighter than the rest. The circle became a tunnel of light proceeding from some distant sun in the heart of the Self. Swiftly and smoothly I was borne through the tunnel and as I went the light turned from silver to gold. There was an impression of drawing strength from a limitless sea of power and a sense of deepening peace. The light grew brighter, but was never dazzling or alarming. I came to a point where time and motion ceased. In my recollection it took the shape of a flat-topped rock, surrounded by a summer sea, with a sandy pool at its foot. The dream scene vanished and I am absorbed in the Light of the Universe, in Reality glowing like fire with the knowledge of itself, without ceasing to be one and myself, merged like a drop of quicksilver in the Whole, yet still separate as a grain of sand in the desert. The peace that passes all understanding and the pulsating energy of creation are one in the centre in the midst of conditions where all opposites are reconciled.[5]

59

GEORGE IVANOVICH GURDJIEFF
1874[1]–1949

Gurdjieff's chronicle of his *Wanderjahre*, begun in 1927, was first published in France in 1960 by his pupils. There is no way of ascertaining how much is fact and how much didactic fiction in these stories, now familiar to an even wider public through a popular film. What is certain is the part that music played, and continues to play, in the "Work" initiated by Gurdjieff for what he called, significantly enough, "the harmonious development of man."

This extract describes the progress of Vitvitskaïa, one of the book's remarkable women, through the successive stages of musical knowledge. She begins with the practical side, and becomes an accomplished pianist. Next she studies music history and theory, ancient and modern. A book on vibrations alerts her to the wider implications of music as a cosmic force. She tries naïvely to apply theories based on this insight, but meets with no success until given specific information by the "Monopsyche" (= Monophysite?) Brethren as to the adjustment of pitch to climatic and other conditions. How this works, she does not tell us. Her experiments, more carefully adapted to character and race, now meet with some success. But she has not yet found the key to the universal and infallible power which the monotonous singing of the Turkestan monks seems to have possessed over the psyches of all who heard it. Gurdjieff counters with his own experience among the Essenes, of a music that like the mythical songs of Orpheus has a magical effect even on the physical plane.

Vitvitskaïa's researches may be taken as an outline of Gurdjieff's own quest for the secrets of music.[2] He introduced the results as the "Temple Music" of his institute at Fontainebleau during the 1920s, played either by himself on the piano or harmonium, or by his faithful pupil the composer Thomas de Hartmann. A private recording by the latter is in circulation, and must be judged for effectiveness by those who have used it in conjunction with Gurdjieff's exercises.

275

Source From *Meetings with Remarkable Men*, by G.I. Gurdjieff, translated by
A.R. Orage, revised anonymously, New York, Dutton, 1963, pp. 127-34. Copyright
© 1963 by Editions Janus. Reprinted by permission of Triangle Editions, Inc., and
the publisher, E.P. Dutton, a division of New American Library.

Vitvitskaïa's Musical Researches

To illustrate the character of the inner world of Vitvitskaïa – this
woman who had stood on the brink of moral ruin and who later,
thanks to the aid of persons with ideas who chanced to cross the
path of her life, became, I may boldly say, such as might serve as an
ideal for every woman – I will confine myself here to telling about
only one aspect of her many-sided inner life.

Among other interests she was particularly drawn to the science of
music. The seriousness of her attitude towards this science may be
shown clearly by a conversation we had during one of the
expeditions of our group.

On this journey through the centre of Turkestan, thanks to special
introductions, we stayed for three days in a certain monastery not
accessible to everyone. The morning we left this monastery,
Vitvitskaïa was as pale as death, and her arm, for some reason or
other, was in a sling. For a long time she could not mount her horse
by herself, and another comrade and I had to help her.

When the whole caravan was under way, I rode beside
Vitvitskaïa, a little behind all the others. I very much wanted to
know what had happened to her and questioned her insistently. I
thought that perhaps one of our comrades had acted the brute and
had dared in some way to insult her – a woman who had become
sacred for us all – and I wished to find out who the scoundrel was, in
order, without dismounting and without words, to shoot him down
like a partridge.

To my questions Vitvitskaïa finally replied that the cause of her
state was, as she expressed it, that "damned music," and she asked
me if I remembered the music of the night before last.

I did indeed remember how all of us, sitting in some corner of the
monastery, had almost sobbed, listening to the monotonous music
performed by the brethren during one of their ceremonies. And
although we had talked about it afterwards for a long time, none of
us could explain the reason for it.

After a little pause Vitvitskaïa began to talk of her own accord,
and what she said about the cause of her strange state took the form
of a long story. I do not know whether it was because the scenery
through which we were riding that morning was indescribably
glorious or whether there was some other reason, but what she then
told me with such sincerity, I still remember almost word for word
even after all these years. Each of her words was so strongly

imprinted on my brain that it seems to me I hear her at this moment.

She began as follows:

"I do not remember whether there was anything in music that touched me inwardly when I was still quite young, but I do remember very well how I thought about it. Like everybody else I did not wish to appear ignorant and, in praising or criticizing a piece of music, I judged it only with my mind. Even when I was quite indifferent to the music I heard, if my opinion was asked about it, I expressed a view, for or against, according to the circumstances.

"Sometimes when everyone praised it I spoke against it, using all the technical words I knew, so that people should think I was not just anyone, but an educated person who could discriminate in everything. And sometimes I condemned it in unison with others, because I thought that, if they criticized it, there was doubtless something in it which I did not know about, for which it should be criticized. But if I praised a piece of music, it was because I assumed that the composer, whoever he might be, having been occupied with this matter all his life, would not let any composition see the light if it did not deserve it. In short, in either praising or blaming, I was always insincere with myself and with others, and for this I felt no remorse of conscience.

"Later, when that good old lady, the sister of Prince Lubovedsky, took me under her wing, she persuaded me to learn to play the piano. 'Every well-educated, intelligent woman,' she said, 'should know how to play this instrument.' In order to please the dear old lady, I gave myself up wholly to learning to play the piano, and in six months I did indeed play so well that I was invited to take part in a charity concert. All our acquaintances present praised me to the skies and expressed astonishment at my talent.

"One day, after I had been playing, the prince's sister came over to me and very seriously and solemnly told me that, since God had given me such a talent, it would be a great sin to neglect it and not let it develop to the full. She added that, as I had begun to work on music, I should be really educated in this field, and not just play like any Mary Smith, and she therefore thought that I should first of all study the theory of music and, if necessary, even take an examination.

"From that day on she began sending for all kinds of books on music for me, and she even went to Moscow herself to buy them. Very soon the walls of my study were lined with enormous bookcases filled to overflowing with all kinds of musical publications.

"I devoted myself very zealously to studying the theory of music, not only because I wished to please my benefactress but also because I myself had become greatly attracted to this work, and my interest in the laws of music was increasing from day to day. My books, however, were of no help to me, for nothing whatsoever was said in them either about what music is, or on what its laws are based. They merely repeated in different ways information about the history of music, such as: that our octave has seven notes, but the ancient Chinese octave had only five; that the harp of the ancient Egyptians was called *tebuni* and the flute *mem*; that the melodies of the ancient Greeks were constructed on the basis of different modes such as the Ionian, the Phrygian, the Dorian and various others; that in the ninth century polyphony appeared in music, having at first so cacophonic an effect that there was even a case of premature delivery of a pregnant woman, who suddenly heard in church the roar of the organ playing this music; that in the eleventh century a certain monk, Guido d'Arezzo, invented solfege, and so on and so forth. Above all, these books gave details about famous musicians, and how they had become famous; they even recorded what kind of neckties and spectacles were worn by such and such composers. But as to what music is, and what effect it has on the psyche of people, nothing was said anywhere.

"I spent a whole year studying this so-called theory of music. I read almost all my books and finally became definitely convinced that this literature would give me nothing; but my interest in music continued to increase. I therefore gave up all my reading and buried myself in my own thoughts.

"One day, out of boredom, I happened to take from the prince's library a book entitled *The World of Vibrations*, which gave my thoughts about music a definite direction. The author of this book was not a musician at all, and from the contents it was obvious that he was not even interested in music. He was an engineer and mathematician. In one place in his book he mentioned music merely as an example for his explanation of vibrations. He wrote that the sounds of music are made up of certain vibrations which doubtless act upon the vibrations which are also in a man, and this is why a man likes or dislikes this or that music. I at once understood this, and I fully agreed with the engineer's hypotheses.

"All my thoughts at that time were absorbed by these interests and, when I talked with the prince's sister, I always tried to turn the conversation to the subject of music and its real significance. As a result she herself became interested in this question, and we pondered over it together and also began to make experiments.

"The prince's sister even bought several cats and dogs and other animals specially for this purpose. We also began inviting some of our servants, served them tea and for hours on end played the piano for them. At first our experiments produced no result; but once, when we had as guests five of our servants and ten peasants from the village formerly owned by the prince, half of them fell asleep while I was playing a waltz of my own composition.

"We repeated this experiment several times, and each time the number of those who fell asleep increased. And although the old lady and I, making use of all kinds of principles, composed other music intended to have different effects on people, nevertheless the only result we attained was to put our guests to sleep. Finally, from constantly working on music and thinking about it, I grew so tired and thin that one day, when the old lady looked at me attentively, she became alarmed and, on the suggestion of an acquaintance, hastened to take me abroad.

"We went to Italy and there, distracted by other impressions, I gradually began to recover. It was only after five years had passed, when we went on our Pamir-Afghanistan expedition and witnessed the experiments of the Monopsyche Brotherhood, that I again began to think about the effect of music, but not with the same enthusiasm as at first.

"In later years, whenever I remembered my first experiments with music, I could not help laughing at our naïveté in giving such significance to the guests' falling asleep from our music. It never entered our heads that these people fell asleep from pleasure, simply because they had gradually come to feel at home with us, and because it was very agreeable after a long day's work to eat a good supper, drink the glass of vodka offered them by the kind old lady, and sit in soft armchairs.

"After witnessing the experiments and hearing the explanations of the Monopsyche brethren, I later, on my return to Russia, resumed my experiments on people. I found, as the brothers had advised, the absolute 'la' according to the atmospheric pressure of the place where the experiment was to be carried out, and tuned the piano correspondingly, taking into consideration also the dimensions of the room. Besides this, I chose for the experiments people who already had in themselves the repeated impressions of certain chords; and I also took into consideration the character of the place and the race of each one present. Yet I could not obtain identical results, that is to say, I was not able by one and the same melody to evoke identical experiences in everyone.

"It cannot be denied that when the people present corresponded absolutely to the mentioned conditions, I could call forth at will in all of them laughter, tears, malice, kindness and so on. But when they were of mixed race, or if the psyche of one of them differed just a little from the ordinary, the results varied and, try as I might, I could not succeed in evoking with one and the same music the mood I desired in all the people without exception. Therefore I gave up my experiments once more, and as it were considered myself satisfied with the results obtained.

"But here, the day before yesterday, this music almost without melody evoked the same state in all of us – people not only of

279

different race and nationality, but even quite unlike in character, type, habits and temperament. To explain this by the feeling of human 'herdness' was out of the question, as we have recently experimentally proved that in all our comrades, thanks to corresponding work on themselves, this feeling is totally absent. In a word, there was nothing the day before yesterday that could have produced this phenomenon and by which it could somehow or other be explained. And after listening to this music, when I returned to my room, there again arose in me the intense desire to know the real cause of this phenomenon, over which I had racked my brains for so many years.

"All night long I could not sleep, but only thought what could be the real meaning of it all. And the whole day yesterday I continued to think, and even lost my appetite. I neither ate nor drank anything, and last night I grew so desperate that either from rage or exhaustion or for some other reason, I almost without knowing it bit my finger, and so hard that I nearly severed it from my hand. That is why my arm is now in a sling. It hurts so much that I can hardly sit on my horse."

Her story touched me deeply, and with all my heart I wanted to help her in some way. In my turn I told her how a year earlier I had happened to come across a phenomenon, also connected with music, which had greatly astonished me.

I told her how thanks to a letter of introduction from a certain great man, Father Evlissi, who had been my teacher in childhood, I had been among the Essenes, most of whom are Jews, and that by means of very ancient Hebraic music and songs they had made plants grow in half an hour, and I described in detail how they had done this. She became so fascinated by my story that her cheeks even burned. The result of our conversation was that we agreed that as soon as we returned to Russia we would settle down in some town where, without being disturbed by anyone, we could really seriously carry out experiments with music.

After this conversation, for all the rest of the trip, Vitvitskaïa was her usual self again. In spite of her injured finger, she was the nimblest of all in climbing every cliff, and she could discern at a distance of almost twenty miles the monuments indicating the direction of our route.

Vitvitskaïa died in Russia from a cold she caught while on a trip on the Volga. She was buried in Samara. I was there at the time of her death, having been called from Tashkent when she fell ill.

Recalling her now, when I have already passed the half-way mark of my life and have been in almost all countries and seen thousands of women, I must confess that I never have met and probably never will meet another such woman.

60

CYRIL SCOTT

1879–1971

As a young composer, Scott was one of the first Britons to feel and absorb the winds of change blowing from the continent of Europe, and for a time he enjoyed considerable fame as one of the English Impressionists. He became a Theosophist shortly before World War I, and alongside his musical activities wrote several books on occultism, among which *The Initiate, by His Pupil* has remained popular.

During the 1920s Scott wrote the book *The Influence of Music on History and Morals: a Vindication of Plato* (published 1933). Our source is its revised and amplified edition, with a new title, in which Scott explained how it came to be written: "I am in a position to acknowledge my indebtedness to the Master Koot Hoomi, who was my Authority for what was previously set forth and for much added information which follows. This High Initiate, who I may mention *en passant*, resides in Shigatse, takes a special interest in the evolution of Western music, a fact which theosophical literature has failed to stress, even though He was one of the two sponsors of the Theosophical Society at its inception towards the end of the last century. Indeed, He considers it advisable that students of occultism of all schools should more fully appreciate the great importance of music as a force in spiritual evolution, and to this end He has revealed much that has hitherto not been revealed, and that cannot fail to prove of paramount interest to all music-lovers" (pp. 31-2). After describing how he contacted K.H. and submitted his writings to the Master through a clairvoyant medium, Nelsa Chaplin, Scott adds: "In this way the book came to be written, inspired and sponsored by Him Who in a former life had been the great philosopher and musician, Pythagoras the Sage" (p. 36). If this be so, then we have here a link with the oldest of our sources and the inspirer of Plato's musical and numerical doctrines (see Iamblichus, no. 7).

Scott is included here as a representative of modern Theosophy.

His initial conversion to the movement came after hearing a lecture by Annie Besant, who headed the Theosophical Society after the death of H.P. Blavatsky in 1891, and his attitudes resemble in many respects those of Besant and of the independent writer Alice A. Bailey (whose books were also composed under the guidance of a Master). Scott refers at the end of our extract to "the great World Teacher, The Christ." This is the Master known by various names to all the great religions – The Jewish Messiah, the Mahdi of Islam, the Kalki or Tenth Avatar of Vishnu, the Buddha Maitreya – for whose advent, imminently expected, Besant, Bailey, and so many others devoted themselves to preparing mankind.

Source *Music, its Secret Influence throughout the Ages*, London, Rider, 1958, reprinted New York, Weiser, 1969, pp. 151-3, 199-204. Reprinted by permission of Marjorie Hartston Scott.

Chapter 26   The beginnings of music and religion

"Whereas Melody is the cry of Man to God, Harmony is the answer of God to Man."

It requires but little imagination to realize that in primitive Man there must have been desires and yearnings which he could not understand, still less put into words, however much he may have tried. Mere speech was a totally inadequate means of expression; he needed something more forceful, yet less definite; he needed an outlet for those strange supplicatory emotions – and he ultimately found it in a rudimentary form of song. He discovered that when he sang, his petitions in some unaccountable way seemed to have been heard, and so his yearnings were stilled; he obtained an emotional relief, as a distraught woman obtains relief when she prays to the God of her own religion. It may seem extravagant to say that through music the first conception of God was aroused in the human mind, yet when primitive Man deemed his prayers were heard, he naturally came to conceive of a Being higher than himself – a Being who could watch over him with parental care. Hitherto his conceptions had been entirely phallic; he had regarded "the portal through which a child enters the world as the actual Giver of life"; but after he had discovered song, he conceived the idea of the Great Mother, the very first deity to whom he turned for consolation and protection from the evils of his precarious existence.[1]

The next stage in the evolution of religion is common knowledge; when once the idea of the Great Mother had been formulated, Man fashioned her image in wood or stone, and carved figures of her in caves, for he felt the need of a concrete object towards which to direct his worship. Finally, having fashioned his idols, he appointed someone to guard them and minister to their supposed needs; and in this manner the office of priest originated. It was the priests who by degrees improved the primitive type of song and transformed it into a species of chanted spell. These spells were committed to memory and handed down from generation to generation. Only much later were they notated. One of their effects was to increase religious fervour, with the result that men began to sway with their bodies, to dance and clap their hands. In the course of time the most elementary form of drum was invented to accentuate the rhythm; this led to the invention of other instruments and so to the actual birth of music as an art.

We see, then, that from the very beginning, music was associated with religion, and that the priests played an important part in its systematization and development. Indeed, according to the Akashic Records,[2] the first priest who was selfless enough pure-heartedly to serve humanity was enabled to hear the music of the higher spheres; and to him it was given to know that whereas "Melody is the cry of Man to God, Harmony is the answer of God to Man." But although, needless to say, he was unable to translate what he heard into earthly sounds – the means being lacking – it inspired him with the idea of introducing a greater variety into the existing musical phrases, so from that time onward music very gradually became more diversified.

The priests, having discovered the potency of the above-mentioned *mantrams* or spells, and realizing that if certain notes were reiterated definite results could be obtained and definite powers brought into action, used this particular form of magic – for magic it was – for noble and constructive ends during the earlier periods of Atlantean history. Under the influence of Initiates, Sound was employed to build beautiful and wonder-inspiring forms; but in the later phases of that mighty civilization it came to be employed entirely as a force for destruction. Discordant sounds were deliberately used to shatter and disintegrate. As every occultist knows, the practice of magic for evil ends was responsible for the downfall of the continent, and thus perished not only that dark phase of its music, but also that scientific knowledge of the application and potency of Sound which had wrought such havoc. Wherever some particular power or aspect of knowledge has become vitiated by abuse, it has been permitted by the Higher Ones to fall for the time being into obscurity, to re-emerge again aeons later, perhaps, as a purified overtone of itself.

Among the first composers to be instrumental in introducing this overtone of the ancient Atlantean music was Debussy. In more occult terms he was unconsciously used by the Higher Ones to carry over Fourth Race sound-vibrations into the Fifth.[3] To this end he made a study of and absorbed the characteristics of Javanese music, which is a remnant, though mellowed and modified, of the Atlantean, and which, I should add, exercises a powerful influence through the astral on the physical body, especially on the solar plexus. An obvious example of this Fourth Race music mingling with that of the Fifth is shown in his *Fêtes* in which ancient chants actually associated with the temples of the past subtly mingle with a wholly modern and irresponsible element.

Debussy was succeeded by composers unconsciously expressing the harsher and more destructive element of the Atlantean music, albeit at a higher point of the evolutionary spiral, since, as I elaborated in Chapter 22,[4] this destructive force is used to disintegrate obsolete and baneful thought-forms of various kinds.

We will now return to the consideration of music in another and earlier phase of its development.

Chapter 36   The music of the future

The future of music is a subject which invites much speculation along various lines. Some persons, in fact, employ an easy catch-phrase to the effect that it is still in its infancy, as if it had been "born" some few centuries ago instead of in pre-historic times. These persons, nevertheless, give us no clue to the features it will assume when it has reached "youth" and finally "manhood." If we consider that the modern orchestra consists of 120 performers or more, are we to suppose that in say, another 200 years it will consist of twice that number and later on of four times the number, and so forth, *ad infinitum*? The answer must perforce be in the negative, because there is, one would imagine, a limit to aural endurance, especially if we pre-suppose the addition of vast choruses. Then along what lines is it profitable to speculate as to the musical future?

Once again we must turn to the results of occult investigation. Indeed, the great Initiates have vast and imposing plans for the musical future, and we are authorized by Them to say that it depends on the reception of the present volume how much more They will feel justified in making known.

Let us first deal with such phases of music likely to appear in the more immediate future, the reader being warned that although we can naturally only treat of each one in succession, some of them may be operating concurrently.

For the next decade or so, the prevailing note of serious music will tend to be unemotional and intellectual in character,[5] and although here and there composers far ahead of their time may be "reaching out towards that Beauty and Mystery which are veritably as the garments of God,"[6] such composers will not receive their due until a much later date, nay, perhaps only after their death.

Meanwhile, as everyone is aware, we are much troubled by the nerve-shattering noise to which in all large towns we are subjected, and which, far from decreasing, is only likely to increase as time goes on. The jarring sounds of motor-horns, whistles, grinding brakes and so forth exercise a cumulative and deleterious effect upon the entire organism. In order to help to counteract this, certain composers will be used to evolve a type of music calculated to heal where these discordant noises have destroyed.[7] For this end, of course, etheric vision or, at any rate, great inner sensitiveness, will be indispensable, so that the value of each combination of notes and its effect upon the subtler vehicles of the listeners may be fully realized.[8] Such men, consciously aware of their responsibility towards humanity, will indeed be as faithful custodians of the sacred two-edged sword of Sound.

Certain gifted composers will further set themselves the task of writing types of music creating thought-forms suited to specific moods or emotional states. With the vast array of musical resources available, they will be able to meet the needs of the most complex of modern psychology.

Again, music in the future is to be used to bring people into yet closer touch with the Devas; they will be enabled to partake of the benefic influence of these beings while attending concerts at which by the appropriate type of sound they have been invoked. Although at the present time music is extant which calls forth the Devas or nature-spirits, the ordinary listener is not conscious of their presence, and thus there is no actual rapport between the members of the two evolutions. The scientifically calculated music in question however will achieve the twofold object of invoking the Devas and at the same time stimulating in the listeners those faculties by means of which they will become aware of them and responsive to their influence. Among these Devas will be those especially concerned with the animal kingdom. The result will be a revolt against that form of cruelty called blood-sports. Efforts are already (1958) being made to bring in a law to prohibit such sports. Further, in the course of time music will become more and more potent to bring humanity into touch with the higher planes, thus enabling them to experience a spiritual joy and exaltation which now can only be experienced by the very few.

Having thus dealt, albeit cursorily, with the esoteric side of the music of the future, we will now give an indication of some of its more apparent characteristics.

Innovations will take place in connexion with concerts. Already there have been complaints from the more fastidious music-lovers that concert-halls are too garishly lighted, and that what is seen detracts from what is heard. Such people, however, have usually been set down as cranks, and concert promoters have paid no heed to their idiosyncrasies. Nevertheless, the time will come when the demands of these so-called cranks will be fulfilled, and in an atmosphere of semi-darkness colours of every variety will be projected on to a screen, expressive of and corresponding to the content of the music. Thus will that dream of Scriabin's be realized, the unity of colour and sound; and through its realization the audiences of the future will experience the healing and stimulating effects of that very potent conjunction.

Meanwhile the discordant element of the present day will have made way for concord; and melody, without which no music can long survive the dust of time, will have been reinstated. As the music of the last twenty-five years has in so large a measure been disruptive in character, the music we may anticipate in the future will be constructive.

From among other information conveyed, we gather that America will be particularly responsive to this new music, for that great continent is the cradle of the coming race, the units of which, in common with the majority of artistic types, will function through the sympathetic system in contradistinction to the cerebro-spinal. The enthusiasm and the keen receptivity to new ideas which already constitute such a marked characteristic of the more sensitive Americans of today makes them peculiarly appreciative of novel combinations of sound. From amongst them many famous executants will be born, some of whom will exhibit great proficiency on a new species of violin to be invented in the future. On this violin it will be possible to convey the more subtle divisions of the tone, and to draw from it the maximum of its potentialities will necessitate on the part of the performer an even greater degree of musical sensitivity than at the present time.

We have been living in the Age of Destruction when, as stated earlier, even ultra-discordant music has been used to destroy certain baneful thought-forms. This type of music, however, has served its purpose already some years ago, and it is now for Concord to rebuild.

"As above, so below. . . ." Just as the denizens of the earth who represent cells in the body of the great Planetary Logos have gone through the purifying fires of two world-wars, so on a much mightier and to us incomprehensible scale has that Logos Himself also passed through the fire, and is now in process of taking a higher Initiation which must inevitably affect each unit within His consciousness. New cosmic currents of force are beginning to circulate throughout His aura, inspiring new and harmonious qualities, tendencies and ideals; and it will be the exalted function of music to help to focus these currents and further their rhythmic distribution. Great floods of melody will be poured forth from the higher planes, to be translated into earthly sound by composers sensitive enough to apprehend them. At first only a faint echo of these melodies will penetrate the spheres of human endeavour, and the music of the next few decades can only be, as it were, a prelude to what will follow.

The National Devas of various countries, working through Sound, will seek to form a bridge between nation and nation by inspiring the harmony of true co-operation and that genuine peace which is not merely the laying down of arms. Through them a new form of patriotism will be inspired, the spirit of which when voiced will be, "How can my country contribute to the international good?" instead of "How can my country show itself superior to others?" Thus in place of the old type of martial national anthem, a type will be substituted which will urge the nations towards the realization of Brotherhood. Already at long last they are beginning to recognize that the form of separateness which masquerades under the name of Nationalism is as unprofitable as, to the few enlightened, it is unspiritual.[9] And so the day is drawing nigh when it will be rejected for the purely material reason that it does not pay. This attitude, of course, falls far short of the ideal which the Great Ones are ever seeking to put before humanity, for only when true Brotherhood is felt in the heart will that ideal be attained.

To this end the great World Teacher, The Christ, will come again; though exactly when He will come must largely depend on Humanity itself and better relations between the Powers. There is hope that He may come at the close of the century. But when He does come it will be to inspire, to construct, to "make all things new." And it will be for music, by creating harmony within Man's subtler bodies, to make ready for and facilitate His advent.

Yet even then music will not have reached the limit of its potentialities. So far, with our earthly music we have only been able to imitate the faintest echo of the Music of the Spheres, but in the future it will be given us to swell the great Cosmic Symphony. In that unimaginable Unity-Song is the synthesis of Love, Wisdom, Knowledge and Joy, and when Man shall have heard it upon earth and become imbued with its divine influence he will attain the eternal consciousness of all these attributes.

I am able to conclude this new edition of the book with a recently received message from the Master K.H.[10] It is:

"To-day, as we enter this new Age, we seek, primarily through the medium of *inspired* music, to diffuse the spirit of unification and brotherhood, and thus quicken the vibration of this planet."

61

KARLHEINZ STOCKHAUSEN

born 1928

In the tradition of Beethoven and Wagner (see nos 44, 54), Stockhausen is a composer fully aware of the transcendent nature of music and of the suprapersonal source of his inspiration. Since 1968 his works have taken on an overtly religious nature – in the broadest sense of the term – and show a concern with the current and future spiritual transformation of mankind. This is obvious even from the titles of such works as *Mantra, Inori* (Devotion), *Für Kommenden Zeiten* (For times to come), *Sternklang* (Starsound), *Tierkreis* (Zodiac) and *Sirius* (the star long recognized by esotericists as having a special connection with the Earth and its destiny). Stockhausen's current work, the opera-cycle *Licht*, is a dramatization of the cosmic background to earthly events, much as Rudolf Steiner envisaged it earlier in the century.

Even more than the transcripts of lectures that form our extracts from Steiner and Inayat Khan (nos 55, 56), these thoughts of Stockhausen are spontaneous and unrevised. They were recorded during a long interview he gave to a Dutch cultural circle, "Kring Nea Mousa," led by Hugo Pit, at Stockhausen's home in 1973. The subtitles of the three excerpts are editorial.

Stockhausen says in plain, modern language what all our authors have been saying. Coming not from a philosopher, a churchman, a music theorist or a literary dilettante, but from a composer who more than any other has shown the way to a new music, his words carry particular weight and significance for the future.

Source   Interview 1: Gespräch mit holländischem Kunstkreis, Kürten, June 2, 1973, in Karlheinz Stockhausen, *Texte zur Musik 1970-1977*, vol. 4, Cologne, DuMont, 1978, pp. 501-2, 506-10, 512-13. Reprinted by permission of Karlheinz Stockhausen.

Music and the Centers of Man

Each of us is, as you know, a person with many levels – there are after all whole cultures which have differentiated them. I have a sexual center, three vital centers, two mental centers and a suprapersonal center. If I can perceive that, I have come far enough to have awoken seven different centers in myself. And with different things I can bring each center into vibration. I can set my sexual center in vibration with a certain sort of music, but with another music I can set my supranatural center in vibration. And I will add to that: have you perhaps gone far enough yet to discover which parts of a type of music, or which pieces of music, set which of your centers especially in vibration?

There is also music that goes through all the centers: hence there are moments in which you are addressed in a purely sacred, a purely religious way; and other moments in which you are addressed purely sensually, purely erotically. That is pretty reckless music. One must be very strong to be able to experience that completely. Above all, this music must be exceptionally well balanced, fantastically composed. If it is not, then there are overloadings, and when one hears it one is overexcited in a certain way, and brought out of equilibrium.

Hence it is naturally better if one hears music that draws one up higher than one is by nature. We are mostly pretty physical sacks, are we not — all of us? Most of us spend most of our time on feeding ourselves, taking care of clothing and shelter, copulating and sleeping: primarily satisfying physical desires, then. Now and again one reminds oneself: "We are spirits, and spirits should be connected with the superhuman, with the Cosmos, with God." Much music also serves for that! But such music is very rare today, extremely rare. Most music is just physical, and speaks to centers in us that belong more to the animal than to the superhuman (I mean here by "superhuman" what we are as spirits, when we are freed from flesh and bones).

That is what should be the most important thing now: that each person should gradually become conscious enough to choose specific music and to be able to say: "I choose that within myself which comes to vibration through this music."

Towards a New Religious Music

The great difficulty in music, but also what is so extraordinarily fascinating and beautiful, is that today we stand so precisely on the borderline between two great world-epochs. Around 1950 one great world-age ended (it runs down gradually at first), and a new one began. I am an artist who must play his role exactly on this borderline. For a musician it is a very special role to have such a double view. I still grew out of the spirit of the passing age: I felt the great opportunities of a mental music that would be built primarily through a man's capacity for construction – and at the same time I see the end of a music which was once, in its best moments, religious music. I see the end of the single religions: there are only a few people who still really find their complete fulfilment in them. One can now see how the earth becomes a united earth. For me Buddha is as significant as the other founders of religions, although I grant Christ a special significance. Christ achieved a phenomenal example: to make the individual conscious of his inextinguishability and to see the face of God in every person – that is an original message. Buddhism tells of the extinction of the individual: the "I" should give itself up and merge in the Whole, and Buddha is the Whole. We have a strong consciousness – we Europeans, above all – that "*I* am also something, I am not just nothing." No one can ever make it credible to me that a man's greatest wish should be the wish to be nothing. To assume that, for me, is not only hopeless, but I also do not want it. I suspect that my innermost self finds a great joy that I should be myself, and you should be yourself. Therefore I believe that Christianity is something unique, though I also no longer practice religion in an orthodox way, and have left the Catholic Church.

What I want to say is this: one sees the end of the traditional religions, and music used to be imbedded, everywhere in the world, in religion. That was so in Europe, in all of Asia. In India it is still so today, although there too music is profaned, emancipated from religion, and so there is more and more secularized *Gebrauchsmusik*.[1] Today people no longer know, in fact, what it is actually for. At best they think it is a psychological medium to get to know oneself better. So they choose a certain piece of music by Mozart or Stockhausen and experience it as if in a mirror: they want to find themselves in the music and vibrate with it. One can withdraw into oneself with headphones and dive into oneself by listening to music; then one needs no one else at all. When you have all learnt this for yourselves, you naturally no longer need Hugo Pit as the center of your group, for each one can make musical discoveries for himself and reveal his own center: one hears a new piece and discovers how one reacts to it. What one says about it afterwards is comparatively unimportant. One certainly sees what happens to oneself. If the inner voice says "Not this music, no, stop!" (which one often hears already in the first bars – and one feels more and more strongly) – "That is not good for me now, it excites me too much, it drags me down," one must say to oneself: "No, I do not want that," and immediately stop it.

There are people who have a sense for what is good or bad for them. But all should learn to ask themselves: "What happens to me when I hear the composition *Stimmung*?"[2] Then one would feel: "Aha, this music awakens my consciousness for something I would otherwise repress; for I am mostly busy with eating, drinking, moving, buying, mending, talking, television, sleep. . . ." When does the question put itself to one: "Who am I, why am I alive at all, where do I want to go from here, what happens when I die?"

Music should above all be a means to keep awake the connection of the soul with the other side. Through religion, music has for a long time been given to people as an atmosphere; the musicians were employed by the Church. Then it was gradually secularized and became more and more a means of cultivated amusement, whose most recent variant is the training of psychological self-knowledge through music.

Today there is however a new branch which is becoming more and more popular: music-therapy. People are experiencing music not only as a mirror that tells them who they are; they are also learning that music can heal. If for instance one is sick – say, we are too nervous or fearful or aggressive or tired of life –, one can cure such sicknesses with music. But at first there are only a few who know what is good for a cure. They can handle music therapeutically. There must have been something like it among the Greeks, even more among the Indians in the form of mantra-techniques. Plato's writings say what specific music is good for. In Europe, unfortunately, this knowledge has disappeared, because we have become scientifically too one-sided, and in medicine think of almost nothing but chemical treatment or surgery. We have no idea of musical therapeutics. Only now we are slowly beginning to discover this again. I know, for instance, a music therapist who was formerly a biologist and now tries to heal the mentally ill with music. Ironically enough, they only begin to heal people with music when they are already mentally ill. They often use my music for therapy, too. Unfortunately they only start with people in the hospital, who are already completely unbalanced. Very few realize that every one of us basically needs music for self-healing. Normally people drink coffee to become lively again. Few are wise enough and know the exact music by which one is always inwardly refreshed and dancing; a few just know that with certain pieces of Stockhausen, their ideas come ten times faster. These listeners use music therapeutically in order to make themselves more lively, become more creative, to be able to speak of connections of which they otherwise had no idea: thus they use music as the preeminent spiritual food.

Then there naturally comes the next step, which religion also originally strove for, namely to bring ourselves through music into relationship with that which we cannot grasp with the understanding, but which we can feel; with the supranatural, with that which gives life to the whole universe – with God, the Spirit who holds everything together, all the galaxies, all the solar systems and planets, and also every single one of us on this little planet. Thus one

291

can evidently make contact with it: there is music that gives one the possibility of doing that. That is not only the music that we normally call "sacred music." We have forgotten that once all music composed was sacred music. That is the greatest problem today: to make music that does not smell of church (so that most people would immediately say "I have nothing to do with that"), yet which is experienced quite obviously as spiritual music, without allying itself to specific forms of religion. Then it is a matter of finding forms which make it impossible for someone to sit in a concert-hall and, when something is played up there on the stage, to say "I have nothing to do with that." Or for anyone to say, as if going into a shop, "I've paid 10 Marks for my ticket, and now I want to have something to my taste." That is certainly the usual situation: one goes to a concert-hall and buys oneself something that agrees with one. Hence it often happens that one is disappointed because the program is made by people whom one does not know and who do not know one. One's well-being functions perhaps for short intervals, perhaps even for a whole piece, but then not at all for several concerts. Perhaps one concert happens by chance to be once again in tune with one's taste, but in between one has gone in vain. . . .

People like you must learn gradually to take spiritual nourishment deliberately, and not simply to consume everything that is set before you. Let it be you yourselves who decide; do not follow a manager and his taste, but your own. But how is one to do that? In the today's music industry it is very difficult. That is why a group like yours is very important: people come together there with relatively similar tastes, and above all their tastes are further educated. This happens all the more, the further you penetrate, for instance, into my music, the further you "climb" with me: I would actually like to make more and more music that is heard above all by people who are religious; and religious in such a way that they will let the whole be set in vibration within themselves, that unlimited Self which allows us to make contact with the fantastic feelings of unity that embrace the whole cosmos. My own difficulty is to find each time a new way through which that becomes completely clear – so that in the very moment when people first hear the title of a work and then the music, they experience the whole atmosphere and immediately feel: "Wait, something different is happening here!"; so that they can already notice that in the way the musicians enter, how they are prepared, how they perform the music, how the tones sound (whether the tones are free, whether they vibrate freely). Judgment should no longer rest on whether a piece of music is intelligent or refined or clever or skilfully made. It must be music in which the mental remains in the background, in which it is mainly a matter of vibrations which produce above all an equilibrium of the soul, not only of the body. Vital vibrations can naturally occur as well: I love the whole circle – to traverse the whole circle of the human at least once in each composition, and thereby to feel at each moment: "That's coming into balance again!", so that then one actually has the feeling at the end that one is in equilibrium, that one has received a harmonious feeling. The best thing would naturally be if, when someone hears a piece of mine then goes afterwards to a stranger, he could embrace him and say: "I find you wonderful!", simply because he is happy. With every new piece I work on making this suprapersonal element in man, which in the past was enlivened by the single religions, able to come ever more precisely into vibration, and on maintaining myself in that condition during the time of composition – also when I am concentrating, listening to a single piece. The chief thing is that I should as far as possible always move in this realm. If then I sometimes become a "physical sack" and notice it, then I must immediately get up – look up – again, so that I can return there.

The Composer and his Spirit

There will be people who will discover this music. That is the wonderful thing on this earth: everything that exists has its meaning. Everything is consumed – that is the most remarkable thing . . . everything is found . . . if you do not eat it, another will . . . what we do not eat, the animals eat, what they do not eat becomes earth again. Everything is alive. So it is not so important for the whole whether anyone likes something or not. It cannot be decisive for me as a composer whether you like my music or not. If you do not like it, someone else will like it; if no one liked it, then that too would not make me despair. I work on something, and when it is finished I make something new. Naturally I am happy if I now meet someone who is sympathetic to me – in whom I detect waves that are beautiful – and who likes what I have made. But that is a purely personal matter, that is Stockhausen. That which in my music is not Stockhausen – the most essential part –, is timeless, universal. "Stockhausen" is only a label, a name. When I have gone, it is no longer there. But the music lives on. Then my name is merely a word, as when I say "Moments" to name something.[3] But that no longer has anything to do with with me. None of you knows "Beethoven." He is a myth! He is a series of letters. None of you knows the person. Seen from the exterior he was a decrepit little man who usually had pains in the ear and belly-aches, who now and then ate a hare and drank a glass of wine, who was usually grousing like a madman and quarrelling with housekeepers: he was certainly a complex and, to many, an unsympathetic man. With a very fine sensitivity to vibrations you might perhaps have understood what kind of a being the other Beethoven was, whom Bettina von Arnim described.[4] She was a wise woman. She got him to talk, and saw what a wonderful soul lay behind this wild façade. So she quoted sentences of his that are fantastic, so wise and so enlightened! She managed it. For the others he was a taciturn type. Today of course, today everyone finds his music wonderful. But what is that? Everyone finds *themselves* wonderful, when they like it. They do not know Beethoven at all. While listening to this music they feel wonderfully alive, full of energy, elevated, divine. In every Beethoven-lover there lies hid this spirit that was in Beethoven. I will tell you: Stockhausen's music is not Stockhausen, but this spirit which is using me. And you, too, are not what you appear to be. Your human personality is quite limited and temporary. You are little lights, as I am, which flicker – which whisper something to one another, to pass the time. What it is that we say is fundamentally also not so important . . . what is important is that we are together like this . . . for twenty lights simply give off more light . . . than a single one. . . .

NOTES

Notes by other authors, translators or commentators are indicated by their initials in parentheses.

1 Plato

1 In choosing the translations of Plato, Iamblichus and Simplicius by Thomas Taylor (1758–1835), I have had regard to Taylor's own position in the transmission of the Perennial Wisdom with which this anthology is largely concerned. It was he who first made Plato's complete works available in English, and more importantly, he was the first to translate the major part of the Neoplatonic corpus into any modern language, publishing in English works of Plotinus, Iamblichus, Damascius, Porphyry, the Emperor Julian, Proclus, and others. Taylor's translations opened the doors of Neoplatonism to the Romantic poets (beginning with Taylor's friend William Blake), the American Transcendentalists, and the Theosophists (including W.B. Yeats). What many of these people knew of the harmony of the spheres, they knew through Taylor's version. I have modified Taylor's text, which follows the original in using indirect speech throughout, by removing the "thats" which begin every clause, hence turning it into a direct report. I have also altered his description of the Siren's song, in the interests of clarity and consistency of musical terminology (see note 12).

2 Odysseus' tale to Alcinus fills four books of Homer's *Odyssey*.

3 In *The Pythagorean Plato*, pp. 41-55, Ernest McClain argues for a musical allegory underlying not only the description of the Sirens and their songs, but all the numbers in this myth. His interpretations are included briefly in these footnotes. The tenth day corresponds to the Tetraktys $\therefore$, the Pythagorean symbol of the space-time world developed in three dimensions (1=point, 2=line, 3=plane, 4=solid) and making, by addition, the number 10. Plato also uses 10 in the *Republic* as a measure of age: 10 years for the oldest child usable to

build a utopia; 100 for the span of life; 1000 years between reincarnations. The ordinary dead decay when they pass this symbolic limit: Er, on the other hand, goes on to 12 and then revives. 12 is the limit of the *musical* Tetraktys 12:9:8:6 which gives the ratios for the framework of two interlocking fifths (e.g. D' A G D) within which all Greek tuning system fitted. This alerts the musical reader to one possible sense of what follows: the "place" in which Er reawakens is this framework.

4   The sequence of events through which the souls pass is as follows: 1. Life on Earth; 2. Death; 3. Judgment; 4. 1000-year period of rewards (upwards opening A) or expiation (downward chasm A); 5. Return through upward opening B or downward chasm B; 6. Journey to the Throne of Necessity; 7. Random distribution of the lots; 8. Free choice of lives in allotted order; 9. Drinking of Lethe and oblivion; 10. Descent to Earth and rebirth in a new body.

5   In McClain's musical interpretation, the downward chasms are the endless progressions through integers to the infinitely large (∞) and through fractions to the infinitely small ($\frac{1}{\infty}$). The upward openings both lead eventually to the One, whether reached at the end of the integer sequence $\infty \ldots 3, 2, 1$, or the fractional sequence $1/\infty \ldots 1/3, 1/2, 1/1$. These are respectively the contraharmonic and harmonic series (McClain, *op. cit.*, pp. 42ff).

6   The fate of Aridaeus shows that we are to distinguish a permanent Hell (or Tartarus, as opposed to the place of 1000-year purgation), from which exit into another incarnation is impossible. This would obtain only in cases where the being in question has lost all contact with its immortal soul, hence any possibility of purgation and salvation.

7   The 7 days spent in the meadow of the musical Tetraktys 12:9:8:6 are the 7 steps of the scale which fill out its framework. The 8th step is the higher octave, D' or G, beyond which five further stages remain in the harmonic series; 6:5 (minor third), 5:4 (major third), 4:3 (perfect fourth), 3:2 (perfect fifth), 2:1 (octave) (McClain, *op. cit.*, p. 45).

8   This is the octave, the purest ratio of 2:1, seen after 4 "days" and reached after 5. It is the undergirding of the musical cosmos. Thus the journey from 12, the top of the Tetraktys (or the bottom, if it is interpreted as the reciprocal, contraharmonic series), to the unity of the cosmos has taken Er 12 days in all (McClain, *op. cit.*, p. 46).

9   The eight whirls or spheres are those of the seven planets and the fixed stars enclosing the Earth, arranged as shown opposite. I have found no explanation of the widths of the lips, beyond suggestions that they must have to do with distances between the planetary orbits, though exactly how this is so, no one can say. Socrates said (530b) that astronomy should be studied not by observation but through solving mathematical problems. This one remains unsolved.

Plato's numbering:	8th	7th	6th	5th	4th	3rd	2nd	1st
Sphere of:	Moon	Sun	Venus	Mercury	Mars	Jupiter	Saturn	Fixed Stars
Order of widths of lips:	5	4	7	3	6	2	1	8 (largest)
Relative speeds:	fastest (1st degree)		fast (2nd)		medium (3rd)	slow (4th)	slowest (5th)	opposite rotation
Colors:	reflected light, from Sun	brightest	white	yellow	reddish	whitest	yellow	variegated

10 There has been much debate on the meaning of Plato's description of the motion of Mars, the 4th planet with the 3rd fastest speed: τρίτον δὲ φορᾷ ἰέναι, ὡς σφίσι φαίνεσθαι, ἐπανακυκλούμενον τόν τετράτον. Sir Thomas Heath translates it as: "third in the speed of its counter-revolution the fourth appears to move" (*Greek Astronomy*, p. 48); Francis M. Cornford as: "third in speed moves the fourth (Mars), as it appeared to them, with a counter-revolution" (*Plato's Cosmology*, p. 88), the term "counter-revolution" referring to all three outer planets whose slower motion makes them seem to drop behind relatively to the Sun group. D.R. Dicks, on the contrary, sees Mars alone as "making an additional revolution" through the very broad loops of its epicycles (*Early Greek Astronomy*, pp. 112-13). Allan Bloom's translation seems to imply the same meaning: "Third in swiftness, as it looked to them, the fourth circled about" (*The Republic of Plato*, 617a).

11 The Sirens in Homer's *Odyssey*, Book XII, are women-headed birds of prey whose singing lures sailors to be wrecked on their rocks and eaten by them. But the ancient Greeks also envisaged them as beneficent deities who guided the dead soul and charmed it by their song to forget the lost joys of life (cf. Plato, *Cratylus*, 403e). In the oldest mythology, souls went after death not to an upper world but to the Fortunate Isles, situated across Ocean, and there the Sirens sang. But with the advent of the idea of astral immortality the Isles, and the Sirens, were translated to the stars, and the Sirens become celestial divinities, as here. This necessitated a re-interpretation of the *Odyssey* episode, according to which Odysseus alone is the philosophical hero who, in his journey on the sea of life, is able to hear the divine music without succumbing to frenzy and insanity. On these interpretations see Franz Cumont, *Recherches sur le symbolisme funéraire des Romains*, pp. 326-31. See also our extracts from Philo (no. 12).

12 Taylor: "uttering one voice variegated by diverse modulations. But that the whole of them, being eight, composed one harmony." Original: φωνὴν μίαν ἱεῖσαν, ἕνα τόνον. ἐχ πασῶν δὲ

ὀκτὼ οὐσῶν μίαν ἁρμονίαν συμφωνεῖν. McClain (*op. cit.*, pp. 51ff) suggests that the Sirens' eight notes are those of the Dorian tetrachord and its inverse, the modern major: D E F♯ G A B♭ C D': the "pattern laid up in heaven" for the filling out of the 6:8:9:12 framework that takes account of the need for symmetry. This is the mode of interpretation that best explains the functions of the three Fates in the following passage. McClain plots the scale on a circle thus:

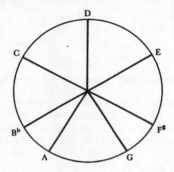

But the three Fates are "at equal distance from one another," which can only be achieved by placing them at equally-tempered major thirds:

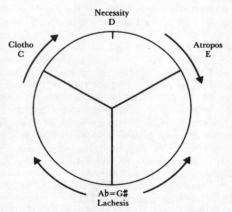

The interval C E in Pythagorean tuning gives a C that is too low, an E that is too high: hence Clotho's and Atropos' adjustments. Lachesis' task is to make A♭ and G♯ coincide, adjusting one with each hand.

The symbolic meaning of such a system is, in McClain's words, that "Plato saw the necessity of temperament for systems meant to function in harmony, be they musical scales, planetary orbits, or communities of just men" (*ibid.*, p. 55).

2 Cicero

1 The sky is the furthest visible heaven, the "celestial" one of the Fixed Stars; the smallest star is the Moon.

2 Cicero's scheme is as follows:

Sphere no.	9	8	7	6	5	4	3	2	1
	Earth	Moon	Mercury	Venus	Sun	Mars	Jupiter	Saturn	Celestial
Pitch	None	1 (lowest)		2	3	4	5	6	7 (highest)

This was to remain the most widely accepted order until the Copernican Revolution. But Plato (*Timaeus* 38d; *Republic* X, 616e) and Aristotle (*Metaph.* XI, viii, 1073b) place Venus and then Mercury above the Sun (see note 9 to our *Republic* extract). Macrobius calls this the Egyptian order, and Cicero's the Chaldean and Archimedean order. See A.E. Taylor, *A Commentary on Plato's Timaeus*, pp. 192-4.

3 Cicero follows the cosmology of Aristotle's *De Caelo* with its two divisions – sublunary and celestial – and heavy, stationary Earth. But he differs from Aristotle (*De Caelo* II, ix, 290b) in allowing the spheres to make music, though unlike that of Plato's Sirens it is of an impersonal and relatively physical nature. Macrobius points out that Cicero nevertheless distinguishes the "eternal fires" of the heavenly bodies from the "divine minds" which animate them (III, 4; Macrobius I, xiv, 17-18).

4 There are eight tones, but, since Mercury and Venus have the same pitch, only seven different pitches. It is clear that Cicero's planet music is not one of proportions between orbits, as may be the case in the *Timaeus*, but of speeds of planetary motion. These motions agree in number with the archetypal Septenary, the number of cosmic manifestation (see Macrobius I, vi), which may be viewed as the lower two rows of the Tetraktys, above which are the unmanifest principles of the One and the Dyad:

> •   One
> • •   Dyad
> • • • •} Septenary

5 Here earthly music is regarded not only as imitation of the celestial, but also as preparation for a transition to the higher worlds. Cicero puts it on a par with the cultivation of *studia divina*, which may mean philosophy but could also refer to theurgy. Stahl's translation reads: "as have those who have devoted their exceptional abilities to search for divine truths." Original: *sicut alii, qui praestantibus ingeniis in vita humana divina studia coluerunt.*

6   *Catadupa*. This comparison, first found in Cicero, is often recalled by later writers.

7   The parallel recalls the Allegory of the Sun in Plato's *Republic* VII, 508. The Sun is the representative in the visible world of the higher order, which cannot be reached with the physical senses – the eyes would be blinded – but only with correspondingly higher senses known collectively as the Intellect (*nous*). Similarly, the harmony of the spheres can only be heard when the normal earthly state and its senses are transcended, as presently by Scipio. Where the parallel fails is in the absence of any audible equivalent to the Sun; the Nile cataracts are cited, but not in the same function.

3   Plutarch

1   Socrates' "daimon" was a spirit-guide or sign (our translators' preferred term for δαιμόνιον) which periodically came to him uninvited to give good advice, always of a warning nature. Plutarch cites an amusing instance of it telling Socrates not to go down a certain street: those of his companions who disregarded his advice found themselves overrun by a herd of muddy swine (580 e-f).

2   A subterranean cave at Lebadeia in Boeotia. Pausanias, ix, 39, 5-14 describes the rituals and oracular procedure.

3   An experience often described by initiates, e.g. "there was a final mad whirl within my brain. I had the sensation of being caught up in a tropical whirlwind and seemed to pass upwards through a narrow hole; then there was a momentary dread of being launched into infinite space, I leapt into the unknown – and I was *free*!" Paul Brunton, *A Search in Secret Egypt*, p. 73.

4   The stars and planets.

5   Plutarch's spheres all make music and harmonize with a gentle whirring sound, apparently caused by their movement through the aether. Cf. Synesius (no. 8), lines 27-9.

6   The sea is the celestial sphere, rotating every day around its poles. The current is its equator, which moves fastest. The fixed stars are carried with it, but the planets also have independent movements.

7   The Greeks imagined a starless zone around the invisible South Pole. The shoals and shallows are indistinct galaxies and the Milky Way.

8   The turbid area is probably the sublunary realm.

9   The planets' spirals arise from the combination of their daily circles along with the celestial sphere from East to West, and their own contrary rotation through the Zodiac from West to East.

10   The eight parts are 8/60 of the meridian, i.e. 48°, close to the actual distance between the tropics. The inclined sea is the Zodiacal belt. For fuller explanations see *ed. cit.*, p. 465 nn.

11   The two openings are the intersections of the Zodiac and the galactic circle, the whiteness that of the Milky Way. On these openings cf. the

Myth of Er (no. 1), note 5. An abyss is also described in the following passage, not reproduced here.

4 Corpus Hermeticum

1 Hermes is the speaker. Poimandres is the personification of the Intellect or higher Mind, and is addressed also as *Nous*.
2 The Angels or lesser Gods.
3 The individual in question, together with the other purified souls residing above the Eighth Sphere (the fixed stars).

5 Censorinus

1 The musical part of this work, beginning with VIII, 1, has so far dealt with the beliefs of the Chaldeans concerning the months of pregnancy in which live births can occur, and relating these to the aspects made by the Sun in these months to its position at conception. These aspects are expressed both in the language of astrology and as musical intervals. A digression on Pythagoras follows.
2 The periods of early fetal development are here grouped in the musical tetraktys arrangement 6:8:9:12 (see note 3 to Plato, no. 1 and text of Zarlino, no. 30).
3 Cf. Macrobius' *Commentary on the Dream of Scipio*, I, vi, 14-17, who explains that the joining of the "Male and female numbers," 8 + 27, make 35, which being multiplied by 6 gives the "earliest complete development of the human fetus, as if it were judge of the proper time."
4 See Macrobius, I, vi, 62-6 on the role of the number seven in embryology. Stahl, in his edition, cites also Aristotle *De gen. animal.* IV, x, 777b; pseudo-Iamblichus *Theologoumena arithmeticae*, ed. de Falco, 62-4; 70-1; Gellius III, x, 7-9; pseudo-Galen, ed. Kühn, IX, 908; Clemens Alexandrinus VI, xvi, 143; pseudo-Hippocrates *De carnibus* xix; *De natura pueri*, ed. Kühn, I, 386; Philo Judaeus, *De opificio mundi* cxxiv.
5 Odd numbers are male, good, and primal in Pythagorean numerology; even numbers reflect the female, evil, indeterminate dyad.
6 Jahn attributes these opinions to the lost works of Aristoxenus and Theophrastus (*c.* 370-288/5 BC: Aristotle's successor), both entitled περὶ μουσικῆσ, referring to Mahne de Arist, p. 137 sqq. and to Menag. ad Diog. L, V, 47. No reference is given for Socrates' opinion.
7 *tibicine aut tubicine*, the latter word hesitantly inserted by the editor. Perhaps *tubicine* alone would make better sense.
8 Asclepiades of Prusa, first-century BC materialist physician with theory of disease as hindering of corpuscular movement. Music would presumably help to set the corpuscles in motion again. Works lost.
9 Herophilus of Chalcedon, earlier third-century BC Alexandrian

physician and anatomist. Works lost. His theory of the musical rhythm of the pulse was to be taken up again by Robert Fludd, *Pulsus*, 1629.

6 Plotinus

1 I.e. like actors in a play.

2 The Rational Soul of the World, experienced as the universal plan and law.

3 Does Plotinus actually refer to the formants or harmonics present in a single note (in which case he is the only person in Antiquity to have remarked on this phenomenon), or to something more vague like the "harmony" made by the eight Platonic Sirens (see no. 1)?

4 After the birth of polyphonic music, this idea took on new strength through the comparison of harmonic discord and concord, both necessary to music, with relative evil and good.

5 Plotinus has previously explained that the cosmos has its own periodic cycles, independently of human souls. The voluntary or semi-voluntary descent of the latter, accepting the cosmic harmony (= planetary positions) prevailing at the moment of birth, brings the soul into temporary unison with the cosmos. See also *Poimandres* (no. 4).

6 A reference to the theory of Empedocles (*c.* 493-*c.* 433 BC), legendary Sicilian philosopher, mystic, and statesman associated with Pythagoras, known especially for naming Love and Strife as the twin generators of the cosmos. Plotinus accepts these as permeating all levels of existence: as natural laws of attraction and repulsion susceptible to exploitation by the mage – or scientist. On this and on Plotinus' musical philosophy in general, see Abert, *Die Musikanschauung des Mittelalters*, pp. 43-51.

7 The magician works largely through trained imagination, coupled with a powerful will. Often he literally imagines himself to be the force or divinity whose particular powers he seeks to use. This putting of himself in tune with the patterns of cosmic energy is contrasted with the "standing outside the All" which is the ultimate goal of the mystic who follows the Plotinian path of *theoria*.

8 The "reasonless soul" is the part of the soul where the emotions lie, and it is at this level that the magi operate upon their subjects, leaving unaffected the rational or higher souls of the latter. Similarly, the real soul of a star is not affected by ceremonial magic; only the lower degrees of energy emanating from it are, as it were, tapped.

7 Iamblichus

1 For a thorough summary of the sources, see S.K. Heninger, *Touches of Sweet Harmony*, pp. 19-68, and for a reconstruction of Pythagoras' life and doctrines, emphasizing his differences from Plato, Peter Gorman, *Pythagoras, a Life*.

2   See Ernest G. McClain, *The Myth of Invariance*, "Babylon and Sumer,"
    pp. 129-60; also summarized in McClain's *Meditations through the Quran*,
    "The Holy Mountain," pp. 125-61.

3   The oaths used by the characters in the Platonic dialogues were
    interpreted by the Neoplatonists as being hidden indications of the
    particular divinity associated with, or presiding over, the matter under
    discussion. Perhaps this expletive, apparently so incongruous, is a hint
    that this psychological use of music is an "expansion of the spirits" (as
    Ficino would say – see no. 27) and as such ruled by Jupiter.

4   I.e. "preparations" and "touchings."

5   It is a Platonic dogma that the soul's movement is always circular;
    therefore the only change that can be wrought in it is to make it turn in
    the opposite direction. Cf. Plotinus (no. 6), VI. 9.8.

6   Cf. the same gift reported, after Nicomachus, by Porphyry in his *Life of
    Pythagoras*, 30, and our extract from Simplicius (no. 11). It appears that
    Pythagoras was able voluntarily to achieve the kind of trance-vision
    which was granted in exceptional circumstances to Er and Scipio, and
    that he retained from this, as they did, a memory both of music and of
    moral teachings, the latter expressed in his *Golden Verses*.

7   Fragment 129 Diehls. On Empedocles, see note 6 to Plotinus (no. 6).

8   Pythagoras' springtime ritual was held while the Sun entered its sign of
    exaltation (Aries), and symbolically represented the Sun-god, Apollo,
    with his attribute of the lyre, surrounded by the signs of the Zodiac: a
    motif found repeatedly in ancient iconography. The paean is a hymn
    addressed to Apollo as god of healing.

9   "Well-instituted polities" (says Proclus in MS. Comment. in Alcibiad.
    prior.) "are averse to the art of playing on wind instruments; and
    therefore neither does Plato admit it. The cause of this is the variety of
    this instrument, the pipe, which shows that the art which uses it
    should be avoided. For instruments called Panarmonia, and those
    consisting of many strings, are imitations of pipes. For every hole of the
    pipe emits, as they say, three sounds at least; but if the cavity above
    the holes be opened, then each hole will emit more than three sounds"
    (TT). The point seems to be that the aulos (reed-pipe) is a symbol of
    inconstancy, since through overblowing and venting (as in modern
    woodwind instrumetns) one can change notes without altering the
    basic fingering.

10 The Phrygian piper, playing a native tune, must have been expressing
    the "feminine" and "passive" qualities which Plato was later to
    attribute to the Phrygian mode (*Republic* 399 a-c), and which made the
    lad unable to resist his impulses. The change to slow and heavy
    spondaic rhythm (– –) probably brought him closer to the Dorian ideal:
    the ethos and the scale favored by Plato both for psychological effects
    and for tonal symbolism.

11 On the Pythagorean vespers, see also Plutarch, *De Iside et
    Osiride* XXXI, 384; Quintilian IX, 4, 12; Censorinus (no. 5), XII, 4.

12 *De Mysteriis* opens with "The Epistle of Porphyry to the Egyptian Anebo," asking for the solution of his questions and doubts concerning the Gods, magic, oracles, theurgy, the Demiurge, astrology, and demons. The body of the work is "The Answer of the Preceptor Abammon" to this epistle, Abammon being Anebo's master (I, i). Thomas Taylor says, on the authority of Proclus (this source, pp. 17-18, 304) that Abammon is a name assumed by "the divine Iamblichus."

13 The examples chosen by Anebo are characteristic of divinities popular in the third century AD: the dancing Corybantes, dashing their swords on their shields, the Thracian Jupiter Sabazius, whose initiations involved drawing a live serpent across the breast, and the Syrian Mother-Goddess in her many guises, with her eunuch priests and bizarre ceremonial. See my *Mystery Religions in the Ancient World*, especially pp. 150-3. Iamblichus in Ch. 10 explains them all as having their effects in the purely divine and intellectual realm (see this source, pp. 134-40, which includes a long note on the Corybantes and Curetes from Proclus, *Plat. Theol.* VI, 13). He is at pains to distinguish between the merely psychological effects of music and the authentically spiritual ones which alone are rightly designated "enthusiasm" (from ἐνθουσιασμός, possession by a god).

14 Taylor's italics emphasize a fundamental tenet of ceremonial magic: that certain earthly phenomena (including melodies) are as it were imprinted with the signature of a deity, who is actually present therein as far as is possible on the terrestrial plane. Iamblichus goes on to correct the assumption, common then as now, that divine possession is only a condition of body and psyche brought about through their native "harmonic" constitution, such as was described in the Pythagorean tales of the efficacy of music: no, it is a direct meeting with the Gods, such as the soul experienced before birth. The sound of instruments puts the soul in touch with *musica divina*, without the mediation of *musica mundana* or *musica humana*.

8 Synesius

1 Synesius uses the old form for Jerusalem, Σόλυμοι.

2 In this refrain it is Christ who is invoked as a spiritual Father.

3 Cerberus. Synesius sets the Harrowing of Hell in the classical Tartarus.

4 The early Church, following Luke 24.50-53 and John 20.17, did not divide the Ascension clearly from the Resurrection. It is the Acts of the Apostles 1.9-11, source of the later church's teaching, that places them forty days apart.

5 The inhabitants of the upper air or lower aether, midway in status between gods and men, sometimes beneficent, sometimes malevolent.

6 The sounds of the seven planetary bodies are caused by their

movement through the aether, called "wise" because this harmony embodies the mathematical laws of the cosmos. We are in a Platonic framework in which the material planets reflect the creative wisdom of the Demiurge.

7   The passage through the sphere of the Fixed Stars brings the voyager to the end of the sensible realm and into the intelligible, sometimes envisaged as a further series of concentric but immaterial spheres.

8   Martianus Capella's Philology, on attaining the Eighth Sphere, knelt and, "concentrating the whole attention of her mind, prayed long in silence" (*The Marriage of Philology and Mercury*, 202).

9   Martianus Capella

1   Stahl and Johnson's date, as suggested in vol. I, pp. 11ff. Henry Chadwick, in his *Boethius*, p. 21, gives the 460s or 470s.

2   I.e. Minerva and Venus.

3   In section 212, among the deified mortals, Orpheus and Aristoxenus were introduced, playing lyres, thus reconciling the two factions of Greek music theory. The following verse passage (indented) celebrates the three most eminent semi-mythological musicians of Antiquity.

4   Olympus, pupil and favorite of Marsyas (WHS).

5   Venus.

6   One wonders what artefact inspired Martianus' description of the shield of Harmony. The other Arts each carry recognizable attributes, some beautiful, others as absurd as those of Renaissance pageants. It seems unlikely that Martianus himself would have invented this one, a kind of musical orrery.

7   The gods revere the harmony of the spheres in which they recognize the grandeur of the supreme harmony of the divine Intellect (the "secret fire," a metaphor reminiscent of the Chaldean theosophy) to which even they are subject.

8   The Great and Little Bears (WHS).

9   Presumably the two octaves of the "earthly" Greater Perfect System, the foundation of Greek music.

10 Referring to Martianus' mixture of prose and verse.

11 Juno, Vesta, Minerva, Ceres, Diana, Venus, Mars, Mercury, Jupiter, Neptune, Vulcan, Apollo.

12 The sun and the moon.

13 A reference to an earlier passage, describing the Grove of Apollo in Cirrha, near Delphi:

> [11] Amidst these extraordinary scenes and these vicissitudes of Fortune, a sweet music arose from the trees, a melody arising from their contact as the breeze whispered through them; for the crests of the great trees were very tall and, because of this tension, reverberated with a sharp sound; but whatever was close to and near the ground, with drooping boughs, shook with a deep heaviness of sound; while the trees of middle size in

their contacts with each other sang together in fixed harmonies of the duple [2:1], the sesquialtera [3:2], the sesquitertia [4:3] also, and even the sesquioctava [9:8] without discrimination, although semitones came in between. So it happened that the grove poured forth, with melodious harmony, the whole music and song of the gods.

[12] As the Cyllenian explained this, Virtue learned that in heaven also, in the same way, the spheres either produce harmony or join in the accompaniments; so it is not strange that the grove of Apollo should be full of harmony, when the same god, in the sun, modulates the spheres of the heavens also.

The same musical tetraktys is expounded again during the marriage, in a passage on the arithmology of Mercury's and Philology's names (sections 107-108).

14 The reference is to Leda, mother of Helen (WHS).

15 Selene, goddess of the moon (WHS).

16 Stahl and Johnson say that this is "the most Neoplatonic passage in the entire *Marriage*, but it does not constitute a sufficient basis for regarding Martianus as a representative of the Neoplatonic school" (ed. cit., vol. I, pp. 204-5). Henry Chadwick, on the other hand, sees him as imbued with the Neoplatonism of Iamblichus, Proclus, and the Chaldean Oracles (p. 21). One might go so far as to say that the title itself has more than a hint of Hermetism about it, for what is this tale but the hierogamy, the sacred marriage or Chemical Wedding, that crowns the quest of the Soul? Philology has faithfully followed the disciplines and learned all that earthly wisdom can offer; now the time has come to spew it forth and leave behind what is, at best, only a shadow of the true Logos or Creative Mind with which she is enamoured. Her promised spouse is Mercury, familiar since his assumption of the mantle of the Egyptian Thoth as the psychopomp who leads souls to the Beyond. His learning and eloquence – his Logos – is not of this world, for he is an immortal god: and Philology, through her marriage, will also partake of divinity; the Soul will leave earth, shake off the psychic trammels represented by the seven spheres, and attain gnostic union with the divine Spirit. Not without reason does Martianus place Harmony, rather than the traditional Astronomy, at the culmination of his work: for, as this passage relates, Harmony has her origins in the very heights of the intellectual (or logoic) hierarchy. Regarded thus, Martianus begins more and more to resemble his great predecessor and model, Apuleius, who could use the form of a picaresque novel (*The Golden Ass*) to convey initiatic truths.

17 The following compilation probably comes from lost works of the great Roman encyclopedist Marcus Terentius Varro (116-27 BC). Other parallels are to be found in numerous other Roman authors (see ed. cit., vol. I., p. 54), but this collection is the most complete of its time. Aristeides Quintilianus is the source for the later and longer part of

Harmony's speech (930-995), here omitted, in which she expounds Greek music theory.

10 Boethius

1 Calvin M. Bower, ed. cit.; see also Bower, "Boethius and Nicomachus, an essay concerning the sources of De Institutione Musica," and for an excellent summary of Boethius' musical contribution, Henry Chadwick, *Boethius; the Consolations of Music, Logic, Theology, and Philosophy*, pp. 78-101.

2 Bower, *Boethius' The Principles of Music* [= our source], p. 369.

3 The Quadrivium: Arithmetic, Geometry, Music, Astronomy.

4 *Timaeus* 37a.

5 *Republic* 424b.

6 *Ibid.*, 424c.

7 Has there ever been a time at which intellectual musicians did not deplore the current state of music as a sad decline from some real or imagined past? This phenomenon should be seen as the writer's "vertical" aspiration towards the more spiritual purposes of art, projected onto the "horizontal" progression of history. Just as there is never a Utopia on earth, so music is always present in both elevating and depraved forms.

8 *Republic* 399c.

9 *Ibid.*, 401d.

10 Boethius returned to the theme of harmonious elements in the *Consolations of Philosophy*; see the passages quoted by Zarlino (no. 30). On the harmony of the elements and seasons as a function of Love, see Erixymachus' speech in Plato, *Symposium* 188a. See also Wisdom of Solomon, 19.18, which compares the changing of the elements to that of the notes on a harp.

11 See Cicero (no. 2).

12 Concerning the music of the human being see Plato *Phaedrus* 86; *Republic* 442-443; *Laws* 653b; Cicero *Tusc. Disp.* I, 10; Ps.-Plutarch *De Musica* 1140b; Ptolemy *Harmonics* III, 5-7 (CMB). Also our extracts from Jacques de Liège (no. 24) and Zarlino (no. 30).

13 Boethius is here probably referring to Aristotle, *De Anima* 423a, 30: "if the movement set up by an object is too strong for the organ, the equipoise of contrary qualities in the organ, which is precisely its sensory power, is disturbed; it is exactly as concord and tone are destroyed by violently twanging the strings of a lyre." Boethius significantly does not cite *De Anima* 407b-408b, where Aristotle refutes the notion that the soul is a harmony (CMB).

14 Cf. Cicero, *de Officiis* I, xlii, on the unacceptability of artisanship or the minor trades. It was well over 1000 years before technical virtuosity in music was regularly valued, as it is today, over theoretical knowledge or compositional skill.

15 In his *De Musica*, VI, vii, 17, St Augustine calls the highest of his several "rhythms" that which judges all the others.

11 Simplicius

1 Sir Thomas Heath, in *Aristarchus of Samos, the Ancient Copernicus*, pp. 163ff., discusses the Pythagoreans' knowledge of the distances between the respective planets and the center of the cosmos. But D.R. Dicks, *Early Greek Astronomy to Aristotle*, pp. 64ff., considers Heath "far too sanguine" and does not even concede Heath's assertion that the Pythagoreans knew of the basic classical picture of a static earth, rotating sphere of fixed stars, and contrarily rotating planets. For further references, see Leo Elders, *Aristotle's Cosmology: a Commentary on the De Caelo*, pp. 223-6.

2 Aristotle's refutation of the music of the spheres can be summarized as follows: large bodies make loud noises; the heavens are immense; therefore their noise, if it existed, would be devastating. Noise is caused by friction of a moving with an unmoving body. If the heavenly bodies moved in a mass of air or fire, as generally supposed, certainly there would be noise. But there is no noise, because the stars are attached to the body which carries them, like the parts of a ship which are attached to the body of the ship carried by a stream (*De caelo* II, 9, 290b-291a).

3 The soul has three vehicles, one etherial, another aerial, and the third this terrestrial body. The first which is luminous and celestial is connate with the essence of the soul, and in which alone it resides in a state of bliss in the stars. In the second it suffers the punishment of its sins after death. And from the third it becomes an inhabitant of earth (TT). These are more generally known as the triad of (Divine) Spirit, Soul, and Body, abolished in the West by the Council of Constantinople, AD 869, in favor of a spiritual-material dualism.

4 At a stroke, Simplicius dissolves the objection of Aristotle (which is also the assumption of the modern scientific method): that for a thing to be true, it must be demonstrable to the senses held in common by all people. He says that other senses are developed in those who (1) are blessed at birth with extraordinary gifts, (2) are unusually virtuous, (3) practise theurgic rituals for their self-improvement.

5 I.e. an immaterial vibration can set in motion the suitably sensitive physical sense-organ and give rise to the experience of sound.

6 The preceding sentences suggested that Pythagoras could actually have experienced the heavenly motions as sound, but here Simplicius seems to make his experience a mathematical one. Perhaps the experience in question is inexpressible in any terrestrial mode. The most thorough discussion of the matter is by Jacques de Liège, in his chapter on *Musica mundana* (not included here).

12 Philo

1 *Phaedrus* 246e. On Philo's use of musical ideas, see Abert, *Musikanschauung*, pp. 35-43.

2 Philo says that mortals will never arrive at a clear solution of the problems of the heavenly constitution and harmony (*On Dreams* I, IV, 23-4).

3 Or "Respiratory" (RM). Cf. the four constituents of man in our introduction to Philo: *logos*, corresponding to air, is here governed by *nous* corresponding to the heavens, in order to make mere voice into melody.

4 *Odyssey*, XII, 39-45. See also note 11 to Plato (no. 1).

5 On nourishment through music, see also the Ikhwān al-Ṣafā' (no. 15) and Majd al-Dīn al-Ghazālī (no. 17).

6 Cf. the descriptions of Pythagoras' hearing celestial music in our extracts from Iamblichus (no. 7), Simplicius (no. 11), and Suhrawardī (no. 18).

7 Philo is commenting on Deuteronomy 32-34, which contains the song, blessing and death of Moses. The song opens with an invocation to heaven and earth (32.1).

8 Perhaps the twelve proclamations to the Twelve Tribes (Deuteronomy 33) suggested this idea to Philo.

9 Cf. the stripping of the soul in *Poimandres* (no. 4).

13 Isaac ben Solomon ibn Sahula

1 For an outline of the part it has played, see Amnon Shiloah, "The Symbolism of Music in the Kabbalistic Tradition."

2 See Ernest McClain, *Meditations through the Quran*, pp. 125-61, "The Holy Mountain."

3 The *Zohar*, or "Book of Radiance" is the principal book of early Jewish Kabbalah (esoteric doctrine), and takes the form of commentaries on the *Torah* (the first five books of the "Old Testament" of the Christian Bible) attributed to the inspired Rabbis Eleazar (third century), Simeon ben Jachai, and others. The author of the main part is believed to have been Moses de León, a Spanish Jew of the thirteenth century, but naturally much of his material was compiled from older sources. The "Radiance" or "Splendor" of the title is the Divine Light that shines from every line of Scripture (even the outwardly insignificant ones). Like the Sufis, the Jewish mystics regarded their sacred texts as a living entity with a superior existence – to some it was the Name, or even the Body, of God – which invited deeper and deeper readings correlative to their own mystical development.

For a key to the many references to music in the *Zohar*, see Amnon Shiloah, *Music Subjects in the Zohar: Texts and Indices*, which has an introduction in English and, although the extracts are given in

Hebrew, is usable in conjunction with an English *Zohar* because it gives all the references in Arabic numerals. On the Kabbalistic books from a Pythagorean point of view, see also Albert von Thimus, *Die harmonikale Symbolik des Alterthums*, vol. II.

4   He may have in mind some such system as that of Ptolemy's *Harmonics* III, 5, which was certainly known by Arab theorists, in which the faculties and powers of the soul are aligned with the musical intervals.

5   This section originally in Aramaic. Translation kindly provided by Professor Masha Itzhaki.

6   I.e. a body of knowledge.

7   The books of Judaic Law.

8   *Gevurah* is the name of the fifth Sefirah of the Kabbalistic "Tree of Life," usually rendered as "Judgment" or "Severity" (as opposed to its counterpart *Hesed*, "Mercy"). In man this appears as the tendency towards "discipline, rigour and discrimination," according to Z'ev ben Shimon Halevi, *Kabbalah: Tradition of Hidden Knowledge*, p. 7. Shiloah, "The Symbolism of Music," p. 61, says: "We repeatedly find the idea that music comes from the north, that is the left, the side of judgment, while speech arrives from the right, the side of mercy."

9   From here onwards the text is a patchwork of quotations from the *Zohar*, III, 18b-19a. The present translation is a literal one.

14   Isaac Loeb Peretz

1   Cf. the wordless melismas improvised by the cantors in the synagogue.

2   Kabbalistic doctrine teaches that the Universe is created from the letters that make the *Torah*. This assimilation of the creative archetype with music and with the World-Soul is remarkably Platonic.

3   On visions of light (the astral world) being succeeded in the mystic's ascent by sound (Devachan), see also Rudolf Steiner (no. 55).

4   The presence of sadness as an element of this mystical epiphany reminds us, in the present context, of the great Jewish philosopher Se'adiah (or Saadya) Gaon (892-942) who lists the virtues promoted by music as: power to reign, fortitude, humility, joy, and sorrow (Werner and Sonne, "The Philosophy and Theory of Music in Judaeo-Arabic Literature," p. 286), and of the Brethren of Purity's (no. 15) allusion to the "saddening" melody as an arouser of desire for God.

5   The Kabbalists speak of a mystical experience which removes the consciousness from the body in such a way that physical death ensues. According to Frances Yates, *Giordano Bruno and the Hermetic Tradition*, p. 99, Pico della Mirandola was greatly preoccupied with this experience. Cf. Psalm 116, verse 15: "Most precious in the sight of the Lord is the death of his Saints."

15   The Brethren of Purity

1   On some of these debates, see Y. Marquet in *Encyclopedia of Islam*, vol. V, pp. 1071-6. For the most complete and sympathetic account in English, with full bibliography, see S.H. Nasr, *An Introduction to Islamic Cosmological Doctrines*, pp. 25-104.

2   *ta'līf* is "composition" in the literal sense of the putting-together of elements, hence is close to the Platonic concept of harmony. The Epistle here divides music into two categories: the harmony found throughout the universe and expressible in mathematical proportions, and the sonorous *musica instrumentalis* represented by *ghīna'* (literally "song") and *sinā'at al-malāhī*, *malāhī* meaning amusements or entertainments.

3   This formula, which is repeated throughout the treatise, and gives a special flavor to the text, is based on a verse from the *Quran* (58. 22). All quotations from the *Quran* are taken from Arthur J. Arberry, *The Koran interpreted* (AS).

4   For details about the poems, their poets and historical context, and for very extensive notes, see Shiloah's French translation of the Epistle, "L'épître sur la musique des Ikhwān al-Ṣafā'."

5   This story appears to be of Arabic, not classical provenance. Unlike the string of anecdotes which commonly illustrate the power of music in Boethius and his imitators, the instances in this chapter lead deliberately from the most violent effects to the most soporific.

6   This, the final chapter of the Epistle, touches on the mystical experiences of listening which are further developed in the treatises of the al-Ghazālī brothers (nos 16, 17).

7   The fact that people are on different gnostic levels, an indispensable assumption in any discussion of gnosis, is exemplified in the distinction made here, as in all schools of Islamic esotericism, between the literal or apparent meaning of sacred texts (*zāhir*) and their hidden or interior meanings (*batīn*).

8   Cf. Philo on the Death of Moses (no. 12).

16   Abū Ḥāmid al-Ghazālī

1   For an account of his life and place in the history of Islamic culture, see F.E. Peters, *Allah's Commonwealth*, pp. 690-716. Peters concludes his book with sad observations on the failure of al-Ghazālī's ambition.

2   The *Sidratu-l-muntahā*, the farthest point in heaven to which the knowledge of creatures reaches (*Quran* 53. 14) (DBM). Presumably equivalent to the Eighth Sphere of European cosmology.

17   Majd al-Dīn al-Ghazālī

1   He has been citing instances from the *Quran* and the legends of the

Prophet Muhammad to justify the use of music for ritual purposes. His strong words on those who disapprove of it are due to the warrant he draws from the Prophet's own conduct.

2 The Sufis were careful not to let novices indulge too freely in audition because, like any mystical practice, it could be misused and do more harm than good.

3 *Quran* 6.52; 18.27.

4 This refers to the procedure of *ta'wīl*, the reading of deeper meanings into the outward "forms" of the sacred text, indispensable to Sufis.

5 One of the Companions of the Prophet.

6 *Quran* 18.

7 The divine Presence; a term borrowed from Hebrew *shekina*.

8 In Islamic mysticism, the *Quran* has a distinct existence in the spiritual world, where its surahs are perceptible as objective entities or beings. The Kabbalists of this period had the same view of the *Torah*.

9 Cf. the allegorization of musical instruments by the Church Fathers. See H. Abert, *Die Musikanschauung des Mittelalters*, pp. 211-23.

10 Cf. the poem of Rūmī (no. 19) on the human being as a reed-flute.

11 *Quran* 7.171.

12 *Quran* 15.29; 38.72.

13 The text now moves from static symbolism to the actual experience of the mystic who, on hearing the music, begins to dance, whirl, tear and throw off his clothes, yet experiences in the midst of this frantic activity the center of spiritual Peace. Outward quiescence (see points I and V below) is only the sign of material existence.

14 For light on the meaning behind this practice, see Henry Corbin, *Creative Imagination in the Ṣūfism of Ibn 'Arabī*, pp. 64-7, on the ritual of investiture with a mantle. The action has the intention of bestowing on the receiver the present spiritual state of the donor.

15 On the multifarious lights experienced by Sufis, see H. Corbin, *The Man of Light in Iranian Sufism*, pp. 61-120.

16 See Philo (no. 12); also point II below. The Sixth Imam, Ja'far Ṣādiq, reported that for the inhabitants of Jābalqā and Jābarṣā "their nourishment is hymnology" (H. Corbin, *Spiritual Body and Celestial Earth*, p. 260).

17 The repetition of the word *huwā* (He) with lengthening of the second vowel, is a mystic practice (JR).

18 The "pillars" of Islam are the five daily prayers, the pilgrimage to Mecca, and the affirmation that there is one God and that Muhammad is his prophet.

19 *Fanā'* is the extinction of the individuality in the state of Union with God; *baqā'*, which is superior even to this, is the state of subsistence in Pure Being. See R.A. Nicholson, *The Mystics of Islam*, pp. 162-4, but also Shahidullah Faridi's critique in Hujwīrī, *The Unveiling of the Veiled*, pp. ix-x.

20 On the situation of music, dance, and other external means to

spiritual realizations in the general economy of Muslim ascesis, see Titus Burckhardt, *An Introduction to Sufi Doctrine*, pp. 132-5.

21   This paragraph analyzes the three different letters of the word *samā'* (audition) in their various combinations.

22   Muhammad.

23   *Quran* 5.86f.

18   Suhrawardī

1   On his life and works, besides our source see S.H. Nasr, *Three Muslim Sages*, pp. 52-82. Other relevant articles by Nasr are "The Influence of Sufism on Traditional Persian Music," and "Islam and Music."

2   The images and forms perceived in the intermediate world – some would say on the "subtle plane" – of Hūrqalyā. The commentator has already said (ed. cit., p. 128) that they "exist neither in thought, since the great cannot be imprinted in the small, nor in concrete reality, otherwise anyone with normally healthy senses would be able to see them. But they are not merely non-being." He describes them further below.

3   The four worlds are not given here in their hierarchical order, which is as follows:

   A.   World of Archangelic Lights (Jabarūt)
   B.   World of Souls governing bodies (Malakūt)
   C.   World of the Active Imagination (Hūrqalyā)
   D.   Material World (double barzakh)

Worlds C and D correspond to one another except in extent: each has both an Earth and Heavenly spheres. Christian cosmology has omitted C, joining the upper limit of D (the Primum Mobile) directly to the lowest rank of B (the Angels, or in some cases the souls), hence losing the concept of a subtle realm and compounding the difficulties that arise from an unmediated dichotomy of spirit and matter. See also note 3 to Simplicius (no. 11).

4   The Heavens of the seven planets (*Quran* 78.12).

5   The last sentence is the most puzzling of all. In Hūrqalyā, we are told, what is impossible or inconceivable on earth actually takes place, but none of the descriptions of it suggest for a moment that, even there, the laws of number are suspended. Numerical symbolism, in fact, is one of the threads that relates it both to the Archangelic and to the material world. And where there is number, there is, at least by implication, tone. Perhaps Pythagoras' belief in the absolute primacy of these principles derived from his perception of them there as universal constants. In Suhrawardī's visionary recital, *The Chant of the Wing of Gabriel*, the disciple is also instructed in the science of the esoteric meaning of letters and words based on their numerical symbolism (Nasr, *Three Muslim Sages*, p. 78), an experience which may relate to the same body of knowledge.

19 Rūmī

1 The *nay* or reed-flute was the poet's favorite musical instrument . . . and has always been associated with the religious services of the Mawlawī Order, in which music and dancing are prominent features. . . . A great deal – much of it, I think, fantastic – has been written about the meaning of *nay* in this and the following verses. There can be no doubt that it symbolizes generally the soul of the Saint or Perfect Man lamenting its severance from "the reed-bed" (the spiritual world where it dwelt in a state of pre-existence) and waking in others the same longing for their true home; and that, in particular, it is used here as an emblem either of Ḥusāmu'ddīn [= Shāmsoddīn, Rūmī's devoted disciple and amanuensis] (with whom the poet is mystically one) or of the poet itself, filled with the Divine spirit which he pours forth in song . . . (RAN). On Rūmī's other uses of musical imagery, see Annemarie Schimmel, *The Triumphant Sun*, pp. 210-22.

2 Literally, "rent our veils" (RAN).

3 Seventh/early eighth-century poet, known as the "obsessed": a type of mystical self-abandonment.

4 A prince of Balkh (d. *c.* 776) who was called from a life of dissipation to become a Sufi.

5 The connexion of this passage with the preceding verses, which is not made very clear, becomes evident if we consider the poet's intention, namely, to show that Ibrāhīm ibn Adham, with all the Kingdom of Balkh at his command, was nevertheless an unworldly prince. Although, like other monarchs, he had his bodyguard and court-minstrels, no motive of self-interest or self-indulgence could be imputed to him. His justice secured him against attack; and if he was not insensible to the pleasures of music, for him they were only a means of bringing the spirit into harmony with its own proper world (RAN).

6 Nicholson suggests that this refers either to the proclamation "Am I not your Lord?" (*Quran* 7.172) to which all human souls respond in eternity, to the trumpet of spiritual resurrection which is heard as the Voice of God in the mystic's heart, or to the Last Trump (*Quran* 74.8) announcing the Day of Judgment.

7 Sufis hold that in the state of pre-existence all human souls were with Adam in Paradise, where cacophony is unknown (RAN).

8 See Wagner, p. 238, for an example of this put into practice.

9 A reference to the next story (not included here), of the thirsty man who was entranced by the sound of the walnuts dropping into water he could not reach.

20 Dionysius the Areopagite

1 The Seraphim, Cherubim, and Thrones, who "are established about God, immediately encircling Him; and in perpetual purity they

encompass His eternal knowledge in that most high and eternal angelic dance" (ch. 7).

2   The Dominions, Virtues, and Powers.

3   The Principalities, Archangels, and Angels: the latter are the actual "messengers" (ἄγγελοι) who appear to us.

4   The ecclesiastical hierarchy of the Christian Church, which Dionysius describes as reflecting on earth the orders of Heaven.

5   Isaiah 6.3.

6   The threefold division of all spiritual powers occurs also in Neoplatonism. In this insistence on "first, middle and last powers" we may also hear an echo of *Timaeus* 31 b-c: "But it is impossible for two things alone to cohere together without the intervention of a third; for a certain collective bond is necessary in the middle of the two." John Scotus Eriugena, in his Commentary on Dionysius (*PL* 122, 225-6), emphasizes the universality of the mean which brings about the harmonies between and within the Hierarchies.

21   Aurelian of Réôme

1   Aurelian's sources are Boethius, Cassiodorus, Isidore of Seville, and a music treatise ascribed to Alcuin. See Lawrence Gushee on "Aurelian" in *The New Grove Dictionary of Music and Musicians*, vol. I, pp. 702-4.

2   On learning songs from angels, cf. Dionysius the Areopagite, *Celestial Hierarchies*, ch. 13, describing how Isaiah was instructed in the divine praise-song by a Seraph.

3   I.e. Monte Sant' Angelo, on the Eastern spur of Italy.

4   *Dialogues* IV, 26.

22   Anonymous of the School of Chartres

1   Ed. cit., p. 101. The notes are in a Florentine MS., Naz. Conv. Soppr. I. 1. 28 (PD).

2   Quoted in John of Salisbury's *Metalogicon*, III, 4 (*PL*, 199, 900).

3   The passage in Martianus reads: "Sacred principle of unity amongst the gods, on you I call; you are said to grace weddings with your song; it is said that Camena was your mother." Dronke comments on this: "The God Hymenaeus, it would seem, is both the natural sexual creative force, and the glory of mutual love. And this mutual love is no purely human concept: with the help of Boethius' famous hymn on cosmic love, which he cites, the author glimpses such a loving bond in the harmony of the parts of the physical universe. Thereupon he proceeds to identify the god who has revealed himself in so many aspects of the universe – sexual, procreative, mutually loving, and elemental – with the Christian Holy Spirit. Charity is theologically the gift that the Holy Spirit infuses (*infundit*) in mankind. In this text,

however, the activities of the divine power throughout the universe have been evoked so comprehensively and with so deep a sense of unity that concepts become interchangeable and can stand as metaphors for one another. Thus it is *caritas*, the theological virtue, which is said to be infused in all things. It is the third person of the Trinity, the Christian Hymenaeus, who is now said to fulfil the elements of the fable, presiding over the nuptials, brought forth by the 'Camena' of heavenly harmony."

4 (*Hymeneus est membranula, in qua concipiuntur puerperia, matrix videlicet, que septem continet cellulas: impressione humane forme signatas.*) The manuscript appears to suggest that the *membranula* and *matrix* are identical, but this must, I think, be due either to faulty syntax or faulty preservation of the text, rather than faulty anatomy (PD).

5 Pre-microscopic embryology assumed that it was the actual seminal substance that formed the basis of the foetus. The simile of a seal may derive from Macrobius I, vi, 63: "Once the seed has been deposited in the mint where man is coined."

6 Boethius, *Consolations of Philosophy* II, metrum 8.

7 From Isidore of Seville's *Etymologia* (sixth century) throughout the Middle Ages, assonance served as a substitute for scientific etymology. The resultant meanings, often absurd, can only be taken seriously if we remember that the association of a truth of another order satisfied the medieval mind to the same degree that the tracing of historical roots does the modern. Which is ultimately more productive of truth, is hard to say.

8 *Camena est una ex octo earum facta*; Dronke omits "of them." Even so, the meaning is not altogether clear; the writer seems to draw a parallel between the eightfold harmony of the spheres influencing the ninth sphere, Earth, and the eightfold Camena whose child is Hymenaeus, equivalent to the ninth Muse.

23   Adam Scot

1 The interval of a perfect fourth.
2 The interval of an octave.
3 The interval of a perfect fifth. These are the three "perfect consonances" of Greek and Medieval music theory.

24   Jacques de Liège

1 For an appreciation of the opening chapters of this work, see Walter Grossmann, *Die einleitenden Kapitel des Speculum Musicae von Jean de Muris* (then believed to be the author).
2 Gregory the Great, *Moralium Libri*, VI, 16 (*PL*, 75, 740c).
3 *De Institutione Musica*, I, 1 (see no. 10).
4 *Ibid.*, I, 2.

5 Aristotle, *Nicomachean Ethics*, III, 6.
6 *De Musica*, VI, 4; *De genesi ad Litteram*, XII, 35.
7 *De Institutione Musica*, I, 2.
8 Loc. cit.

26 Henry Suso

1 On Suso in his context, and on the authenticity of this *Life*, see James
   M. Clark, *The Great German Mystics: Eckhart, Tauler and Suso*, pp. 55-74.
2 See especially *Paradiso* X, 64-81; XII, 1-9; XIII, 1-30.

27 Marsilio Ficino

1 *Spiritual and Demonic Magic*, p. 3n.
2 Cf. Plotinus IV. 4. 40 (no. 6): "a significant cry," etc.
3 The "image" is a talisman of the planetary metal inscribed with
   appropriate words and symbols. Cf. Fournier, no. 49.
4 Ficino invokes as authorities some of those *prisci theologi* who
   constituted the perennial chain of wisdom in Antiquity: the Hebrew
   Kabbalists, Zoroaster, Hermes, Orpheus, Pythagoras, Plato and the
   Platonists, Apollonius of Tyana, and the more mystical Christian
   Fathers such as Origen, Clement of Alexandria, and Dionysius the
   Areopagite. This concept was brought to the West early in the century
   by the Byzantine scholar George Gemistos Pletho, who influenced
   Cosimo de' Medici in his grand scheme for the revival of all this
   ancient theology.
5 A new type of planetary scale, devoid of musical meaning but
   comprising steps of increasing subtlety of means, corresponding to
   different levels of being. Man, as microcosm, can operate on all of
   them, and beyond them, too.
6 Again, Ficino is vague about how this is to be done, except that it is
   very hard! But he avoids the obvious course of simply assigning modes
   to the planets, preferring to recommend what we would call deductive
   reasoning and experimental science as the proper way to find the right
   music for each planet. He had obviously done so himself, as we hear of
   him singing planetary songs to his own accompaniment on the viola de
   braccio. See D.P. Walker on "Ficino and Music" in *Spiritual and
   Demonic Magic from Ficino to Campanella*, pp. 3-24.
7 *Spiritus*, not to be confused with the highest element in man sometimes
   called the Spirit (Divine Spark, etc.), is a material but subtle substance
   which permeates the body, carrying the life-forces and acting as a
   vehicle for psychic influences. In pre-Cartesian perception-theories the
   act of seeing, especially, was believed to consist of an emission of
   spiritus through the pupil of the eye which returned, laden with an
   image. Ficino describes the workings of music as follows:

But musical sound by the movement of the air moves the body: by purified air [inside the ear] it excites the aerial spirit which is the bond between body and soul: by emotion it affects the senses and at the same time the soul: by meaning it works on the mind: finally, by the very movement of the subtle air it penetrates strongly: by its contemperation it flows smoothly: by the conformity of its quality it floods us with a wonderful pleasure: by its nature, both spiritual and material, it at once seizes, and claims as its own, man in his entirety. (Quoted from Ficino's *Commentary on the Timaeus*, ch. 28, in Walker, *op. cit.*, p. 9)

8   Ficino is only concerned with drawing down the influences of the benefic planets, hence ascribes no music to the malefics Saturn and Mars, or the at best indifferent Moon. Although in one respect Saturn is the noblest planet of all, representing the state of pure intellectual contemplation from which alone one can break through to the heavens beyond, his influence in the earthly direction is destructive. Pure contemplation, after all, annihilates all earthly things for one who attains it.

9   See our extracts from these writers.

10   This is the tale of the Tarantula, the effects of whose bite can only be cured by the Tarantella: a favorite example of music's marvelous effects. On tarantism see Henry E. Sigerist, "The Story of Tarantism," in Dorothy M. Schullian and Max Schoen, eds, *Music and Medicine*, pp. 96-116, and Luis Robledo, "Poesía y música de la tarántula," pp. 223-32.

28   Matthaus Herbenus

1   *Phthongoi* is the Greek term for single notes. Herbenus is probably referring to pre-Renaissance errors in understanding the Greek system.

2   *Nat. hist.* II, 20.

3   *Mundus* in Latin, like *kosmos* in Greek, carries the meanings of neatness, cleanliness, and beauty (cf. "cosmetics").

4   Note the humanist emphasis on Man's dignity and potentially divine condition.

5   Empyrean literally means "fiery," but was used in the Renaissance for the Christian heaven beyond the eighth sphere.

6   The absolute summit of music is here reached in the *vox Dei*, which is in a sense also the creative Word.

7   Herbenus is evidently not a Pythagorean: the angelic music surpasses number and is expressed in intellectual modes inconceivable to man. Therefore, like most Christian authorities from St Augustine onwards, he would reject the mathematical sciences as conveyors of absolute wisdom in favor of direct, supra-rational experience.

29 Henry Cornelius Agrippa

1 Hebrew was considered, by those acquainted with it, a more efficacious language for magical purposes than any vernacular; Greek, similarly, as being a more "worthy" language than Latin, perhaps because of the use, since ancient times, of the numerical equivalents to the letters (found also in Hebrew and Arabic) in speculative numerology. Not long after Agrippa's time, John Dee was to receive through angelic revelation the even worthier language of Enochian, on whose remarkable nature research still continues. This hierarchy of languages reflects the Renaissance's search for sources and origins, and for the pure and unadulterated tongue of man's unfallen state: a search continued, among our later authors, by Fabre d'Olivet.

2 Luke 10.20.

3 *Life of Apollonius of Tyana*, IV, 45.

4 No concordance available to me enables me to locate this passage.

5 *Res reconditae*.

6 *The Golden Ass*, VI, 2.

7 This is the *spiritus* with which Ficino (no. 27) was also concerned. See note 7 to Ficino.

8 The "species" is the incorporeal essence of objects, existing on the same plane as *spiritus*. An intermediate or subtle realm is posited here as the mediator between body and soul, or – which comes to the same thing – between the physical cause of the sound and the inner perception of it. It is the "collective bond" necessary between any two disparate entities, as Plato says in *Timaeus* 31b-c. For a vivid description of the emission of the species of light from the eye, and its effects on the *spiritus*, see Ficino's *Commentary on Plato's Symposium*, VII, 3, p. 223.

30 Giosefo Zarlino

1 O. Strunk, *Source Readings in Music History*, p. 228.

2 See the *Institutioni*, 1573 ed., pp. 231-3.

3 See Marco Pallis, "The Metaphysics of Musical Polyphony."

4 *Book of 83 Questions*, question 56 (GZ). Cf. Censorinus (no. 5).

5 *Harmonics*, III, 5 (GZ).

6 Ch. 4 (GZ).

7 *Aeneid* VI, 545 (GZ).

31 Luis de León

1 The (subtle) air is the vehicle literally moulded by the vibrations of music; cf. note 7 to Ficino (no. 27).

2 Here sound is converted into vision. This verse combines the image of the musical Demiurge with his lyre with an allusion to Amphion's

musical building of Troy, the temple in question being of course the cosmos.

3 The Pythagorean music of the spheres answers the Demiurge's harmony with its own.

4 Cf. Rudolf Steiner on the experience of Devachan (no. 55). Willis Barnstone, in *The Unknown Light*, a translation of selected poems of Fray Luis whose title is taken from this poem, line 2 (*luz no usada*), writes a perceptive analysis of the poem to support his claim for the authenticity of Fray Luis's mystical experience, as against those critics who have been at pains to reduce it to the aesthetic level. Barnstone's translation is fine poetry but not sufficiently literal for the present book.

5 These are his fellow poets who formed the "School of Salamanca," especially Francisco Sánchez, D. Juan de Almeida, and D. Alonso de Espinosa.

32 Guy Lefèvre de la Boderie

1 *Spiritual and Demonic Magic from Ficino to Campanella*, p. 124, n. 4. See also Walker's *The Ancient Theology, passim*; Frances A. Yates, *The French Academies*, pp. 43-4 *et passim*, and *The Occult Philosophy in the Elizabethan Age*, pp. 65-7.

2 See Anne Macaulay, "APOLLO: The Pythagorean Definition of God."

3 Levèvre had added the four "vestures" to the traditional tetrads of the elements, times of day, seasons, and humors. See S.K. Heninger, *Touches of Sweet Harmony*, pp. 146ff. The comparison with the four strings of an instrument is found also in Arab sources, such as al-Kindī (ninth century) and the Brethren of Purity. See A. Shiloah, "Un ancien traité sur le 'ud d'Abu Yusuf al-Kindī."

4 Apocalypse 5.8-10.

5 Cf. the bow of the musical archer-god Apollo.

6 The Tetragrammaton Jod, He, Vau, He.

7 Cf. also the heavenly rose of Dante's *Paradiso*.

8 The highest string of a lute, viol, or violin.

9 The planetary spheres.

33 Robert Fludd

1 On Fludd's work in general, see Joscelyn Godwin, *Robert Fludd, Hermetic Philosopher and Surveyor of Two Worlds*. On Fludd and music, see Peter J. Amman, "The Musical Theory and Philosophy of Robert Fludd," and Todd Barton, "Robert Fludd's Temple of Music."

2 For the text of the *Confessio* in English, see Paul M. Allen, *A Christian Rosenkreutz Anthology*, pp. 180ff., or Frances A. Yates, *The Rosicrucian Enlightenment*, pp. 251ff.

3 Quoted from *Confessio Fraternitatis R.C., Ad Eruditos Europae*, first published Cassel, 1615.

4 For Jerome Cardan's writings on music, see the forthcoming edition by Clement A. Miller, American Institute of Musicology.

5 Fludd was most enthusiastic about the weapon-salve, a medicine applied not to a wound but to the object which caused it. As a physician he seems to have made very little use of it, but since its ingredients included, *inter alia*, moss from the skull of a hanged man it cannot have been easily concocted. The theory behind it is that it heals by acting "magnetically" at a distance.

6 These are common instances from the medieval bestiary, based in turn on travelers' tales and the Latin encyclopedists, especially Pliny. On the catoblepas, Pliny (VIII, 77) says that its head is so heavy it hangs down towards the ground – fortunately for the human race, because all who meet its gaze expire immediately (T.H. White, *The Bestiary*, p. 55n.).

7 Part of *Utriusque Cosmi Historia*.

8 In Fludd's scheme of cosmic music, Saturn's note stands an octave away from that of the fiery sphere, Mars' from that of air. See diagrams in Godwin, *Robert Fludd*, pp. 45, 49.

9 Cf. the theory of musical perception via the subtle *spiritus* or etheric matter, which occultism recognizes as the carrier of the formative forces of Nature. (See note 7 to Ficino.)

10 Fludd is thinking of making music on Ficinian principles, imitating the ambience of a planet in order to attract its virtues. Unfortunately he can give no more practical example of this musical sympathy than the old experiment of the two lutes.

11 One can only guess at the reasons Fludd has in mind, but in the alchemical context – which is a likely one – the lyre would be the series of subtle centers in the human being parallel to the planets and ruled by the heart (= Sun), while the caduceus depicts the positive and negative currents that wind through these centers. See Titus Burckhardt, *Alchemy*, pp. 130-6.

12 The meaning of this and the following sentence is not clear. The human "scale" in Fludd's works covers either 2 or 3 octaves. See Godwin, *Robert Fludd*, pp. 47-9.

13 Like Ficino, Fludd was careful to show that his magic was entirely natural, and involved no traffic with demonic entities or the souls of the dead.

14 The next chapter describes the wonderful insights that Fludd has received from a "certain little book" or "little box" of Nature, but without saying what this is – except, in true alchemical style, that it is very common and as old as the human race. From later works it seems that the reference is to Fludd's experiment on wheat, described in *Anatomiae Amphitheatrum* (Frankfurt, 1623) and available in English in Allen G. Debus, *Robert Fludd and his Philosophical Key*. This experiment, which was central to Fludd's whole philosophy, appears to have been the inspiration for the remarkable series of plates illustrating his

account of Creation at the beginning of *Utriusque Cosmi Historia*; see Godwin, *Robert Fludd*, pp. 24-9 and (with text translated by Patricia Tahil) Adam McLean, ed., *The Origin and Structure of the Cosmos*.

34 Johannes Kepler

1 See Rudolf Haase's articles in J. Godwin, ed., *Cosmic Music: Three Musical Keys to the Interpretation of Reality*.

2 In seven axioms Kepler has summed up what he said earlier in the book concerning the harmonic proportions brought about by dividing the circle by inscribing regular polygons, and the relation of consonance and dissonance to these divisions. The axioms develop the observations first made in his *Mysterium Cosmographicum*, 1596, for which see Godwin, ed., *Cosmic Music*, appendix.

3 *Mens*, capitalized by Kepler and translated here sometimes as Mind, sometimes as Intellect, means more than the human mind in the usual acceptance of the term. Equivalent to the Greek *nous*, it stands above Spirits and Soul and is the organ for the perception of the intellectual world of Platonic forms to which geometrical axioms belong.

4 "Meteorology and Music are likewise different peoples, stemming from the common fatherland of Geometry" (Book IV, ch. 6). Kepler had found, over years of observations, that certain planetary aspects or angles have an effect upon the weather.

5 *Species immateriata*. Kepler assumes the theory of perception according to which the sense-organs grasp not the objects in themselves but a "species" of etheric emanation from them. See note 8 to Agrippa (no. 29).

6 We would say "every other impulse," but Kepler counts inclusively.

7 Kepler's marginal note here reads: "What is the cause of the pleasure derived from chords?"

8 Kepler touches here on one of the mysteries of perception: the fact that, unlike the pleasures of touch and taste, that of hearing is not actually felt in the ear itself, but in an abstracted domain of the mind. His explanation is, however, at least a semi-physical one, for in the next sentence he envisages the immaterial "species" entering the ear, then being carried by the etheric "spirits" of the body into the realm of understanding or the "common sense."

9 He seems to refer to music that is too loud, but which can be enjoyed when modified in volume.

10 The chief speaker in Plato's *Timaeus*.

35 Athanasius Kircher

1 On Kircher and music, see Ulf Scharlau, *Athanasius Kircher als Musikschriftsteller*.

2 See Valerio Rivosecchi, *Esotismo in Roma Barocca: Studi sul Padre Kircher*, p. 63 *et passim*.

3 On Werckmeister, see no. 36; on Nassarre, see introduction to Luis da León (no. 31); on the violinist, composer and theorist Giuseppe Tartini, see D.P. Walker, *Studies in Musical Science in the Late Renaissance*, and Tartini's *Scienza Platonica*.

4 For an alternative musical system of correspondences based on the number ten, see Angelo Berardi, *Miscellanea Musica*, pp. 31-6.

5 Parts of Kircher's *Ars Magna Lucis et Umbrae*.

6 This refers to the apparent stases and retrogradations of the planets.

7 The largest of Kircher's three books on magnetism, also entitled *Magnes*, Rome, 1641.

8 The immediate source for this table is Giambattista Porta, *Magiae Naturalis*, Book I, *passim*. Similar tables are to be found in Agrippa's second book of *Occult Philosophy* (for examples, see Heninger, *The Cosmographical Glass*, pp. 116-22), but Agrippa's lists of fish, birds, quadrupeds and gemstones are quite different (see especially this sevenfold table, where these are assigned to the planets). So are those in the *Magical Calendar of Tycho Brahe*.

9 See the chart, Enneachord II (the planets), for the Greek note-names. The modern pitches added editorially are only relative.

10 He refers to the resolution of discords in polyphonic music by off-beat resolution, as in a suspension or appoggiatura. In the same book he attributes such "syncopations" to the planets.

36 John Heydon

1 *Dictionary of National Biography*, vol. 9, p. 769.

2 Seth Ward (1617-89), bishop and astronomer. Thomas Heydon: no works or biographical details known. Henry More (1614-87), Cambridge Platonist and Christian Kabbalist. Eugenius Theodidactus: Heydon's own pseudonym, under which he wrote *Advice to a Daughter*, London, 1658.

3 Sir Christopher Heydon, d. 1623, a distant relative of John; writer of astrological treatises, especially *A Defence of Judiciall Astrologie* and *An Astrologicall Discourse*, both London, 1603.

4 Thomas Hobbes (1588-1679), scientific associate of Galileo, Bacon, Mersenne and Gassendi before his concentration on political philosophy which resulted in the *Leviathan*, 1651. Thomas Barlow (1607-91), Calvinist principal of Queen's College, Oxford, and later bishop of Lincoln. Not known as an astrologer. Mr Fisk – no works or biographical details known.

5 Cf. p. 87 of the same work: "For as in *Music* there be but three perfect concords, viz. the diapason, diapente, and diatessaron: so in the *Harmony* of the *Beams*, by which the *Genis* come down, there are but three perfect aspects answerable to the *Harmony* of the *Heavens, Spheres and Planets*."

6 Cf. Leibniz's definition of music as "exercitum arithmeticae occultum

nescientis se numerare animi," i.e. "An occult exercise of arithmetic on the part of the soul, acting unconsciously." (G.W. von Leibniz, *Letters*, ed. Kortholt, no. 154.)

37   Andreas Werckmeister

1   Sethus Calvisius (1556-1615), author of *Melopoeia*, Erfurt, 1592; Johannes Lippius (1585-1612), author of *Synopsis musicae novae*, Strasburg, 1612; Heinrich Baryphonus (1581-1655), author of *Pleiades musicae*, Halberstadt, 1615; Abraham Bartolus: see note 5 below; Michael Praetorius (1572-1621), author of *Syntagma Musicum*, Wolfenbüttel, 1615-9. All of the foregoing seem to have known one another. Wolfgang Caspar Printz (1641-1717) was author of *Phrynis Mitilenaeus*, Quedlinburg, 1676-9, and many other works. An even later member of the tradition, Johann Heinrich Buttstedt (1666-1735), in his *Ut Mi Sol, Re Fa La*, Erfurt, 1716, relies heavily on Fludd, Kircher and Werckmeister in an attempt to preserve the modal system.

2   For this chapter of Agrippa, see our no. 29.

3   Not known. Presumably the Latinized version of the German name Eschholz.

4   *Non modo forma ali quem, Sed et omnia membra venustant,*
     Si numeris constant harmoniisque suis.
     Est in membrorum totâ compage venustas,
     Harmonia in cunctis conspicienda venit.

   Source unknown.

5   This is appended to part 6 of Heinrich Zeisingk's *Theatrum Machinarum*, pp. 89ff. It is a very curious work, somewhat resembling Robert Fludd's *De Templo Musicae*, showing musical machines and fountains, applying the world-system to the lute, etc. It also contains correlations of the keynotes C, D, E, F, G, A, and B♭ and B♮ respectively with Mars, Jupiter, Saturn, Moon, Mercury, Venus, and Sun. One's taste in music, Bartholus says, may be taken as an indication of one's sun-sign or ascending planet.

6   Werckmeister's most occult remark. In addition to music theory, he had read the Renaissance magi: Ficino, Pico, Bruno, and as he says Agrippa and Paracelsus. On his sources, see Rolf Dammann, "Zur Musiklehre des Andreas Werckmeister."

7   Johannes Arndt (1555-1621), theologian and devotional writer. The book referred to is presumably his often reprinted *De vero christianismo* whose fourth book is *Liber naturae*, on the Christian reading of the "Book of Nature."

8   The craftsmen entrusted with making the Ark of the Covenant and other ceremonial objects.

38 Giovanni Marcazi

1 The poem as it stands was compiled by Mayr from two different sources, the first verse from one work (Bergamo, Bibliotèca Civica, MS Cart. 68, No. 2), the remainder a complete ode called *La Musica* (Cart. 77, No. 2). Mayr's note on it reads: "Da Nob.[ile] Sig.[nore] Ab.[bate] Giovanni Marcazi nel Lod.[evole] Man.[oscritto] intitolato *Poesie Originali* d'alcuni Bergamaschi da essi donate a Sebastiano Muletti fra gli arcadi Liudresio Ferrate. Bergam.[o] 1782. Tom. III." (JA) I.e. "By the Noble Abbé Giovanni Marcazi in the praiseworthy manuscript entitled *Original Poems* by certain Bergamasques, presented by them to Sebastiano Muletti among the Arcadians 'Liudresio Ferreate.' Bergamo, 1782. Vol. III." The title "The Origins and Powers of Music" is editorial.

2 The soul of man which, reflecting the harmonious structure of the World-Soul, regulates the being who does not recognize it.

3 A reference to God breathing the soul into Adam, made from clay (Genesis 2.7).

4 The spring on Mt Helicon, sacred to the Muses, here equated with the souls of the spheres, following Martianus Capella I, 27-8.

5 Achilles, taught by Cheiron of Apollo's love for Daphne.

39 J.F.H. von Dalberg

1 See especially his short story *Die Aeolsharfe*, Erfurt, 1801, translated by Maynard Schwabe in Andrew Brown, *The Aeolian Harp in European Literature, 1591-1892*, pp. 25-9. I am preparing an edition (in German) of Dalberg's musical writings.

2 See his *Untersuchung über die Ursprung der Harmonie*, pp. iii ff.

3 In *Die Aeolsharfe* a nymph similarly appears and leads the prose-poet to new realms.

4 Probably referring to the fragments of Empedocles. See note 6 to Plotinus (no. 6).

40 François René Chateaubriand

1 Merowech, legendary founder of the Merovingian Dynasty.

2 This refers to the death of Louis XVI. I was writing a year after the death of the martyr-king (FRC).

3 The Angel of America has already risen from Earth, past the globes "which men, plunged in the darkness of idolatry, profane by the names of Mercury and Venus" (p. 489), to the Sun, where he meets the two saints.

4 These must be the twelve "slices" marked off on the Firmament by the zodiacal signs. I do not know of any precedent for this description, but the "different colors" may be borrowed from *Republic* X, 617.

5   On the harmony of stars, see introduction of Kosegarten (no. 41). There is no longer any debate about its manner of audibility: it is heard internally through the organs of the soul.

6   Compare to this passage Plato's "Myth of Er" (no. 1).

7   Doctrine of certain Fathers of the Church (FRC).

8   Several Fathers of the Church have supported these doctrines, which are here not a rule of faith but a subject of poetry (FRC).

9   The imagery of this paragraph is from the Apocalypse.

10 Bartolemé de las Casas (1474-1566), the "Apostle of the Indians"; J. de Bréboeuf, I. Jogues: seventeenth-century Jesuit missionaries to North America.

11 See notes 5 and 6 to Kosegarten (no. 41) on these instruments.

12 In the remainder of the chapter Chateaubriand does not hesitate to proceed where most other authors fear to tread: he describes the very throne of Christ, Jehovah, and the Chaos behind Divinity. In this he goes far beyond Tasso, whose *Gerusalemme Liberata*, with its heavenly and hellish comings and goings, was doubtless another of his models.

41   Ludwig Theobald Kosegarten

1   See John Hollander, *The Untuning of the Sky*, pp. 412ff.

2   See William Vaughan, *German Romantic Painting*, pp. 43ff., 76. Runge was an intensely musical painter, thinking in terms of cosmic harmonies and using harmonic proportions in his work (*ibid.*, p. 63).

3   *Bardale*: rare German word for a female bard.

4   Aödi: from Homeric Greek ἀοιδή, the art of song or the act of singing. Ἀοιδός is a singer.

5   The musical glasses or glass harmonica was a favorite instrument of the Romantic poets, who heard its sound as evocative of the supernatural. Mesmer used it to help induce trances in his patients.

6   An allusion to the Aeolian harp, which shared the above distinction with the musical glasses. See *Aeolian Harp*, series edited by Stephen Bonner. Chateaubriand (no. 40) also refers to these two instruments as he describes the music of heaven.

42   Novalis

1   For an English translation, see J. Godwin, *Harmonies of Heaven and Earth*, ch. I.

2   Novalis believed that the fall into strife and suffering was an inevitable part of cosmic, human, indeed every development, and that eventually all things would be led back to perfection. He felt this intimately in his own life in the tragic death of the girl Sophie, whom he loved. His whole spiritual life thereafter was oriented to the reunion with her in a more perfect mode of being to which he looked forward at his death.

3   Suhrawardī (no. 18) gives the most plausible explanation of this

episode. It seems that the spirits of the stars and their music must be in the Heavenly Spheres of Hūrqalyā, while the old King is the recipient of the laws from the still higher world of Souls (Malakūt) which he mediates through the card-game. The episode could also be interpreted Kabbalistically, as the transition from the world of Briah to that of Yetzirah.

4   Speculative musical writers cannot escape from the imagery of the music of their own time: compare the monophonic planet-scales of Antiquity and the Middle Ages to the polyphonic songs of Kepler and Kircher. Novalis's star-music, in turn, belongs to the period in which contrast had become a major interest of composers; his description would fit the music of Beethoven perfectly.

43   E.T.A. Hoffmann

1   *Odyssey* XVIII, 563. The soul has two gates: one (opaque) of ivory, one (transparent) of horn, through which pass respectively false and true dreams. See also *Aeneid* VI, 893ff.

2   Some other associations between the sun and music, of which the most obvious is Apollo's dual patronage, are collected by Hans Kayser in *Lehrbuch der Harmonik*, p. xxv, and Marius Schneider, *Singende Steine*, p. 13. Kayser cites in particular Friedrich Hölderlin's *Hyperion* and Raphael's Prologue to Goethe's *Faust* II; Schneider the Egyptian "singing sun." See also J. Godwin, *Harmonies of Heaven and Earth*, ch. III.

44   Bettina Brentano von Arnim

1   *Op. cit.*, letter of July 24, 1808; in Bettina von Arnim, *Werke und Briefe*, vol. II, p. 128. On Bettina's philosophy of music, see Roman Nahrebecky, *Wackenroder, Tieck, E.T.A. Hoffmann, Bettina von Arnim*.

2   For a considered and positive evaluation of Bettina's veracity, see Alexander W. Thayer, *The Life of Ludwig van Beethoven*, vol. II, pp. 179-85.

3   Beethoven's "electrical" imagery has to be read in context. The late eighteenth and early nineteenth century was the golden age of electrical experimentation, unaffected as yet by practical applications, and filled with speculations on the nature of this mysterious force. Electricity would also have been associated, in the layman's mind, with the "magnetism," both material and animal, popularized by Mesmer: hence with ideas of immaterial, etheric or spiritual realms.

4   Beethoven's use of the rare term *raptus*, apparently in use in his circle at the time, is a powerful argument for the authenticity of Bettina's account, first published in 1839, long after the term had fallen into disuse. Anton Schindler's objection that he had never heard Beethoven speak in this way is answered by the contrast between the dull and

unimaginative Schindler and the brilliant and spiritual Bettina, to whom Beethoven was strongly attracted, to say the least. See the end of our extracts from Stockhausen (no. 61).

45 Heinrich von Kleist

1 He shot himself in a suicide pact with Henrietta Vogel, who was suffering from cancer.
2 Goethe, who considered his own researches and discoveries in color theory (*Farbenlehre*) even more significant than his work as a poet.

46 Rahel Varnhagen

1 See Hannah Arendt, *Rahel Varnhagen: the Life of a Jewess*, pp. 114f.

47 Antoine Fabre d'Olivet

1 Fabre's cosmology is based on the three principles of Providence, which wishes to lead all things to unity, Destiny, which is restrictive and coercive, and Will, which enables man to choose between them.
2 It is interesting to see the list of composers which a well-educated musical amateur draws up in the Paris of 1813 or so. For Fabre, as for Dalberg (no. 39), Pergolesi (1710-36) comes first to mind.
3 Rameau said: "Music is lost; taste changes at every moment." Marcello said it before him in Italy, at the very time of Pergolesi and Leo (*Essai sur la Musique*, vol. III, p. 377, and in the supplement, p. 468) (F d'O).
4 Herodotus, II, 79.
5 *Laws*, II, 676e.
6 For Fabre, the Egyptian era was one of relative decline after the breakup of the Universal Empire of Aryan India.

48 Arthur Schopenhauer

1 Schopenhauer belongs to the side of those who grant the primacy in musical symbolism to melody rather than to harmony: to the side of Rousseau, against Rameau (see J. Godwin, *Harmonies of Heaven and Earth*, ch. IV). In his later collection of essays and brief observations he acknowledges Rameau's theoretical work: "The grammar of this universal language has also been regulated with the utmost exactitude: though the causes of it have only been set forth since Rameau" (*Parerga et Paralipomena*, p. 463), but in the following section he says: "In the compositions of today more attention is paid to the harmony than to the melody: but I am of the contrary opinion and consider melody the core of music, to which the harmony is related as sauce to the roast" (ed. cit., p. 464). The issue had been taken up not long before in one

of the seminal works of literary romanticism, Etienne Pivert de Senancour's *Obermann* (1804), who believes that the whole universe is certainly regulated by number and numerology (see the extremely Pythagorean "Letter 47"), but says that "It is above all the melody of notes which, joining extension without precise limits to a sensible but vague movement, gives the soul this sentiment of the infinite which it believes it possesses in duration and extension" ("Letter 61"). See Marcel Raymond, *Senancour: Sensations et révélations*, pp. 163-6. Senancour's sentiment of the infinite beyond time and space is probably to be identified phenomenologically with Schopenhauer's "laying hold of the real," mentioned at the end of this extract.

49   Charles Fourier

1   The pros and cons of its authenticity are discussed (inconclusively) by Adrien Dax in "A propos d'un talisman de Charles Fourier: Analyse critique et essai de reconstitution," in *La Brèche, Action Surréaliste*, No. 4 (1963),pp. 18-25.

2   In his *Théorie de l'Unité Universelle*, edition of 1846, vol. II, p. 145, Fourier gives the following correspondences of colors and metals with the notes of the scale:

C	Violet	Iron
E	Azure	Tin
G	Yellow	Lead
B	Red	Copper
D	Indigo	Silver
F	Green	Platinum
A	Orange	Gold

The only planetary names which could be inserted in this series, following Fourier's cosmology, are the Earth at C, Herschel (Uranus) at E, Jupiter at G, and Saturn at B. There is consequently no relation whatever to the traditional planetary metals, colors, or notes. Yet the next instruction seems to assume that one is inserting seven planets. If I were to construct the talisman, I would use one of the accepted systems of correspondences, and discount Fourier's altogether. Did he, as Dax suggests, perhaps make this talisman before his own cosmological system was developed?

50   Honoré de Balzac

1   See his unequivocal statement: "I am not orthodox at all and I do not believe in the Roman Church . . . Swedenborgianism, which is only a repetition in the Christian sense of ancient ideas, is my religion, with the addition which I make to it of the incomprehensibility of God." *Oeuvres posthumes, Lettres à l'Etrangère*, vol. I, p. 403; quoted in

Gwendolyn Bays, *The Orphic Vision: Seer Poets from Novalis to Rimbaud*, p. 103. The evidence for his Martinist connections is summarized on the same page of Bays's book, but unfortunately without clarifying whether this "Martinism" is the occult freemasonry of Martinez de Pasqually or the contemplative theosophy of Louis-Claude de Saint-Martin. I would assume the latter.

2   See especially Auguste Viatte, *Les Sources occultes du romantisme*, and Brian Juden, *Traditions orphiques et tendances mystiques*. Max Milner gives this movement its full due in his contribution to the multi-volume survey *Littérature Française*, published by Arthaud. In his preface to vol. 12, *Le Romantisme I, 1820-1843*, Milner alludes significantly to the "fecundity of a period [Romanticism, taken in the most general sense] which has been for our culture, in every sense of the term, that of an initiation" (p. 6).

3   Cf. one of the 22 *Pensées* of Balzac's *Louis Lambert*: "Perhaps one day the inverse sense of the ET VERBUM CARO FACTUM EST [And the Word was made flesh] will be summarized by a new Gospel which will say: AND THE FLESH SHALL BE MADE WORD, IT WILL BECOME *THE WORD OF GOD*" (Paris, Calmann-Lévy, 1896, p. 141).

4   Arnold Schoenberg was a great lover of this story, and drew from it the text and title for one of his *Four Orchestral Songs* of 1913-16. In 1912 he had actually contemplated setting the last chapter to music. He wrote in his essay of 1941, "Composition with Twelve Tones": "The unity of musical space demands an absolute and unitary perception. In this space, as in Swedenborg's heaven (described in Balzac's *Séraphîta*), there is no absolute down, no right or left, forward or backward." This is quoted in Dore Ashton, *A Fable of Modern Art*, p. 99, a book whose last chapter deals with Schoenberg's own links with esoteric philosophy.

5   Cf. *Louis Lambert*, ed. cit., p. 138: "The four expressions of matter in relation to man – sound, colour, perfume, and form, have the same origin." Similar ideas of correspondences between the senses recur in Gérard de Nerval, Baudelaire, Victor Hugo and Rimbaud. See John Senior, *The Way Down and Out: The Occult in Symbolist Literature*, pp. 85, 89.

51   George Sand

1   Cf. the imagery in Hoffmann's *Ritter Gluck* (no. 43).

2   Thou canst not stir a flower
    Without troubling of a star.

Francis Thompson, *The Mistress of Vision*

52   Gérard de Nerval

1   For an introduction in English to Nerval's occultism, see John Senior, *The Way Down and Out*, pp. 74-88.
2   Cf. the Creation of the World-Soul in Plato's *Timaeus*.
3   The forget-me-not.

53   Robert Schumann

1   Letter to Ritzhaupt, August 14, 1832.
2   Cf. the words of Philo on those who go mad on hearing divine music (no. 12), and St Gregory's anecdote related by Aurelian (no. 21). One cannot help noticing the number of contributors to this section of the anthology who have met with disaster on the earthly level: Hoffmann's alcoholism, Kleist's and de Nerval's suicide, and Schumann's insanity.
3   Printed in the supplementary volume of the critical edition, as No. 9, *Thema (E-flat major) für Pianoforte* (BL).

54   Richard Wagner

1   From a conversation between Wagner and Engelbert Humperdinck while the latter was assisting with the presentation of *Parsifal*, written down by Humperdinck and reported by him to Arthur M. Abell in 1905. See Abell, *Talks with Great Composers*, pp. 137-9. Although Abell's book is not a recognized scholarly source, his credibility and Humperdinck's are at least as good as Bettina von Arnim's (see no. 44), and Wagner's understanding of the practical "magical" use of the Imagination is something neither Abell nor Humperdinck would have been capable of inventing.
2   In the original we have the words "durch seine hiermit verbundene tiefsinnige Hypothese" &c., – literally "through his profound hypothesis linked herewith," or perhaps "allied hereto." This "dream" hypothesis does not appear in the "*Welt als W. u V.*," however, but in a lengthy essay on "Ghost-seeing" in Vol. I of the "*Parerga und Paralipomena*," written after the publication of the larger work; so that the "connection" must be regarded in a purely subjective light, that is to say, as Wagner's own discovery. In fact our author, partly by re-arranging the "material supplied [elsewhere] by the philosopher," partly by his independent observations, has carried Schopenhauer's Theory of Music infinitely farther than its originator could ever have dreamt (WAE).
3   Cf. "In lichten Tages Schein, wie war Isolde mein?" and in fact the whole love-scene in *Tristan und Isolde*, act ii (WAE).
4   Cf. *Tristan und Isolde*, act iii: "Die Sonne sah ich nicht, nicht sah ich Land noch Leute: doch was ich sah, das kann ich dir nicht sagen" (WAE).

5 In this paragraph Wagner is saying, in effect, that just as physical bodies make absolute light visible, so rhythm focuses tone into perceptible music. This is a profound observation, inasmuch as without rhythm there can be tone but no motion in time, whilst without objects there can be light but no motion in space. It could be an argument in favor of the primacy of harmony ("belonging to neither Space nor Time") over melody and the rhythm that is inseparable from melody.

6 "Die Musik, welche einzig dadurch zu uns spricht, dass sie den allerallgemeinsten Begriff des an sich dunklen Gefühles in den erdenklichsten Abstufungen mit bestimmtester Deutlichkeit uns belebt, kann an und für sich einzig nach der Kategorie des *Erhabenen* beurtheilt werden, da sie, sobald sie uns erfüllt, die höchste Extase des Bewusstseins der Schrankenlosigheit erregt." – A very difficult sentence to render justice to, even in a partial paraphrase, without appealing to Schopenhauer's convincing theory of the Sublime (*Welt als W. u V.* I. § 39). As an element of that theory is formed by the recognition that in the Sublime, whether in Nature or Art, we are brought into direct contact with the *universal* Will, our author's argument as to the nature of Music is really far more strongly supported by his present paragraph, to the ordinary mind, than by Schopenhauer's assumption of a "dream-organ"; which latter, however, Wagner explicitly has adopted by mere way of "analogy" – a purpose it admirably serves, though it has given offense to those who have been misled by the oft-repeated *illustration* into considering it a main factor in the *exposition*, whereas each several reference to "dreams" might be omitted without in the slightest degree affecting the philosophic basis of Richard Wagner's remarkable contribution to a much-needed Science of Music (WAE).

55 Rudolf Steiner

1 Blavatsky did not write much on the subject of music, but for tables of note-planet correspondences, with some important comments, see the supplementary material of *The Secret Doctrine*, 6-volume "Adyar Edition," vol. 5, pp. 435-63.

2 The background to this lecture, including an analysis of sleep, dream and death and the references to the Bach and Bernouilli families, is available in Steiner's own book *An Outline of Occult Science*, pp. 55ff.

3 Steiner was the editor of the volume of the 12-volume Schopenhauer edition (Stuttgart, Cotta, 1895) which contains the section on music we have quoted.

4 Steiner's lectures were usually taken down in shorthand and only published after his death in unrevised form. He drew a clear distinction between them and his written books, which he regarded as his most authoritative teaching. This lecture was one of four on music

which he gave in various cities late in 1906. It was first published in *Das Goetheanum*, vol. 24, nos 28-29 (1945). The four lectures were collected by Helmut von Wartburg, together with Steiner's other principal lectures and question-answerings on music, in the Steiner Gesamtausgabe, Dornach, 1969, and re-issued with an additional lecture, Dornach, 1975. Some of our notes are from von Wartburg's edition.

5 Steiner had given more details on the Bach and Bernouilli families in his lecture of November 26, 1906 (given in our source, pp. 22-9). The distant ancestors of the Bach family, he says, had developed a particular physical configuration of the ear that is indispensable for musical genius. The ego of a great composer must wait in a discarnate state until such a suitable body has been bred.

6 Goethe, *Spruche in Prosa*, section "Das Erkennen"; literally "In the works of Man, as in those of Nature, only the intentions are worth noticing." Cf. also Eckermann's *Conversations with Goethe*, October 20, 1828 and April 18, 1827 (HvW).

7 Goethe, *op. cit.*, section "Kunst"; literally "The Beautiful is a manifestation of secret laws of Nature, which without this revelation would have remained forever concealed from us" (HvW).

8 Goethe in the book on Winckelmann, in the chapter "Antike"; literally: "If the healthy nature of Man works as a whole, if he feels himself in the world as in a great, beautiful, worthy and precious whole, then the Universe, as if it could feel itself reaching its goal, will leap up and admire the peak of Becoming and Being" (HvW).

9 Cf. the composer Olivier Messiaen: "In my dreamings I hear and see ordered melodies and chords, familiar hues and forms; then, following this transitory stage I pass into the unreal and submit ecstatically to a vortex, a dizzying interpretation of superhuman sounds and colours. These fiery swords, these rivers of blue-orange lava, these sudden stars. . . . Behold the rainbow!" Introduction to his *Quatuor pour la fin du Temps* (1941).

10 Cf. Synesius (no. 8) on the journey through the Astral planes of sounding spheres concluding in the "silence-filled Heaven."

11 Devachan: a word borrowed by H.P. Blavatsky from Hinduism, meaning the place of the *devas* (angels or lesser gods), to indicate the state of the higher ego between incarnations. Steiner's explanation illuminates many of our ancient texts, and in particular vindicates the geocentric cosmos through which the soul traditionally ascends. The astronomical picture is a symbol in objective mode of a subjective experience, and as such has nothing to lose by advances in physical astronomy. The parallel is as follows:

Objective Cosmos	*Subjective Experience*
Heavens of the Angels	Devachan: experience of tone and absolutely true meaning

Objective Cosmos	Subjective Experience
Eighth Sphere, fixed stars	Threshold of Devachan
7 Planetary Spheres	Astral World: states of purgation, as described in *Poimandres*
Earth, 4 Elements	Physical Body, left behind at death or dormant in sleep

12 Charles Webster Leadbeater (1847-1934), follower of H.P. Blavatsky and, after her death, co-director with Annie Besant of the Theosophical Society. He was a clairvoyant and wrote, among other works, *The Astral Plane: its Scenery, Inhabitants, and Phenomena* and *The Devachanic Plane*.

13 Steiner, and occultists in general, assume that the present historical and "prehistoric" ages of man known to science were preceded by other civilizations, of which the latest was the Atlantean, named after the continent of Atlantis whose final destruction is recorded by Plato in the *Critias*.

14 Steiner is expressing in ordinary language the ancient belief that *musica instrumentalis* acts on *musica humana* by virtue of its resemblance to *musica mundana*.

15 *Empfindungsseele* and *Empfindungsleib*: a division which takes place within the Astral body, as it were into active and passive components. See especially Steiner's *An Outline of Occult Science*, p. 45.

16 Cf. the similarity of ancient journeys through the spheres, whether taken in dreams, as Scipio's (no. 2), in visions, as Er's and Timarchus' (nos 1, 3), or after death, as in *Poimandres* (no. 4) or Synesius (no. 8).

17 Quotation from the *Emerald Tablet of Hermes*.

18 Cf. Goethe, "Gesang der Geister über den Wassern": *Des Menschen Seele/Gleicht dem Wasser:/Von Himmel kommt es,/Zum Himmel steigt es,/Und wieder nieder/Zur Erde muss es,/Ewig wechselnd.*

56 Hazrat Inayat Khan

1 See Victor-Emile Michelet, *Les Compagnons de la hiérophanie*, p. 75.

2 Also published separately: see Bibliography. Karlheinz Stockhausen (see no. 61) has spoken highly of this book: "And please *read* – there are much wiser men than I – please read the little book of Hazrat Inayat Khan: *Music*. Please, please. You really *should* read this book, above all the whole second volume of *The Sufi Message of Hazrat Inayat Khan*," *Texte* 1970-1977, p. 533, second interview with the Dutch cultural circle, following that from which our extract no. 61 is taken.

3 First described by Ernst Chladni in *Entdeckungen über die Theorie des Klanges* (1787).

4 A common mythological theme, treated above all by Marius Schneider; see his essays in J. Godwin, ed., *Cosmic Music*.

5 But one could write a whole study of rocks and stones that do have musical properties and associations. E.g. the fallen obelisk of Karnak, where "an interesting test can be performed. Put your ear to the angle of the pyramidion and hit the obelisk with your hand. The entire enormous block resounds like a tuning fork at the slightest blow," John Anthony West, *The Traveler's Key to Ancient Egypt*, p. 252.

57 Pierre Jean Jouve

1 Allusions to Leibniz's definition of music; see note 6 to Heydon (no. 36).

2 The first performance in Paris was conducted by Paul Sacher in November, 1937; the second by Charles Münch on the 2nd of May [1938] (PJJ).

58 Warner Allen

1 Conjecture based on the opening lines of this extract and the dates "March, 1931" and "March, 1946" given in the address to the reader, p. 7.

2 *The Timeless Moment*, p. 162.

3 Job 38.7.

4 In "Little Gidding," from *Four Quartets*.

5 For Nicolas of Cusa, the coincidence of contradictories, the reconciliation of the opposites, is the wall that encloses Paradise, the place where God is found by revelation. – *Visio Dei*, cap. 9, etc. (WA).

59 George Ivanovich Gurdjieff

1 Date as given, with extensive argument, by James Webb in *The Harmonious Circle*, p. 70. The birthdates given in other Gurdjieff literature are variously 1872 and 1877.

2 His findings at the speculative level bore fruit in his theory of "cosmic octaves," which describes the workings of all energetic systems in the terms of a major scale. See P.D. Ouspensky, *In Search of the Miraculous*, pp. 122-40. In the same book, pp. 296-8, Gurdjieff expounds his theory of "objective art" which can be relied on to produce a definite and always identical impression. "Objective music is based on 'inner octaves.' And it can obtain not only definite psychological results but definite physical results. There can be such music as would freeze water. There can be such music as would kill a man instantaneously. The Biblical legend of the destruction of the walls of Jericho by Music is precisely a legend of objective music. . . . In the legend of Orpheus there are hints of objective music, for Orpheus used to impart knowledge by music. Snake charmers' music in the East is an approach to objective music, of course very primitive. Very often it is

simply one note which is long drawn out, rising and falling very little; but in this single note 'inner octaves' are going on all the time and melodies of 'inner octaves' which are inaudible to the ears but felt by the emotional center. And the snake hears this music or, more strictly speaking, he feels it, and he obeys it. The same music, only a little more complicated, and men would obey it" (p. 297).

60   Cyril Scott

1   See *Through the Eyes of the Masters*, by David Anrias (CS).
2   The Theosophical term for the memory of all past events enshrined in the *Akasha* (Sanskrit term for the ether).
3   The Atlantean was the Fourth Root-Race, according to H.P. Blavatsky; the Fifth is the Aryan, in the broadest sense that embraces all the peoples from the Himalayas to Western Europe.
4   Chapter 22, "The Ultra-discordants and their effects," dealt with the dissonant music of Schoenberg and his followers, saying that "it is an occult musical fact that discord (used in its moral sense) can alone be destroyed *by* discord, the reason for this being that the vibrations of intrinsically beautiful music are too rarefied to touch the comparatively coarse vibrations of all that pertains to a much lower plane" (p. 136).
5   See *Through the Eyes of the Masters*, by David Anrias (CS).
6   *Ibid.* (CS).
7   Karlheinz Stockhausen (see no. 61) has actually suggested using "acoustical garbage machines" or "sound swallowers" in public places which are computer-programmed to counter every noise with the contrary vibrations, thus cancelling it out and producing silence. See Jonathan Cott, *Stockhausen*, pp. 80-1.
8   See *The Initiate in the Dark Cycle*, pp. 205 and 208 (CS). This book was published anonymously by Scott.
9   See *ibid.*, ch. X (CS).
10   See Introduction to this item.

61   Karlheinz Stockhausen

1   "Utility music."
2   Stockhausen's composition of 1969 in which six singers, seated in a circle, sing with subtle variations the notes of a harmonic chord, interspersed with Divine Names from all cultures and with two erotic poems.
3   Reference to Stockhausen's composition *Momente* (1962-4).
4   See no. 44.

BIBLIOGRAPHY OF WORKS CITED IN THE INTRODUCTIONS AND NOTES

Abell, Arthur M., *Talks with Great Composers*, New York, Philosophical Library, 1954.

Abert, Hermann, *Die Musikanschauung des Mittelalters*, Halle, 1905, reprinted Tutzing, Schneider, 1964.

Allen, Paul M., ed., *A Christian Rosenkreutz Anthology*, Blauvelt, N.Y., Rudolf Steiner Publs., 1968.

Amman, Peter J., "The Musical Theory and Philosophy of Robert Fludd," in *Journal of the Warburg and Courtauld Institutes*, vol. 30 (1967), pp. 198-277.

Anrias, David, *Through the Eyes of the Masters*, London, George Routledge & Sons, 1932.

Arberry, Arthur J., *The Koran Interpreted*, London and New York, Macmillan, 1955.

Arendt, Hannah, *Rahel Varnhagen: the Life of a Jewess*, London, Leo Baeck Institute, 1957.

Arnim, Bettina von, *Werke und Briefe*, Frechen, Bartmann, 1959.

Ashton, Dore, *A Fable of Modern Art*, London, Thames & Hudson, 1980.

Barnstone, Willis, *The Unknown Light: Poems of Fray Luis de León*, Albany, State University of New York, 1979.

Barton, Todd, "Robert Fludd's Temple of Music: a Description and Commentary," MA thesis, University of Oregon, 1978.

Bays, Gwendolyn, *The Orphic Vision: Seer Poets from Novalis to Rimbaud*, Lincoln, Nebraska University Press, 1964.

Berardi, Angelo, *Miscellanea Musica*, Bologna, 1689.

Blavatsky, H.P., *The Secret Doctrine*, Adyar Edition, 6 vols, Adyar, Theosophical Publishing House, 1938, reprinted 1971.

Bonner, Stephen, ed., *Aeolian Harp*, 4 vols, Cambridge, Bois de Boulogne, 1968-1972.

Bower, Calvin, "Boethius and Nicomachus, an essay concerning the sources of De Institutione Musica," in *Vivarium*, vol. 16 (1978), pp. 1-45.

Brahe, Tycho, attrib., *The Magical Calendar*, ed. Adam McLean, Edinburgh, Magnum Opus, 1980.

Brentano, Bettina, *see* Arnim.

Brown, Andrew, *The Aeolian Harp in European Literature 1591-1892*, Cambridge, Bois de Boulogne, 1970.

Brunton, Paul, *A Search in Secret Egypt*, New York, Dutton, 1936.

Burckhardt, Titus, *Alchemy: Science of the Cosmos, Science of the Soul*, trans. William Stoddart, London, Stuart & Watkins, 1967.

Burckhardt, Titus, *An Introduction to Sufi Doctrine*, trans. D.M. Matheson, Lahore, Muhammad Ashraf, 1963.

Buttstedt, Johann Heinrich, *Ut Mi Sol, Re Fa La*, Erfurt, 1716.

Chadwick, Henry, *Boethius; the Consolations of Music, Logic, Theology, and Philosophy*, Oxford University Press, 1981.

Chladni, Ernst, *Entdeckungen über die Theorie des Klanges*, Leipzig, 1787, reprinted Bärenreiter, 1980.

Clark, James M., *The Great German Mystics: Eckhart, Tauler and Suso*, Oxford, Blackwell, 1949.

Corbin, Henry, *Creative Imagination in the Sufism of Ibn 'Arabi*, trans. Ralph Manheim, Princeton University Press, 1969.

Corbin, Henry, *Spiritual Body and Celestial Earth*, trans. Nancy Pearson, Princeton University Press, 1977.

Corbin, Henry, *The Man of Light in Iranian Sufism*, trans. Nancy Pearson, Boulder, Shambhala, 1978.

Cornford, Francis M., *Plato's Cosmology*, New York, Kegan Paul, Trench & Trubner, 1937.

Cott, Jonathan, *Stockhausen: Conversations with the Composer*, New York, Simon & Schuster, 1973.

Cumont, Franz, *Recherches sur le symbolisme funéraire des Romains*, Paris, Geuthner, 1942.

Dalberg, J.F.H. Freiherr von, *Untersuchung über die Ursprung der Harmonie*, Erfurt, Beyer und Maring, 1800.

Dammann, Rolf, "Zur Musiklehre des Andreas Werckmeister," in *Archiv für Musikwissenschaft*, vol. 11 (1954), pp. 206-37.

Dax, Adrien, "A propos d'un talisman de Charles Fourier," in *La Brèche*, no. 4 (1963), pp. 18-25.

Debus, Allen G., *Robert Fludd and his Philosophical Key*, New York, Science History Publs., 1979.

Dicks, D.R., *Early Greek Astronomy to Aristotle*, London, Thames & Hudson, 1970.

Elders, Leo, *Aristotle's Cosmology: a Commentary on the De Caelo*, Assen, Van Gorcum, 1966.

Fabre d'Olivet, Antoine, *Histoire philosophique du genre humain* (1824), trans. N.L. Redfield as *Hermeneutic Interpretation of the Origin of the Social State of Man*, New York, Putnam, 1915.

Ficino, Marsilio, *Commentary on Plato's Symposium*, ed. and trans. Sears Jayne, Columbia, University of Missouri Press, 1944.

Fludd, Robert, *The Origin and Structure of the Cosmos*, ed. Adam McLean, trans. Patricia Tahil, Edinburgh, Magnum Opus, 1982.

Giorgi, Francesco, *De Harmonia Mundi*, Venice, 1525, trans. G. Lefèvre de

La Boderie as *L'Harmonie du Monde*, Paris, 1578 (reprinted in facsimile).

Godwin, Joscelyn, *Robert Fludd, Hermetic Philosopher and Surveyor of Two Worlds*, London, Thames & Hudson, 1979.

Godwin, Joscelyn, *Mystery Religions in the Ancient World*, London, Thames & Hudson, 1981.

Godwin, Joscelyn, "The Revival of Speculative Music," in *Musical Quarterly*, vol. 68 (1982), pp. 373-89.

Godwin, Joscelyn, ed., *Cosmic Music: Three Musical Keys to the Interpretation of Reality* (Essays by M. Schneider, R. Haase, H.E. Lauer), West Stockbridge, Mass., Lindisfarne Press, 1986.

Godwin, Joscelyn, *Harmonies of Heaven and Earth*, London, Thames & Hudson, 1986.

Goodenough, Erwin R., *By Light, Light: the Mystic Gospel of Hellenistic Judaism*, New Haven, Yale University Press, 1935.

Gorman, Peter, *Pythagoras, a Life*, London, Routledge & Kegan Paul, 1979.

Grossmann, Walter, *Die einleitenden Kapital des Speculum Musicae von Jean de Muris*, Leipzig, 1924, reprinted Nendeln, Kraus, 1976.

Halevi, Z'ev ben Shimon, *Kabbalah: Tradition of Hidden Knowledge*, London, Thames & Hudson, 1979.

Hammerstein, Reinhold, *Die Musik der Engel: Untersuchungen zur Musikanschauung des Mittelalters*, Bern and Munich, Francke, 1962.

Heath, Sir Thomas, *Aristarchus of Samos, the Ancient Copernicus*, Oxford University Press, 1913.

Heath, Sir Thomas, *Greek Astronomy*, London, Dent, 1932.

Heninger, S.K., *The Cosmographical Glass: Renaissance Diagrams of the Universe*, San Marino, California, Huntington Library, 1977.

Heninger, S.K., *Touches of Sweet Harmony: Pythagorean Cosmology and Renaissance Poetics*, San Marino, California, Huntington Library, 1974.

Hollander, John, *The Untuning of the Sky*, New York, Norton, 1970.

Hujwīrī, *Kashf-al-Mahjub* (The Unveiling of the Veiled), trans. R.A. Nicholson, London, 1911, reprinted Lahore, Islamic Book Foundation, 1976.

Inayat Khan, Hazrat, *Music*, Lahore, Pakistan, Sh. Muhammad Ashraf, 1971.

Juden, Brian, *Traditions orphiques et tendances mystiques dans le romantisme français (1800-1855)*, Paris, Klincksieck, 1971.

Kayser, Hans, *Lehrbuch der Harmonik*, Zürich, Occident, 1950.

Kepler, Johannes, *Mysterium Cosmographicum*, Tübingen, 1596.

Kircher, Athanasius, *Ars Magna Lucis et Umbrae*, Rome, 1646.

Kircher, Athanasius, *Iter exstaticum*, Rome, 1656.

Kircher, Athanasius, *Mundus Subterraneus*, Amsterdam, 1665, 2nd ed. 1678.

Kleist, Heinrich von, *Die heilige Cäcilie, oder die Gewalt der Musik*, trans. Linda Siegel in her *Music in German Romantic Literature*, Novato, Calif., Elra, 1983.

Lippius, Johannes, *Synopsis musicae novae* (Strasburg, 1612), ed. and trans. Benito V. Rivera, Colorado Springs, Colorado College Music Press, 1977.

Macaulay, Anne, "APOLLO: The Pythagorean Definition of God," in *Homage to Pythagoras*, Lindisfarne Letter no. 14, West Stockbridge, Mass., 1982, pp. 85-109.

McClain, Ernest G., *The Myth of Invariance*, New York, Nicolas-Hays, 1976.

McClain, Ernest G., *The Pythagorean Plato: Prelude to the Song Itself*, New York, Nicolas-Hays, 1978.

McClain, Ernest G., *Meditations through the Quran*, York Beach, Maine, Nicolas-Hays, 1981.

Mathers, S.L. MacGregor, *The Kabbalah Unveiled*, London, Redway, 1887.

Michelet, Victor-Emile, *Les Compagnons de la hiérophanie*, Paris, Dorbon Ainé, 1937, reprinted Nice, Bélisane, 1977.

Milner, Max, *Le Romantisme I, 1820-1843*, Paris, Arthaud, 1973.

Nahrebecky, Roman, *Wackenroder, Tieck, E.T.A. Hoffmann, Bettina von Arnim; Ihre Beziehung zur Musik und zum musikalischen Erlebnis*, Bonn, Bouvier, 1974.

Nassarre, Pablo, *Escuela Musica*, Zaragoza, 1723-4.

Nasr, Seyyed Hossein, "The Influence of Sufism on Traditional Persian Music," in *Studies in Comparative Religion*, vol. 6 (1972), pp. 225-34.

Nasr, Seyyed Hossein, "Islam and Music," in *Studies in Comparative Religion*, vol. 10 (1976), pp. 37-45.

Nasr, Seyyed Hossein, *Three Muslim Sages*, Delmar, Caravan Books, 1976, repr. of 1969 ed.

Nasr, Seyyed Hossein, *An Introduction to Islamic Cosmological Doctrines*, rev. ed., Boulder, Shambhala, 1978.

Nicholson, Reynold A., *The Mystics of Islam*, London, Routledge & Kegan Paul, 1966 repr. of 1914 ed.

Ouspensky, P.D., *In Search of the Miraculous*, New York, Harcourt, Brace & World, 1949.

Pallis, Marco, "The Metaphysics of Musical Polyphony," in *Studies in Comparative Religion*, vol. 10 (1975), pp. 105-8.

Peters, F.E., *Allah's Commonwealth*, New York, Simon & Schuster, 1973.

Porta, Giambattista, *Magiae Naturalis libri XX*, Naples, 1558.

Raymond, Marcel, *Senancour: Sensations et révélations*, Paris, Corti, 1965.

Regardie, Israel, *A Garden of Pomegranates*, St Paul, Llewellyn, 1935.

Rivosecchi, Valerio, *Esotismo in Roma Barocca: Studi sul Padre Kircher*, Rome, Bulzoni, 1982.

Robledo, Luis, "Poesía y musica de la tarántula," in *Poesía* (Madrid), nos 5-6 (1979-80), pp. 223-32.

Rudhyar, Dane, *The Rebirth of Hindu Music*, Adyar, Theosophical Publishing House, 1928, repr. New York, Weiser, 1979.

Rudhyar, Dane, *The Magic of Tone and the Art of Music*, Boulder, Shambhala, 1982.

Scharlau, Ulf, *Athanasius Kircher (1601-1680) als Musikschriftsteller*, Marburg, Studien zur hessischen Musikgeschichte, 1969.

Schaya, Leo, *The Universal Meaning of the Kabbalah*, trans. Nancy Pearson, London, Allen & Unwin, 1971.

Schimmel, Annemarie, *The Triumphal Sun*, London, Fine Books, 1978 [on Rūmī].

Schneider, Marius, *Singende Seine*, Kassel, Bärenreiter, 1955.

Scholem, Gershom, *On the Kabbalah and its Symbolism*, trans. Ralph Manheim, London, Routledge & Kegan Paul, 1965.

Schopenhauer, Arthur, *Parerga et Paralipomena*, Leipzig, Brockhaus, 1877.

Schullian, Dorothy, and Max Schoen, eds, *Music and Medicine*, New York, Henry Schuman, 1948.

Scott, Cyril, *The Initiate: Some Impressions of a Great Soul, by his pupil*, London, George Routledge, 1919.

Scott, Cyril, *The Initiate in the Dark Cycle*, London, George Routledge, 1932.

Senancour, Etienne Pivert de, *Obermann*, Paris, 1804.

Senior, John, *The Way Down and Out: The Occult in Symbolist Literature*, Ithaca, Cornell University Press, 1959.

Shiloah, Amnon, translator, "L'épître sur la musique des Ikhwan al-Safa," in *Revue des Etudes islamiques*, vol. 32 (1965), pp. 125-62; vol. 34 (1967), pp. 159-93.

Shiloah, Amnon, "*Un ancien traité sur le 'ud d'Abu Yusuf al Kindi*," in *Israel Oriental Studies*, vol. 4 (1974), pp. 179-205.

Shiloah, Amnon, *Music Subjects in the Zohar: Texts and Indices*, Jerusalem, Hebrew University, Magnes Press, 1977.

Shiloah, Amnon, "The Symboli m of Music in the Kabbalistic Tradition," in *World of Music* (Mainz), vol. 22 (1978), pp. 56-69.

Steiner, Rudolf, *An Outline of Occult Science*, trans. H.B. Monges, London, Rudolf Steiner Publishing Co., 1949.

Strunk, Oliver, *Source Readings in Music History*, New York, Norton, 1950.

Tartini, Giusseppe, *Scienza Platonica fondata nel cerchio*, ed. Anna Todeschini Cavalla, Padua, Cedam, 1977.

Taylor, A.E., *A Commentary on Plato's Timaeus*, Oxford University Press, 1928.

Taylor, René, "Hermeticism and Mystical Architecture in the Society of Jesus," in R. Wittkower and I.B. Jaffe, *Baroque Art: the Jesuit Contribution*, New York, 1972.

Taylor, Thomas, *The Mystical Hymns of Orpheus*, new ed., London, 1896.

Taylor, Thomas, *The Theoretic Arithmetic of the Pythagoreans*, London, 1816, reprinted New York, Weiser, 1978.

Thayer, Alexander W., *The Life of Ludwig van Beethoven*, New York, Beethoven Association, 1921.

Thimus, Albert Freiherr von, *Die harmonikale Symbolik des Alterthums*, 2 vols, Cologne, M. DuMont Schauberg, 1869, 1876, reprinted Hildesheim, G. Olms, 1972.

Vaughan, William, *German Romantic Painting*, New Haven, Yale University Press, 1980.

Viatte, August, *Les Sources occultes du romantisme*, 2 vols, Paris, Champion, 1979 repro. of 1928 edn.

Walker, D.P., *Spiritual and Demonic Magic from Ficino to Campanella*, London,

Warburg Institute, 1958, repr. Kraus, 1969.

Walker, D.P., *The Ancient Theology: Studies in Christian Platonism from the Fifteenth to the Eighteenth Century*, London, Duckworth, 1972.

Walker, D.P., *Studies in Musical Science in the Late Renaissance*, London, Warburg Institute, 1978.

Webb, James, *The Harmonious Circle*, London, Thames & Hudson, 1980.

Werner, Eric, and Isaiah Sonne, "The Philosophy and Theory of Music in Judaeo-Arabic Literature," in *Hebrew Union College Annual*, vol. 16 (1941-2), pp. 251-319; vol. 17 (1942-3), pp. 511-73.

West, John Anthony, *The Traveler's Key to Ancient Egypt*, New York, Knopf, 1985.

White, T.H., *The Bestiary*, New York, Capricorn, 1960.

Yates, Frances A., *The French Academies of the Sixteenth Century*, London, Warburg Institute, 1947, repr. Kraus 1973.

Yates, Frances A., *Giordano Bruno and the Hermetic Tradition*, London, Routledge & Kegan Paul, 1964.

Yates, Frances A., *The Rosicrucian Enlightenment*, London, Routledge & Kegan Paul, 1972.

Yates, Frances A., *The Occult Philosophy in the Elizabethan Age*, London, Routledge & Kegan Paul, 1979.

Zeisingk, Heinrich, *Theatrum Machinarum*, Altenburg, 1614.

The Zohar, trans. Harry Sperling and Maurice Simon, 5 vols, London and Bournemouth, Soncino Press, 1949.

INDEX NOMINUM

INDEX RERUM

ARKANA – NEW-AGE BOOKS FOR MIND, BODY AND SPIRIT

With over 150 titles currently in print, Arkana is the leading name in quality new-age books for mind, body and spirit. Arkana encompasses the spirituality of both East and West, ancient and new, in fiction and non-fiction. A vast range of interests is covered, including Psychology and Transformation, Health, Science and Mysticism, Women's Spirituality and Astrology.

If you would like a catalogue of Arkana books, please write to:

Arkana Marketing Department
Penguin Books Ltd
27 Wright's Lane
London W8 5TZ

ARKANA – NEW-AGE BOOKS FOR MIND, BODY AND SPIRIT

A selection of titles already published or in preparation

Weavers of Wisdom: Women Mystics of the Twentieth Century Anne Bancroft

Throughout history women have sought answers to eternal questions about existence and beyond – yet most gurus, philosophers and religious leaders have been men. Through exploring the teachings of fifteen women mystics – each with her own approach to what she calls 'the truth that goes beyond the ordinary' – Anne Bancroft gives a rare, cohesive and fascinating insight into the diversity of female approaches to mysticism.

Dynamics of the Unconscious: Seminars in Psychological Astrology Volume II Liz Greene and Howard Sasportas

The authors of *The Development of the Personality* team up again to show how the dynamics of depth psychology interact with your birth chart. They shed new light on the psychology and astrology of aggression and depression – the darker elements of the adult personality that we must confront if we are to grow to find the wisdom within.

The Myth of Eternal Return: Cosmos and History Mircea Eliade

'A luminous, profound, and extremely stimulating work . . . Eliade's thesis is that ancient man envisaged events not as constituting a linear, progressive history, but simply as so many creative repetitions of primordial archetypes . . . This is an essay which everyone interested in the history of religion and in the mentality of ancient man will have to read. It is difficult to speak too highly of it' – Theodore H. Gaster in *Review of Religion*

Karma and Destiny in the I Ching Guy Damian-Knight

This entirely original approach to the *I Ching*, achieved through mathematical rearrangement of the hexagrams, offers a new, more precise tool for self-understanding. Simple to use and yet profound, it gives the ancient Chinese classic a thoroughly contemporary relevance.

ARKANA – NEW-AGE BOOKS FOR MIND, BODY AND SPIRIT

A selection of titles already published or in preparation

The Networking Book: People Connecting with People
Jessica Lipnack and Jeffrey Stamps

Networking – forming human connections to link ideas and resources – is the natural form of organization for an era based on information technology. Principally concerned with those networks whose goal is a peaceful yet dynamic future for the world, *The Networking Book* – written by two world-famous experts – profiles hundreds of such organizations worldwide, operating at every level from global tele-communications to word of mouth.

Chinese Massage Therapy: A Handbook of Therapeutic Massage
Compiled at the Anhui Medical School Hospital, China
Translated by Hor Ming Lee and Gregory Whincup

There is a growing movement among medical practitioners in China today to mine the treasures of traditional Chinese medicine – acupuncture, herbal medicine and massage therapy. Directly trans-lated from a manual in use in Chinese hospitals, *Chinese Massage Therapy* offers a fresh understanding of this time-tested medical alternative.

Dialogues with Scientists and Sages: The Search for Unity
Renée Weber

In their own words, contemporary scientists and mystics – from the Dalai Lama to Stephen Hawking – share with us their richly diverse views on space, time, matter, energy, life, consciousness, creation and our place in the scheme of things. Through the immediacy of verbatim dialogue, we encounter scientists who endorse mysticism, and those who oppose it; mystics who dismiss science, and those who embrace it.

Zen and the Art of Calligraphy
Ōmori Sōgen and Terayama Katsujo

Exploring every element of the relationship between Zen thought and the artistic expression of calligraphy, two long-time practitioners of Zen, calligraphy and swordsmanship show how Zen training provides a proper balance of body and mind, enabling the calligrapher to write more profoundly, freed from distraction or hesitation.

ARKANA – NEW-AGE BOOKS FOR MIND, BODY AND SPIRIT

A selection of titles already published or in preparation

Judo – The Gentle Way Alan Fromm and Nicolas Soames

Like many of the martial arts, Judo primarily originated not as a method of self-defence but as a system for self-development. This book reclaims the basic principles underlying the technique, re-emphasizing Judo as art rather than sport.

Women of Wisdom Tsultrim Allione

By gathering together the rich and vivid biographies of six Tibetan female mystics, and describing her own experiences of life as a Tibetan Buddhist nun and subsequently as a wife and mother, Tsultrim Allione tells the inspirational stories of women who have overcome every difficulty to attain enlightenment and liberation.

Natural Healers' Acupressure Handbook
Volume II: Advanced G-Jo Michael Blate

Volume I of this bestselling handbook taught the basic G-Jo – or acupressure – techniques, used to bring immediate relief to hundreds of symptoms. In Volume II Michael Blate teaches us to find and heal our own 'root organs' – the malfunctioning organs that are the true roots of disease and suffering – in order to restore balance and, with it, health and emotional contentment.

Shape Shifters: Shaman Women in Contemporary Society
Michele Jamal

Shape Shifters profiles 14 shaman women of today – women who, like the shamans of old, have passed through an initiatory crisis and emerged as spiritual leaders empowered to heal the pain of others.

'The shamanic women articulate what is intuitively felt by many "ordinary" women. I think this book has the potential to truly "change a life"' – Dr Jean Shinoda Bolen, author of *Goddesses in Everywoman*

ARKANA – NEW-AGE BOOKS FOR MIND, BODY AND SPIRIT

A selection of titles already published or in preparation

On Having No Head: Zen and the Re-Discovery of the Obvious
D. E. Harding

'Reason and imagination and all mental chatter died down . . . I forgot my name, my humanness, my thingness, all that could be called me or mine. Past and future dropped away . . .'

Thus Douglas Harding describes his first experience of headlessness, or no self. This classic work truly conveys the experience that mystics of all ages have tried to put into words.

Self-Healing: My Life and Vision Meir Schneider

Born blind, pronounced incurable – yet at 17 Meir Schneider discovered self-healing techniques which within four years led him to gain a remarkable degree of vision. In the process he discovered an entirely new self-healing system, and an inspirational faith and enthusiasm that helped others heal themselves. While individual response to self-healing is unique, the healing power is inherent in all of us.

'This remarkable story is tonic for everyone who believes in the creative power of the human will' – Marilyn Ferguson.

The Way of the Craftsman: A Search for the Spiritual Essence of Craft Freemasonry W. Kirk MacNulty

This revolutionary book uncovers the Kabbalistic roots of Freemasonry, showing how Kabbalistic symbolism informs all of its central rituals. W. Kirk MacNulty, a Freemason for twenty-five years, reveals how the symbolic structure of the Craft is designed to lead the individual step by step to psychological self-knowledge, while at the same time recognising mankind's fundamental dependence on God.

Dictionary of Astrology Fred Gettings

Easily accessible yet sufficiently detailed to serve the needs of the practical astrologer, this fascinating reference book offers reliable definitions and clarifications of over 3000 astrological terms, from the post-medieval era to today's most recent developments.

ARKANA – NEW-AGE BOOKS FOR MIND, BODY AND SPIRIT

A selection of titles already published or in preparation

The Ghost in the Machine   Arthur Koestler

Koestler's classic work – which can be read alone or as the conclusion of his trilogy on the human mind – is concerned not with human creativity but with human pathology.

'He has seldom been as impressive, as scientifically far-ranging, as lively-minded or as alarming as on the present occasion' – John Raymond in the *Financial Times*

T'ai Chi Ch'uan and Meditation   Da Liu

Today T'ai Chi Ch'uan is known primarily as a martial art – but it was originally developed as a complement to meditation. Both disciplines involve alignment of the self with the Tao, the ultimate reality of the universe. Da Liu shows how to combine T'ai Chi Ch'uan and meditation, balancing the physical and spiritual aspects to attain good health and harmony with the universe.

Return of the Goddess   Edward C. Whitmont

Amidst social upheaval and the questioning of traditional gender roles, a new myth is arising: the myth of the ancient Goddess who once ruled earth and heaven before the advent of patriarchy and patriachal religion. Here one of the world's leading Jungian analysts argues that our society, long dominated by male concepts of power and aggression, is today experiencing a resurgence of the feminine.

The Strange Life of Ivan Osokin   P. D. Ouspensky

If you had the chance to live your life again, what would you do with it? Ouspensky's novel, set in Moscow, on a country estate and in Paris, tells what happens to Ivan Ososkin when he is sent back twelve years to his stormy schooldays, early manhood and early loves. First published in 1947, the *Manchester Guardian* praised it as 'a brilliant fantasy . . . written to illustrate the theme that we do not live life but that life lives us'.

ARKANA – NEW-AGE BOOKS FOR MIND, BODY AND SPIRIT

A selection of titles already published or in preparation

A Course in Miracles: The Course, Workbook for Students and Manual for Teachers

Hailed as 'one of the most remarkable systems of spiritual truth available today', *A Course in Miracles* is a self-study course designed to shift our perceptions, heal our minds and change our behaviour, teaching us to experience miracles – 'natural expressions of love' – rather than problems generated by fear in our lives.

Medicine Woman: A Novel Lynn Andrews

The intriguing story of a white woman's journey of self-discovery among the Heyoka Indians – from the comforts of civilisation to the wilds of Canada. Apprenticed to a medicine woman, she learns tribal wisdom and mysticism – and above all the power of her own womanhood.

Arthur and the Sovereignty of Britain: Goddess and Tradition in the Mabinogion Caitlín Matthews

Rich in legend and the primitive magic of the Celtic Otherworld, the stories of the *Mabinogion* heralded the first flowering of European literature and became the source of Arthurian legend. Caitlín Matthews illuminates these stories, shedding light on Sovereignty, the Goddess of the Land and the spiritual principle of the Feminine.

Shamanism: Archaic Techniques of Ecstasy Mircea Eliade

Throughout Siberia and Central Asia, religious life traditionally centres around the figure of the shaman: magician and medicine man, healer and miracle-doer, priest and poet.

'Has become the standard work on the subject and justifies its claim to be the first book to study the phenomenon over a wide field and in a properly religious context' – *The Times Literary Supplement*